THE LAND OF
STONES AND SAINTS

BY

Frances Parkinson Keyes

Garden City, New York

DOUBLEDAY & COMPANY, INC.

1957

Nihil obstat: John A. Goodwine, J.C.D.
           Censor Librorum

Imprimatur: ✠ Francis Cardinal Spellman
           Archbishop of New York
           August 17, 1957

The nihil obstat and imprimatur are official declarations that a book or pamphlet is free of doctrinal or moral error. No implication is contained therein that those who have granted the nihil obstat and imprimatur agree with the contents, opinions or statements expressed.

THE LAND OF STONES AND SAINTS

The Street of Life and Death, by Leonor Veretas

BY FRANCES PARKINSON KEYES

Fiction

BLUE CAMELLIA

THE ROYAL BOX

STEAMBOAT GOTHIC

JOY STREET

DINNER AT ANTOINE'S

CAME A CAVALIER

THE RIVER ROAD

ALSO THE HILLS

CRESCENT CARNIVAL

ALL THAT GLITTERS

FIELDING'S FOLLY

THE GREAT TRADITION

PARTS UNKNOWN

HONOR BRIGHT

SENATOR MARLOWE'S
  DAUGHTER

THE SAFE BRIDGE

LADY BLANCHE FARM

QUEEN ANNE'S LACE

THE CAREER OF DAVID
  NOBLE

THE OLD GRAY HOMESTEAD

Nonfiction

THE LAND OF STONES
  AND SAINTS

THE FRANCES PARKINSON
  KEYES COOKBOOK

ST. ANNE; GRANDMOTHER
  OF OUR SAVIOUR

THE COST OF A BEST
  SELLER

THÉRÈSE: SAINT OF A
  LITTLE WAY

ALL THAT IS LOUISIANA

THE GRACE OF GUADALUPE

BERNADETTE OF LOURDES

ALONG A LITTLE WAY

CAPITAL KALEIDOSCOPE

SILVER SEAS AND GOLDEN
  CITIES

LETTERS FROM A
  SENATOR'S WIFE

Juvenile

ONCE ON ESPLANADE

Verse

THE HAPPY WANDERER

TO

THE PRIOR AND COMMUNITY

OF THE

DOMINICAN CONVENT OF SANTO TOMAS, AVILA,

THE ABBESS AND COMMUNITY

OF THE

CISTERCIAN CONVENT OF SANTA ANA, AVILA,

ALSO

MARIA LUISA CATURLA OF MADRID,

A LADY AS LEARNED AS SHE IS LOVELY

AND

LUIS BOLIN, INFORMATION COUNSELOR

OF THE SPANISH EMBASSY IN WASHINGTON,

A DIPLOMAT AS KIND AND COMPETENT

AS HE IS DISTINGUISHED.

WITHOUT THE THOUGHTFUL, EFFICIENT

AND SCHOLARLY HELPFULNESS

OF THESE KIND FRIENDS

THIS BOOK COULD NEVER HAVE BEEN WRITTEN.

CONTENTS

PROLOGUE   xi

I   THE GIRL WITH THE FIRM MOUTH   3
    (*Isabel the Catholic, 1451–1504*)

II THE GIRL WHO WAS TOO HIGH SPIRITED   65
    (*St. Teresa of Avila, 1515–1582*)

III THE MAN WHO SANG WHEN HE SUFFERED   127
    (*St. John of the Cross, 1542–1591*)

IV THE STRONG WOMAN OF SANTA ANA   177
    (*The Venerable María Vela, 1561–1617*)

V   HIS EXCELLENCY, THE AMBASSADOR
    OF SPAIN TO JAPAN   229
    (*San Pedro Bautista, 1545–1597*)

NOTES   289

BIBLIOGRAPHY   342

INDEX   349

LIST OF ILLUSTRATIONS

The Street of Life and Death, by Leonor Veretas   *Frontispiece*

Isabel of Castile   2

Cloister of the Convent of Santo Tomás   47

St. Teresa of Avila   64

Blessed Alonso Orozco   113

Modern Fiesta of St. Teresa   122

St. John of the Cross   126

Reproduction of title page in 1649 edition of THE WORKS
OF ST. JOHN OF THE CROSS   163

María Vela with the Virgin and Child   176

The Gothic cathedral in Avila   178

San Pedro Bautista   228

Inscription commemorating the site where Doña Isabel was declared heiress of the Kingdoms of Castile and León   296

Genealogy Chart   298

Map of Spain and Portugal at the beginning of the reign of the
Catholic Kings   301

Tomb of Prince Juan   303

Prologue

THE BOOK which I have called THE LAND OF STONES AND SAINTS would not have been written except for two great disappointments and what seems to me an even greater opportunity.

I first undertook to produce a work of religious character more than twenty years ago, when I was given as an assignment a biography of the "Little" St. Theresa, to be written in Lisieux, while living among persons who had known this sanctified soul in the flesh, and conferring with them. This biography, originally published under the title, *Written in Heaven*, and later reissued under the title, *Therese: Saint of a Little Way*, was hardly finished when I decided I would like to make a comparative study between its heroine and the "Great" St. Teresa, and to do the work in Avila. The project met with prompt editorial approval. Before it could be put into effect, however, World War II had rendered all European travel impossible; and before this was feasible again, Sackville-West's *Study in Contrasts, St. Teresa of Avila, St. Thérèse of Lisieux*—to which she gave the primary title of *The Eagle and the Dove*, had been brought out by Doubleday & Company (1944). I read it with absorption and admiration, but also with a feeling of great frustration; I knew there was nothing I could say, by way of comparing the two saints, that Sackville-West had not said much better already.

But Avila continued to beckon me. I had been there, very briefly, in the course of my first trip to Spain, at which time I was writing about kings and courts, not about saints and cloisters; but I had always wanted to go back, for, even in that short incidental visit, it had "said" a great deal to me, although I had barely glimpsed its wonders and although I had approached it—as it never should be first approached if this can be avoided—by the road from Madrid, which means that, after a long stretch of barren and rocky countryside, you enter drab suburbs before you get even a momentary glimpse of the matchless walls. On the other hand, if you first approach it by the road from Salamanca, you see two entire sides of these encircling walls, in all their majesty, before you see anything else of the city. Thus beheld, it is one of the greatest sights, not only in all Spain, but in all the world, especially if you come upon it in the afternoon when each of its eighty-odd semi-circular towers casts a dark, castellated shadow on the sunny surface beyond, or when all its battlements are bathed in moonlight. Edward Hutton, the English author whose *Cities of Spain* is one of the most perceptive as well as one of the most sensitive travel books that I have ever read, was fortunate enough to approach it first from this direction; and his description of the impression it made on him is, in my opinion, a masterpiece:

"Suddenly, like a vision, at a turning of the way, Avila rose before me on her hill, a beautiful mediaeval city, surrounded by perfect rose-coloured granite walls—a city out of a Missal, as it were, forlorn in the wilderness, indestructible amid the ruin of a world. Around her, some ancient civilisation seems to have been destroyed; everywhere immense titanic rocks, strange and fantastic, piled one upon another as though commemorating some wild, forgotten religion, or strewn on the hills, the last remnant of some colossal palace, or solitary, prostrate on the plain, as though hurled from heaven in some battle of archangels, surround her, as in a world before the creation of the first five days. It is impossible for me to convey in words to you anything of that immense ruin or its strength. It is like a passionate and difficult silence over everything. But the aspect of the city upon the infinite stretches of sierra, in a country as stony as Judaea, I shall never forget. She seems to sum up in herself, and to express with a sort of tragic precision, as it were, all the chaos and ruin that lie about her in that world of rocks and stones. Where the very boulders are writhing in agony to find expression, she alone has understood everything and been reconciled. She is the visible image of the word Amen."

If anything had been needed to intensify my desire to visit Spain again, Hutton's book, which I read after my return to the United States, would certainly have done so; and when I finally did go back— again very briefly, but possessing somewhat better acquaintance with saints and cloisters than I had the first time—Avila said even more to me than it had before. The cathedral, even in its severity, seemed no less a sanctuary because it had been a fortress; and the stone lions, linked together with iron chains suspended from one powerful jowl to the next, which serve as its guardians, are the most imposing form of enclosure with which I am familiar. (As a matter of fact, these lions are not in the least fierce looking; some of them actually have a rather smug expression; and the same is true of the stone lions in the Plaza de Santa Teresa, whose tongues are exposed in such a way that they appear to be licking, with relish, the stone pillars to which they are attached.) I walked all around the cathedral, through the narrow Street of Life and Death—so-called because of the wonderful carved medallion of a beautiful young girl and a grinning skull which adorns the cathedral's façade—and into the wider streets of Tostado and San Segundo. Inside the cathedral, I lingered in the Sacristy and the Museum, entranced even more by the wonderful old illuminated missals than by the primitive paintings and richly embroidered vestments and jeweled vessels and ornaments of gold and silver, among them a monstrance hung with bells, arresting as these were, also. In fact, I spent so much time in the cathedral that there was less time than I had hoped for other sight-seeing; but, late that afternoon, as I left the Church of the Encarnación, which is attached to the convent where Teresa spent the first twenty years of her cloistral life, I said to Don José, the Spanish friend who had devoted the day to showing me as much as possible, "I still realize it would be folly to attempt the comparative study which I had planned and of which I told you; but perhaps I might try to write a simple biography of your great saint, without any attempt of comparing her to another—merely a record of her life, unconnected with that of any other person, except, of course, those of her contemporaries and associates. I know that a great many biographies have been written about her already; and then, there is her *Autobiography*, besides her *Letters* and her *Essays*. But perhaps there might still be a new approach. . . ."

Don José was so encouraging in his response to this suggestion that I went home determined that when I next returned to Avila—which would be at the earliest possible moment—it would not be for just a day or two, but for a long stay, and everything seemed to justify a hope of going back the following summer. Meanwhile, I read whatever I could lay my hands on about St. Teresa—in English, in French, in Spanish; and when "spring came round again next year," my plans were made, my passage was engaged. Then, just as I was about to set sail, an American friend who had followed my quest for information told me that a new book had just come out which I should certainly add to my collection of Teresiana. She would give it to me, she said, as a *bon voyage* present. . . .

The book was Marcelle Auclair's *Teresa of Avila*.[1] Once I had begun it, I went on with such avidity that I could hardly bear to put it down. When I finally did so, it was with an even stronger feeling of frustration than when I had finished *The Eagle and the Dove*. I was now convinced there was no research I could do which had not been so thoroughly done already that mine would be superfluous; there was no viewpoint I could express which would still be original; there was no writing I could achieve which would glow with the clarity and vitality that illumined the pages of the book I was so reluctantly closing.

I went on to Avila just the same because it seemed impossible, at that late moment, to change all my plans; but I did so rather aimlessly. I could not shake off the conviction that, much as I might enjoy the city, this enjoyment would be unproductive; I could, of course, continue work on the novel I was writing, but it so happened that this might just as well have been done in New England or New Orleans as in Spain. Instead of putting in my usual long working hours, I took things at an easier pace, because there was no incentive to do otherwise; and, consequently, one afternoon, I accepted an invitation—which, normally, I should have declined—to while away an hour at the Restaurante de Pepillo with my friend, María Luisa Caturla, drinking *leche helada*—the Spanish version of a milkshake.

The Restaurante de Pepillo, like the Oro del Rhin and El Aguila de Gredos which adjoin it, is an agreeable place at which to drink a *leche helada* in a leisurely manner and there is plenty to see between sips. The three restaurants are at right angles to each other at one end of the plaza; beyond them, underneath an arcade, are some of the best shops in the city: the Pajarita, a confectioner's; Iselma, a bakery; the Relojería Kaiser Platería, a jewelry store; La Perla, a fancy grocery; the Abulense, a stationery and souvenir shop. Across the street—the Calle del Duque de Alba—is the beautiful Romanesque Church of San Pedro and, near this, the Post Office, where the letter slot is in the form of a lion's open mouth; also, several more shops with living quarters above them, and the Church of Santa Magdalena. At the opposite end of the plaza is the magnificent Puerta del Alcázar and, beyond this, the Paseo del Rastro, one of the pleasant gardens outside the walls; at the right of the Puerta, a busy commercial street, the Calle de San Segundo. In the center of the plaza is a rather mediocre statue of Santa Teresa and a plot of land hemmed in by the aforementioned stone lions who appear to be licking, with relish, the pillars

to which they are attached. At the hours of the *paseo*—midday and
evening on Sundays, evening every day of the week—one side of the
plaza is closed to vehicular traffic; but at nearly all times it is crowded
and noisy. Donkey carts and heavily laden donkeys whose vociferous
drivers walk beside them are almost as numerous as small honking
motorcars; bent, wrinkled women, shabbily clad in rusty black, and
unshaven, unkempt old men, who have somehow managed to retain
their look of dignity, are almost as numerous as men and women who
are either fairly or very well dressed and—in the case of the women—
especially noticeable for their neat shoes and carefully arranged hair.
The shabby old women are muffled in black shawls which cover their
heads and arms and are tightly clutched against their flat breasts; but
the beautiful shoulder-length ringlets, the thick glossy black braids of
the pretty girls and handsome matrons are unobscured. Only when
they approach San Pedro or Santa Magdalena—and then, at the very
last moment before entering—do they throw mantillas of gossamer
lightness over their shining tresses. The young men about town have
black hair of patent leather sleekness, trim figures and roving eyes,
and it is no wonder that their admiring glances are cast first in one direction and then another. The stranger within Avila's noble gates,
quietly sipping *leche helada* on a warm summer day, is stirred to admiration, too, even while nursing a disappointment which is rapidly
becoming a grievance.

María Luisa, the friend who had lured me into unaccustomed idleness and unaccustomed enjoyment of it, persisted in disrupting this
enjoyment by arguing with me about the book I had decided to abandon. She is probably the foremost living authority on the great Spanish painter, Zurbarán, and spends much of her time doing further research about him; but her artistic and intellectual activities are by no
means confined to one subject; they embrace almost every phase of
Spanish history. There are plenty of things which could be said about
St. Teresa, she insisted, that had not been said already. Or, if I would
not consider a work of monumental size, why would I not at least
write something for the benefit of the many persons who did not have
time or inclination to read major biographies? Something without too
many names and dates, without too many classical references, at least
in the body of the book? Or perhaps just something in pamphlet form?
I set down my unemptied glass of *leche helada* and shook my head.
There were, to be sure, still some things that might be said about
Santa Teresa that hadn't been said before, or at least that hadn't been

emphasized; but, as far as I was aware, while there were enough of these for a biographical sketch, there weren't enough to justify practical publication. Books, I told her, trying to speak patiently, had to run to something like standard length; for at least the hundredth time, I endeavored to explain to a non-professional the requirements of publishing houses, the demands of the book trade, the terms of contracts. But while I was doing so and feeling more and more that it was futile, my gaze wandered from the magnificent Puerta del Alcázar, at the further end of the square, to that rather mediocre modern statue, encompassed by satisfied lions, which was nearer the Restaurante de Pepillo and which I had never attentively observed before. As I did so, I noticed for the first time that the four sides of its pedestal were carved with names and, partly to escape further importunities and partly because my interest was really aroused, I sauntered over to the statue and began to read.

"Apparently," I announced, going back to María Luisa and the *leche helada* after a prolonged perusal, "a good many famous persons besides Santa Teresa came from Avila—that is, I take it those names on her statue belong to fellow citizens of hers or they would not have been put there. But you remember what Edward Hutton said." I had quoted this favorite author of mine to María Luisa before, and she had agreed with me that his description of the first view of Avila, as seen from the Salamanca road, was a masterpiece. Now I quoted from him again: " 'Even as Assisi is nothing without the light of St. Francis, of which she is the almost perfect expression, so Avila is a ruin, a beautiful, a curious ruin, it is true, but still just a ruin without the life of Santa Teresa, which is, as it were, the soul of this fierce solitary place.' " María Luisa shook her head. "This time, Hutton is wrong," she said vehemently. "It isn't a ruin, is it? And it certainly isn't solitary!" She waved her hand, first in the direction of the crowded tables around us, then toward the thronged plaza and, finally, toward a white-helmeted, white-gloved policeman, standing near the Puerta del Alcázar, who was, by this time, having trouble with the dense and somewhat unruly traffic. "It's certainly very much alive," she added, laughing. "And it always has been—thanks not only to Teresa, but to those fellow citizens of hers that you are so tardily discovering."

"Of course, I knew that Juan de la Cruz was an *Avilés*," I said defensively, "and the nuns at Santa Ana's Convent, the day Don José took me to see them, told me it was there Isabel first declined the

crown of Castile. But did she have any other special connection with
the city or the province?"

"Why, she was born in Madrigal de las Altas Torres! And she grew
up in Arévalo! You ought to go to both those places and many others
associated with her. All her early life was centered in the province
and much of her later life right here in its capital. Didn't you know
that?"

"I certainly didn't and I imagine a good many other people don't
know it, either. I believe they think of Avila wholly in terms of St.
Teresa—just as Hutton did."

"Well, they shouldn't. Why do you suppose the hotel where you're
staying is named the Reina Isabel? And why do you suppose Avila has
been called the City of Knights and the City of Kings? It never would
have been if it hadn't produced a good many celebrities in both categories. And the province wouldn't have been called the Land of Stones
and Saints—*Tierra de Cantos y Santos*—if it hadn't produced almost
as many saints as stones. I don't see why you think you need to confine
yourself to Teresa. I don't see why *Avila* shouldn't be the heroine of a
book, so to speak, with all her famous children—some of them, anyway
—as the supporting characters. Have you ever thought of it that way?"

"No," I said, truthfully and apologetically. "I hadn't before. But I'm
thinking about it now. I believe you're right. I believe I've found my
story after all."

So, once again, I have come back to Avila, not for a day or two this
time, but for a prolonged sojourn, and not in a state of discouragement, but in a state of eagerness and hope. And never, in the course
of all my wanderings, have I felt that my reward was richer. This is,
of course, partly due to the enthralling nature of my work; but it is
also due to the fact that I have not tried to accomplish this in a hurry.
Most visitors and some students still seem to feel that they can "do"
Avila in a day or two and no traveller could fall into greater error. No
hasty survey would provide time for penetration to the tiny patio,
reached only by a short steep flight of steps, leading from the room in
which St. Teresa was born, which is now a chapel in the lower part
of the church dedicated to her; and this patio, so secluded that it seems
like a place of secret retreat, so simple that it is adorned only by a few
vines, a tiny fountain on one wall and a tiny statue on another, affords
the privilege of one of the most exquisite sights in Avila. Neither
would a hasty survey provide time to go down the steep hill to the tiny

hermitage of San Segundo, separated from the River Adaja only by
its lovely little courtyard, which is carpeted with green grass and dot-
ted with green trees; and, once inside the shrine, to find that it shelters
a sculptured tomb of Avila's first saint which is one of Juan de Juni's
masterpieces, and furthermore to learn detailed stories of this saint
and, also, of Santa Barbada and the Venerable María Vela, of whom
more hereafter. Neither would a short stay provide time to wander at
leisure through the Park of San Antonio, far beyond the limits of the
walled city, and thereby find the statue of San Pedro Bautista, whose
name, for some strange reason, is omitted from the lists of the great
Abulenses on St. Teresa's pedestal,[2] though he achieved both fame
and glory, first as missionary to the Philippines, and later as Spanish
Ambassador to Japan, where he suffered martyrdom. Moreover, there
is a certain atmosphere of secrecy about many aspects of Avila: the
façades of the churches, the convents and palaces reveal almost nothing of the spaciousness and splendor and absolutely nothing of the
life that lie beyond them. To be sure, this is no truer of Avila than
it is of many another ancient city; but it does constitute a valid reason
why it is impossible to become familiar with it quickly, and to discover
that though the secrecy may be real, this does not indicate emptiness
or isolation—for again, I must differ with Hutton, who calls it a "fierce
solitary place" and refers to "the quietness of its deserted convents."
Solitary? Its shops may lack wares, but they never seem to lack cus-
tomers and its streets, like its plazas, are crowded day and night. Moreover, these crowds, for the most part, are noisy—indeed, H. V.
Morton, another writer whose work I have greatly enjoyed, complains
that he gets very little sleep there; he is especially disturbed by persons
gaily shouting good-night to each other at two in the morning; and
I must confess that I have similarly found great apparent reluctance
on the part of Spaniards, not only to sleep themselves—except late
in the afternoon—but to let anyone else sleep. Every morning, since
we have been living on the Calle de los Reyes Católicos—of which
more hereafter—we have been wakened early by the cries of the
lottery vendors, most of them blind, who go through the streets tap-
ping on the narrow sidewalks with their canes and loudly hawking
their wares. Next come the muleteers, berating their patient beasts of
burden and urging them forward. Then the corrugated metal shutters
on the shops, which went down with a clatter late the evening before,
are rolled up with even more of a clatter, while the shopkeepers and
their tenants, who live upstairs, are lustily saluting each other; and

there are a good many shopkeepers and tenants, for the Calle de los Reyes Católicos is now a prosperous commercial street and only a few *palacios* are left which have not been put, at least partially, to practical business use. Groups of soldiers from the barracks begin to saunter along and they, too, hail the comrades who are out for a leisurely stroll, apparently unimpeded by any military duties. And, every now and then, there is the blare of a band, playing such tunes as "Anchors Aweigh" and "Beer Barrel Polka," which seem somewhat incongruous in such a setting.

As for the "deserted" convents, I cannot help wondering which ones Hutton had in mind for, according to the list given me by my friends at Santa Ana, who are Cistercians, there are 334 nuns belonging to thirteen different Orders in Avila; 216 monks, friars and seminarians belonging to four different Orders; and this, of course, does not include the secular clergy attached to the cathedral and the almost innumerable churches. Only the Franciscan Monastery, as far as I know, is a deserted ruin, and this is indeed tragic, from many points of view, not the least of them mine, because, with it, have perished all the local records of its "Guardianship" by Fray Juan de Zumárraga, who later became the first Bishop on the Western Hemisphere.

The religious of Avila, both men and women, regular and secular, are more than disposed to be helpful to the student whose purpose is known to be serious, as several writers besides myself, among them Marcelle Auclair and E. Allison Peers, have already freely testified; personally, I should like to express special gratitude to the Cistercian Nuns of Santa Ana and the Dominican Fathers of Santo Tomás in the provincial capital and to the Dominican Nuns in Madrigal and the Cistercian Nuns in Arévalo. Besides, many of Avila's great houses are still owned by old and noble families who proudly uphold the traditions of the past. History seemed doubly real to me when I was invited to lunch at the *palacio* that had belonged to St. Teresa's grandmother and ate this delicious meal—the weather being warm and pleasant—along with other guests, in the walled garden, under the shade of a tree planted by the saint herself when she was a young girl. The story of Isabel also seemed very much a part of my own life when I found two of Christopher Columbus' descendants among my fellow guests at the *merienda* at the Quinta San Segundo, which is flanked by no less than seven of the great wall's battlements. If any country has a history more rich and glowing than that of Spain, I do not know which it is; and fittingly, much of this is told in splendid

paintings and gorgeous tapestries and ancient illuminated parch-
ments. In like measure, the best way to study it is in the places where
such things belong and form its background and not so far removed
from it in space and time that, though the authenticity of available
records may remain unchallenged, half of its vitality is lost.

Usually my feelings are those of almost uncontrollable impatience,
combined with helpless rage, when someone says to me gushingly,
"How wonderful it must be to do nothing but write! Just to sit down
quietly and comfortably and wait for an inspiration!" I believe that
this feeling of exasperation is shared by many authors, for it is hopeless
to try to explain to a person who has never attempted it that writing,
pursued as a profession, is hard work, like any other profession, and
that the author who sat tranquilly waiting for inspiration before getting words on paper would soon be a public charge. But such a statement is so generally received with incredulity that it is a source of
untold satisfaction to me that, for once, I can say, "Yes, the writing
of that book was a joy." To be sure, I did not sit around waiting for
inspiration, and though I had neither time nor strength to do much
of anything except the writing and the research and incidental travelling connected with it, while I was working on this book, I had no
desire to do anything else. For I was writing about Isabel and Teresa
and John and the others in the places where they themselves had
lived, among their own people, and they became my friends. And very
wonderful friends they are to have.

Moreover, the latter part of my work in Avila has been done not
only in the city and the province which are so essentially a part of
these great persons and they of the locality, but in a house which is
an ideal setting for such work. Primarily through the good offices of
mutual friends—Don Agustín de Amezua, a distinguished member of
the Spanish Academy of History, whose untimely death has robbed
me of invaluable assistance, and the Princess von Hohenlohe-Langenburg, whose achievements in both artistic restoration and agricultural
reclamation have brought her national renown—and later, because of
their own interest in the type of writing I was doing, this house was
put at my disposal by the present owners, the Count and Countess
of Montefrío. It was not a *palacio*, the Countess told me, in the
course of her kindly call; and she further explained that, for the last
few years, she and her husband and children had divided their time
between their *finca* in the country and their apartment in Madrid;
they had, consequently, removed much of their furniture, and all dra-

peries, glass, china, silver and linen to use elsewhere. But if I felt like
supplying such of the missing items as were absolutely indispensable,
and could "make do" without the others, I was more than welcome to
the house. I would find the caretaker, Segunda, reliable and efficient;
and Segunda's elder son, Pepe, a bricklayer, had recently married the
former cook of the Duchess of Nájera, and was leaving Pedrosillo
because it was too far out of town for him to commute back and
forth; possibly this bride, who was very cheerful and pretty and whose
name was Pepita, would come and cook for me. . . .

This generous offer and these practical suggestions resulted in an
experience, the memory of which I shall always treasure. Though it is
true that the Casa Montefrío is not actually a *palacio* of great antiquity
—as age is judged in Spain—it certainly may properly be termed a
palacete—a minor, younger, but wholly worthy companion of such famous houses as those in which the Dávilas, the Abrantes and other
great families have lived in Avila, and also worthy of comparison to
them in interest and atmosphere. It is situated on the Calle de los
Reyes Católicos—the Street of the Catholic Kings—which, in itself,
has a certain symbolism for me; and it stands foursquare around a
central patio which, in turn, is surrounded on two sides by a wide,
interior gallery, whose broad windows afford an unobstructed view of
the beautiful Spanish sky and which is flooded with golden sunshine
all day. From this gallery lead the two formal drawing rooms, the spacious dining room and the Count's book-lined study; the numerous
bedrooms and the extensive kitchen quarters lie beyond. It was built
by a certain Don Fernando Larrondo y Etchepara, who was not a
native of Avila, but of St. Jean de Pied de Port, whither he returned
when conditions along the Basque border quieted down again after
the French Revolution. By a strange coincidence, this noble Basque
was the great-great-grandfather of the present Countess, though, when
he sold the house, it was to her husband's ancestors and not to hers!
The purchasers in question belonged to the Aboín family of Avila,
which, at that time, was not numbered among its nobility, but were
agriculturists, merchants and statesmen, though one of its members,
Don Manuel Pinto y Fonseca, had been a Grand Master of the
Knights of Malta, and all of them had been faithful Monarchists; so
it was not surprising that, in due course of time, a certain Mariano
Aboín, who had been Mayor of Avila and a member of the Cortes,
first as Deputy and then as Senator, was given a title—Count of
Montefrío—in recognition of his services to Isabella II and her son,

who eventually became Alfonso XII. The present Count is the grand-son of the first bearer of the title, while his wife is descended from the Canarian family of De Massieu and the *Avilés* family of Orozco, the latter being the same to which belonged the Blessed Alonso de Orozco, whose name is carved on the statue of St. Teresa, among those of the persons who have given special distinction to the Land of Stones and Saints.

Enchanted as I was with the *palacete* and its history, and gratefully surprised at the kindly gesture which had made my installation in it possible, I cannot truthfully say that, in less time than it takes to tell, everything was running smoothly there. I have kept house before, out-side of my own country, but only in a large city where equipment and supplies were approximately like those in the United States; and, since then, I have become an addict, not only to large refrigerators, but to even larger deep freezes. This was my first experience with an icebox approximately the size of a medicine closet—which automatically in-dicated daily marketing—and with a market which was a tax on the ingenuity, if not on the imagination. Delicious melon there was in-deed—as long as the melon season lasted; string beans, eggplant, cauliflower and squash abounded in like measure and for the same length of time. But there were never any green peas, there were no oranges after mid-September and, except for lettuce and tomatoes, there was a corresponding lack of nearly all fruits and vegetables to which we are accustomed as the autumn advanced. When it came to fish, poultry and meat, the situation was even worse. *Merluza*—hake —seems to be the favorite product of the sea, as far as this region is concerned, and often proves to be the only one available; it was dis-tasteful to us from the beginning and repulsive after an unrelieved diet of it. Veal is a specialty of Avila, but there are days when even that is not obtainable, especially late in the season when, presumably, all the poor little calves have already been slaughtered; and despite the size and number of flocks in the nearby countryside, lamb and mutton are scarce because wool is of greater value to the shepherds. Beef becomes something to dream about; and the small, stringy chick-ens are almost unbelievably tough. Only the partridges, almost as small, stringy and tough as the chickens at the beginning of the season, gradually become more plump and tender until they are really deli-cious. Their fame is certainly as well founded as that of the veal; and the charming story of St. Teresa's retort to a serving maid, who was astonished to see such a holy woman help herself liberally to the dish set before her by lavish hosts, takes on a new meaning as we enjoy a similar delicacy ourselves. "My child," Teresa allegedly remarked, "there is a time for penitence, but there is also a time for partridges!" There certainly was, as far as we were concerned; also, for the *croquetas* and *empanadas*, for which the tough meat could be ground up fine, and the *paellas* of shrimp and clams—fortunately always available—in the making of which Pepita, the pretty bride, excels.

The greatest handicap of all, for the American housewife, is a total lack of cream and the danger of using any milk that has not been thoroughly boiled; not until she tries to set a table in which these fundamentals are lacking does she thoroughly realize how great are the resources which she has hitherto accepted as a matter of course. Shopping for kitchenware and dry goods is not much simpler than shopping for food; coffee pots may be purchased only in conjunction with large numbers of cups. Double boilers and muffin tins are, apparently, non-existent. Napkins can be bought only in conjunction with large expensive tablecloths; a single sheet will be found in one shop and two in another, but never many or even several in the same place; and Turkish towels are the only ones that come ready made. Bolsters are available, but no pillows. Mattresses can, indeed, be made up in a day by the *colchonero* whose shop is only a few doors down the street; but it is such a mattress as, in all my travels, I have never encountered before and—I may say, in passing—hope I shall never encounter again!

However, my friends, the nuns of Santa Ana, came to my rescue with all the sheets and blankets they could spare, María Luisa loaned me platters, and an excursion to Medina del Campo to see the Castle de la Mota resulted in the incidental purchase of plentiful if unremarkable pottery. Gradually, Deanie Bullock, the faithful secretary who continues to share my work and my wanderings, and I settled in at the *palacete* after having dealt with most of our basic needs; and, from the beginning, the mainstay, the light and the joy of our household existence was Segunda, the Contessa's caretaker.

As far as we are concerned, it is entirely inadequate to refer to her merely as a caretaker. Despite her diminutive size—she is less than five feet tall and certainly weighs less than a hundred pounds—she stands sturdily on her sneakered feet, moves with noiseless but almost incredible speed and is, apparently, as indefatigable as she is efficient. She brings us both our breakfast trays, Deanie her midmorning coffee and callers their afternoon tea. She serves sherry before lunch in the

sunny gallery and cocktails before dinner in front of a cheerful wood
fire. She keeps bottles of Solares water embedded in ice at my bedside. She waits on table. She washes, irons and presses our clothes,
our table linen and our towels. (Alfonsa, the jovial portress at Santa
Ana, takes away the sheets to wash them, but Segunda irons them.)
She makes our beds and, by this I mean that, every morning, she dis-
mantles them completely, kneads the mattresses until the lumps of
cotton with which they are filled are distributed as evenly as possible
to the thickness of at least six inches, and then spreads them out again
under layers of bed clothing. She lays out our night clothes, changes
our towels and scrubs our bathroom. She summons, in turn, the *car-
pintero*, the *fontanero* and the *electricista*, of whose services we frequently stand in need, and supervises their labors of reparation. And
every day she not only dusts the premises from one end to the other,
but goes scuffling and sliding over the floors with large floppy pieces
of Canton flannel under her shoes, until the parquetry shines with her
polishing.

This parquetry forms the flooring of the wide interior gallery surrounding two sides of the patio (the other two sides and Deanie's
bedroom have tiled flooring, which is scrubbed), the two drawing
rooms, the dining room, the library and the two bedrooms in use for
our guests and myself. This seems to me a very considerable amount of
space, and I am thankful to observe that Pepe, the happy bridegroom
(who, since the weather grew cold, has attended the furnace located
in the lower regions) also takes advantage of his trips between the
kitchen and the basement to scuffle and slide in the same way and
with the same equipment as his mother, which supplements her labors
to the extent of lightening them somewhat. However, Segunda also
supervises pretty Pepita and makes sure there is a loaf of fresh homemade bread for breakfast toast—*pan de molde*—and fresh homemade
cake—pronounced kay-kay—for tea every day. She does the marketing,
sometimes accompanied by Deanie, who has struck up a very helpful
friendship with the vendor of partridges; she also does all the minor
errands and some of the major ones, sometimes accompanied by
Deanie and sometimes alone. She is always smiling, but her smile is
never quite so broad as when she is out shopping. She delights in buy-
ing anything, even a spool of thread or a bunch of carrots, and when
she has brought home her purchases, she shows them to me with an
air of triumph. At that, she does not invade the library, where I sit
writing, and she fiercely defends me from intrusion by anyone else;

she waits until the day's work is over and then she comes proudly to
me.

How quiet it is in that library, empty except for the bookcases which
line the walls, the big desk in the center and my own chair, unless I
see fit to draw in another! It does not connect with any other room,
just with the wide gallery overlooking the patio, and it has no windows
—only a skylight which almost covers the ceiling. So no street noises
penetrate to it and neither does the insistent ringing of a telephone
ever interrupt a train of thought. The telephone in the *palacete* had
long since been disconnected and, though the Countess kindly offered
to have one installed again, I quickly declined the offer. I remember
that, as a child of nine, I was greatly astonished upon my arrival in
France for the first time to discover that all the little dogs were addressed in French and that they appeared to understand. This astonishment gradually abated, as it was made to seem logical; but my
astonishment over the fact that Spaniards not only understand each
other—and even foreigners—over their telephone, but that they use
this instrument as casually as we do ours and actually with more apparent enjoyment, will never abate. The most trying ordeal to which
I can be subjected, in the course of a trip to Spain, is a telephone
conversation. Even a house call, at a hotel where I am staying, can
reduce me to such a state of exhaustion that I do not recover for
hours; a call which involves any distance has even more disastrous
effects. When I say "any distance," I refer only to local calls; to others
I am, fortunately, almost never subjected, as two hours must be allowed to get through from Avila to Madrid, for instance—a distance
of about seventy miles—and even that reckoning is only approximate;
so, if there is anything else that needs to be done in the course of a
morning, afternoon or evening, nothing else is attempted by the person who puts in the call. Even a call to Aravaca, a suburb of Madrid,
which bears about the same relation to this capital as Chevy Chase
does to Washington, requires the leeway of an hour; and, after a connection has been established, the conversation which ensues is subject
to the accompaniment of sounds which combine those of whistling,
crackling and pounding; also, to frequent interruptions and to complete disconnection. Decidedly, a telephone is the modern improvement with which I can most readily dispense in Spain!

Without it, and with the other advantages I have mentioned, it is
no wonder that I have been able to write and write and write, and
that I have done so with more happiness and with a greater sense of

fulfillment than I have ever before had in my work. No wonder that included in my fondest hopes is the one that I may return to the *palacete* to write again. Among the many legends that you hear in Avila is the story that Christ shed tears when he passed through the naked sierra and that these tears, now petrified, form the rocks in this Land of Stones and Saints. It is a lovely legend, just as most of Avila's legends are lovely, but to me personally, it has less significance than many others since, in my experience, this is a place where tears are not shed, but where they are dried. "For me, at least, Spain remains a sort of refuge, a land of sun and desert. If that be the obscure need of your spirit, go to her and she will heal you."[3]

FRANCES PARKINSON KEYES

THE LAND OF STONES AND SAINTS

Isabel of Castile from the portrait which hangs in the room she occupied at the Convent of Santa Ana, Avila. By special permission of the
Prioress and Community of Santa Ana.

PART I

The Girl with the Firm Mouth
(Isabel the Catholic, 1451—1504)

1

On a warm July day, in the year of Our Lord 1468, a tall, fair-haired girl, with hazel eyes, beautiful rosy skin and a firm mouth, sat sewing by the deep-set window of her room in the Cistercian Convent of Santa Ana at Avila.

The room was unlike the one in which she had been born in the great family house at nearby Madrigal de las Altas Torres, where a small inner chamber, without windows, led to a slightly larger one which, in turn, led to the covered gallery surrounding an immense patio—a gallery so deep that the outer chamber did not have much light or air, either; nevertheless, a great Queen—Isabel, cousin of King Alfonso V of Portugal and wife of King Juan II of Castile—had chosen this apartment for her confinement. The room at the Convent of Santa Ana was very large, with a raftered ceiling and high pale walls; and though it had only one window, this was very large, too, and sunlight streamed into it the greater part of the day. For, instead of looking out on a covered gallery, which in turn looked out on a patio, it "gave" directly on the kitchen garden of the convent and the orchard beyond this, where the foliage of the fruit trees, now at the peak of their summer luxuriance, hid the wall behind them. Some white hens had strayed from the nearby poultry yard and were busily selecting feed for themselves among the plentiful vegetables at which they pecked. Two little spotted heifers, tied to an apple tree, were sleeping contentedly in its shade. It was a scene almost pastoral in character, but permeated with the still greater calm of the convent. Every now and then the girl looked out on it, finding peace and reassurance in the sight; then she returned to her needlework, which she executed with skill, and to her thoughts, which were troubled, and which she was prayerfully trying to keep tranquil.

She had need of all her resolution and all her faith to accomplish this purpose, and the missal she herself had illuminated lay close at hand, so that she could turn to that, too, whenever she felt she required the support of a power stronger than her own. But she believed in herself as well as in God and both beliefs upheld her in these difficult hours, the most critical as well as the saddest through which she had ever passed, though all her life she had lived close to both danger and sorrow.

Her mother, Isabel of Portugal, always somewhat inclined to melancholy, had been a nervous invalid from the time of her daughter's birth, when a well-founded suspicion of attempted poisoning added to the complications of a hard confinement. Her father, Juan II of Castile—a widower with a half-grown son when he married her mother —excelled in sports, for which he was well fitted by his strong physique, and was also an enthusiastic patron of the arts, for which he had talent, as well as taste. But he was dissolute as a man and weak as a ruler; he had died when his daughter was only three years old and she had never been able to look to him for maintenance of any kind. Enrique, the son by his first wife, succeeded him to the throne and his disconsolate widow withdrew to a small property at Arévalo with her two children—for by then the little girl had a baby brother—and lived in a state of greater and greater seclusion and depression all the time.

It was in the frail, fair-haired baby, Alfonso, that the sturdy little girl, who had been named Isabel for her mother, and who was stronger in both body and will than her brother, found her greatest joy and her most constant companionship. She had been sent to receive part of her early education at the famous Convent of Santa Ana in Avila, which was founded by the great Bishop, Sancho Dávila, who later became Regent for King Alfonso XI of Castile during the latter's minority; and it was to this convent that she had now returned for refuge; the ties between the nuns and herself had remained very close.[1] But as soon as Alfonso was old enough, he and Isabel generally studied together. Their teachers came from the great University of Salamanca and, though Latin was not included in their curriculum, they learned to speak, read and write Castilian with fluency and grace. From earliest childhood, Isabel had loved fine needlework and excelled in it and, naturally, the nuns had done much to foster this talent, as well as her gift for illuminating parchment.[2] She had also loved music and poetry from an early age, and occasionally the brother and sister devised entertainments; on these occasions, Alfonso was the audience and Isabel appeared clad as a muse or recited lilting verses. But by no means all their time was devoted to cultural pursuits. They went to the great fairs, held three times a year in the spacious market place at Medina del Campo, to which merchants came from far and wide. Business was brisk in Cordovan leather, Sevillian sugar, Valencian silks and spices, Toledano steel and Andalusian horses, mules and steers; and all these were traded for cloths and tapestries from Flanders and paper and trinkets from France. Turbaned Moors and bearded Jews, Provençal peasants, who spoke a strange tongue, and Flemish weavers whose tongue was stranger still were in charge of such wares and the children wandered from booth to booth in fascination. Medina del Campo was more than twenty miles from Arévalo, but Isabel and Alfonso went galloping gaily back and forth over the flat plain; they would have laughed at the very idea that the journey might tire them, for they spent endless hours in the saddle without the slightest thought of fatigue. They both also enjoyed hunting and regarded every sort of game as their natural prey; Isabel could kill a bear with a javelin almost as casually as she could shoot a deer with a bow and arrow; and if she did not handle a sword and lance like her brother, it was not because she lacked the ability, but only because these would not have been considered feminine accomplishments.

The Dowager Queen's habitual melancholy cast only a slight shadow over her children's exuberant spirits; and the state of frugality to which her household had been reduced by the parsimony of her stepson and his favorites—as far as she was concerned—made little impression on Isabel and Alfonso, for they had never known any existence less restricted by necessity. Their life at Arévalo seemed perfect and complete to them; and, far from longing to widen their horizon, they were almost as much appalled as their distracted mother when they were suddenly summoned by their half-brother, Enrique, to the old Moorish Alcázar in Segovia,[3] where he was holding court.

The brother and sister had greater need of each other's affection and support than ever before. Seldom had any monarch given less dignity and luster to a crown than Enrique. He was repulsive to look at, with puffy cheeks, protuberant eyes and a wide flat nose; the rest of his person was no more pleasing than his face; but his habits, tastes and outlook on life were even more revolting, for all were vile beyond description. He surrounded himself with male favorites, among them a certain Juan Pacheco whom he had created Marqués of Villena and who went about smelling of scent and loaded with jewels, though he did not lack virility and could be charming when he chose. His evil characteristics were by no means unique; the whole court was corrupt to the very core and honeycombed with intrigue. The King's childless first marriage to the meek unfortunate Blanche of Aragon had been annulled on the grounds of impotence and from that time onward he had been known as *Enrique el Impotente*. The fact that, as far as was known, he had no illegitimate children gave great weight to the contention that he was incapable of begetting them; at this period, continence in a male was regarded as a weakness rather than a virtue, nor was he expected to take his marriage vows seriously. Far from drawing a veil of secrecy over his amorous pursuits, he was apt to parade their consequences with pride.

Enrique's second wife, Juana of Portugal, a lively and engaging brunette, was also childless for seven years; then she gave birth to a daughter who, apparently, was regarded as legitimate by practically no one, least of all the King. At all events, though she was named Juana for her mother, with young Isabel standing sponsor at her baptism, she was universally known as La Beltraneja from the beginning. One of the King's most charming courtiers was a certain magnificent specimen of robust manhood and also an incomparable knight of arms, by name Sir Beltrán de la Cueva. The King and Queen were both fascinated by this charmer; neither hesitated to acknowledge him tacitly as the little Princess' father through her nickname. She could not be the lawful heir to the throne, despite the King's vainglorious proclamation of her as such—a proclamation accepted by the Cortes under duress and with much murmuring; the bar sinister, however lightly regarded upon occasion, was still an almost insuperable impediment to such inheritance; and since, admittedly, Enrique could not hope to produce an heir himself, the question naturally arose: who would next wear the crown? Would the cuckold King continue his attempts to foist his wife's child on his people, or would he bow to the inevitable, recant his outrageous order of allegiance to La Beltraneja, and admit that his young half-brother, Alfonso, should rightfully be the next King of Castile?

Inevitably, both Alfonso and Isabel heard all this discussed, sometimes through innuendo, sometimes in whispers and sometimes with brazen openness, over and over again. A court so dissolute in its behavior was even more offensive in its speech. As far as book learn-

ing was concerned, the two children were given the education Enrique
had promised their distracted mother when he tore them away from
her. They had studied grammar and rhetoric, history and philosophy
at Arévalo; and they now continued these studies. Thanks to the nuns
at Santa Ana Convent, Isabel could embroider and paint long before
she came to Court and her natural gift for poetry and music had also
been evident from childhood. After all, had not her father been pas-
sionately addicted to both? And did the nature of her birthplace—the
little city of the high towers, to which the most popular songs of the
day owed their name of madrigal—count for nothing? Now she continued her lessons "in music, painting, poetry, grammar and sewing"
while Alfonso "learned all the accomplishments of a cavalier." Unfortunately, they learned other things as well. The day came when
Isabel fled from the sordid importunities of the Queen, whose gaiety
had long since taken a turn toward depravity, and ran to throw herself,
sobbing, in her brother's arms. Child that he was, he buckled on his
sword and went straight to Juana's apartment, where he informed her,
unequivocally, that she "had spoken more like a harlot than a Queen
and that he, Alfonso, Prince of Castile, forbade her to mention any
further evil to his sister, Doña Isabel." He next visited the Queen's
ladies-in-waiting and "forbade them, under pain of death, to address
his sister." Juana and her minions pretended to be amused by this
rebuke from a thirteen-year-old boy. However, it had its effects: Isabel
was not molested any more. But the experience had left its mark.
Never again was she free from a feeling of contempt and loathing
for her half-brother's court. Her rosy face and classic features took on
the look of firmness and reserve which they never wholly lost again,
except in her first happy year of love; and that was still far away on
this day when she sat sewing and thinking and praying in the deep
window seat of her raftered room at the Convent of Santa Ana in
Avila.

The disposition of her hand was a matter which, from her earliest
years, had also been of grave concern to her. "She had been promised
at various times to Fernando of Aragon, to Carlos of Viana, to Alfonso
V of Portugal, and there had been much talk . . . of her marrying a
brother of Edward IV of England . . . all had royal blood, all had
qualities she could respect."[4] Then Enrique made a disgraceful bargain with the Marqués de Villena, who had joined the rebellious
faction led by Alonso Carrillo de Acuña,[4-a] the powerful Archbishop
of Toledo, but who had been lured back to loyalty by the conviction

that allegiance to the King would be more profitable in the long run. According to this agreement, Enrique would banish Don Beltrán, whom Villena hated, and give the Infanta Isabel in marriage to Villena's brother, Don Pedro Giron, Master of Calatrava.

Isabel found the very mention of his name abhorrent; she knew him to be evil through and through. On the occasion of her first meeting with him, when she was still a child, he had made insulting proposals to her mother, encouraged to do this—or so he said—by the King himself. Isabel had never forgotten her horror over this episode, vaguely as she grasped its meaning at the time. When she understood it, her beloved younger brother was no longer near her to be her mainstay; he had been seized and imprisoned at the command of Enrique, while the rest of the Court was making a state visit to Gibraltar, where they had effected a meeting with the King of Portugal. Enrique and Juana had been at some pains to present Isabel as a desirable consort to this monarch since, at that moment, she was their most precious pawn. Meanwhile, further attempts had been made to corrupt the unfortunate boy, even in his dungeon cell; poison had also been tried, and both had failed. So had his desperate attempts to communicate with his sister. But he had finally succeeded in getting a message through to Carrillo, who immediately sent him a promise of help and, eventually, through force of arms, precipitated his release. Far from being reunited with his sister however, he had been removed to a safe distance and incomprehensibly placed under the guardianship of Villena, who was then still hand in glove with Carrillo.

Only Isabel's childhood friend, Doña Beatriz de Bobadilla, of Arévalo, who had been closer to the little Princess than anyone except her brother and who was to prove her lifelong friend, was with her when the King's will, regarding her marriage to Don Pedro, was made known. Beatriz vehemently offered her a dagger. Isabel refused it and took refuge in prayer, remaining secluded in her room while the preparations for the wedding went on, and the King stormed outside her locked door—he would show his stubborn sister who was master in Castile! Don Pedro, who was at his castle in Almagro, hastily prepared for departure to Segovia, well pleased with the instructions he had received to expedite his coming. Beatriz continued to finger her dagger and Isabel continued to pray. Meanwhile, Don Pedro, having started his journey, was obliged to break it at the little village of Villareal, after having been overtaken by darkness; he consoled himself for his primitive accommodations with the boast that, in a few nights,

THE GIRL WITH THE FIRM MOUTH

he would be sleeping with the Princess. Instead, he was sleeping in his coffin after a horrible end, brought on by a sudden attack of quinsy, in which he choked to death. Beatriz sheathed her dagger and Isabel changed her petition for rescue to a song of thanksgiving.

But who could say that prayers would always be answered? Certainly not Isabel. For all her faith, the ways of Providence were inscrutable to her. She had been delivered from a marriage that would have been a nightmare, and she was still free to hope that, someday, she might know the full experience of love with the man of her choice, even if she were a princess. The Convent of Santa Ana, already so familiar and so dear to her, was her preferred refuge in this time of her present trouble, and she was thankful for the comfort and the consolation it had given her. But while she watched the novices from her high wide window, she knew that she would never have chosen as they did, to live out their lives as cloistered virgins. True, the Court had revolted her; but not her country, not her people, not her life in the open. Soon she would be chafing to ride abroad again with her liegemen about her; and in their goodly company she would find the freedom and the friendship and the wisdom she craved.

So she told herself resolutely, as she sat sewing and thinking and praying; and so she tried, with all her might and main, to believe. But she did this with the bitter knowledge that she would never again have the companionship and the support which had meant more to her than anything else in the world and she could not help dwelling on the events which had led up to this tragic lack. Carrillo and Villena, at that time still working together, had caused little Alfonso to be proclaimed King at Valladolid. They were planning for a large meeting of the Insurgents at Avila, and they sent a secret message to Isabel, inviting her to attend it. She had carefully weighed the pros and cons, with a caution already characteristic of her, and then she had decided against it. But shortly thereafter, the Archbishop and the Marqués, with the little Prince between them, rode into the turreted city at the head of a great procession of horsemen, and the people on every side had acclaimed the child as King of Avila.

A pageant had then been enacted, before a heterogeneous multitude, with the mighty walls as a backdrop and the Archbishop as master of ceremonies. On the throne which formed the central property was placed a figure of Enrique in caricature. The Archbishop said Mass. Afterward, he advanced to the throne, removed the crown from the head of the hideous image and shouted, "Thus lose the dignity you have guarded so ill!" The next instant a nearby nobleman seized the scepter, crying, "Thus lose the government of the realms, as you deserve!" while a second noble pulled the caricature from the throne and kicked it about in the dust. Immediately, the great crowd was in a state of tumult. The frail little Prince was led to the empty throne, and the crown placed on his fair head, to the sound of trumpets and the shouts of his partisans.[4-b]

But there was another sort of outcry, too, a murmur, gradually growing louder and louder, against the outrage done the man who was still lawfully King of Castile, whatever he had done and been, and who would be lawfully King until he died. It was not long before this outcry became a mighty roar. The blasphemous performance proved a boomerang and civil war began in earnest, with the vacillating Villena now firmly entrenched on the side of the Archbishop. Since the death of his infamous brother, Don Pedro, had robbed him of a royal sister-in-law, he calculated he had nothing to lose by renewed or continued allegiance to the wretched King.

Eventually, a great battle was fought near Olmedo. At the very beginning of the fray Carrillo was wounded, but he fought on and on, a gorgeous figure clothed in mail and cloaked in scarlet. Whatever happened, and for all his faults of double-dealing and disloyalty, he remained a leader of tremendous power and prestige, and he did not need to rely on his position for the latter attributes; his strategy was brilliant, his physique superb, his courage indomitable. At the moment, the safety of little Alfonso, who was fighting beside him, was his chief concern. The boy was revealing extraordinary valiance and military skill beyond his years; but his life was too precious to be risked, for political as well as personal reasons. Don Beltrán, splendid in silver and steel, was fighting with the contestants on the other side and, despite his lack of principle, his bravery could never be questioned, either. He made a magnificent showing while defending himself successfully against the twoscore fighters who deliberately sought his death. The King, who, over and over again, had proclaimed himself a pacifist, though he made no objection when others waged war in his behalf, took no part in the battle himself, but watched it from the safe vantage point of a hill. At the end of the day, his army was still in possession of the field, but the rebels had a larger number of prisoners and pennants, including the royal standard. After being informed of this, Enrique decided that victory for his side was still problematical;

when Don Beltrán, flushed with triumph, went to seek him out, he was nowhere to be found.

A few days later, the King was discovered hiding in a small nearby village, a craven and miserable figure. The Queen and La Beltraneja presently joined him at the town of Olmedo, and there he remained with a limited but efficient guard, while Carrillo went to Avila to recover from his wounds. For the moment, both armies remained quiescent. But Carrillo was never known to be idle long, wound or no wound; his mind was as active and as tireless as his body and he used it more like a politician than a priest; moreover, ways and means never bothered him, if he could accomplish his ends. He ferreted out some hirelings who were willing, for a consideration, to seize the King. They very nearly succeeded in doing so, for they actually penetrated to the royal residence. But Enrique managed to elude them, borrowed some clothes from one countryman and a mule from another, and somehow reached safety. The Queen found refuge in Segovia, keeping La Beltraneja and Isabel with her.

They did not remain there long, however. The rebels were hot on their trail, and the Queen fled hastily again, taking her little girl with her. She would have taken Isabel, too, if the Infanta had been willing to go. But Isabel had made one of her thoughtful decisions: this was, perhaps, a golden opportunity for escape, not from the army but from the dissolute Queen. Besides, her brother Alfonso was with the approaching cavalry. Calmly, she anticipated his arrival.

Their reunion, so long delayed, was a joyous one. For a few brief happy days, they remained together, reviewing the past, planning the future. Then Alfonso returned to Avila, where Carrillo was expecting him, and Isabel stayed behind in Segovia, awaiting developments.

She did not have to wait long. Shortly thereafter, she was abruptly informed that a courier had come posthaste from Cardeñosa and was demanding to see her at once. Cardeñosa? A poor little village on the outskirts of Avila! The name was familiar, but hitherto without significance. All too soon it acquired this. The tidings that the courier brought concerned her brother, the "King of Avila." With the Marqués de Villena and other nobles he had ridden to Plasencia, in the hope of gaining support from that city, while Carrillo was engaged in a similar errand elsewhere. They had ridden back to Avila by way of Cardeñosa and, without previous arrangements, had decided to stay there for the night. And then Alfonso had been taken suddenly and violently ill. He was asking for his sister. . . .

She reached the little village with almost incredible swiftness. But, as she slid from her horse, it was the Archbishop, who had arrived before her, and not the poor little mock King who came out to meet her. Carrillo started to tell her that he had been in time to administer the Last Sacraments, but that was all; the poor boy's death had been as sudden as his illness. The day before he had eaten trout, of which, as she knew, he was particularly fond. Perhaps he had eaten too much, considering the heat of summer; or perhaps the trout had not been as fresh as it should have been; or perhaps. . . .

Isabel did not want to hear any more and she had nothing to say in reply. She went into the room where her brother lay and knelt beside his lifeless body. There, in prayer and seclusion, she tried to make up her mind what to do next. She could not see very far ahead. But she was determined that she would never return to Enrique's Court and equally determined that she would never trust Villena again. She took not the slightest stock in the theory that Alfonso might possibly have overeaten; and if the trout had been bad, the heat of summer had nothing to do with this. Though she had no means of proving it, no one would ever make her believe that this was not another case of poisoning. For some reason, Villena had once more shifted allegiance and might well be as dangerous to her as he had been to her brother. She resolved that she would seek sanctuary at the Convent of Santa Ana and that she would stay there until her course had been made clear to her. . . .

So there she remained, clad in her white mourning, busying herself with her needlework and her prayers, but most of all with her thoughts, as she looked out from her high window at the thriving garden and the fruitful orchard beyond it, at the little heifers resting under a shade tree, and at the novices, in their snowy veils, going quietly back and forth on their appointed tasks. It occurred to her that, a little later, she might go down to the chapel and look up at the statue of the good Bishop, Sancho Dávila,[5] who had founded the convent, and read the verses[6] about him which were carved on a great tablet underneath. The verses had always intrigued her, even though there was no mention in them of his greatest achievement—that of serving as Regent for young Alfonso XI during the boy King's minority: a service which had won him the title, "Wielder of the Kingdom of Castile." If, someday, justice should prevail and the rightful heir would again be Castile's ruler, this heir would owe a great deal to Bishop Dávila, who had written one of the greatest chapters in Avila's history.

It did not occur to Isabel that she herself would write the most important chapter of all.

2

The next morning, the Abbess herself came to the great raftered room and told the thoughtful girl that she must present herself immediately in the parlor.

No sound of tumult had reached the cloister. But in the town everyone was already talking about the cavalcade that had come clattering over the pavements of Avila with Carrillo, Archbishop of Toledo and Primate of Spain, at its head. And people were telling each other excitedly that when the cavalcade reached Santa Ana's Convent, the Archbishop had dismounted and knocked on the gate with the hilt of his sword, demanding audience of Doña Isabel. Why had he come and what was going to happen next?

They could get no inkling of why he had come and he, least of all, could have foreseen what would happen next.

In order to reach the parlor from the great raftered room, it was necessary to traverse a long stretch of the paved upper gallery surrounding the patio, into which the interior doors of both these apartments and many others led. This stretch had its advantages. The Abbess was able to prepare Isabel, to a certain degree, for the audience. If she chose, Her Royal Highness might remain behind the grille and the Abbess would stay at her side. The Archbishop of course had a right to enter the cloister, but this was not the prerogative of the nobles who accompanied him; they must remain in the parlor and, as their leader and spokesman, he would naturally remain with them while addressing her, from the outer side of the grille. There was no reason why Her Royal Highness should be alarmed. . . .

She was not alarmed, but she preferred to accept the invitation of the Abbess to remain behind the grille. They entered the rear of the parlor together, and the dark draperies which curtained the grille were drawn back, permitting the cloistered women and the armed men to regard each other through the heavy tracery of iron bars. The two women saw a great company in glittering mail and a powerful prelate in a scarlet cloak ornamented with a great cross; the armed men saw a black-veiled nun and a young girl whose white wool dress trailed on the ground and whose fair, unbound hair fell in shining waves over her shoulders. The men, who had expected that, one by one, they would kneel to kiss Isabel's hand, could only kneel. She remained standing at a safe distance, waiting for Carrillo to speak.[7]

He told her that now her brother Alfonso was dead, she was their one hope. They had come to offer her their allegiance—and the crown of Castile.

She heard him through quietly. Then, just as quietly, she reminded him that her other brother, Enrique, was still the lawful King of Castile, as he had legally inherited the crown from their father, Juan II. Since this was the case, no one had a right to wrest his throne from him, especially as kings derived their authority from God as well as man. The crown was his to keep as long as he lived. She did not blame her brother Don Alfonso—for the repose of whose soul she now constantly prayed—because his viewpoint had been different; no doubt he had acted as he believed right. But as far as she was concerned, Enrique IV could count on her loyalty as long as he lived.

Yes, she had said that twice. Had anyone noticed that she had said nothing as to where her loyalties would lie after his death? Probably not. . . .

"For if I should gain the throne by disobedience to him, how could I blame anyone who might raise his hand in disobedience to me?" she inquired, bringing her reply to an end by asking a question herself. Then once more she stood silent.

Instantly Carrillo's booming voice resounded through the room again. Did Her Royal Highness realize what would happen if she persisted in a refusal? Her life, as well as the lives of all these her loyal subjects, would be in danger from the vengeance of the King and Queen. More than that: Castile—her country—would face almost certain ruin. If it met with a horrible fate, the blame for this would be at her door, for she alone embodied its salvation in this critical hour.

To all appearances, the passionate plea left her unmoved. Finally it was obvious to the Primate of Spain that there was nothing he could say or do which would change the mind of this girl with the firm mouth. He bowed, and turned toward the outer door of the parlor, the same by which he had entered it; then, followed by his cavaliers, he went down the short flight of stone steps leading to the paved vestibule of the convent and thence out into the courtyard, and on to the street where the gaping multitude awaited him. Isabel and the Abbess remained standing in their places until the last man had disappeared. Then the Abbess drew the dark curtains across the grille again and led the girl back into the upper gallery. As they looked down from it into the patio, they could see the lay sisters putting the laundry out on the grass to dry. It was spread white and clean and fragrant in the sun, all around the central stone well, crowned with a cross, and some of the sisters, conscious that they were observed at their work, looked up and smiled; they were very proud to have Doña Isabel as their guest.

The Infanta and the Abbess bade each other good-bye at the door of the great raftered room. Then both returned to their prayers.

3

For two months more, Isabel remained secluded at the Convent of Santa Ana in Avila. Outside its walls, tumult still raged. But it was a tumult subsiding in waves.

The dire predictions of Carrillo had not come to pass. Enrique was bankrupt; he was willing to make almost any concession to the rebels if this would mean money, and their fear that, if they sued for peace, this would mean their destruction, was quite unfounded. Villena, again at odds with Carrillo, though they were still nominally on the same side of the fence, informed his hated rival that he thought Isabel had done quite right in refusing the crown; at the same time, he counseled the King, with whom he was again *en rapport*, that he thought it would be a good thing to acknowledge her as his heir temporarily. Without a struggle, Enrique agreed to do this; he also agreed to meet the rebel barons in the place of their choice—Toros de Guisando, a field some leagues distant from Avila, where Julius Caesar had won a great victory hundreds and hundreds of years before. Its name came from the nearby Hieronymite Monastery of Guisando and the four stone bulls, rudely sculptured in some age even more remote, which marked the field's approach from the rough roads winding down to it over the stark hills. Straggly bushes, scrubby trees and great gray boulders served as natural boundaries to an enclosure which provided sufficient space for a great company to assemble, and sufficient seclusion to keep such an assemblage screened from general observation. Moreover, its location was central enough to make it accessible from many different directions.

When word was brought to Isabel of the proposed meeting, she announced her intention of attending it. Carrillo waited on her again and counseled her against such a course; he had reason to fear that the proposed agreement would amount to nothing and, what was far more serious, he also had reason to fear for her personal safety. If she herself had been given to fears, she might well have been afraid of the latter, too, especially since Villena was manipulating the terms between the rebels and the King. But, as usual, her judgment proved sound. She rode out to Toros de Guisando at Carrillo's side, and remained beside him while the extraordinary contract, to which Enrique signed his name, was read aloud to the assembled nobles drawn up with great ceremony and solemnity on either side of the field guarded by the four stone bulls:

(1) He granted a general amnesty to all the insurgents.
(2) He agreed to ask the Pope to annul his marriage to Queen Juana and to send her back to Portugal within four months.
(3) He acknowledged Isabel as Princess of the Asturias and heiress to the throne of Castile and León.
(4) He agreed to convoke a Cortes within forty days, to give legal sanction to Isabel's title, and to discuss necessary reforms in government.
(5) He promised never to compel Isabel to marry against her wishes on condition that she would not marry without his consent.
(6) He agreed to give Isabel the cities of Avila, Huete, Molina, Medina del Campo, Olmedo, Escalona and Ubeda, for her proper maintenance as heiress.[8]

The date of this extraordinary document was September 19, 1468.

If Isabel was surprised that the terms of this treaty were so favorable to her, or shocked that her brother would consent to insult his wife so publicly, her feelings were not apparent. With the same imperturbability that she had shown throughout, she accepted Enrique's embrace, and his salutation of her as his heiress. Then she received the nobles who came to pledge allegiance to her. This time, they were also able to kiss her hand.

4

Avila was her own now, more significant and more splendid than any of the other cities which had been ceded to her. Olmedo was important to her, not only because it was a well-fortified town, but be-

cause she would always associate it with the gallant defense in which
her beloved brother, Alfonso, had played such a valiant part. True,
no decisive victory had taken place and, therefore, he did not personify
the truth of the old saying that "whoever wants to be master of Castile
has only to conquer Olmedo and Arévalo"; but he had proven his mettle and helped to prevent actual defeat with a skill far beyond his
years. Medina del Campo was also closely associated with him in his
sister's mind, for it had been the scene of their happy carefree outings
which he and she had shared when they went to the great fairs held
in the spacious square; and above this plaza loomed the mighty castle
suitable for a royal residence because of its size and splendor, besides
being impregnable as a fortress. Escalona was also castle crowned,
besides being beautifully situated on a river; and Ubeda was as rich
in the olive groves, silvering the slopes which it surmounted, as in the
architectural marvels which surrounded its squares and lined its streets.
But none of these had the grandeur of Avila. Its tawny walls, indestructible as they were magnificent; its superb gates, which could be
relentlessly closed against an invader or opened wide to admit a welcome cavalcade; its great gray cathedral, which was no less a place of
worship because it was also a mighty fortress; its monasteries and its
churches, its mullioned palaces and pleasant plazas—all these were
now encompassed by her prerogative. Moreover, it was the city which
had accepted and hailed her beloved brother, Alfonso, as its sovereign.
He would not alas! go down in history as the King of Castile; but he
would always be known lovingly and locally as King of Avila. Isabel
was no more likely to forget its touching tribute to him than she was
likely to forget that it was here she herself had been offered the crown.

True, she had declined that offer; but that was only because reason
as well as conscience told her that she should bide her time. Now
she could have a palace of her own in the walled city if she chose,
or she could ask to have part of the Convent of Santa Ana set aside
for her use and that of her ladies-in-waiting until she actually became
Queen or until she desired to marry. A procedure of this sort would
have been by no means unusual and such an arrangement would have
suited her spirit perfectly. But she did not need Carrillo's reminder
that, though the treaty of Toros de Guisando had been signed, it had
not yet been ratified by the Cortes, which was about to assemble at
Ocaña.[9]

To Ocaña, Isabel wisely decided to go herself. It was one thing
to receive reports from a distance; it was quite another to watch the

progress of events with her own eyes, to think them over and to decide what to do next in the light of what she saw.

It was just as well that she made this decision. The delegates took the oath of allegiance to Isabel, but Enrique, after making many vague promises for the betterment of his people, dissolved the Cortes before this body could formally ratify the treaty of Toros de Guisando.

This was more or less what Carrillo had expected. He rightly guessed that Villena was up to his usual wiles, and that the treaty was only a stopgap until some convenient means to get rid of Isabel could be found. The most convenient means was naturally a foreign alliance and opportunely—almost too opportunely to have it appear simply a coincidence—an impressive delegation arrived from Portugal. The question of a marriage between King Alfonso V and Isabel had been in abeyance since the state meeting at Gibraltar; now it was raised again, more urgently than before. Almost simultaneously, an envoy arrived from Aragon, with a fresh request that Isabel would graciously bestow her hand on Prince Fernando.

There was nothing new about this request, either. Isabel had been only six when she had first heard Enrique discussing such an alliance with her mother. At that time, she had not understood what it all meant. But since then she had heard the proposal repeated rather frequently, sometimes with a half promise attached to it; gradually, she had come to grasp better what it meant or at least what it might mean, and to like what she did understand. She had already decided, at Gibraltar, what she thought of the Portuguese King; now she felt it would be a good idea to find out a little more about Fernando and also, about a third suitor who, though unrepresented at the moment, was also a serious contender: the Duke of Guienne, brother of King Louis XI of France and, until recently, heir prospective to the French crown. Somehow, she contrived to send her chaplain secretly to look these two suitors over. He returned with a very unflattering report of the Frenchman and an enthusiastic one of the Aragonese.

Intuitively, Isabel had begun to feel that Fernando was her man, but this was no moment to trust to instinct alone. Cautiously and confidentially, she discussed the situation with Carrillo, permitting him to point out various angles of it which she had considered already. If she married either Alfonso V or the Duke of Guienne, she would have to leave her own Castile and live as a foreigner in her husband's country; nothing would suit Enrique and Villena better than this, but it was doubtful whether it would suit her. She would not be a Queen Regnant in either case, but a Queen Consort in one and a mere Duchess in the other. Neither could she count on having her future children reigning monarchs, as Alfonso V had a son by his first wife and Louis XI, in his old age, had belatedly got a son. On the other hand, if she married Fernando, they would jointly reign over the two largest and most important kingdoms in the Iberian Peninsula and their own union might well unite these; in that case, such an alliance would lay the foundations of a new order. Both kingdoms were bent on the destruction of the Moor; with this common aim as an incentive—not to mention the fact that Castile had an army and Aragon had a navy—it was well within the realm of possibility that they could accomplish their purpose; once this was done, they could become the most powerful nation in Europe. They already had the advantages of a common tradition, a common tongue and common customs; these, in themselves, were tremendous assets. Besides, everyone spoke well of Fernando. He was vigorous, accomplished and good-looking, just about her own age, too—well, just a little younger and not quite so tall, either. But these were trifling differences, according to Carrillo.

Isabel agreed with him. Then, having listened to Carrillo, she listened first to Gutierre de Cárdenas, her *maestresala*,[10] and next to Don Fadrique Enriquez, the wiry, fiery little Admiral of Castile, who had long been friendly to her cause. "'Since the modesty customary to damsels prevented them from deciding concerning their own marriages,' she had certain scruples. Cárdenas managed to overcome them by arguing that, as her father was dead, and her mother incapacitated by illness, she must be guided by public opinion. The three estates— nobles, clergy and common people—wished her to marry Fernando, he said. After a moment of reflection, the girl replied,

"'God, the witness of hearts, knows that before my own affection I look first to the welfare of these kingdoms. And since the votes of the nobles appear to point in this direction, and it seems pleasing to God, I will conform to His will and submit to the opinion of all.'"[11]

Having made this praiseworthy declaration, Isabel received the Portuguese delegation with courtesy, dwelt on her awareness of the compliment that had been paid her and said that she would give it her most careful consideration. This was a little too vague to satisfy either her brother or the Portuguese King's envoy and, for the second time, Enrique threatened to incarcerate her until she came to her senses; but she was older and more adroit now than when he had succeeded in appalling her with the prospect of marriage to the loathsome Don Pedro and her position was infinitely stronger. It was not so easy to browbeat her. She conversed again with the delegate from Lisbon, pleasantly reminding him that she and the King were within the forbidden bounds of consanguinity, since he was her mother's own cousin. Was she not right in believing that, so far, the Pope had failed to grant a dispensation? Ah! Well, if and when he did, that would, of course, make a difference. Meanwhile. . . .

Meanwhile, she unobtrusively sent her faithful *maestresala*, Gutierre de Cárdenas, and her friend, Alonso de Palencia,[11-a] to Aragon with instructions to accept Fernando's proposal.

It was a bold step, actually a dangerous one, even though Carrillo, Cárdenas and Fadrique told her she was justified in taking it, since Enrique had already broken the terms of the treaty of Toros de Guisando by trying to force her into a marriage with the Portuguese King. Fadrique could hardly be considered an impartial adviser, since he was Fernando's maternal grandfather,[12] and had everything to gain and nothing to lose by such a match; and Carrillo was obliged to flee from Ocaña somewhat hastily, for, if Isabel had her secret messengers, Enrique had his spies, and he soon learned both of the Archbishop's advocacy of the Aragonese suitor and of the departure of Isabel's two emissaries. Foaming with rage, partly because Carrillo and Cárdenas were both beyond his reach, and partly at this fresh proof of his sister's insubordination, Enrique ordered Isabel's arrest.

But the next morning, when she awoke, she was unexpectedly still at liberty; and below her window was an armed mob—all sorts and conditions of men, women and children, bearing every sort of primitive weapon along with the pennants of Aragon and Castile. They were lampooning the King of Portugal and the Court of Spain, they were improvising ribald verses about La Beltraneja and her parents, and finally they burst forth into lusty song:

> *"Flores de Aragon*
> *dentro Castilla son!*
> *Pendon de Aragon!*
> *Pendon de Aragon!"*[12-a]

These were the sort of people on whom Cárdenas had told her she could count. She had trusted him and her own heart, and neither her judgment nor her intuition had played her false. In the face of this new uprising, Enrique had little choice and no courage. He countermanded the order for Isabel's arrest and set off for the south, giving as his excuse that there was even worse trouble in that vicinity and that when this was settled, he would come back and deal with the Princess as she deserved.

She did not await his return or risk a change in the popular feeling. Taking immediate advantage of the opportunity afforded by her brother's absence, she set off at top speed for Madrigal, and was soon safely installed in the place of her birth—the little city of lilting songs and high towers.

5

What happened next would seem to belong to the realm of romance rather than the realm of history, were it not for the fact that history, interpreted through its most vital figures, is so much more glowing and arresting than any tales peopled by imaginary characters.

Isabel's envoys to Fernando, Gutierre de Cárdenas and Alonso de Palencia, managed to arrive safely in Aragon, but they heard many disquieting rumors along the way: the Bishop of Burgos, a relative of Villena, was hostile to Isabel; so were some of the most powerful nobles along the Aragonese border, who had sworn to ambush Fernando if he attempted to cross this. Cárdenas managed to relay these alarming tidings to Isabel by a trusty messenger who tracked her from Ocaña, where her emissaries had left her, to Madrigal, where she had so confidently taken refuge. And to the disquieting news, Cárdenas added a word of advice—she had better ask for help from Carrillo—speedily.

She did so, but her appeal brought no immediate response. Meanwhile, Cárdenas and Palencia had found Aragon in a state of turmoil. Fernando was fighting on one front, his father, Juan II, on another, and his mother, Juana Enriquez, on another. The King was almost blind with a double cataract; the Queen had cancer. But they were a doughty pair and there was nothing on which they had more stubbornly set their will than the marriage of their son with the Castilian Princess. It cannot be said that their purpose was disinterested: Juan saw in the alliance a safeguard against the ever-increasing menace of a powerful France; Juana saw in it further gratification of her ever-vaulting ambition; both refused to admit that the situation was hopeless. The King submitted to an operation, recovered his sight and resumed leadership of his troops at the age of eighty; forging his way through the enemy lines which surrounded him, he entered Barcelona in triumph. The Queen died, but she had kept death at bay until her army had been reinforced by Fernando's near Gerona and she had witnessed the victory of their joint forces over John of Lorraine. It was hardly to be expected that the son of such parents would abandon his courtship merely because there was still no law and order in the land and no money in the treasury, or because a few robber barons, with whom he would know how to deal in short order, tried to frighten him with threats. He gaily signed the marriage contract, ransomed— with borrowed funds—a necklace that had belonged to his mother and, entrusting this to Cárdenas, sent it to Isabel with the message that he would soon be with her, but that, meanwhile, the bauble would serve as a token of his love.

The necklace was not only the most beautiful article of personal adornment which Isabel had ever possessed or even seen; it was more beautiful than any of which she had ever dreamed. Its pearls gleamed, its rubies glowed, as she took it in her white hands and then proudly clasped it around her slim throat. She was still at Madrigal when her emissaries returned with their joyous message and their magnificent gift and, during their absence, she had managed to deal singlehanded with the Cardinal of Albi, who had learned of her presence there and had come to plead the cause of the Duke of Guienne. This suit had previously been presented to her and adroitly evaded. Now that it had been renewed, she was even more adroit in her answers, claiming that the responsibility for her choice must lie first with God and secondly with the grandees of her kingdom. No mention had been made of her representatives' journey to Aragon. Though the Cardinal was, of course, aware of their mission and suspicious of Isabel's favorable interest in it, he had been obliged to leave Madrigal without securing from her an acknowledgment of this. Once more, she had played for time and time had been on her side.

She knew that its sands were running low. Villena's uncle, the Bishop of Burgos, decided that the moment had come when it would not be amiss for him to visit Madrigal, too, and Isabel was now wearing her necklace not only proudly, but openly. She realized that, when Villena and the King were supplied with the detailed description of it which would soon be on its way to them, their fury would have no bounds. It was not hard to guess that a detachment of cavalry would be ordered to Madrigal with instructions to seize the troublesome girl who seemed bent on flouting her brother's authority. But though she had not heard from the Archbishop of Toledo, she had not ceased to trust him and her confidence was not misplaced: before the cavalry of Enrique could reach Madrigal, the horsemen of Carrillo were there, three hundred strong. Without hesitation, without question, Isabel rode away with him at their head in the middle of the night. By morning—the morning fixed for her seizure—she was safe in Valladolid.

That is to say, comparatively safe. The cavalry of Enrique, though larger than that of Carrillo, could not prevail against such an army as the friendly city of Valladolid could raise—overnight, if necessary—in defense of Isabel. No such foolish and futile move would be attempted, especially as Don Fadrique, Fernando's grandfather, was using Valladolid as his headquarters and could add the power and prestige of his position as Admiral of Castile and the forces at his disposal to the troops which the citizenry could supply. However, given a little more time, Enrique was quite capable of sending not a mere detachment, but a sizable army. Swiftness and secrecy of action on the part of Isabel and her advisers was now more essential than ever. If worse came to worst, she could, as Fernando's wife, take temporary refuge in Aragon. But the chances were that no such desperate measures would be necessary. As a married woman, her position would be infinitely stronger than at present in Castile, especially since Fernando's reputation as a successful warrior was already well established. When she had such a man as that for a husband, it would be much more difficult and dangerous to cope with her than ever before. . . .

So again a trusty emissary was sped away, with instructions to urge disguise as well as haste on the recipient of the message. The reply was prompt but cautious: The Prince of Aragon would come "if he could." Isabel did not doubt that he would manage. And he did. Less than three weeks elapsed between the arrival of Cárdenas and Palencia in Saragossa and the arrival of Fernando in Valladolid.

Fernando had a tall tale to tell and every word of it was true. The barons on the border had been shamelessly outwitted. The Prince had travelled as a muleteer, serving a group of "merchants" going eastward from Aragon. They had taken back roads and stopped only at small squalid inns. No suspicions were roused when they crossed the frontier. But there had been a near accident after they reached Castile. The "muleteer," feeling that he could now throw caution to the winds, had ridden ahead of the "merchants" and pounded on the gate of a castle near Burgo de Osma, which belonged to the Count of Treviño, one of Isabel's most loyal supporters. But it was already locked for the night, and a sentry, suspicious of a raid, and too greatly alarmed to wait and discover whether these suspicions were well founded, began heaving rocks from the top of a battlement. One of these—a stone the size of a man's head—grazed Fernando's ear and he raised an out-cry in his own name. After that, of course, there had been opened gates, swift apologies, a warm welcome for him and the members of his household who, no longer posing as merchants, came swiftly rid-ing up after him. No, he really had not been hurt at all—a mere scratch, a mere bruise, hardly any blood drawn to speak of. How could he help but lead a charmed life, considering his errand? . . . He had stopped at Dueñas only long enough to change into more suitable apparel and then he had been officially escorted to Valladolid. And now here he was in the palace of his good friend, Juan de Vivero, ready to present himself to his betrothed and receive her as his bride.

What knight had ever approached his liege lady with so thrilling a story and so valid and urgent a claim? None, Isabel felt very sure. From the moment that she first beheld Fernando, she looked at him with eyes of love. Everything about his appearance was pleasing to her: his fine build, his erect carriage, his courtly manner, his high brow, his vivid coloring, his quick flashing smile and quick flashing glance. The coloring seemed, at first, to be confined to different shades of brown—a deep tan, chestnut-tinted hair, dark, heavy eyebrows; but Isabel soon saw that his mouth was red and that the same red glowed under the brown of his cheeks. The smile was not there all the time; Isabel watched for it to come and go. Without it, his face was grave; with it, suddenly illumined. The glance was roving; Isabel waited for it to rest on her. She recognized it as bold, shrewd and searching when it darted first in one direction and then in another. It would be hard to browbeat or hoodwink this man. The glance was still bold and shrewd and searching when it rested on her, but at such times it softened and lingered. Its audacity, already tinged with ardor, was a tribute to her charm; its shrewdness bespoke recognition of her char-acter and courage; its quest discovered nothing that did not arouse respect and admiration. She knew that his appraisal of her was as re-warding as hers of him and she hoped that, when she addressed him directly, the effect would be satisfactory to the same degree. For if his appearance had pleased her, his voice thrilled her through and through. In this there was no similarity when he spoke to others and when he spoke to her; its harshness turned to melody, its arrogance to solicitude. As she looked and listened, she knew that her instinct had been true: no man should ever be her master, but this was the one she wanted for her mate.

She was ready to let him know this. He had thrown caution to the winds in coming to her and she was too great a lady to play the coquette or feign an indifference she did not feel. There was no mock modesty about her. But there was one reason for hesitation: she and Fernando were within the prohibited bonds of consanguinity, for their fathers, Juan II of Castile and Juan II of Aragon, were own cousins.[13] It would require a Papal Bull to afford the necessary dispensation. Oh, if the lack of this were the only impediment to their immediate union, she need not give the matter another thought! Such a contingency had long been foreseen and Fernando had come prepared for it. He stood by, his smile resting lovingly upon her, while his grandfather, the Admiral of Castile, handed a document to the Archbishop which bore the signature of the previous Pope, Pius II, and was dated five years earlier; it authorized Fernando to marry any person within the third degree of kinship. It did not occur to Isabel that she should question its authenticity.[14]

The provisions of the marriage settlement which, like the lack of a dispensation, might have presented difficulties if either of the high-contracting parties had been disposed to make them, were also accepted without demur, though, in this case, it was Fernando who made the greatest concessions. "He agreed to respect all the laws and usages of Castile; to reside there and never leave the country without his wife's consent; to make no appointments, civil or military, without her approval; to leave all nominations to Church benefices in her hands; to alienate no property belonging to the Crown; to continue the Holy War against the Moors of Granada; to provide always for the maintenance and comfort of Isabel's mother, the Queen Dowager, at Arévalo; to treat King Enrique with respect and filial devotion as the lawful ruler of Castile. All public ordinances were to be signed jointly by Isabel and Fernando unless one of them happened to be out of the kingdom. Isabel, if she succeeded Enrique, was to be the undisputed sovereign of Castile—Fernando was to have the title of King only by courtesy."[15] Isabel was in love and she was ready to go to great lengths to prove this; but she was still the Princess, still the heiress to a throne —still the girl with the firm mouth which did not quiver even at the prospect of the kisses which would make it redder than ever before.

Fernando had arrived in Valladolid on the eleventh of October; the very next day, Isabel wrote to her brother, Enrique, that she intended to be married at once. She gave reasons for this immediacy, but made no excuses, though she could hardly have forgotten that when he promised she should never be forced, against her will, to marry, she had likewise promised never to marry without his consent. She intimated that she would have been glad to await his blessing, had not the Archbishop, the Admiral and the Prince overpersuaded her, and convinced her that delay would be disastrous. It is one of the few recorded cases in which she prevaricated. The wedding day could not possibly have come too quickly to suit her and, within a week, she and Fernando were married in the palace of their friend, Juan de Vivero, with some two thousand well-wishers as witnesses. For six days thereafter, Valladolid gave itself over with joy to the celebration of this propitious event. The bridal couple withdrew to realms of rapture.

As the weeks lengthened into months, they discovered to their joy that their bridal happiness had the firm foundation of so many mutual or correlative habits and tastes that it could not fail to be enduring. They were not only blissful lovers; they were good companions and thoughtful partners. Both went daily to Mass as a matter of course. Both were abstemious at table. Both preferred simplicity of dress to ostentation, though both recognized the importance of parading a regal role to the full on great occasions. Both liked to make lists of persons who might be useful to them and record these neatly in little notebooks. Both were accomplished riders and skilled hunters. Isabel did not care for cards and Fernando did; on the other hand, she was fonder of reading than he was, so neither of these pursuits interfered with the other. He was the better chess player, but she was glad to have him enjoy the games he liked while she did needlework. She was busier than ever with this now, for she made all his shirts, spinning the thread, weaving the linen, sewing the seams, embroidering the collars. It was a labor of love, but it was also a proud pursuit. She would have been ashamed to have her husband wear a garment that was not worthy of his station.

It was not until after Christmas that Isabel was roused to real uneasiness by her brother's long and silent inactivity. She had written him a second letter, shortly after her marriage, claiming that, since he had failed to abide by the terms of the treaty of Toros de Guisando when he tried to force her into marriage with Alfonso V, she had been justified in breaking a pledge in her turn. It was unfortunate that she had not stressed this point in her first letter, instead of blaming her precipitancy on her betrothed, his grandfather and the Archbishop of Toledo. Her argument would have had far more weight if it had not been so tardy, and it is not surprising that Enrique's only answer to it was a brief message to the effect that he would consult his ministers. Months went by before he sent her any further word and then the word was disquieting: Isabel, he said, had broken the treaty of Toros de Guisando. (He, naturally, did not admit that he had broken it first.) Therefore, he proposed to treat her like any other rebel.

This, she knew, meant discord and strife at the very least. At the worst, it might well mean another civil war.

She was not frightened, but she recognized the gravity of the situation. The idyllic interlude was over. And though the memory of it would illumine the rest of her life, she must now prepare for rough going. Tranquilly, she accepted the decision on the part of her advisers that she should leave Valladolid, which was no longer safe for her. The Archbishop suggested Dueñas, where his brother, Don Pedro de Acuña, would be glad to offer the hospitality of his house to the young couple. They accepted the invitation.

It was a quiet place. Fernando had plenty of time for chess. Isabel had plenty of time for needlework. She welcomed it. For she was not only making her husband's shirts now; she was making baby clothes.

6

The baby, a beautiful, fair-haired, little girl, was born on the first of October and named after her mother.

Now that the care of a child had been added to her other responsibilities, Isabel decided that the time had come to make a further appeal to Enrique. Her daughter was only a few days old when she sat up in bed and wrote another long letter, in which she reviewed everything that had been said and done by him at Toros de Guisando and much which he had said and done since. She reminded him of all the important witnesses to his words and deeds, piously placing the Almighty at their head, but not failing to mention the more accessible archbishops, bishops and noblemen who were present in person. She then dwelt on the dire consequences which might result if her brother failed to keep faith with her, at first rather obliquely and then in a manner so direct that it took the form of a threat.

All in all, this was one of the most tactless documents that ever bore her signature, and though it is easy enough to understand why she wrote in this vein, if she were going to write at all when she was exhausted and angry, it is also easy to understand why the King sent her an indignant letter in reply and why his retort to his sister soon assumed the proportions of a dare. He recalled Queen Juana and her daughter from the virtual exile into which they had been sent; required the ever-obliging Villena and several other equally complacent noblemen to take the oath of allegiance to La Beltraneja on the ground that he had changed his mind as to who was the rightful heiress to Castile and León; and betrothed the poor little girl, who must, by this time, have been in a state of complete bewilderment, to the Duke of Guienne. Then he and his Court repaired to Segovia, where they proceeded to eat, drink and be merry.

It was only one short year since Isabel had felt that her cup of joy was full. Now she had to swallow one bitter pill after another and her husband was not with her to comfort and support her. His aged father's affairs had taken a turn for the worse and he was recalled to Aragon, in the forlorn hope that his presence might be helpful in the war against the French King, Louis XI. Isabel did not try to prevent him from going; but she could not help feeling that it was easier for him to go without her than it was for her to remain behind without him. And this was not only because the excitement of war would act as a stimulant which the dreary life at Dueñas could not provide. Rumors had reached her that she had not been Fernando's first and only love, as he had been hers; worse yet, that the beautiful, blonde baby girl was not even his first-born. If Isabel had given the matter sober thought, she would have known that she could not expect him to be as singlehearted as she was herself or to have the same standards of chastity. Male promiscuity was so generally accepted as a matter of course that her very claim to the throne was based partly on the fact that Enrique was not known to have any illegitimate children and that, therefore, he was undoubtedly impotent. But she had not expected that she would so soon have cause for jealousy. The other woman—the other baby's mother—was in Aragon with her little boy; it was unthinkable that Fernando would not see them both again. And perhaps the sight of his son, if not the sight of his former mistress, would stir within him longing for a renewal of an association which it had been hard for him to forego and he would yield to this desire. Isabel had to fight against the fear that it might be so.

When the cold Castilian winter set in, Isabel was alone with her baby, and such news as reached her from the outside world brought no cheer with it. Crime was rampant, fear and famine were in the land. How was she to know that even these were on her side, that time and death were still also her allies? The wretched people who, not without reason, blamed Enrique and his favorite for their want and misery, felt hope stirring within them at the thought that, with a different ruler, their hard lot in life might be better—certainly it could not be worse. They were ready and eager to risk the change. Many of the nobles shared this feeling and, whereas, poor peasants could only murmur and groan, *caballeros* could act. The day came when Isabel heard that the town of Sepúlveda, which Enrique had given to Villena, refused to admit the favorite within its walls; instead, it swore allegiance to Isabel. Agreda acted in a similar manner by rejecting the powerful Duke of Medinaceli and declaring for her. Aranda de Duero, where Queen Juana's officers had been quartered, sent them packing and ran up Isabel's standard. She left her isolated refuge in Dueñas and went to Aranda to receive the homage of these gallant soldiers. And it was there that the faithful friend of her girlhood, Beatriz de Bobadilla, who was now married to the powerful governor of the Alcázar in Segovia, Andrés de Cabrera, came to tell her that she, Beatriz, believed the time might be ripe for a reconciliation with Enrique. . . .

Things were not going so well with him and his plans after all. The Duke of Guienne had died, under suspicious circumstances, so nothing had come of the French match for La Beltraneja. Nothing would come of a proposed alliance with Portugal, either, for its King had managed to make excuses when the unfortunate little girl was offered to him. The child seemed to have lost her usefulness as a pawn and, therefore, as a prospective heiress. At the moment, Enrique was at his hunting lodge, where he was sulking rather than shooting. If Isabel would come to Segovia and stay at the Alcázar as the guest of its governor and his lady, and Enrique were tactfully informed of her presence, Beatriz could not help thinking. . . .

Isabel did not wait for her to think differently. The suggestion of a precipitate descent upon Enrique embodied the type of challenge which the Princess was never slow to accept. Beatriz had slipped off to Aranda in the guise of a poor country woman and Isabel had cherished a weakness for such disguises ever since the band of "merchants" served by a "muleteer" had made their way from Saragossa to Valladolid. That masquerade had come to a triumphant conclusion; why should this one not do likewise? And had she ever hesitated to go riding off into the darkness? What about that midnight gallop from Madrigal, with Carrillo at her side and Enrique's cavalry hot on her trail? Oh—so the Archbishop was to be her escort again this time, if she consented to the scheme? Better and better! They would ride through the night again and be at the Alcázar before dawn on whatever day Beatriz had in mind.

It was no sooner said than done. Enrique, whose inconsistencies would be unbelievable if they were not a matter of record, received her with enthusiasm. He speedily left his hunting lodge and hastened to the palace, for he could hardly wait to welcome and embrace his sister. The pleasure she had given others in coming to Segovia, he assured her and everyone else who would listen, was as nothing to the pleasure she gave him by so doing. The next day they must go through the city together, she on a fine white horse, he on foot, with his hand on her bridle rein. The populace must see them like that. And then, of course, there must be a round of feasts. . . .

Unfortunately, at the first of these, which was celebrated on Epiphany, Enrique ate something that disagreed with him. He took to his bed, doubled up with pain and convinced that poison had been part of the picture. The finger of suspicion did not point in any one direction and, after a few days, he was well enough to get up again. But when he did so, he shook the dust of Segovia from his feet and went as fast as he could to Madrid. In little or no time he had so far forgotten his transitory enthusiasm for his sister that he was more than ready to listen to a plot for assassinating Beatriz and Cabrera and for seizing Isabel and Carrillo with the idea of disposing of them later.

But time, always so beneficial to Isabel, was less advantageous to Enrique. The first person he approached for approval of this plot was Don Pedro González de Mendoza, Bishop of Sigüenza, who had once been one of his most loyal supporters; and Mendoza's recoil from the suggestion was so violent that Enrique was frightened by this vehemence. The Bishop not only denounced the plot as infamous to the last degree; he went on to point out that the whole realm was convinced the succession belonged to Isabel and that such an act as

Enrique was contemplating would result in actual danger to the King himself.

It was this argument, far more than any appeal against a hideous crime, which caused Enrique to hesitate. He was essentially a coward. And, while he was hesitating, death, which, like time, played such a part in Isabel's destiny, dealt the King a body blow by striking down Villena at the very moment when he was besieging the latest town of which Enrique had made him a present. The King, who had been ailing ever since that ill-fated feast at Epiphany, could not rally from the shock of this loss, though he tried to console himself with Villena's son. He died, as he had lived, in a state of vacillation and ignominy. As his end drew near, Mendoza, who had become Cardinal of Spain, tried to persuade him to make a will and settle the question of succession forever. He simply sighed and turned away. His only reference to La Beltraneja was an injunction that she should do what was required of her by Mendoza, the new Marqués of Villena and certain other great personages. The only wish he expressed was that he should be buried beside his mother at Santa María de Guadalupe.

Isabel, who had been biding her time in Segovia, was still there when the news of his death came flashing through that same day. She gave immediate orders that the flags of Castile and of the city should be lowered and covered with black. Then she, herself, dressed in black, and went to the Church of San Miguel to pray for the repose of her brother's soul. When she emerged from the gloom of the sanctuary into the crisp, bright air, the streets were already thronged with shouting people who waited to hail her as their rightful ruler.

The next day she was crowned Queen of Castile.

7

The coronation of Isabel took a magnificent form.

The December day was clear and crisp, with a bright blue sky overhead and white frost upon the ground. There was a sparkle to it which it owed partly to the sky and partly to the frost. And, as the trumpets sounded and the great gates of the Alcázar opened to let Isabel pass through into the crowded streets beyond, her people saw that she was riding a white palfrey, that she was dressed in white brocade and ermine, and that jewels were glittering not only at her throat and on her fingers, but even on the arch of the small foot which rested lightly on her shining stirrup. The radiance of the day came not only from the elements; it also emanated from the Queen.

Directly in front of her rode a herald, holding aloft the Castilian "sword of justice" to signify that this radiant girl in white had power of life and death over ten million subjects. Directly behind her came two pages, bearing on a golden cushion the crown of her ancestor, Ferdinand III, the King who had effected the permanent union of Castile and León and who had been venerated as Ferdinand the Saint for many generations. On one side of her rode Andrés de Cabrera, stately in his robes of office as Governor of the Alcázar; on the other, Carrillo, Archbishop of Toledo, his shining armor veiled but not concealed by his vestments of purple and gold. And following in their wake came a magnificent procession of prelates and nobles, soldiery and citizenry. The churchmen chanted *Te Deum Laudamus!* The rabble roared *Viva la Reina!* The narrow streets resounded with the singing and the shouting.

A high platform had been erected on the plaza and here the waiting throne had been placed. Isabel dismounted from her white palfrey and ascended the steps, her shining mantle floating out behind her. Once more the trumpets sounded. Then there was a moment of breathless silence as the Archbishop placed the crown of St. Ferdinand on her golden hair and Cabrera knelt to hand her the keys of the city and of the citadel. The stillness was broken by the voice of a herald proclaiming, "Castile! Castile! Castile for the King Don Fernando and his wife Doña Isabel, Queen Proprietress of this kingdom!" And while his words were still ringing through the frosty air, the singing and the shouting began again, louder and more vehement even than before. Guns roared from the Alcázar, cannon boomed from the city walls and all the bells of Segovia rang out. *Viva la Reina! Viva la Reina!*

In the midst of this pandemonium, Isabel sat on her throne, serene and smiling, inclining a crowned head and extending a jeweled hand as she accepted the oath of allegiance from the dignitaries who came forward to swear it. Many of her oldest and most trusted friends were there, among them those two faithful messengers, Gutierre de Cárdenas and Alonso de Palencia. A new, but no less valued friend, was Gonzalo de Córdoba, the "Golden Youth" who had come forward to offer her his sword and service during her dark days of waiting and uncertainty. More unexpectedly, came Don Beltrán de la Cueva, Duke of Alburquerque; and as he bent to kiss the outstretched hand, there was again a moment of silence, and this time it was a shocked stillness. His very presence attested to the proof of Isabel's claim to the throne on which she now sat, to the crown which rested on her fair hair. But it also stigmatized anew the frail widow of the weak and wicked King who still lay in state at his palace in Madrid, and the helpless child who was her daughter.

Some of the great nobles whose allegiance was not only wanted but needed were missing in the glittering throng and there was subdued murmuring and suppressed anxiety because of their absence. Don Fadrique, Admiral of Castile, however, was in the very forefront of the celebration, apparently undisturbed, for the moment, because his grandson was receiving no share in the honors that were being heaped upon Isabel. Fernando was very far from feeling the same way about it, when the news of his wife's coronation reached him in far-off Perpignan. At the time of Isabel's brief, theatrical reconciliation with Enrique, Fernando had been hastily recalled to Segovia so that he might share in the love feast. Then he had returned to the support of his aged and destitute father and had given this gladly and efficiently.[16] But it had not occurred to him that, in his absence, Isabel would act so independently; above all, that she would accept such supreme honors unless he were present to share them. True, he had promised to make no civil or military appointments without her approval; to leave all nominations to Church benefices in her hands; and never to leave Castile, where he was henceforth to reside, without her express consent. He had gone even further: he had agreed that he was to have the title of King only by courtesy. But he had done all this when he was a hot-headed suitor. At such times, all men said and did things they regretted afterward; they did not expect to have their words taken too literally or their actions regarded as indicative of permanent habit. He was especially enraged at the mention of the lifted sword which had been carried in the procession—a feature of the coronation glowingly described to him in a letter from Gutierre de Cárdenas. Fernando called upon a historian of his acquaintance to say whether he had ever heard of such a thing as carrying this symbol of power over life and death before a *Queen*. "I have known it only of Kings!" the injured Prince declared with vehemence.

His wrath was contagious. Very naturally, his father shared it and, presently, his grandfather also took his side, repenting the characteristic impetuosity with which he had acted in taking the oath of allegiance. Carrillo also expressed tardy doubts as to whether any woman should be given so much power, revealing for the first time the streak of smallness in a strong character which was soon to dim the splendor of his long loyalty. Neither Fernando's temper nor those of his supporters was improved when he arrived in Segovia, after sweeping down from Catalonia with the same speed that had sent him headlong on his ride to his betrothed; for he was met at the city gates by a group of nobles who greeted him as King of Castile—not through his own right, but through courtesy, as Consort of their Queen. Within the city, another group of nobles, calling itself the Aragonese faction, clamored for Fernando's "rights." He was all too ready, not only to listen, but to join the clamor.

An open breach between husband and wife was very close, for Isabel was angry, too, and deeply hurt besides. The *cédula*, or decree, wherein she announced her brother's death and proclaimed herself Queen, had already been read in Avila and elsewhere. If it had not occurred to Fernando that she would take their marriage contract seriously, neither had it occurred to her that he would not do so. Moreover, she was deeply concerned lest the Salic Law, which prevented a woman from becoming a Queen Regnant, and which operated in Aragon but not in Castile, might eventually disbar her daughter from the throne. The differences in viewpoint between the royal pair soon reached such proportions that Cardinal Mendoza—of whom Carrillo was furiously jealous—was called upon to represent the Queen and Carrillo—of all persons!—the King at a formal conference.

It was Isabel who saved the day. Fortunately, Pulgar, one of the foremost chroniclers of the period, who called her a "woman of great heart," preserved the wording of the speech which she made on this hazardous occasion. Addressing herself directly to Fernando, she said:

"'This subject, *señor*, need never to have been discussed, because where there is such union as by the Grace of God exists between us, there can be no difference. Already, as my husband, you are King of Castile, and your commands have to be obeyed here; and these realms, please God, will remain after our days for your sons and mine. But since it has pleased these cavaliers to open up this discussion, perhaps it is just as well that any doubt they have be clarified, as the law of these our kingdoms provide.' She turned briefly from her husband to confront the troublemakers with a level gaze and then looked back at Fernando again. 'This, *señor*, I say, because, as you perceive, it has not pleased God thus far to give us any heir but the Princess doña Isabel our daughter,' she went on. 'And it could happen that after our days someone might come, who, being descended from the royal

House of Castile, might allege that these realms belong to him, even by the collateral line, on account of her being a woman. . . . Hence you see well, *señor*, what great embarrassments would ensue for our descendants. And . . . we ought to consider that, God willing, the Princess our daughter has to marry a foreign Prince, to whom will belong the government of these realms, and who may desire to place in command of the fortresses and royal patrimony other people of his nation, who will not be Castilians; whence it may follow that the kingdom may pass into the hands of a foreign race. And that would be a great burden on our consciences, and a disservice to God, and a great loss to our successors and subjects. And it is well that this declaration be made now to avoid any misunderstandings in the future.' "[17]

This subject need never have been discussed . . . but since it has arisen, it is well that there should be no misunderstandings in the future. These statements, made by a girl with a firm mouth who was also a powerful queen, a rightly displeased wife and a careful mother, almost automatically prevented any further argument. Fernando was not slow to see this. Our chronicler goes on to relate that the King "knowing this to be true, was much pleased." There is no doubt that he knew it to be true. There may be more as to whether he was pleased. Be this as it may, he "gave orders that nothing further be said on the subject." Nothing was. From then on, the reign of Fernando and Isabel was one of singular unanimity. Their motto became:

Tanto monta, monta tanto
Fernando como Isabel, Isabel como Fernando.[18]

Pulgar put it differently, but quite as effectively. "The favorite of the King was the Queen; the favorite of the Queen was the King." No showy adventurer, like Beltrán de la Cueva, no vulgar page elevated to a marquisate like Juan Pacheco, was ever to come between them to cause public scandal and private shame. The little boy who had been born in Aragon, prior to Fernando's marriage, was eventually to have three sisters, "on the wrong side of the blanket."[19] But their mothers were not flaunted in Isabel's face, nor was there ever a *"maitresse en titre"* at the Court of the Catholic Kings. As for Isabel, the extreme chastity of her life was an example and an inspiration to everyone who moved within her orbit. Like her firmness, it was inviolable.

8

As far as her husband was concerned, Isabel had, indeed, clarified for all time the official status of their relationship to each other and to the Kingdom of Castile. It still remained for her to make completely clear to her people that she intended to brook no question as to her absolute authority and no interference with it.

The second ultimatum, like the first, was delivered in Segovia. Isabel had been enjoying a period of well-earned rest at Tordesillas, which was still rightly regarded as a pleasant place of residence for a queen who did as she pleased and not as a gloomy prison for one who was forcibly imprisoned.[20] A series of battles, constituting a long-drawn-out war with Portugal, had finally ended in a signal victory at Toro; but Fernando, who had played a conspicuous part in these, besides going once again to the succor of his father, Juan of Aragon, had not yet returned to join her. During the earlier part of the war, Isabel, too, had been at the front a large part of the time and had been tireless in scouring the countryside for men and supplies. Each time she appealed for these from her people, she ended her call for aid with a fervent prayer which she recited aloud in the presence of the multitude:

" 'Thou, O Lord, who knowest the secrets of the heart, of me Thou knowest that not by an unjust way, not by cunning or by tyranny, but believing truly that these realms of the King my father belong to me rightfully, have I endeavoured to obtain them, that what the kings my forebears won with so much bloodshed may not fall into the hands of an alien race. Lord, in whose hands lies the sway of kingdoms, I humbly beseech Thee to hear the prayer of Thy servant, and show forth the truth, and manifest Thy will with Thy marvellous works: so that if my cause is not just, I may not be allowed to sin through ignorance, and if it is just, Thou give me wisdom and courage to sustain it with the aid of Thine arm, that through Thy grace we may have peace in these kingdoms, which till now have endured so many evils and destructions.' "[21]

Such words as these, so publicly and yet so devoutly uttered, could not fail to impress her hearers and spur them on to greater and greater action. The penetration of the enemy to her own homeland, especially its encampment at Arévalo, acted as a continual goad to her resourcefulness and courage and she accomplished wonders. But exertion and exposure had taken their toll and she had suffered a miscarriage, which, besides playing havoc with her health, robbed the nation of the eagerly awaited male heir. She allowed herself to be persuaded that she must take time for convalescence, not only for her own sake, but for the sake of her people.

If her active mind had been more at rest, she would probably have made a more rapid recovery, for her constitution was amazingly sound. But she was troubled about many matters and grieved over many others. Not the least of the latter was the defection of Carrillo, whom she had so long regarded, and with reason, as one of her most loyal friends. He had taken umbrage, shortly after her accession to the throne, at her failure to fulfill immediately certain promises in regard to giving him still more lands and titles than he already possessed. Isabel had no intention of going back on her word; but there were certain other powerful claimants to these proud possessions, and she felt it wise to temporize by asking the Archbishop to be satisfied with certain other benefits of equal value and importance. Like many another man before and after him, he had no faith in "something just as good." He sulkily left Segovia, where the Court was still in residence, and went, almost secretly, to Alcalá de Henares, where he began to spend most of his time and money dabbling in alchemy. In this unworthy pursuit, one of his boon companions was a certain Fernando de Alarcar, who had been a close friend of Isabel's arch-enemy, the first Marqués de Villena. The fact that the latter was incidentally Carrillo's nephew had never carried weight in times past. Now it began to look as if the second Marqués were in league with his great-uncle and his great-uncle with him. Moreover, the jealousy which Carrillo had been at no pains to conceal, when Don Pedro González de Mendoza had been given the Cardinal's hat, had not diminished with time; it continued to rankle and increase.

At this point, Mendoza made a generous gesture: he went himself to Alcalá de Henares, begged Carrillo to give the young King and Queen his valuable support in their attempt to avert war, both foreign and domestic, and to bring law and order to their troubled land. The Cardinal even agreed to efface himself in Carrillo's favor and to allow the latter to take the lead in directing affairs at the coming session of the Cortes. The only satisfaction he received was a stiff and formal reply to the effect that Carrillo had always considered Isabel the rightful heiress to the throne and that he would be glad to see the Cortes assemble. And it was not long afterward that a communication was placed in Isabel's hands from the King of Portugal. It stated that he proposed to invade Castile in the name of his niece, Juana—whom he now tardily and contradictorily acknowledged as the legitimate daughter of Enrique and whom he proposed to marry; while outstanding among the names of those who had promised him support in this enterprise was that of Alonso de Carrillo, Archbishop of Toledo. . . .

This had been the body blow which almost felled Isabel and from which she was now so slow in recovering. That the scum of the earth —the thieves and cutthroats to whom she was meting out stern justice but showing no mercy—might desert her, when the going was hard, this she could understand, this she could accept. But that a great churchman, a splendid knight who wore armor under his vestments, a loyal friend who had sponsored her cause by offering her the crown when she sought sanctuary at Santa Ana and came riding through the night with three hundred horsemen to take her from Madrigal to meet her bridegroom—that such a man among men as this should fail her in her hour of need passed all comprehension and all credence. Impetuously, she wrote him a letter in which protest was mingled with appeal. His only answer to it was the indirect comment, made to one of his friends, that he intended no harm either to Isabel or to her husband.

In the face of such a slight, she felt that there was only one course left to her: she would go to Alcalá de Henares herself and plead with him in person. To the horror of her more conservative advisers, she set out, as usual on horseback, accompanied only by Count Haro, the Duke of Infantado, and the Duke of Alba. When she neared her destination, the Count Haro was sent forward to announce her visit. The reply which he brought back to her was the epitome of effrontery:

"Tell the Queen that if she comes into the city by one gate, I will leave it by another. I took her from the distaff and gave her a sceptre and I will send her back to the distaff."

The words were as unwise as they were presumptuous. If Isabel had needed anything more to call forth her latent powers, here it was. It was then that she began to ride among her people, wearing a breastplate over a plain dress, and calling on them to rally around her and on God to help her righteous cause. . . .

Well, victory, like hope, had been long deferred, but it had come at last. Carrillo had joined the King of Portugal with five hundred lances and something like two thousand men. But these were not enough to turn the tide. When the second battle of Toro ended in a glorious triumph for Isabel's side, the Archbishop found that the Portuguese had no further use for him. His star had set; hers was still on the ascendant.

It was with no personal pride that she sat thinking of this, in her quiet retreat at Tordesillas. She would always grieve over Carrillo's downfall, not only as it affected her, but as it affected him: that a man once so majestic should have so far fallen from the seats of the mighty that he should waste his great substance and his great talents in the company and in the pursuits of a charlatan was a shameful and dreadful thing. She would always be conscious of the tragedy of his betrayal; but she would try not to forget what he had been to her in the past in brooding over what he had failed to be in the present. And, for the time being, her thoughts were centered happily on her husband. He had proved himself a glorious leader in her cause, as brilliant in strategy as on the battlefield. But though he seemed to all the warriors, nobles and churchmen with whom he came in contact to be singularly favored by fortune, privately he was nursing a deep disappointment over the loss of the expected child and blaming Isabel for her lack of prudence in safeguarding her health. She could not make that loss up to him, at least not now; so she felt she must try to compensate for it, in as far as she could, in some other way than by giving him an heir. She must arrange some great public celebration in his honor, at which he would receive the tribute which was his due.

It was while she was considering what form this should take that the news reached her of a serious revolt in Segovia: a disappointed office seeker, Maldonado, during the temporary absence of the Governor, Cabrera, had smuggled several armed men, disguised as laborers, into the Alcázar. These men had killed the guards, seized the keys and captured Mosen de Bobadilla, the Governor's father-in-law. The Queen's only child, little Isabel, was in a tower of the fortress with her nurse; her faithful guardian, Beatriz de Bobadilla, was at Tordesillas with Isabel, which made the child's peril all the greater. At the Alcázar, she was protected only by a few loyalists. Maldonado had first taken possession of another tower and then of the entire building, except for the corner where the Infanta's defenders still held out. A general siege had started and the whole city was in an uproar. Even the Bishop, Don Juan Arias de Avila, was siding with Maldonado, because of a grudge against Cabrera, though the Bishop, like the Governor, was a *converso*, a "new Christian" and the son of Jewish parents.

His support was so powerful that almost none had stood out against it. Only a few of Isabel's faithful soldiers, barricaded at the Gate of San Juan, were still holding out. The messenger who brought her the bad news, riding all night to do so, had come from there himself.

Besides Beatriz, Isabel had with her, at Tordesillas, only the Cardinal of Spain and the Count of Benavente. She did not stop to assemble troops, only to order that four horses should immediately be saddled. Then, without a moment's delay, she and her three friends started for Segovia, sixty miles distant. She rode all day, stopping to give her horses the brief rest which was all she would allow herself or her companions. At dawn, on the second day, she came within sight of Segovia.

Her mad dash to rescue the Infanta and crush the revolt did not take the rebels by surprise; knowing her mettle, they were well aware of the sort of action they might expect, once the situation was made known to the Queen. That is, the first action. They were unprepared for the second.

The Bishop and several other prominent citizens came out to meet her and greeted her with respect. However, the Bishop ventured to make two requests: the first was that she should not attempt to enter the city by the Gate of San Juan, where the fighting was most furious; it would not be safe, even for the Queen, to do so. The second was that neither Beatriz de Bobadilla nor the Count of Benavente should enter at all. Beatriz was Cabrera's wife, Benavente his great friend; since the feeling against the Governor was running so high, it certainly would not be safe for them to brave the fury of the crowd. The Bishop's companions tried to corroborate his words of warning. Isabel interrupted them, with a rage and a boldness of which they would have believed her incapable, well as they thought they knew her.

"'Tell those cavaliers and citizens of Segovia that I am Queen of Castile, and this city is mine, for the King my father left it to me; and to enter what is mine I do not need any laws or conditions that they may lay down for me. I shall enter the city by the gate I choose, and the Count of Benavente shall enter with me, and all others that I think proper for my service. Say to them further that they shall all come to me, and do what I shall command like loyal subjects, and cease making tumults and scandals in my city, lest they suffer hurt in their persons and their property.'"[22]

Without waiting for any sort of a reply, she dug her spurs into her horse's sides and went charging through the Gate of San Juan, followed, at a gallop, by her three companions. Somehow, they forged their way through to the Alcázar, threatened at every step of the way not only by howls of fury, but by spears and swords. Somehow, they reached the small courtyard enclosing the tower where the Infanta was imprisoned. When they had gained this much ground, the Queen suddenly wheeled her horse around. The Cardinal, who had reached her side, leaned toward her and besought her to have the gates of the Alcázar closed, before an even greater and more furious mob than thronged the courtyard already could get inside. Her only answer was to shout an order that everyone who desired to enter should be admitted. The seething crowd pushed forward and, still shouting and screaming, still brandishing spears and swords, jostled around her. She sat still as a statue, silent as the grave. Her immobility, her silence, the sternness of her set face were more effective than her daring and her defiance. It was one thing to go dashing through a mob; that might be sheer bravado. It was quite another to remain facing such a mob without a tremor; that was fortitude. Slowly, the screams and shouts subsided to a murmur; slowly, the waving swords were sheathed, the uplifted spears grounded. When even the murmuring had ceased, the Queen spoke.

" 'My vassals and my servants, tell me what you want. If it is for the good of my city and my kingdom, I want it, too.' "

A spokesman stepped forward. The first demand of the people was for the removal of the Governor. The second——

He never got as far as the second. Isabel announced that, in Cabrera's absence, she herself was taking possession of the Alcázar, and that later she would see it was committed to the care of someone who would be both faithful to her and acceptable to her people. The words were hardly out of her mouth when the fickle crowd began the cry of, "Viva la Reina!" The mob outside echoed the refrain. "In a trice the men who had been cursing Cabrera were clamouring for the blood of Maldonado and his partisans. The rebel leaders fled for their lives. By noon the towers and walls had been cleared of them, and the Queen was in complete possession of the Alcázar. Her first thought was to embrace the Princess, from whom she had so long been separated. Then she rode in weary triumph through the streets to the palace near the church of St. Martín, followed by a mob that all but smothered her in their joy and admiration. From the steps of the palace she made a brief speech, promising them protection from the tyranny of Cabrera and all others, bidding them go peacefully to their homes, promising that if they would send a committee to her to explain all their grievances, she would have justice done. The multitude melted away. The Queen entered the palace, threw herself on a bed, and slept."[23]

Of course, Isabel had, never for a moment, seriously considered dismissing Cabrera as Governor of the Alcázar. She was well aware that, had it not been for his decisive support, at the time of Enrique's death, she could not have instantly been crowned Queen of Castile; and his wife's loyalty to her had never wavered from the time the two little girls had been bosom friends at Arévalo. She did, indeed, receive the committee chosen by the people and listen gravely to its complaints. However, she convinced the malcontents that such minor offences as had been committed were not Cabrera's fault but that of his subordinates. Then she gave it as her considered opinion that he should be "reinstated." The committee, with equal gravity, agreed.

She had called these people of Segovia her vassals and servants. She had reminded them that the city and the country where they lived were also hers. They never again dared to question her verdict that this was so.

9

The first part of Isabel's story, as I set out to tell it, logically ends with the ultimatum which Fernando accepted in those tumultuous days which followed his wife's coronation and her subsequent display of triumphant authority in Segovia. Other writers much abler than I, other historians far more learned, have presented her as the great reformer of a chaotic land;[24] the severe but upright judge in hitherto corrupt courts; the tireless and victorious warrior at Toro, Granada and numerous other places; the Defender of the Faith so zealous that she became the disciple of the relentless Torquemada; the sponsor of Christopher Columbus who made possible the discovery of a new world; in short, as the "Queen of Queens." There is nothing I feel I can add on these subjects. But other writers and historians, in dwelling on the supremely important aspects of her character and her achievements, have necessarily left untold or but briefly recorded much about the earlier events of her life and the setting for these. So I have ventured to set them down, as a prologue, so to speak, of what came afterward, in the way I have learned them, not in great centers, but in Madrigal and Arévalo, in Medina del Campo and Toros de Guisando and Cardeñosa and elsewhere throughout the Province of Avila, as well as in its capital city. It is not the most scholarly way to learn history, but—to me, at least—it seems the most refreshing and illuminating. And there is a sequel to the story of Isabel's reforms and achievements and triumphs, which, like the prologue to them, has its setting in the Land of Stones and Saints. It is a sad story, so perhaps some readers would rather skip it. But it forms the second part of the one which I set out to tell and it belongs in the record, so I must go on with it.

For nearly twenty years, Isabel spent little or no time in Avila or, for that matter, in any one place. The Catholic Kings held court, just as the Cortes met, wherever it seemed most expedient: in Toledo, in Segovia, in Valladolid, all nearby; in Seville, in Córdoba, in Granada, all distant. But their headquarters were by no means always in a palace. Sometimes they were in a tented camp, near a battlefield; sometimes in the home of a friend—a spacious one in some city, a simple one in the country; in any case, not only temporary but more or less haphazard. True, all Isabel's connections with her homeland were not severed; her mother continued to live, if living it could be called, in Arévalo. But she had withdrawn further and further into the shadows of melancholia, until her mind had given way completely. Isabel had continued to supervise her care and provide, as far as material wants were concerned, for her well-being. Other persons, unrelated to the Queen, were not forgotten or overlooked, either: Fernán Gómez Dávila was appointed Chief Superintendent in the household of the Catholic Kings; and they had chosen Alonzo Díaz de Montalvo, a distinguished native of Arévalo, who had acted as Royal Counselor to both Enrique IV and Juan II of Castile, to serve them in the same capacity; Isabel selected her former confessor, Fray Hernando de Talavera, who had become Bishop of Avila, as a member of Mendoza's suite when the great Cardinal entered Granada; and it was this Bishop's privilege to hoist the standards of the victorious army and to consecrate a former mosque, where the first Mass was said in the city of the Moors, as a Christian church.[25] But it was not until after the Moorish conquest that Isabel and Fernando felt they were entitled to some rest from their labors, a closer association with their friends and a more settled abode. They then decided that Avila would be an ideal place to spend their summers and took up residence in a palace built especially for them which adjoined the magnificent new Monastery of Santo Tomás.

Funds for the erection of this monastery and the adjacent palace, which were begun in 1483, had been supplied partly by the Catholic Kings and partly by Doña María de Avila, widow of Hernán Núñez Arnalt, the monarchs' trusted paymaster, who had greatly desired to supply a suitable residence and teaching center for his friends the Dominican Monks and whose will had provided amply for this purpose. Beyond the beautiful church, whose superb altar was high literally as well as figuratively, and whose elaborately carved choir stalls were supplemented by thrones for the King and Queen, were three cloisters: the *Claustro del Noviciado*—Cloister of the Novitiate—also known as the *Claustro Toscano*—the Tuscan Cloister—and the Old Cloister, as it was the first built, which was spacious but comparatively simple of design; the Cloister of Silence, also called the Cloister of the Dead, because it was here that the burial of the monks took place, which was somewhat more stately of design; and the Cloister of the Kings, ornamented by two tiers of arcades connected by a magnificent staircase and elaborately carved with pomegranates, the glowing fruit to which Granada owes its name.

It was in the beautiful apartments surrounding this third cloister, and reached through a private entrance which opened direct from their own orchards and kitchen garden, that the Catholic Kings established their pleasant and restful headquarters during the warm months and gathered around them their children, every one of whom had been born in a different place: Isabel the Younger, as we have already seen, in Dueñas; Juan, the long-awaited male heir to the throne, in Seville; Juana in Toledo; María[26] in Córdoba and Catalina in Alcalá de Henares. Now, instead of being dragged from pillar to post and separated from each other for long periods of time, they were settled and united. Young Isabel was already a widow, and had returned to the shelter of her parents' roof after only six months of singularly happy marriage to Prince Alfonso of Portugal; his cousin, Manoel, who had apparently fallen in love with her at first sight, had repeatedly asked for her hand; but so far she had steadfastly refused to listen, and Fernando and Isabel did not press her, much as they desired to perpetuate a Portuguese alliance. She was her mother's favorite daughter, as lovely in character as in looks; and though grief had clouded her natural joyousness and revealed a hitherto unguessed strain of stubbornness in her habitual docility, she was still much easier to deal with and much pleasanter to live with than her sister, Juana, who had been a fretful ailing baby and had slowly developed into a sullen and backward child. In appearance, Juana so greatly resembled Fernando's mother, for whom she had been named, that Isabel playfully called her "little mother-in-law." But this playfulness hid an ever-increasing anxiety, for in disposition, Juana was far more like her other grandmother, the tragic recluse of Arévalo. María and Catalina were agreeable girls, still without pronounced characteristics of any kind; but Juan, the only boy, had, from birth, seemed to his parents "a child of grace and an inheritor of the Kingdom of Heaven." His mother called him her angel, and he was indeed seraphic in every way: his golden hair glowed like a nimbus; his eyes were as blue as the heavens; his smile had a celestial sweetness. This ethereality occasioned no alarm; it seemed as different from the sickliness of Juana as from the sturdiness of the other girls; and the resemblance he bore to Isabel's brother, Alfonso, was a cause for rejoicing, not for anxiety. As he advanced from infancy to boyhood and from boyhood to adolescence, he lost none of the rare and winning attributes which he had possessed as a little child; he simply added to them. He had a natural talent for music and learned with ease to play the flute, the clavichord and the organ. His tenor voice, though not powerful, was pleasing and he enjoyed singing both alone and in chorus. He also enjoyed amateur theatricals and often shared in them at the Duke of Alba's palace. Latin and philosophy presented no difficulties and he took an added interest in them because his mother, who had always regretted their omission from her own education, now studied them with him. Moreover, he rode well, hunted and jousted as a matter of course. At the age of twelve, he was knighted by his father as prepared for that honor and worthy of it. At fourteen, he renewed the oath to respect the privileges of the joint Kingdoms of Castile and Aragon, which his parents had taken in his behalf, at the splendid ceremony held in Calatayud when, at the age of three, he had been acknowledged the rightful heir to the throne and the people had sworn allegiance to him. At fifteen, when Columbus returned from his first triumphant trip to the "Indies," Juan sat on a throne beside his parents, under a golden canopy, to welcome the Discoverer of the New World back to Spain. At the same age, he was considered sufficiently advanced in his education to act as judge, in the presence of learned counselors, on various questions regarding problems, both real and imaginary, which were put to him by statesmen and lawyers. Not only to his family, but to everyone with whom he came in contact, he seemed to increase "in wisdom and in stature and in favor with God and man."

With Aragon and Castile forming a united kingdom;[27] with law and order established and maintained throughout the land; and with the conquest of the Moors assured, the upbringing and education of their son became a matter of passionate preoccupation to Fernando and Isabel. Since he had no brothers, ten young male companions were carefully chosen to share his pastimes and his studies and to live in the palace with him; their numerous teachers were selected with the utmost care. The most famous among these was, undoubtedly, the Milanese, Pietro Martire,[28] who organized a school modeled on Charlemagne's *Schola Palatina*, for the Prince and his friends. But two brothers, Antonio and Alessandro Geraldino, were also outstanding, and later, Lucio Marineo Siculo, a Sicilian who afterward became Professor of Poetry and Grammar at Salamanca, was added to the little faculty. Less widely known, but more greatly loved by the Prince, were Juan Dávila of Avila and his wife, Doña Juana de Velázquez, who had been the Prince's nurse and had remained an important figure in the royal household; while their son, Juan Velázquez, became a leading figure among the young companions. All three of these were closer to the Prince than any of his other teachers and schoolmates. He regarded Juan Dávila not only as his tutor but as his foster father; and he made Juan Velázquez his personal treasurer and called him "my bosom friend." It was due in no small measure to the affection and esteem in which this family was held that Avila was chosen as a summer residence by the Catholic Kings.[29]

Long before his thorough and comprehensive education was completed, the question of the Infante's marriage, like those of his sisters, had become a matter of careful consideration on the part of his parents. They were not blind to political advantages; but they were also sincerely anxious that their children should be happy. After pondering and dismissing several other projects, they decided upon one which they believed had every prospect of success from both viewpoints. A double wedding should take place: their difficult daughter, Juana, should marry Philip—son of Maximilian I of Austria, Emperor of the Holy Roman Empire—who could not fail to please and cheer even so moody a girl as she was, for he was known to be one of the handsomest and most beguiling young princes of the era; their beloved son, Juan, should marry Philip's sister, Margaret, who, according to reliable report, exceeded even her brother in pulchritude and charm.

Cloister of the summer palace of the Catholic Kings, adjoining the Convent of Santo Tomás, Avila (now part of the convent). From a photograph by Mayoral, Avila.

Juana accepted her parents' suggestion with more obvious satisfaction than she generally displayed and Juan responded with enthusiasm. The harmony and happiness which pervaded the royal household became contagious and the little widow who had grieved so long agreed to put aside her mourning weeds and marry again. Catalina was already formally betrothed to Arthur, Prince of Wales; only María, among the children of the Catholic Kings, was unprovided with an advantageous mate. However, since England, Hungary and Portugal were now all aligned, there would be plenty of time to decide, later on, where she might best be placed.

The fleet which bore Margaret as a bride to Spain, like the one which bore Juana as a bride to Flanders, met with fierce storms and was long in deadly danger. Isabel, lacking news from either one, was inevitably the prey of great anxiety; and during the long period while she waited for glad tidings, she received some that were sad: her mother, who had lived so long in the obscurity of dark thoughts, as well as a dark room, was now groping her way toward the shadow of the Valley of Death. Isabel went back, as in duty bound, a last time to Arévalo. In one way, the loss of her mother was not a source of poignant grief, for it had been years since the poor deranged woman had recognized her daughter—or anyone else—so there had been no vital ties to bind them together; but her death severed the last link with Isabel's memories of a happy childhood and the manner of it roused fears for the future. The dying Dowager had covered her face so that no one could look at her and turned morbidly away from those who sought to comfort her. Isabel had seen her daughter, Juana, make just such gestures. Must she believe that there was too great a resemblance for either joy or safety between grandmother and grandchild?

Resolutely, Isabel tried to dismiss such gloomy forebodings, and began the arrangements for her mother's burial at the Monastery of Miraflores, near Burgos, where her father, Juan II of Castile, and her brother, Alfonso, the poor little "King of Avila," were already entombed. In the midst of funeral preparations, her sad spirits were lightened by the long-awaited report from Flanders: Juana had arrived safely and all was well with her. Not long thereafter, the Admiral of Castile, Don Fadrique the Third, to whom had been entrusted the honor of bringing Juan's bride to Spain, sailed buoyantly into port and Margaret stepped ashore at Santander.

Everyone had been prepared to welcome her warmly as well as suitably; but no one had realized how quickly this would require no conscious effort, because she would capture all hearts by her winsomeness, or how soon she would seem less the great heiress of the Holy Roman Empire than the fairy Princess of song and story, happily come to life. That her bridegroom should fall head over heels in love with her might have been expected; that his parents, his teachers, and his friends would also find her irresistible was less a matter of course; that even a crusty old sailor by the name of Christopher Columbus should have so fallen beneath her spell as to name an island for her, in the course of his next voyage, was a still greater tribute to her fascination.[30]

The Princess arrived in Lent and Juan pleaded in vain for a secret wedding before the forty-day period of penance was over. After what seemed to him like an eternity, though it was actually only a few weeks, he and Margaret were married with all due ceremony at the Burgos Cathedral. Banquets, tournaments and merrymaking of every sort celebrated the glad event; it was years since the Court, always under the necessity of functioning economically, and grown more sedate with the maturing years of its sovereigns, had abandoned itself so unreservedly to rejoicing. This went on all summer. But, though unheeded, there had been warnings that so much excitement was putting an undue strain on the constitution of the Prince. In character, in intellect, in appearance, nothing was lacking as far as he was concerned; but there had always been that quality of ethereality; and the quiet and temperate life he had led, which had, so far, served to safeguard him, had not adequately prepared him for a ceaseless round of gaiety or for an uxorious form of life. His teacher, Pietro Martire, in writing to a friend, was outspoken in his fears and gave the reasons for them with the candor of the age:

"A few days back I wrote to you telling of the happenings in Burgos upon the arrival of the royal daughter-in-law, Margaret. But I omitted describing to you the qualities of her person, not very evident at the time. If you could see her, you would believe that you were contemplating Venus herself. Even as Mars desired the Goddess of Chipre for her beauty, nobility, and age, thus has come to us from Flanders this lovely woman, without any coquetry in her makeup or dress. . . . But it is to be feared that these very qualities bring with them the misfortune and ruin of Spain, because our young Prince is becoming pallid, consumed with passion. The doctors and the King himself beg the Queen to intervene and separate the newlyweds. They ask her to seek a respite in the incessant acts of love and they warn of the dangers that these will incur. Again and again they call her attention to the paleness of her son's face and his fatigued manner, adding that the sickness is attacking his marrow and weakening his very being. They urge that a remedy be applied before it is too late. But they achieve nothing. The Queen answers that Man does not have the power to tear asunder those whom God has joined together."[31]

The Queen was not thinking only of the biblical injunction. She was also thinking of the blow Juan's manhood would sustain and the personal grief he would suffer if he were separated from his beautiful bride. She could not bear to have him hurt. Nor had she forgotten those blissful days and nights at Dueñas, where she had spent her honeymoon. She and Fernando would both have given short shrift to anyone who suggested that they should curtail their "acts of love." She would expect her son and his wife to do the same. . . .

With the passing of summer, the Court divided into two groups. Juan and Margaret went on to Salamanca, where fresh festivities awaited them. Fernando and Isabel accompanied their eldest daughter to Alcántara, where her formal betrothal to the faithful Manoel of Portugal took place. She had not previously laid aside the mourning garments she had worn for her first husband. Now, at last, she consented to be dressed in bright colors again.

She did not wear them long. The ceremonies connected with the betrothal were hardly completed when a breathless messenger arrived from Salamanca. Juan had been stricken with a terrible fever after a great feast in his honor. His condition was grave.

Isabel was ill herself; she had managed to keep up until the celebrations were over, but now, for the first time in her life, she found that her body would not respond to her will. She had no choice but to lie helplessly in bed and let her husband leave without her. But Fernando could still undertake a reckless ride at top speed. He leaped on a horse and covered the hundred miles between Alcántara and Salamanca in record time, reaching his son's bedside in time to hear the boy's last words: He had known nothing but happiness all his life and he could die without regret. It added to his sense of peace to know that Margaret already had hopes of a child; the baby would comfort her and his parents in their bereavement. He had already made a good Confession. He wanted to be buried in Avila, at Santo Tomás, where they had all been so happy together, and where his foster father, Juan Dávila, had already been laid to rest. His bosom friend, Juan Velázquez, would make all the necessary arrangements. . . .

The state funeral, inevitably, was held in Salamanca. But shortly thereafter, Fray Diego Deza, in whose arms Juan had died, received the following letter:

Venerable Dean and Chapter of the Church of Salamanca:
We are sending Juan Velázquez to you in order that he may transfer the body of our illustrious son, Don Juan—may he have eternal glory. We charge you that you deliver it to him immediately and that you place complete confidence in everything that the afore-mentioned Juan Velázquez says to you on our part and that which our Confessor, the Bishop of Salamanca, says to you, as if we were writing it ourselves.

I, the King—I, the Queen
From Avila, the 2ᵈ of November, 97th year.[32]

Under the guidance of this faithful friend, the members of the funeral train, shivering with cold and drenched with rain, slowly made their way over the muddy, rutted road leading from Salamanca to Avila: great prelates whose costly vestments were buffeted about by the gale; hooded monks who vainly tried to shield from the wind the long tallow candles which they carried; men of war mounted on black-draped horses; knights wrapped in flowing capes. The white flowers which had formed a mound over the coffin, borne in the midst of these mourners, had been scattered along the roadside or trampled in the mire; but the arms of Castile, emblazoned on its pall, still glittered through the gloom. Beside the bier, with bowed heads, walked Diego Deza and Juan Velázquez.

The icy wind howled over the dreary countryside and the driving rain and withered, swirling leaves obscured the swollen rivers, the fields of stubble and the huddled flocks and herds. In the cities, all the towers and gates of the walls, all the seignorial palaces were hung with black pennants. The common people, their sad faces blue with cold, took such refuge as they could find in the vestibules of noble houses, in the porticoes of the churches and in the public arcades and spoke to each other, in hushed voices, of the terrible tragedy which had befallen them. Silence had fallen even on the brawling taverns; the dice had ceased to rattle; the air was no longer thick with oaths. Roisterers and wastrels, marketmen and muleteers, gathered quietly around the fire to pray for the soul of Prince Juan.

As the cortege approached the bridge over the Adaja, the weary marchers saw that the millers, tanners and dyers, who lived in this quarter, were drawn up along the road to pay a last tribute to the

Prince and to show their respect to his escort. The water wheels had ceased to turn, the hides remained undressed, the great vats no longer boiled over. All the bells were tolling now and the clergy of the city, headed by the Bishop, Don Francisco de la Fuente, had joined the procession, together with a standard bearer carrying a black pennant embroidered in a heraldic design, the sheriff accompanied by his shield bearers, the nobles, the justices and the councilmen, followed by minstrels, and all clad in *márraga tosquísima*.[32-a] Gradually they wound their way through the Ghetto, where the wails and moans of the Jews mingled with the sound of the ringing bells, for the dead boy was one of the few who had shown compassion to these unfortunate people. Further on, a band of weeping farmers and weavers had foregathered; even the guttersnipes and ragamuffins, the panders and prostitutes were sorrowfully waiting for the passage of the Prince whom even the very worst and least of them had loved.

Without stopping, the procession continued by way of the Market of Small Animals to the cathedral, where a moving ceremony took place. Thence, accompanied by several thousand persons, it went through the Market of Great Animals,[32-b] afterward taking the road to the Royal Convent of Santo Tomás. There, in the covered portico and the patio behind it, the stricken parents were waiting, surrounded by their Court and the Community of Dominicans; monarchs and subjects knelt together in a prayer. When they rose, Juan Velázquez lifted the pall from the coffin and Fernando and Isabel bent to kiss their son's cold brow for the last time. As they did so, Juan Velázquez could see that in Fernando's face was a greater gravity than ever before; but that he was completely collected; and that Isabel's face was nearly as white as her son's and that the dark rings which encircled her eyes were as black as the shades of death; but she was tearless and her lips did not once quiver; she did not shrink away from the icy touch. The weeping, the wailing, the gnashing of teeth was for those who could readily give way to their grief without loss of dignity. The man who had deemed his little son worthy of knighthood on the eve of a great battle could confidently believe in the victory of the soul over death. The woman who had brought this boy into the world without uttering a cry, in the extremity of travail, could now, with the same self-control, watch him leave it.

The doors of the church were flung open and, as the bier was carried into the nave, the crowd closed in around it. But, when the bearers had set it down in the chancel, only those nearest and dearest to the

dead boy remained beside it. The bells were stilled, the last notes
of the organ trailed away into silence. The slanting shadows fell across
the glittering arms of Castile and the coffin sank further and further
below the pavement. Then came darkness.

That all Avila should have so grieved and so shown its grief was
intensely moving to the monarchs, but it was not astonishing, for this,
more than any other one place, had been the Prince's home. However,
never in the history of Spain had a death caused such universal and
profound grief, never had general mourning been so deep and so prolonged. Black banners floated from the towers and gateways of every
town and the very mules were draped in black down to their knees.
The entire Court, instead of wearing white mourning, was garmented
in sackcloth. All public buildings and places of business were closed
for forty days.[32-c]

Isabel knew that this public display was more than an outward
show of respect; there was genuine love, genuine grief behind it. She
tried to comfort herself with the knowledge of this and to fix her
thoughts on a future which would bring with it solace. She was ill
much of the time now; she could not fill her days with tireless activities, as she once had done, which would have helped to keep her
from giving way to grief. But she pinned her hopes on Margaret's unborn child, she dwelt on the renewed happiness which her daughter,
Isabel, was finding with Manoel.

Margaret's baby, a little girl, was stillborn. Manoel's wife died in
childbirth. Her baby, a boy, died within two years. The tide had
turned. Time and death were no longer allies of Isabel.

10

Isabel could still face the world with the same show of resolution
that had marked her bearing when, standing behind the grille at Santa
Ana's Convent, she had declined the nobles' offer of a crown and
when, seated in the Council Chamber at Segovia, she had told her
husband that, though he was King of Castile by courtesy, she was its
Queen by inherent right. But from the time she lost her little grandson, Miguel, the child whose birth had cost his mother her life and on
whom Isabel had pinned all hopes for the future, she was never again a
well or happy woman. For years, she had drawn unremittingly on her
reserves of fortitude in behalf of her country, her Church, her law

courts, her husband and her children; now that she needed to draw on them in her own behalf, there were none left.

More and more, she relegated affairs of state to Fernando, making only such public appearances as were unavoidable. He was, necessarily, absent a great deal from Spain, waging intermittent war with both France and Italy. While he was gone, her daughters became Isabel's chief preoccupation; but, increasingly, they were a source of anxiety and grief. Manoel, who had been so persistent a suitor and so loving a husband of the Queen's eldest daughter, recovered from his loss and the cause of it with surprising swiftness, under all the circumstances, and asked for the hand of her younger sister, María. An enduring alliance with Portugal was so important politically that it could not be overlooked, and María herself seemed quite unperturbed at the prospect of marrying the newly-made widower. But Isabel saw her depart with many misgivings—misgivings which, fortunately, were to prove baseless, for María bore eight children without difficulty, and though she died at thirty-five, her seventeen years of married life were happy ones. However, Isabel did not have the prophetic vision to see this; and hardly had María left her, when she was forced to face permanent separation from her youngest daughter, Catalina.

Negotiations for this unfortunate girl's marriage with Arthur, Prince of Wales, had been going on for years. At first they were blocked by the niggardly attitude of her prospective father-in-law, Henry VII of England; then by Isabel's reluctance to let her last child leave home. In this case, her forebodings of disaster were all too well founded. She discovered one excuse after another for delay, and Catalina herself was extremely apt at supplying still more: she was ill with the ague and could not leave Granada; she suffered so intensely with the heat that, once started for La Coruña, close to seven hundred miles distant, she had to keep stopping to recover. When she finally set sail, terrible storms drove the Armada back to port more than once and inclement weather continued throughout the crossing to England. All in all, it took the poor little bride nearly five months to get from Granada to Portsmouth, and another month elapsed before her dilatory bridegroom and his father set out to meet her. The wedding finally took place at St. Paul's Cathedral in London, with all due ceremony; and Isabel, who had been ill herself with fever at the time of Catalina's unwilling departure, and whose convalescence had been retarded by anxiety, received with joy the glowing accounts which came to her. From the beginning, she had been disturbed and displeased by

THE GIRL WITH THE FIRM MOUTH   55

the behavior of Henry VII, and she would not have put it past him to retreat, at the last moment, from his hard-driven bargain; now, apparently, there was nothing more to fear from that quarter.

She soon saw that, in this respect, she could not have been more mistaken. Within six months, the puny little Prince was dead, and Catalina, a widow at sixteen, was an almost friendless small stranger in a foreign land. Isabel immediately begged that her youngest daughter might be returned to her, as her eldest daughter had been returned, under similar circumstances. Only, it seemed, the circumstances were not so similar after all. First, there was the troublesome question of money, which had never arisen in connection with Portugal. The Catholic Kings demanded that certain provisions, in regard to Catalina's dowry, should be fulfilled, in cash and in kind; the King of England, on the other hand, not only failed to make funds and lands available, but reduced Catalina to such a state of penury that, in desperation, she was on the point of borrowing money to meet her most pressing needs. Fernando and Isabel charged their Ambassador, Puebla, to tell the Princess that she must do nothing of the sort, and reminded him that "when the Queen of Portugal, their daughter, became a widow, she received all she wanted from the new King of Portugal, and they had never had to send her a farthing. When the Princess Margot was widowed in Spain, they provided for all her wants, as though she had been their own daughter. Neither her father nor her brother Philip had sent her the smallest sum of money; if they had done so, Fernando and Isabel would have considered it an insult, and would not have accepted it."[33] Despite such indignant messages, poor Catalina was finally obliged to accept a pittance from her miserly father-in-law, since this was all she could get, and to await the deliverance which would enable her to return to Spain.

Its hour never came. To a certain degree, she herself was the unsuspecting cause of its failure, for she innocently announced that her marriage with Arthur had never been consummated, and her statement was duly corroborated. Inevitably, Isabel received this information with mingled amazement and scorn: was the Prince to whom she had given her cherished daughter such a laggard in love that he had not claimed her for his own, at the earliest possible moment? Or had he been a poor creature like Enrique, as lacking in virility as in passion? If she and Fernando could only have divined what manner of weakling they had mistaken for a consort worthy of an infanta, how quickly they would have put an end to the negotiations which Henry of England had delayed through avarice!

Now that the evil was done, however, their pride would not allow them to admit that there was no remedy for it. To the first suggestion of one, they recoiled with abhorrence: Arthur's mother, the kindly Queen of England, died soon after he did; her widower smoothly suggested that everything could now be patched up if he married his daughter-in-law. "The mere mention of it offends the ears; we would not for anything in the world that it should take place," Isabel wrote her Ambassador. But she considered less repugnant the next proposal made to her: that Catalina should become the betrothed of Arthur's younger brother, Henry, who had now acquired the title Prince of Wales in the former's stead. A Papal dispensation would, of course, be necessary; but then, Isabel's own marriage could not have taken place without one. Catalina would eventually become Queen of England after all—and, next to being Queen of Spain, that was the most exalted rank any woman could hold! Her prestige as an infanta, which had suffered such a blow in the mock marriage to Arthur, would be restored to its rightful position of supreme importance. Perhaps everything might yet turn out for the best. . . .

Isabel was still assailed with doubts, and expressed these in a letter to Estrada, another of her ambassadors: "Should the King of England not be willing immediately to settle the betrothal of the Princess of Wales with the Prince of Wales . . . the Princess of Wales shall depart at once for Spain. She shall do so, moreover, without waiting to recover the hundred thousand *scudos* of the portion of which the King of England has to make restitution, should he not immediately give them."[34] At the time, she meant what she said. But her attention had been diverted from Catalina, whose affairs were certainly going badly, to Juana, whose affairs were, unfortunately, going still worse. The latter was the legitimate heiress to the throne of Spain, now that Miguel, the little son of her elder sister, the Queen of Portugal, had died at the age of two; and Juana herself had given birth to a healthy boy, Charles—or Don Carlos, as he was called in Spain—who would eventually inherit a great empire. Her own secure position and the glowing prospects of her child should have served to cheer her; but, as time went on, she had become increasingly morose. There were, undoubtedly, some sound reasons for this: the Spanish subjects who had formed her entourage had been very badly treated in Flanders and, to a large degree, arbitrarily replaced by strangers; many of them were in actual want and Juana was troubled on their account. She could not help them, for her husband and his favorites kept her short of the money which was hers by right. What was even worse, as far as she was concerned, was Philip's flagrant unfaithfulness; despite the way he was treating her, she was still madly in love with him, and so jealous that she was not willing he should exchange a civil word with any other woman. She was mistrustful of everyone, even her confessor, and failed to fulfill her religious duties. Isabel, to whom reports of all this were, naturally, most disquieting, wrote her loving letters which were meant to convey comfort; Juana left them unanswered and, as far as her mother could tell, unread. But at last the difficult girl accepted an invitation urging her and her husband to visit Spain.

This invitation was issued about the same time that Catalina was married; but, owing to a prolonged and very gay sojourn in France along the way, Juana and Philip did not reach Madrid until January of the following year.[35] They had hardly arrived at the Alcázar, where Fernando had gone to meet them, when Philip came down with the measles; and he made the acquaintance of his father-in-law while peevishly tossing about in bed. Fernando treated him with great kindness and tact, and the spoiled boy, who had expected to find the King formal and forbidding, could not help taking a reluctant liking to him. By the time the patient had recovered sufficiently for the young couple to undertake the next stage of the journey—to Toledo, where the Queen was awaiting them—something like an *entente cordiale* seemed to have been created. Isabel greeted both her daughter and her son-in-law warmly and, temporarily, Juana seemed to respond to the affection which was lavished upon her. Unfortunately, this response was of short duration.

Far from feeling honored by the official acknowledgment of Juana and himself as rightful heirs to the thrones of both Aragon and Castile, or enjoying the celebrations arranged for his pleasure, Philip found court life in Spain both tedious and trying. The frequent periods of mourning decreed for persons of whom he knew little and cared less seemed to him a needless ordeal; the round of religious services unending; and the constant presence of the clergy at private gatherings, no less than at all state functions, oppressive beyond words. He "had never been exposed to such a beehive of business activity. . . . Every waking hour was dedicated to affairs of state, and the new Prince was aghast when the Queen explained to him that she had faithfully maintained a fixed weekly program following the counsel given to her many years ago by her confessor, Hernando de Talavera. Every Thursday, and Saturday, one hour was dedicated to signing briefs and documents; mails and petitions were handled each evening; Monday afternoon was allotted to the Prior of Prado (Talavera himself). Tuesday to the cabinet meetings, Wednesday to the royal auditor, Thursday to memorials, Friday to fiscal matters. . . . Philip was frankly bored with the thought of such a schedule and began to cast longing eyes toward his homeland."[36] He soon announced that important business, the nature of which he did not disclose, was calling him back to Flanders; and, as he was hankering for a repetition of the carefree activities in France, which had been so much more to his liking than the stilted banquets at Toledo, he suggested that he might use his good offices as a representative of the Catholic Kings at the Court of Louis XII. Lightheartedly and alone—since it was out of the question for Juana, who was expecting another baby, to accompany him—he took his glad departure.

His actions as a so-called representative were not only futile but treacherous, and the war with France continued under the leadership of Gonzalo, the "Great Captain." This state of hostilities made it impossible for Juana to follow her husband, even after the birth of her second son, who was named Fernando for his grandfather; and her despondency over her enforced separation from Philip began to take a violent form. Hitherto, she had been given to gloom, stubbornness and suspicion rather than bursts of anger. Now she "raged like a lioness" in the Castillo de la Mota, the palace at Medina del Campo. The Court had moved there from Toledo, as it was a favorite residence of Isabel's, and Juana and her baby had been temporarily placed in the care of the Bishop of Burgos while the Queen went to Segovia to raise supplies for Fernando's army, which he was commanding again in person. She was gone longer than she had expected, for she had overtaxed her strength and, once more, fallen ill; but she struggled out of bed and took one last long perilous ride through the darkness, when she received tidings more alarming than any that had reached her from the front: Juana had been begging for permission to take the long and dangerous road to Flanders, war or no war. When her pleas fell on deaf ears, she began to threaten that she would find a way to go despite all opposition. At first, her threats were not taken seriously; but, to everyone's horror, she had eventually fled, half clad, from the palace in the dead of a cold November night. The city gates were already closed and she ordered the guards to open them. The Bishop, who had managed to catch up with her, quickly countermanded her orders, and his were respected, as far as the guards were concerned. But he could do nothing with Juana. Throughout the rest of the night and the next day, she continued to cling to the closed gates, shaking them and screaming at the Bishop, meanwhile fighting off all efforts to protect her against the bitter wind by clothing her more suitably. When at last she was persuaded to take shelter, she would go no further than the nearby hut of one of the guards at whom she had railed, and she was still there when her mother reached her, to be greeted by "words of such disrespect and so beyond any that a daughter should use in speaking to her mother that, if it had not been for the frenzied state she was in, they would never have been tolerated."[37]

The Queen at last succeeded in quieting her distraught daughter and in getting her back to the palace. But this was not before Isabel had heard the murmurings of the crowd which had witnessed the disgraceful scene. "*Juana la Loca*—Joan the Mad." That was what the very peasants were calling the heiress to the throne of Spain; it was what they continued to call her from that day on. The words echoed through the Queen's consciousness in her every waking hour and soon she seemed to be hearing them in her feverish dreams as well.

Spring came round again before Juana at last realized her dream of returning to Flanders and, when she went, she seemed greatly improved in both body and mind. She left her baby, Fernando, behind her, and his beguiling presence was a great source of comfort and pleasure to his grandmother, for the amiable disposition, which was later to make him so general a favorite, was already apparent. But Isabel was completely exhausted by the strain to which she had been subjected during the winter; and the first news which reached her after Juana's arrival in Brussels was so shameful that it caused a serious collapse: Philip had received his wife kindly; there had been every prospect of a happy reunion. Then, at a court function, in the presence of many foreign ambassadors, Juana had attacked the young noblewoman whom she believed to be her rival, scratching and striking her and cutting off her beautiful blond hair. In turn, Philip had cursed his wife and sworn that he was through with her forever. . . .

This time, Isabel could not rally from the shock she had received. In as far as peace and contentment could come to her anywhere, she found them at Medina del Campo. It was a place permeated with memories of a happy girlhood, one that would always be associated in her mind with her friend, Beatriz, and her brother, Alfonso, with great gorgeous fairs and wild gallops over the plain. There were later associations, too: it was here that she had taken her beloved son, Juan, as a child of three, to escape the pestilence, and had seen him grow strong and rosy. It was here that she had made one of her earliest and most significant court decisions, in favor of a poor widow whose husband, a notary, had been murdered by a powerful and greedy noble who coveted his victim's property; and thus she had done away forever with the theory that might and right were the same in Spain. It was here that she had summoned her subjects before the great battle of Toro, triumphantly gathering in men and money from every side; and it was here that she and Fernando had held a long conference with Cardinal Mendoza after that victory, before going on to Madrigal for the gathering of the Cortes, which was to result, after a stormy session, in the revival of the *Santa Hermandad*—the Holy Brotherhood—in the efficiently revised form which was to constitute one of her greatest contributions to law and order. Now, she loved to look out, from the moated castle which crowned the hill, on the fertile fields—golden with summer wheat, purple with summer saffron; and she loved them no less in the autumn, when the promise of the harvest was fulfilled. But when the last of the wheat had been threshed and the last of the saffron dried, she was not gazing out of her high window any more.[38] She was lying quietly in her great bed, too tired for even the slight effort which would have permitted her to have a last look at the land which was so dear to her.

Nevertheless, her weariness did not prevent her from thinking clearly and from making careful provision for the welfare of her people and her country.[38-a] "The money that would have provided an elaborate funeral was to be spent on dowries for twelve poor girls and the ransom of Christian captives in Africa. The poverty of the Castilian treasury . . . weighed on her mind and she gave orders that the number of officials in the royal household should be reduced, and gifts of lands and revenues, that had been alienated by the Crown without sufficient cause, revoked. . . . The future government of her kingdom was her special care. . . . While acknowledging Joanna as her successor, she begged both her and Philip 'to be always obedient subjects of the King, and never disobey his orders.' This injunction was amplified by the command that if Joanna should be absent from Spain, 'or although present . . . unable to reign and govern,' Ferdinand should act as regent, until his grandson Charles was of an age to undertake this task for himself.

"Such were the most important clauses of the document, by which Isabel strove to safeguard her loved Castile from the dangers threatening her. In others, she insisted that Gibraltar, which she had acquired for the Crown should never be alienated from it; that her daughter and son-in-law should not appoint foreigners to any office or post of trust, that the tax of the *alcabala*,[39] if found illegal on inquiry, should be abolished; that a new and more accurate code of laws should be compiled; and that steps should be taken to secure the kindly treatment of natives in the New World."[40]

She now saw to it that her wishes in regard to such weighty matters were duly recorded. But these had not been her first consideration. Her will began with the expression of the desire that her body might be taken to Granada and laid to rest in the Franciscan Monastery there. But she added, " 'Should the King my lord prefer a sepulchre in some other place, then my will is that my body be transported there and laid by his side, that the union we have enjoyed in this world, and through the mercy of God may hope again for our souls in heaven, may be represented by our bodies in the earth.' "[41]

So much for the beginning. The end was equally moving and equally personal. She asked that an alabaster tomb should be raised in the Monastery of Santo Tomás of Avila, where her beloved only son, Juan, was buried. And she added, " 'I beseech the King my lord that he will accept all my jewels, or such as he shall select, so that, seeing them, he may be reminded of the singular love I always bore him while living, and that I am now waiting for him in a better world; by which remembrance he may be encouraged to live the more justly and holily in this.' "[42]

The son she had lost so early. The husband she had kept until the end. The two great loves of her life. These were the last and only persons of whom she was still thinking as she signed the document to which she had given such careful thought and such comprehensive expression. The date—October 12[43]—did not seem important to her. She did not think of it as the anniversary of the day when—thanks to her generosity and her vision—Columbus had found a new land and taken it for Spain, giving it the name of San Salvador—Holy Saviour.

But if the world of human beings was slipping away from her, as she lay so still in her great bed, already clad in the Franciscan habit she had chosen for her shroud, Heaven, the true land of the Holy Saviour, was coming closer and closer to her and she to it. When she heard that, all over Spain, her people were marching in processions and going on pilgrimages to ask for her recovery, she sent them messages, begging them to pray not for the welfare of her body, but for the salvation of her soul. She gratefully welcomed Ximénez, the humble Franciscan whom she had raised to the Cardinalate, who had left the college he was founding and the Bible he was revising that he might come to her; she made her last confession and, for the last time, received Holy Communion. There was no need for firmness any more—nothing to renounce, nothing to challenge, nothing to defend. And there was no struggle, no agony at the last. Death came so quietly and so gently that even her husband, who was close beside her, could hardly believe that she would never clasp his hand and smile at him again as she had just done, that she had left him, this time, forever. There was a great silence in the room, and when it was broken by the sound of weeping which came from those who had not stood so near, it seemed like an intrusion on his grief, a clamor that separated him from a peace that passed all understanding.

He left the death chamber and gave orders that a stand should be built in the market place, according to tradition. When this had been done, he went to it on foot, accompanied by the Archbishop of Toledo, the Bishop of Palencia and all the Court, "to witness the ceremony that was customarily enacted upon the death of a monarch. Preceded by heralds blowing trumpets, the Duke of Alba mounted the stage and raised the standard of Queen Isabel on high three times and proclaimed in a loud voice: 'Castile, Castile for our Sovereign lady, Queen Juana.' "[44]

The next day, after Fernando had taken the oath as Regent, the simple cortege which accompanied the plain black litter left Medina del Campo on its long and mournful journey. Its course took it, eventually, to beautiful Granada, which Isabel had chosen for her sepulchre, because it was the scene of her greatest victory, and symbolized, for her, the victory of immortality over the grave. But first the funeral train wound its way slowly through her own barren homeland of Avila and, as she left it, never to return, she gave it as her legacy a share in her immortal glory.

St. Teresa of Avila. From the statue by Gregorio Fernández in the National Museum of Sculptures at Valladolid.

PART II

The Girl Who Was Too High Spirited

(St. Teresa of Avila, 1515—1582)

1

Doña María de Briceño y Contreras, headmistress of the boarding school for young ladies of rank, maintained by the Augustinian Nuns at the Convent of Our Lady of Grace in Avila, suppressed a discouraged sigh. Then she attempted a fresh conversational approach to her new and obviously reluctant pupil, Teresa de Cepeda y Ahumada.

It was not often that Doña María felt herself so completely baffled, so very nearly defeated, as she was by this beautiful and rebellious girl. True, rumors had reached the convent to the effect that Teresa was too high spirited, not only for her own good, but for the peaceful and contented existence of others. But Doña María was accustomed to dealing with girls who were high spirited, as well as with girls who were sullen, stubborn, mournful, sickly or otherwise difficult to manage. She was now thirty-six years old and she had gained wisdom through long experience, besides being naturally intelligent, patient, gracious and devout. Her pupils loved her as much as they respected her, and she had no difficulty in keeping order throughout the dormitory which she shared with them, or in the schoolroom over which she presided; the young ladies of rank went gladly to chapel with her and did not resent her presence in the parlor when their relatives visited them. Never, since she had been elected by acclamation to her present position, had she been obliged to confess failure with one of her charges. Now it looked very much as if such a failure was staring her in the face. She hoped and prayed that she might be able to avert it.

These hopes and prayers were not based on vainglorious self-assurance; she was still humble in the sight of God, conscious that, like all human beings, she had her limitations and shortcomings and that it was only through the Saviour's Divine Assistance and that of His Holy Mother—The Lady of Grace to whom her life was dedicated—that she could overcome these failings. But with all her heart and soul, Doña María longed for the assurance that such providential help would not be lacking in this case; she felt genuine pity for the girl who was facing her so defiantly.

In the first place, Doña María realized that Teresa's new surroundings, in themselves, must seem prisonlike to a girl who had grown up in a beautiful large house, with a still larger garden, and who had always enjoyed the run of her godfather's palatial residence next door. Both houses faced a noble plaza, dominated by a great tree that grew in the center and left the rest of the square open, so that shade could always be found there, even on the hottest day, and sunshine even on the coldest. Moreover, these houses, set on the very summit of the city, were built flush to the walls and allowed free access to them; from the wide windows at the rear and even more fully from the walls themselves, there was a magnificent view of the fertile fields that were spread out like a vast carpet—emerald green in springtime, golden in the summer and early autumn, sparkling with snow in the winter—and extending as far as the mountains, purple in the distance except when they, too, were mantled with snow. It was a superb sight at any time of year, and a sight that suggested freedom as well as spaciousness, for only the mountains hemmed in the fields and these mountains were far away; only the pleasant little river Adaja, winding its unobtrusive way through the verdure or reflecting the snowy covering on its own frozen surface, severed the great expanse; while the white dusty roads that traversed the fields beckoned to other wonderful cities, unseen by the eyes, but envisioned by the mind: Salamanca, with its great seat of learning towering, rose-colored, into a blue sky; Toledo with its white mosque transfigured into a Christian church by the Catholic Kings; Valladolid, which had been the scene of their marriage and the place where they had spent their first happy year of love.

It was a far cry from such vistas to the confines of Our Lady of Grace. The convent did not even have a real road leading down to it, only one of those passages, typical of Avila, which are at one and the same time a series of broad low steps and a cobblestone street—hard on the feet and a strain on the heart; and as soon as you reached the foot of this passage, there was the façade of the chapel with the convent behind it, both hemmed in by the city walls and the buildings on the further side, and so deep set below them that, quite contrary to offering a view to far-flung glories, they shut out every cheerful sight, even the most close and the most homely. In winter, the buildings were bitterly cold; in summer, the stale chill of centuries still pervaded them, for no sunlight penetrated within them or warmed their surroundings. To nuns, vowed to a life of solitude and austerity, the seclusion of their convent was welcome and the gloom seemed appropriate; if these characteristics were occasionally depressing to the young ladies of rank, these girls were not usually overwhelmed by such conditions. Besides, some of them were considering the cloister as a vocation in any case; it was just as well they should learn beforehand that being a nun meant more than wearing a becoming veil and assuming a rapt expression; it meant abstinence, self-denial, discipline of the mind, mortification of the flesh. Other girls were already pledged in marriage or expecting to be; happy dreams of the future, coupled with the natural optimism of youth, enabled them to endure present discomforts philosophically or even lightheartedly; and it would do them no harm, either, to live austerely for a while before they went forth to dwell sumptuously in a frivolous world.

But this one girl, Teresa de Cepeda y Ahumada, did not seem to fit into either of these categories. She had no idea of becoming a nun; indeed, she had said herself that she was "extremely opposed" to the very mention of such a thing. On the other hand, she was not betrothed, formally or informally. To be sure, there had been rumors about some sort of a love affair, rumors which had reached Our Lady of Grace even before Don Alonso Sánchez y Cepeda had come to the convent, gravely requesting the Abbess to receive his daughter as a pupil at once: a request which automatically indicated that, if there were a love affair, it was not one which he approved or so much as countenanced, and which naturally gave some weight to reports that might otherwise have been dismissed as malicious or mendacious. Vague as these rumors had been, there was nothing about them which suggested that marriage was in the offing. Following the death of his second wife, Doña Beatriz, several years earlier, Don Alonso had closed the main portal of his house to visitors and prolonged his period of mourning; but his inclosed garden led directly into the inclosed garden of his brother, Don Francisco, by a private gate. In Don Alonso's family there were two children, Juan and María, by his first wife, Doña Catalina, and nine by his second: Hernando, Rodrigo, Teresa, Lorenzo, Antonio, Agustín, Pedro, Jerónimo and Juana. In Don Francisco's family were his sons, Pedro, Francisco, Diego and Vicente, and his daughters, Beatriz, Anna, Jerónima and Inés; altogether a group of nineteen own cousins mingling—presumably—almost like brothers and sisters. But Don Alonso's eldest daughter, María, a serious-minded girl, eventually married an equally serious-minded young man and went to live in the nearby village of Castellanos de la Cañada; and, without her restraining influence, there had apparently been—well, indiscretions. Harmless enough flirtations, very probably; but the brotherly and sisterly atmosphere had become charged with something more inflammable; and, after all, these poor young creatures were within the forbidden degrees of consanguinity and they came of pious as well as princely stock. No doubt, Don Alonso had acted wisely in removing Teresa from such a milieu, especially as Don Francisco's daughter, Beatriz, had the reputation of being a good deal of a flirt and something of a gossip.

The headmistress was ready and willing to give Teresa the benefit of the doubt. She could not believe there had been a crisis—at least, not a serious crisis; but there might well have been something secret, even though there had been nothing shameful, in Teresa's relationship to one of her cousins, her clandestine parting with him a source of tragedy to her. After all, she was young and beautiful and, as everyone said, too high spirited; it stood to reason that she must also be naturally ardent. If this natural ardor had been quickened to love for the first time and Teresa had been torn away from the sweetheart responsible for such quickening, it was to be expected that she would take the enforced separation very hard, for a time at least. Doña María was thirty-six now, to be sure, but she had not forgotten how a girl felt at sixteen; therein lay much of her power.

Besides, she said to herself, it was not only the parting with one particular cousin which must have been very hard for Teresa; of course the girl was fond of them all and, likewise, of all her brothers and sisters, from whom she had never before been separated. Then the timing of the separation must have been the final blow.

"For the City of the Liegemen, 1531 was a glorious year: the Empress Isabella arrived there in May with little Prince Philip; it was there that the ceremonies in the course of which the future Philip II, then four years old, was to exchange his childish dress for his first princely breeches took place. The severe taste of the Portuguese princess had to give way before the official programme. Avila glistened with gay tapestries and bright-coloured hangings that sparkled against the granite and was completely invaded by the court. Its sombre streets came to life with gay processions, in the squares tourney followed joust and there was a continual but pleasant hubbub intermingled with the sound of music and the clash of bells.

"It would not do for one of the prettiest girls of rank in Avila to be away from these festivities, and Teresa, who could always adapt herself to any set of circumstances, enjoyed them. . . .

"For two months she went from one festivity to another."[1]

The twenty-sixth of July was fixed as the date when Don Philip was to receive his "princely livery." It was on the thirteenth that Don Alonso decided to send his daughter to Our Lady of Grace. By a margin of less than two weeks, she had missed the splendid ceremonial in which all of her friends would be sharing. The occasion itself was one in which she would have reveled; but it must be gall and wormwood to her to know that, in the midst of their enjoyment, those friends of hers must be speculating on why she had suddenly been deprived of her freedom and shut away from them. If there were no real reason for scandal, if the girl were actually as innocent as she was high spirited, must not the fact that she had been generally adjudged capable of scandalous behavior be doubly hard to bear? Was it not Julius Caesar, who had won that notable battle centuries before at nearby Toros de Guisando—the same place now noted for the treaty which had given Isabel the crown—who had said that his wife must not only be innocent but above suspicion? Was Teresa wounded to the quick because she was not above suspicion?

Doña María was inclined to believe that she was, and the nun's sense of sympathy deepened with her growing understanding. She had heard that Teresa de Ahumada was inordinately fond of finery, that she had loved dressing up in her mother's castoff brocades after Doña Beatriz had renounced costly apparel and gone about, the latter years of her life, as soberly dressed as if she had belonged to a religious order. Then Teresa had had a dress of her own, an orange-colored satin trimmed with black velvet ribbon, which had been so much her favorite that she had worn it constantly over quite a long period; everyone in Avila had recognized her, even from a distance, by this gay orange-colored dress, and had admired her in it and kept on talking about it even after the dress was outgrown or outworn. Doña María could visualize just how Teresa, who now confronted her in the drab, nondescript costume, which all the pupils were obliged to wear, must have looked in that orange-colored dress; and, indeed, she wished that she herself might have seen Teresa in it, for it must have been vastly becoming. The girl had the face and the figure, yes, and the coloring, to wear just such a dress. She was a trifle too plump, perhaps, for perfect symmetry, but she belonged to the type that could afford to be rounded rather than slender; and were those three little warts near her full red lips? Well, never mind, they really looked more like dimples. Of course you could go on finding flaws if you chose, and say that her flashing black eyes were a little too round; but why should you wish to find flaws, when there was so much to admire: the magnificent chestnut-colored hair, falling in natural curls over her shoulders; the translucent skin, which revealed her brow and neck as so white and her cheeks as so delicately rosy. Her hands were lovely, and she sat and stood and moved with grace; her carriage was superb.[1-a] If only that red mouth would curve into a smile, if only those black eyes would glow with happiness. . . . Well she, María de Briceño y Contreras would still find a way to make them. But she must feel her way a step at a time, she must frame her words carefully. Perhaps all the poor child needed was someone to share her secrets now, as she had shared them with that empty-headed daughter of Don Francisco, who could, no doubt, be blamed for most of all Teresa's troubles. The headmistress decided that she would invite the girl's confidence in the kindest and most tactful way of which she was capable. She knew that Teresa was brilliant and accomplished, that she excelled in both homely and lofty arts. She was a good needlewoman and a good cook, a daring horsewoman, a skillful chess player; and when she wrote, words flowed from her pen in easy graceful sequence. But this was no time to challenge her pride or appeal to her intellect. That would come later. For the moment. . . .

"My dear," she heard herself saying, "let us open our hearts to each other."

2

"At first I was very much upset; but I was already weary of vanity and frivolity; when I offended God I was afraid and I forced myself to confess what I had done as soon as possible. I was so troubled on this account that at the end of a week, perhaps sooner, I was much happier there than in my father's house."[2]

This was what Teresa herself wrote later on, in recalling her experience at Our Lady of Grace. María de Briceño's prayers had been answered. "Her good companionship gradually rid me of the habits which bad company had given me and awakened in me afresh the desire for what was eternal," Teresa went on to record, in speaking of the headmistress. "My hostility toward the religious state lessened a little." She prayed more and more herself, following the advice and example of her now beloved mentor, and she begged God to show her the state in which she could best serve him. "I still hoped it would not be in the religious life . . . yet I dreaded marriage."[3]

It is not in the least surprising that these should have been her sentiments at the time, in spite of the support, consolation and good counsel that María de Briceño had given her. Teresa was by no means the first—nor has she by any means been the last—to find that a mutual cousinly caress could suddenly and unexpectedly become a mutual loverlike embrace; and, while recognizing the hard and bitter truth that such a caress could never lead to the full experience of sanctified love, has also faced the harsh fact that she could not find such fulfillment with any other man because, for her, there was only one man in the world. Besides, she had still not been able to see her youthful love affair in its true light, or in its normal relationship to life in general. "My father loved me so much and my dissimulation was such that he did not think me capable of as much evil as was in fact the case. . . . My evil inclinations were sufficient in themselves. In addition there were the servants and I found them quite ready to encourage me in anything wrong. If one of them had given me good advice I might perhaps have listened to her, but self-interest blinded them . . . just as my propensity blinded me. I was not wholly bad and everything dishonourable was abhorrent to my nature, but I loved to spend my time in pleasant chatter; that does not alter the fact that the occasion of falling was there, the danger within a hand's grasp, and I was exposing my father and brothers to it. God guarded me so well that he preserved me from falling, even against my will."[4]

That she did not actually "fall" is evident from this passage, but so is the revelation of the temptation and desire to take the ultimate step. Quite aside from the fact that she knew she could never wholeheartedly love another man as she had loved her cousin, she must also have known that, considering her essential candor, she could not have married another man without telling him everything there was to say about this first love affair; and naturally, for all her frankness, she would have dreaded doing so. Confessions are no doubt good for the soul, but under certain conditions they can be very tearing to the heart.

These conditions did not apply when she bared her soul under the seal of secrecy in the confessional. There she unburdened herself freely, dwelling so insistently on her "guilt" that her priestly confessor wisely decided that she was taking her indiscretion too seriously; as far as he could see, he told her, she had done nothing that could "not have a happy issue by way of marriage."[5] Apparently, neither he nor she made any secret of this opinion, for it was passed on to others who shared it; and evidently the slight stir which had been caused by her abrupt and enforced withdrawal from the social scene was of short duration, for soon her fellow townspeople were voicing their general admiration for her beauty, her distinction and her character by saying to each other, "Teresa de Ahumada? She will marry whom she chooses!" But she did not choose to marry anyone, and if her "evil" conduct had been forgotten by others and minimized by her confessor, she neither forgot it nor minimized it; and though it was easy enough in those days to obtain a dispensation permitting marriage within the forbidden degrees—even the Catholic Kings had done so! —Teresa did not choose to take advantage of that opportunity, either.

With her "dread" of marriage still at the forefront of her consciousness, Teresa knelt in the confessional tucked away in one corner of the chapel at Our Lady of Grace, and afterward knelt to communicate at the small grille on the left of the large one which divided the part of the chapel used by the nuns from the part used by the pupils and the public. She ate her frugal meals in the refectory—later transformed into a sacristy—at the rear of this same chapel, and slept with the other young ladies of rank in the dormitory, where the beloved headmistress presided with such watchful care. She spun, embroidered and made lace, recited the catechism in which she was already letter perfect, and improved her accomplishments as a musician. She was no longer mutinous either in behavior or in spirit; she accepted the conventual pattern, adapted herself to it, and, little by little, came to adorn it. But it still had no appeal to her. Even María de Briceño had not been able to make it seem attractive, devoted as Teresa was to her. The girl's delight in spaciousness and sunlight, wide vistas and distant horizons, had not abated; and though she had ceased to chafe because

she was temporarily deprived of them, she still looked forward eagerly
to the moment when she would be free to enjoy them again. Everything about life at Our Lady of Grace seemed to her cold, confined,
gloomy and grim; and this opinion applied to the austere rule of the
Augustinian Nuns, as well as to the chilly, hidden convent where they
observed it. That was why she still hoped she would not be called
upon to enter the religious life. This, as far as she could see, meant
mortification carried far beyond the realm of reason and solitude
which was nothing more or less than incarceration.

Gradually, however, she began to dwell less on her dread of marriage and more on the state in which she could best serve God. Inevitably, her thinking was somewhat confused; she was still very young,
and she could not get far enough away from her special problems,
either literally or figuratively, to see them in their proper perspective
to life as a whole. She remained for a year and a half at Our Lady
of Grace, and that was a long time to keep turning things over in her
mind, without any more means of mental escape than she had of
physical escape. She came very close to having a nervous breakdown
and, at last, she was sent home to recuperate. But her release had come
too late for her peace of mind. She neither gave nor felt pleasure in
her return to her father's house. At last it was decided that she should
make her married sister, María, a prolonged visit at Castellanos de la
Cañada, breaking her journey at the home of her uncle, Don Pedro
Sánchez de Cepeda, at Hortigosa.

The decision was a singularly wise one. Both Castellanos and
Hortigosa were tiny villages and neither could offer social distractions;
but both could offer other advantages which had been lacking elsewhere and of which Teresa stood in great need just then. Though
Don Pedro's residence was called a palace by his fellow villagers,[6] it
was actually only a pleasant country seat, maintained with tranquil
dignity, and he himself lived a life of the utmost simplicity. He was
a widower, with an only son to whose education he was giving
scrupulous attention; but he hoped that, when this boy was safely
launched in the world, he might retire to a monastery, thus following the practice, then common, of countless men and women whose
habits were devout and whose tastes studious, whether or not they
actually had what could strictly be called a vocation. Meanwhile, he
observed the biblical injunction of visiting widows and orphans in
their affliction and keeping one's self unspotted from the world. He
lived a retired life, except when his charitable deeds took him abroad,

and he kept these benefactions as quiet as possible. For the rest, he spent endless hours in prayer, in meditation and in reading; his splendid library was his one extravagance and his one self-indulgence. To this library he welcomed his niece, with the calm assumption that she would enjoy it as much as he did.

According to her own admission, she was far from being overjoyed at the prospect of spending her time in such a setting and in such pursuits. But she was "extremely anxious to please people," and it had been part of her training to accept, with graciousness, whatever diversions were offered her by her host of the moment. And she had her reward. Her uncle began by quoting poetry to her; then he turned to more weighty tomes and invited her to read aloud to him. *The Letters of St. Jerome* were among the classics which he chose; and later, she freely confessed that, though she stayed with Don Pedro only a short time, his good influence and the words of God, both those she heard and those she read, made a profound impression on her. The influence was merely one of example, for Don Pedro was both too gentle and too wise to attempt any kind of coercion; and the words of God were, in many cases, familiar to her already. It was the *way* she heard them and read them now which made the difference.

At Castellanos the conditions were not the same, but they were no less salutary. Here there was no "palace," or even any kind of a country seat which rural imagination could conjure into the semblance of one; neither was there a voluminous library, dominated by a solitary and inspired scholar who could interpret its contents. Life was pastoral and patriarchal in the extreme. Less than a dozen humble dwellings were grouped around the one occupied by Teresa's elder sister, María de Cepeda, the latter's young husband, Don Martín de Guzmán y Barriento, and their little son, Juanito. Their house was somewhat more spacious than those of their shepherds, for it was two stories high and provided with little balconies; but it was almost as primitive in its appointments; and financially, despite María's sizable dowry, the young couple was in straitened circumstances. A central fountain in the village provided water for all purposes; and while there was no lack of this, since springs and brooks were plentiful in the countryside, only endless drudgery maintained the standards of cleanliness on which the Cepeda family insisted. The surrounding landscape was typically barren, its long stony stretches broken only by clumps of cork trees and by small fields which had been made productive by infinite toil; and the sound of the sheep bells was all that broke the engulfing silence. But the crystalline air supplied a natural tonic and the habit of reading which Teresa had formed at her uncle's house stood her in good stead during the hours which might otherwise have dragged. And there were not many of these. She had always excelled in cookery and had found little chance to practice the art in her father's well-staffed house; now it proved a diverting occupation for her; and she also had a freer hand in the care of her little nephew than she had ever managed to get with her younger brothers and sister. Moreover, María, sweet, gentle and meek, was a living example of all the qualities the girl who was too high spirited lacked, and which she knew she ought to emulate, at least to some degree. If her sister's submissiveness to the rather domineering and demanding man she had married did nothing to incline Teresa more favorably toward wedlock, at least it gave her a deeper understanding of true Christian virtues and a greater appreciation of her own fortunate lot in life.

So, first at Hortigosa and then at Castellanos, Teresa found the freedom and the peace which she craved. Solitude in itself had not oppressed her; it was only solitude associated with imprisonment. Gradually, her confused thoughts became calm; then they became clearer. She did not doubt the consecration of the Augustinian Nuns, though she knew their way of serving God could never be hers; but, increasingly, she thought there must be some other way. She would ponder, she would pray, she would search and, eventually, she would find it.

Probably she herself could not have told when she first began to visualize the Convent of the Encarnación as the predestined scene of her religious life. She had been familiar with it from her earliest years, for it was inaugurated on the very day of her baptism, and one of her dearest friends, Juana Suárez, had taken the habit there as a Carmelite Nun of Mitigated Observance. It was pleasantly situated outside the walls, with open country all around it, and the buildings themselves were attractive, and spacious enough to accommodate the hundred or more nuns who dwelt there in very agreeable fashion. Their ample parlors were open to visitors most of the time, and lay visitors were made as welcome as the clergy. Moreover, though the nuns were theoretically cloistered, this stricture was not taken very seriously; it was no unusual thing for a sister to obtain permission from the Prioress to visit her family or even her friends, for weeks at a time. In other words, Encarnación had become a favored, in fact a fashionable, place of residence for ladies who did not object to wearing a habit or who actually rather enjoyed this; who found a well-ordered life, in which prayer formed a factor, restful and congenial; and who, for one reason or another, either did not wish to marry or had regretfully decided that no one wished to marry them. Certainly they observed such rules and regulations as were laid down for them, unless properly released; but there were not too many of these, there were no penances carried to extremes, there was no discipline under duress. Yet no one said these Carmelites were not devout, no one criticized their Order as a whole. Here was a way of life far more comprehensible, as well as far more appealing, than the austere existence of the imprisoned Augustinians; yet this was a religious order, too. Well then, why was it not the perfect answer to all her probing?

Teresa did not make the decision hastily. After the long visit at Castellanos and two shorter ones at Hortigosa, she returned to her father's house and ran it with great competence. Don Alonso was delighted to have her at home again. So were the brothers who were still there themselves, though Hernando had left to join Pizarro in Peru while she was still at Our Lady of Grace; and now Rodrigo was setting out, as a member of Pedro de Mendoza's expedition, for the Río de la Plata. Incidentally, Teresa's cousins were also delighted at her return, though she never resumed the garden frolics in which she had once been such a magnet; and far from considering her too high spirited now, they thought she had become rather too serious minded. She seemed to read a great deal, all kinds of learned books, not the romances that had enlivened her mother's otherwise dull life, and that Teresa herself had eagerly devoured as a young girl. Not that she was a spoilsport though; she could still be very gay upon occasion. She went out a good deal in general society, and when Charles V came to make a state visit in Avila, she took a leading part in the festivities. (No sudden departure for a convent this time, as there had been when Philip II assumed his "princely attire!") It did not occur to anyone that she was not perfectly contented with the life she now led, that it did not satisfy her completely. Her father assumed that she would marry "some time" and when she did, she would have a very handsome dowry; for Rodrigo, when he sailed away, superbly equipped, had insisted that this accoutrement was all he merited, that his inheritance should be added to that of his sister. But Don Alonso could be forgiven for hoping that "some time" might be in the comfortably distant future. She was companionable, this daughter of his, as well as competent; and she was such a credit to him! So handy about the house, so talented in the matter of needlework. And withal, so pleasing to look at, so stimulating to converse with, so ready with her merry laugh! Yet always discreet now, always gracious—certainly she had the makings of a really great lady! Like everyone else, he had forgotten the episode which had been the cause of such anguish to her. The past was unimportant anyway; what counted was the future, which she could make so happy for him and so glorious for their city. . . .

She was to make it glorious for their city, though not in the way that he envisioned. But she was not to make it happy for him. He was entirely unprepared when she came to him and told him that she had decided to become a nun.

He recoiled from the declaration with a violence which made his earlier refusal to countenance any innocent dalliance with her cousins seem mild indeed. A *nun!* This beautiful girl who could marry anyone she chose, and who would therefore of course select a handsome knight of unquestionable valor and high degree; this girl on whom every sort of Fortune smiled; this girl who, in short, had the world at her feet! She must have taken temporary leave of her senses to so much as suggest such a thing! When she persisted in the suggestion until he saw, unmistakably, that it was a purpose, he told her angrily that he supposed, after he died, she would do as she pleased, but that, as long as he lived, she would never, never, never have his consent. . . .

She waited a reasonable length of time for him to change his mind and, in the meanwhile, she was more than once very close to changing hers. Her decision had not been based on overwhelmingly religious fervor, but on the conviction that she could better serve God in the cloister than on the hearth; the conviction was well founded on thought and prayer, but it lacked warmth and impulse. If she had not felt increasingly sure that while she still could not see the distant path, she saw the first steps leading toward it, she might have wavered. Probably the knowledge that this was still possible was partly responsible for the fact that she persuaded her younger brother, Antonio, to join the Dominicans at the same time that she joined the Carmelites. She knew that if they left the parental roof secretly together, and this gentle boy showed no signs of wavering, she could not do so, either.

Very early one autumnal morning, before anyone else in the house was stirring, they stole out of it and made their way quietly through the town. Even if they had met people they knew, their presence in the streets at such an hour would have caused no astonishment; it was not unusual for them to attend Mass before daybreak. Outside the door of Encarnación, Teresa said good-bye tenderly to her brother; inside, her friend, Juana Suárez was waiting to welcome her with equal tenderness. Even if the Prioress told her that she could not be definitely accepted as a postulant without her father's consent, she knew that he would not withhold this long, now that she had shown her decision to enter Encarnación was not the result of an ephemeral whim, but of an unalterable resolution. Don Alonso passed for a pious man; he could not give the lie to his own reputation by declining to dedicate his daughter to God. So she reasoned and she reasoned rightly. "On 31st October 1536, he gave an undertaking before a notary to make over to the convent of the Incarnation every year, twenty-five measures of grain, one half being wheat and one half barley, or, in their default, two hundred gold ducats. Teresa renounced all claims on the family inheritance and made over Rodrigo's eventual legacy to her sister Juana. Her father also gave the novice a bed, blankets and quilts, six linen sheets, six pillows, two mattresses, two cushions, a carpet, as well as the clothing she would need during the noviciate and after profession: 'the habits, one of fine black cloth and the other of thicker material; three underskirts, one of red wool, another white and the third of fine serge; a sheepskin cloak, her veils, undergarments and shoes; and finally the books which it is customary for nuns to be given.'"[7]

It was the Vigil of All Saints. There was nothing to indicate that the novice, who kept her own name of Teresa de Ahumada, and whose very presence in the chapel throughout the night was due to determination, rather than to devotion, would ever have a place in their calendar.

3

Determination, rather than consecration, had been the primary force which impelled Teresa to become a nun. It continued to be her outstanding characteristic throughout her novitiate and for some time beyond that—indeed until she became so ill that her extraordinary will power was at low ebb for the first and only time in her life.

The transition from life in the world to life in the convent apparently caused her no trouble. In a surprisingly short time, she looked and acted like a nun; there was no awkward or embarrassed period of adjustment. She wore her habit as if with accustomed ease, she kept her hands under her scapular, she walked at the even, unhurried pace which characterizes the seemingly effortless speed of the religious. The manual labor assigned to her was dispatched in the same gracefully efficient way, and she was never tardy in either the refectory or the chapel. It came as a surprise to her fellow novices when she confessed—and this she did rather tardily—that she was not as familiar as she should have been with all the prayers, in fact, that she knew relatively few of them, and that she had not the slightest idea what to do in the choir. It was a blow to her pride to admit this; many a prescribed penance had seemed much easier.

Once she had confessed her ignorance, however, she was swift to learn the things she did not know; and, on the whole, she was happy, or rather, on the whole, she was content, with some joyous moments of exaltation, some sad ones of depression, and some longer periods of the "aridity" which, centuries later, was to constitute one of the greatest trials which her namesake at Lisieux was called upon to bear. After several years of indecision, Teresa de Ahumada had finally made up her mind what was best for her to do and she had done it; consequently, she was aware of the relief that comes from taking definite action after much procrastination and much vacillating. She was slightly confused because the conventual rules seemed elastic enough to provide for extremes of both austerity and luxury. Some of the nuns carried their ascetic practices to excess; others did not even pretend to deny themselves any comfort or pleasure they could afford. Teresa tried to steer a middle course between the two: she accepted, with gratitude, the two private rooms to which she was entitled—so long as she could pay for them—and did not insist, like one self-denying lady of exalted rank, on sharing the dormitory of those who could afford nothing better. On the other hand, she tried to make up for her inadequacy at chapel by taking on tasks which were not obligatory and for which other novices did not volunteer, because they felt such duties to be too distasteful. Among these was the care of a very sick nun who was dying slowly—much too slowly—of an unspeakably loathsome disease; Teresa nursed her day and night, without once betraying the almost uncontrollable repugnance which the sight of blood, pus and excrement aroused, until death brought the poor victim release. True, the zealous young novice could not always control her nausea, but she invariably succeeded in doing so until she was out of the sick woman's sight; and lest this nursing task should not be penance enough, she took it upon herself to administer private discipline far beyond the requirements of the Rule. The Prioress wisely forbade this, when she discovered what Teresa was doing; but by that time the girl's health was already seriously undermined by insufficient sleep and food.

Her Profession, a year after her Clothing, took the usual magnificent form on such occasions; the chapel was ablaze with light and filled with the friends who had come to the ceremony in their most splendid attire. Afterward, Don Alonso, who had supplied the candles, also supplied a sumptuous dinner, and there was dancing and singing to follow; it was not considered in the least inappropriate that all this should take place in the convent or that Teresa should have a part in it. Amidst the merrymaking, an old nun suddenly recalled that, years before, a *zahorí*—a diviner seeking for gold—had come to the convent and predicted that some day Encarnación would have in its community a nun named Teresa who would become a saint. Immediately, Doña Teresa de Casada—the ascetic who slept by choice in the common dormitory—exclaimed, "God grant that it may be I!" Laughingly, Teresa de Ahumada said the same.

Actually, she did not feel very much like laughing. She had pronounced her vows firmly, she had prostrated herself humbly and unhesitatingly before the grille and had touched her head to the ground. But, years afterward, in trying to describe something which had hurt her very much, she was to say, "I do not think that anything in my life hurt so much, *not even my profession day*";[8] and soon she was assailed with fears that her jesting remark might have been an expression of vainglory, however involuntary, however unconscious. She renewed her excessive acts of penance, carrying them far beyond the realm of reason. One day she actually appeared in the refectory on all fours, a pack saddle loaded with stones on her back, while a fellow nun dragged her along by the halter which she had fastened around her neck.

Viewed across the span of centuries, this seems the least appealing period of her life; she was certainly neither cheerful nor charming in the course of it; and, at no other time, as far as I know, did she lack these endearing qualities, did she cease being "anxious to please," or did she fail in common sense, in rationality and in moderation. At no other time, though she was to suffer all her life from various ailments, some slight and some grave, did she deliberately bring these upon herself. Now, naturally enough, she began to experience intervals

of extreme exhaustion and to have serious fainting fits. When her father came to see her, it was occasionally necessary to carry her to the
grille, though, at other times, she managed to drag herself there somehow. Her eyes, always slightly protuberant—one of the few defects in
her beauty—now seemed to be "starting out of their sockets."⁰ Her
fainting fits became so frequent and so prolonged that more than once
her fellow nuns thought that she was dead; and when they succeeded
in rousing her, she gave them to understand that she would really
rather have died. Her physical weakness and her morbid outlook on
life were so interwoven that no one could understand her or help her.
The best physicians then available, not only in Avila but for miles
around, were summoned to see her, but none of them could suggest
any treatment or medication that would be helpful. It seems a wonder
to us now that those which they did suggest—and try—did not kill
her outright; as it was, since her constitution was basically sound and
since probably nothing more serious than a nervous breakdown was
the matter with her, she only grew weaker and weaker and more and
more depressed. At last, in desperation, her father decided to put her
in the charge of a so-called "healer," a woman who lived in the village
of Becedas, not far from Castellanos de la Cañada, where Teresa
had spent such happy months with her married sister, María. There
was nothing in the Carmelite Rule which prevented such a departure
and such an absence from the convent; in fact, when Don Alonso
asked that his daughter's friend, Juana Suárez, should be permitted to
go with her, the Prioress readily agreed to this also.

As on a previous journey, the first stop was made at Hortigosa; Don

Accordingly, one cold, snowy day in late March, a small cavalcade
left Encarnación and took the road leading toward Salamanca. Teresa
was placed recumbent in the litter which had served her delicate
mother as a conveyance when Doña Beatriz travelled between the
town house in the city of Avila and the family *finca* at Gotarrendura,
three leagues distant. The litter's framework was supplied with substantial webbing, its ornamentation was elaborate, and it was suitably
transported by richly caparisoned horses; reputedly, it had cost a thousand *maravedís*. Beside it, rode Don Alonso, astride a horse ac-
coutred with a black saddle and black breast strap; he had never
ceased to wear mourning and to surround himself with the trappings
of woe since the death of his wife. Juana was more humbly mounted;
like the servants who accompanied their master, she went on mule-
back.

As on a previous journey, the first stop was made at Hortigosa; Don

Pedro had not yet retired to a monastery; he was still living in his "palace," in the tranquil atmosphere of learning and devotion which suited him so well. Although he was shocked to see the emaciation of his niece, his welcome took the same form that it had before; while awaiting the preparation of a warm and heartening meal, he installed her in his library.

Evidently, he disposed of the rest of the party elsewhere, for she opened her heart to him in a way that she had not been able to do in talking with Don Alonso and Juana Suárez, and she would hardly have done this if they had also been in the room. She told him about her depression and her discouragement, both of which were, of course, quite evident to him. In return, he urged her to pray and she protested that she did.

"How?"

She outlined the prayers which she recited by rote. He shook his head. Those were not enough. He spoke to her about mental prayer and recollection; then he rose and crossed over to his bookshelves. The volume which he took down this time was not *The Letters of St. Jerome*; it was the so-called *Spiritual Alphabet* of Fray Francisco de Asuna. Teresa leafed through it and then opened it and read at random.

". . . Vocal prayer, as thou hast seen, is a petition we make to God to ask him for what is necessary for us.

". . . The second form of prayer, that is without pronouncing the words with the lips, leaves us free so that our heart alone speaks to Our Lord . . .

". . . The third, which may be termed mental or spiritual, is that in which the highest point of the soul, sustained by love, soars upward to God in the purest and most loving way possible on the wings of desire . . ."[10]

Here were the definitions and the explanations which she had been seeking and, for so long, seeking in vain. Through the wise and tender counsel, committed to writing by a gentle Franciscan, who had also been a valiant soldier, a dim way was clarified for her, a hard way made easier. For the first time in months, her depression lifted. She read on and on. Then she began to copy stray sentences here and there. She was still doing so when she was told it was time to continue her journey. Don Pedro took the precious volume from her and closed it, but only to put it back into her hands.

"Take it with you," her uncle said, "it is your book now."

The day marked the beginning of a new life for Teresa: a life of such prayer as she had hitherto never known. Without this new life burgeoning within her, she would almost certainly have died, physically and spiritually, before another year had passed. For the stay at Becedas was destined to be a fiery crucible.

4

When Don Alonso rode away from Becedas, astride the horse with the black saddle and the black breast strap and followed by the empty litter and his personal servants, he did so with a comparatively easy mind. He had seen his daughter comfortably installed in a suitable house, the property of the Guzmán y Barriento family into which María had married. And María herself had temporarily left nearby Castellanos de la Cañada, in order to be with her sister; between them, she and Juana Suárez should see that Teresa had the best of care. Moreover, his first impressions of the medicine woman had been favorable; she prescribed only what she called "holy remedies" and he liked the sound of that; they came largely from herbs and long experience had proved they could not be harmful in any case, and that they might well have healing powers, with the help of Divine Providence. And Teresa seemed much more at peace than she had in a long while; she spent most of her time reading the book Don Pedro had given her. Well, it was a holy book, not at all like the romances to which, as her father knew very well, she had been addicted to reading in secret, like her mother before her, and which they had always tried to conceal at his approach, as if they were stolen sweets. Perusal of a holy book, in conjunction with the absorption of holy remedies might be just what she needed most. Certainly she could have the complete quiet and isolation at Becedas which had been lacking at Encarnación. There would not be a lot of coming and going, of distracting parlor visits, of whispered gossip along the corridors and small collations in the so-called cells which were actually pleasant little private apartments. Instead of a fountain for its center, like Castellanos, Becedas had a church; its water supply came from a stream that encircled it, making a little island of it. Don Alonso thought it unlikely that Teresa would be disturbed by visits from any of the peasants who lived in the clustering huts between the church and the stream. Her only callers would be the medicine woman and the priest. . . .

In this last assumption Don Alonso was right; the medicine woman, who was to act as Teresa's physician, and the priest, who was to act as her confessor, were, indeed, her only callers; but in judging what their effect upon her would be, he was completely wrong. The medicine woman's holy remedies soon began to take an increasingly violent form; they were no longer confined to simple and beneficent herbs, but included more and more powerful and painful purges; in comparison with them even the injections, the bleedings, the massages with scorpion oil and other treatments to which the unfortunate patient had previously been subjected were comparatively mild; instead of improving physically, Teresa grew frailer and frailer. Spiritually, her condition was even more potentially dangerous.

For the village priest, finding that she had little to confess, but that her general conversation was delightful, fell into the habit of prolonging his pastoral calls. He was a man with a reasonably good education and, doubtless, he found little to stimulate him, mentally, in the society of his regular parishioners, who were simple and ignorant folk. And he was young, personable and virile, as well as intelligent; his very entrance into the invalid's room seemed like a restorative, for it was immediately permeated by his vitality and good cheer. His visits were as pleasing—and as provocative—to Teresa as they were to him. After all, she could not read or rest all the time; and she was young, too, young and essentially feminine and, without conscious effort or intention, almost irresistibly charming. The inevitable happened; their relationship became one of *une amitié fervente*; before long, they were drawn to each other by strong mutual attraction.

It was not an evil attraction, and to say or even suppose that it was, would be in the nature of self-accusation, for it would betray a suspicious nature, prone and even eager to find scandal where no reasonable cause for it exists. But it was a dangerous attraction, not only because she was a nun and he was a priest, but because some men and women are so constituted that they must constantly be on their guard in their association with the opposite sex, because of the strong appeal which they have for it, however unconsciously or involuntarily; and they usually do not know this by instinct, any more than a child with his first paint box knows by instinct that a combination of blue and yellow results in a cool green, whereas a combination of blue and red results in a brilliant purple. Teresa was such a woman, but she was only just beginning to find this out; and, having made this discovery, she soon learned to guard her actions and govern her life accordingly. Apparently, the parish priest was such a man, but he was of more common clay and he was less self-controlled and less guarded; it was not long before he was confessing to Teresa, rather than she to him, and doing so in a rather vehement fashion, with mortal instead of venial sins on his conscience. For seven years, he told her, in a burst of candor, he had been living in sin with a woman of the village; and though this was well known, he had never been publicly or officially rebuked for his concubinage and he had been celebrating Mass and administering the Sacraments all the time.

Teresa was deeply shocked and even more stricken by what he had told her. When he left her and she had recovered herself somewhat, she called María and Juana—whose chaperonage seems to have been rather casual, to say the least—into her presence and, as inconsequentially as possible, said she would like to know something about the persons who made up her confessor's household. To her continued amazement and distress, she found that her sister and her cousin were already well informed on this subject, and that they accepted the situation without much surprise or strain. This attitude apparently eased Teresa's own mind and conscience somewhat; at all events, when the priest next came to see her, she did not refuse to receive him. Whether this was wise or not is, perhaps, open to doubt. Teresa apparently doubted it herself, for, in writing about it, she says, "My intention was good, but my conduct bad; for however great the good, one may never do anything wrong, however small, to bring it about."[10-a]

The immediate good which she hoped to achieve was to persuade her friend that he should part with a little brass idol which his concubine had given him and which he wore on a long cord around his neck. Others had tried in vain to so persuade him and he had remained adamant; now he tore it off and flung it at Teresa's feet. They both wept and she sent him away. Then she called María and asked her to pick up the idol and cast it into the little stream which encircled the village; evidently, Teresa was not willing to touch it herself. When the priest next came to see her he told her that he had broken entirely with "the unhappy woman"—the harshest term Teresa ever used in speaking of her—and "after this, the two [Teresa and the priest] were united in a friendship that was entirely blameless."[11]

Blameless it undoubtedly was, but Teresa must have realized there were still elements of danger in it, for, in writing about it later, she said, "I never saw any harm in the great affection he bore me; *yet it might have been purer.* There were, too, occasions when we might have sinned gravely if we had not had a lively remembrance of God's Presence."[12] It was long afterward that she put these words on paper; but the feeling which inspired them must have already been very strong while she was still at Becedas for, within a few months after her arrival there, she realized that her meetings with the priest must end. She told him this, as gently as she could, but with unmistakable firmness. Then, shaken and bereaved, she wrote to her father and asked him to come and take her back to Avila.

He responded immediately, and when he saw her it was his natural supposition that her summons was based on her desire to die at home. The medicine woman had very nearly finished the work, already unwittingly begun by the doctors in Avila, of preparing to consign her to an early grave. She was tenderly taken to the room which had been hers when she was a child and put to bed there. The physicians, who had been summoned again, now sagely suggested tuberculosis, which they had not mentioned before, as a contributing cause to her moribund condition. But since they tardily admitted there was nothing they could do to cure her, they were willing to spare her further anguish in the way of treatments no less agonizing than futile; they were convinced death was so close at hand that they might as well let her die in peace.

Only her father, after rallying from the first shock of seeing her at Becedas, declined to accept her condition as fatal. Even when she asked for the Last Rites, he soothingly suggested that she should not try to go to confession until she felt stronger. Later, when she lost consciousness, and the priest who came to administer Extreme Unction announced his conviction that she was not dying but already dead, Don Alonso reproached himself bitterly because he had not encouraged her to take Communion before she fell into this state; but he himself refused to admit that the end had already come. A mirror was held over her face and her breath left no mark on it; she was closely examined by the light of a candle and, when it was tilted and some of its drippings accidentally fell on her eyelids, they did not even flutter under the wax. Another candle, in a holder at her bedside, overturned and set fire to the curtains; her brother Lorenzo, who was keeping vigil, had dozed off, and before he was fully roused, the draperies were in flames. Teresa did not wake while he frantically extinguished these. Finally, the nuns came from Encarnación to wash and shroud the body; Don Alonso permitted them to minister to the still form; but when they asked to take it away, for burial in the grave that was already prepared, he shook his head and resumed the place and the position which he had never once willingly left: at his daughter's side, with his fingers on her wrist. If he could be persuaded to speak at all, he insisted that he could still feel her pulse.

After four days, Teresa's eyelids, weighted though they were with wax, twitched slightly. She moved her free hand toward them to release them, touching her shroud as her fingers groped their way along. At first, she was also blinded by tears; but when these ceased to flow and she composed herself, she looked around the *capilla ardiente*[13] in wonderment: at the lighted tapers, at the kneeling nuns, at her father seated beside her, his head bowed but his firm handclasp bringing her back to reality. It was the sensation of endurance and survival he gave her which gradually enabled her to collect her scattered thoughts and to give some coherence to her halting words about heaven and hell, about the work she must still do on earth if she were to earn the one and escape the other, about convents and foundations and souls waiting to be saved. At last the confusion was completely dispelled and she spoke, not only with clarity, but with authority and with the revelation of an uncanny gift of prophecy.

"Never believe I am dead until you see my body covered with cloth of gold."

5

Although Teresa's mind was now wholly clear, and remained so for the rest of her long life, her bodily condition was pitiable. She was so emaciated that she suffered agonies when anyone tried to move her, however gently, in order to make her bed; and she herself could move only the one hand with which she had freed her eyelids from wax. Otherwise, she was completely paralyzed.

No one knew then, and to this day no one can authentically assert, what caused this paralysis. It cannot be explained, any more than the phenomenon of her deathlike trance can be explained. It is futile to try. The only thing we can say, with any degree of conviction, is that we know it happened. The illness which preceded her departure for Becedas can almost certainly be laid principally to a nervous breakdown and there are plenty of valid explanations of why she should have had one, just as there are plenty of valid explanations for her digestive troubles. The protuberance of her eyes, first noticed at the same time, might have been due to a thyroid condition; and there may have been some functional trouble with her heart, though that could not have been very serious, or she certainly would not have lived to the ripe old age she was to attain. Again, her terrible debility after her mistreatment at the hands of the medicine woman and her emotional disturbance because of the abrupt and painful ending to a friendship which had promised so much, are also quite understandable; but the syncope and the paralysis are not. Countless theories, of course, have been advanced, some slanderous, some sacrilegious, some absurd and some reasonably sound; it may be said that, for the next three years, her crippled condition was not unlike that of a person stricken by infantile paralysis and slowly recovering from it, without enlightened guidance. But how to account for the fact that, when her syncope began, she still had the use of her limbs, and that, when she came out of it, she did not, is something that has not been done, as far as I know and—also, as far as I know—cannot be done.

It is, however, noteworthy that, this time, there was no trace of the morbidity which had characterized her earlier breakdown, no wild talk about not caring whether she lived or died and, in fact, preferring to die and be done with it. She expected and wanted to live and, what was more, she felt the place for her to make the effort to recover was not in the luxurious room she had occupied as a child, but in the infirmary of Encarnación. She finally persuaded her father to take her back there.

It was still determination, rather than consecration, that drove her on; but it was determination of such force and splendor that we cannot help believing faith was a powerful factor in it. I am convinced that only a person who has once been blessed with physical beauty and vigor, whose movements were once swift and graceful, whose countenance was pleasing and whose manner was charming, can fully grasp what it means to find one's self bereft of all these attributes, to be helpless or, at best, awkward and clumsy, to feel a burden to one's self and others, to know that pain, however bravely borne, takes its toll and shows its ravages. This is the harder to endure when the victim is young; age sometimes brings with it a certain degree of resignation, a feeling that, after all, there have been many good and even glorious years, and that no human being should expect that life can continue indefinitely in such a way. Teresa de Ahumada had been a child favored by fortune: a beloved daughter, a favorite sister and cousin, a desirable match, a substantial heiress; moreover, her wealth and culture, her beauty and breeding, had been coupled with abundant vitality; she had fairly radiated good health and good spirits. Like most Spaniards, she had been a tireless pedestrian, a fearless and accomplished rider and a wonderful dancer; the garden games she played with her cousins almost certainly included blindman's buff, for one of the most famous paintings by a great Spanish artist depicts persons of quality thus disporting themselves; and other similar pastimes were equally general, gay and strenuous. Now Teresa was a Carmelite nun, vowed to poverty, chastity and obedience, she had forsworn her fortune and her friends, she had lost her looks and her health, and she was, apparently, a hopeless cripple. *And she was just twenty-three years old.* I think these are very important factors to remember in considering the next period of her life.

For three years, she remained a complete paralytic, confined to the infirmary of Encarnación; at the end of this time, she began to drag herself about a little. She found she could walk on all fours and she moved around in this way, not as she had once done, in an exaggerated and unreasonable form of penance, but because it was the only way she *could* move; and she thanked God for the progress that had made this possible. She was praying now for a cure—not because she found it hard to accept, any longer, whatever sacrifice and suffering might be required of her, but because she was sure she still had work to do in the world; those murmurings about convents and foundations and saving souls had sounded vague to those who had surrounded the bed they thought was her bier, and her mind had apparently been confused when she voiced them; but back of the vagueness and the confusion had been a will and a purpose. The will was stronger than ever now, the purpose more urgent. She could not do the work which she saw as her destiny while she was creeping around on all fours, thankful as she was for this much activity after years of helplessness. She must stand upright and stride forward.

Suddenly one day, she felt as if she could do it. Slowly, she raised her head, then her arms and then her body. She swayed slightly, but only for a moment. After that, her feet supported her firmly and she stood straight and still. She put one foot forward and then the other. Without faltering and without stopping, she walked on and on through the long corridor and came into the midst of her sisters.

6

Once she had been restored to physical activity, Teresa was soon restored in every other respect. Motion to her was as natural as breathing; the disabilities which had prevented it were even harder for her to bear than the sufferings which went with it. She had shown great courage in overcoming the first and bearing the second; but for all the brave front with which she had faced the world, her essential *joie de vivre* had, inevitably, been impaired. However, she had tremendous powers of recuperation; she was soon aglow with all the bloom, all the vitality and all the charm which had characterized her before her nervous breakdown, her syncope and her years of paralysis; and, with the recapture of these qualities, she began to arrest more favorable attention from the outer world than any other resident of Encarnación.

It has been frequently noted that the parlors of this institution which, according to our standards, had the characteristics of a pleasant private club rather than those of a rigidly sequestered cloister, constituted the recognized meeting place of the best society in Avila. The religious, as well as the laity, received visitors as a matter of course, and no one assumed, much less insisted, that all conversation on such occasions was to be limited in scope to sacred subjects. Thirty years later, St. John of the Cross, coming to the convent as its confessor, was scandalized at the frivolity which he found there; but it had not yet occurred to Teresa that there was anything shocking, or even surprising, about its atmosphere. This was as it had always been, as far back as she could remember; and since Encarnación had been founded the year she was born, her memories of it went back to her happy childhood. One of the factors which had influenced her entrance there had been the agreeable impression she had received of its urbanities, which formed so great a contrast to the bleakness of Las Gracias. She did not neglect any of the duties assigned to her; on the contrary, "in choir as in the parlor or at recreation, Doña Teresa de Ahumada had the gift of putting herself at each one's disposal."[14] She was living in conformity with the usages and customs established in a convent where a multitude of compromises with the constitution were "lawful."[15] If more of her callers were male than female and if more of the former were laymen rather than priests, no one thought the worse of her for that, even when one of these gentlemen began to show a marked partiality for her society. There was no reason why anyone should have. She had learned the lesson at Becedas which she had failed to master in the walled garden where she and her cousins romped together; never again was she to underestimate her powers of attraction for the opposite sex or the dangers that went with them. She continued to be cordial, but there was an unmistakable element of reserve in her cordiality. Her male callers—especially the one toward whom the greatest show of caution was directed—were not slow to understand and respect her attitude; but their numbers did not decrease. Soon her father discovered that she had difficulty in finding enough time to devote to him, there were so many other claimants for her attention; and he was almost the only caller who sought to speak with her on serious subjects.

This was a bitter blow to him. Although he had been a devout Catholic all his life, the healing practice of mental prayer had come to him largely through his daughter, to whom its benefits had first been revealed in the *Spiritual Alphabet*. After that, he and she discussed the subject at length, while she was ill and helpless, and it had been a source of mutual consolation and strength. It was deeply distressing to him to find that, though he had continued the habit they formed together, and was giving more and more time to this special form of devotion, she was giving it less and less. It did not occur to him that, under all the circumstances, this was only natural. His life was drawing toward its end, and it was an increasingly empty and solitary one; in the truest sense, her life was only just beginning; it was full to over-flowing and it was so far from solitary that she had hardly a moment to call her own. Moreover, in the first joyous period after her full recovery, she did not want to dwell on anything intimately associated with the agonizing experience which had preceded it, even the long hours of communion with her father. What she craved now was action, not contemplation; she was to discover, in time, that she could make room in her life for both and that one was as needful to her as the other. But she was still a very young woman and a very human one. She could not make all the important discoveries about the proper pattern for living simultaneously. Nevertheless, it was not overlong before she again realized that mental prayer was not only valuable, but essential to her.

The realization came when she was summoned home to care for her father, who was dying. His establishment had, little by little, become less luxurious; his daughters had been richly dowered, his sons no less richly equipped as, one by one, they had set out for the New World. He had bestowed most of his remaining goods upon the poor; of what use to him was wealth, now that his wife was dead and his children gone? On the other hand, there were many about him in such need that his benefactions would make the difference between comparative well-being and starvation. He had no regrets as far as money was concerned. It was only about Teresa's spiritual welfare that he was anxious.

To a certain degree, she was able to comfort him. The same Dominican priest who ministered to her dying father became her confessor. He proffered her sage advice on several subjects, frequent Communion among them; but he urged that, above all, she should resume the practice of mental prayer. She promised that she would do so and she kept her promise. Though ten years were to pass before she was to modify her way of thinking or living to any marked degree, except in this one, she did have "the strong pillar of mental prayer as her support."[16]

This being the case, what happened next has never struck me as being sudden or surprising; for was that period not as truly one of preparation as is a novitiate before a profession? It seems to me that it must have been and that, even though unconsciously, Teresa was progressing spiritually with as much rapidity as could reasonably be expected of her. It had taken her three years to recover completely from total paralysis, and it was considered nothing short of miraculous that she did so in that length of time. She succeeded in walking the first time she actually stood upright after crawling about on all fours; but during this crawling process her weakened muscles had gradually been growing more powerful, whether she or anyone else knew it or not. Similarly, the "strong pillar of prayer" had been giving her more and more support all the time; she was prepared—indeed, she was ready—for Divine Revelation when she noticed the painting of *Ecce Homo*—the Christ of the Column—in the oratory. I do not think this observance was accidental; I think it was part of the pattern.

It is quite possible, of course, that this painting, which is still one of Encarnación's greatest treasures, had just been given to the convent when Teresa caught sight of it, and that it was in the oratory only because a more suitable place had not yet been found for it. Even so, neither its subject nor its placement could have been astonishing to Teresa. She had lived surrounded by pictures all her life, both in and out of the convent; most of them were religious in character and many of them were painted with considerable emphasis on the more painful parts of the Life and Death of Christ and His Followers; such was and still is the Spanish custom. The crucifixion and the agonies of the week which preceded it; the martyrdom of saints on the rack, the block and the cross—these scenes were as familiar to her as the *paseo* in the plaza where her father's house was situated or the fruit trees in the orchard at Encarnación. Therefore, she certainly did not stop to gaze at an interpretation of Our Saviour's scourging because it was new and strange to her; she did so because the moment had come when she was ready to recognize and confess the meaning and the application that it had for her. "It represented, and in a way so well calculated as to arouse devotion that from the very first glance I was moved at the thought of His sufferings for us, Christ covered with wounds. My heart was shattered with remorse when I thought of those wounds and my ingratitude. I threw myself on my knees before Him, in tears, and begged Him to strengthen me once for always, that I might not offend Him in the future."[17]

The prayer for strength did not go unanswered. From then on, Teresa found it easier to avoid or abbreviate her periods in the parlor, and the time thus gained gave her more opportunity for mental prayer. She frequently became so absorbed in this that she was not instantly aware of her sisters' presence when they sought her out; but, when she did become conscious of it, she gave no evidence of annoyance and, all in all, her conduct was marked by ever-increasing gentleness and consideration for others. For the second time, a book which fell into her hands had a marked effect on her thoughts and actions; this time, it was *The Confessions of St. Augustine*, which had just been translated into Spanish. She also found increasing enjoyment in the sound of running water, which she had always loved; now she heard God speaking to her through the flowing streams. A succession of different confessors—their number and the divergence of their views seems astonishing and confusing to us even now—were intermittently disturbing to her and several of them seem to have failed her in understanding and kindness. Others were sympathetic, if strict, especially a young Jesuit by the name of Juan de Pardiñas. She should "leave everything to God," he told her; it might help her, in her effort to do so, if she would frequently recite the *Veni Creator*.

She was quietly doing this one day when she realized that something strange, something abnormal was happening to her. At one and the same time she seemed to be losing consciousness and finding it in another realm different from any she had previously known. She had fainted, fairly frequently, of course, at the time of her nervous breakdown, and she still continued to do so occasionally. But this joyous, trancelike state in which she found herself now bore no relationship to those silly swoons. It was rapture such as she had never known before. And she thought she could not really be unconscious, after all, for quite distinctly she heard a voice which she recognized as that of Our Lord.

"Henceforth it is My Will that you should no longer converse with men but with angels."

7

Again a new life had begun for her, more full and more wonderful than any she had known before. It was still a life in which mental prayer played a large and important part; but it was a life in which this strong power which continued to supply her with support also supplied her with additional and extraordinary blessings, partly through its medium and largely, of course, through God's Grace. She had become both clairaudient and clairvoyant. To be sure, she had long felt that Our Lord and Saviour had been guiding her and helping her to interpret His purposes and His will to others; but, so far, the feeling had been based largely on faith and intuition. Now His commands came to her with the same clarity and directness as if He had been in the room with her while He was speaking to her, and she believed that, often, He was. She did not try to explain or define these verbal messages; she simply said she had received them, and no one could convince her that she was suffering from hallucinations, as far as they were concerned. In regard to what she saw, she conscientiously and persistently tried to be more explicit. According to authorities on this subject—of which I do not pretend to be one—clairvoyance is divided into three classifications: "the bodily, the imaginary and the intellectual, of which the bodily is the lowest, the intellectual the highest and the imaginary halfway between the two."[18] Of course, Teresa herself was not an authority on the subject and it is not strange that her efforts to explain her certainty of the frequent Presence at her side of Our Lord—His Majesty, as she nearly always called Him in speaking of Him—were discouraging to her and confusing to her hearers, and that, to this day, it is extremely difficult to analyze it. A biographer of St. Frances of Rome has no such difficulty. The statues and paintings of her, some of them very ancient, which have come down to us, all depict her guardian angel at her side, in a corporal form similar to her own; she plainly stated, over and over again, that he always walked beside her, that she could not only see him and speak to him, but touch him, whenever she wished to do so. We have no such representations of Teresa, at least to my knowledge, and her claims to the actuality of Christ's Presence are much less precise. It is quite natural that they should be, for, in one case, the presence was only angelic, whereas, in the other, it was Divine; but this does not help us to dispel perplexity, any more than it helped her.

"Who told you it was Jesus Christ?" one of her confessors asked her, not without impatience, when she reiterated that she had seen Him. "He tells me so Himself. But before He tells me, I know it already," Teresa persisted. "How? How? How?" this confessor and others repeatedly asked. "I don't know how, Father. But I know it's He," was all the answer she could make at first. However, afterward, she became somewhat more explicit.

"Perhaps if I put it that He's there in the same way as in the darkness we know that a person is by our side. It's something like that. But not altogether. It's more like a piece of news which is communicated to the soul, an announcement which is clearer than the light of the sun. Not that you see the sun or any brightness, yet a light enlightens the understanding without one realizing it is a light and disposes the soul to the enjoyment of this great good."[19]

Later, she became more explicit still: she had "seen" first His hands, then His countenance, then His whole sacred humanity "as the risen Christ in all His beauty and majesty." But when she wanted to see still more—the color of His eyes, the actual extent of His stature, not only for her own delectation, but so that she might describe them to others, He "vanished altogether."[20]

I am only too well aware that, in writing about this stage of Teresa's spiritual development, I am bound to create skepticism and arouse scoffing among my readers. There is not very much I can say to counteract such sentiments. However, in passing, I may mention a conversation I had not too long ago, with a very fine man, a devout Episcopalian, whose leanings, like those of so many others, were toward Catholicism, but who—also, like so many others—had been unable to accept some special item of dogma. "I think I would have made the grade," this gentleman told me, earnestly and regretfully, "had it not been for the Promulgation of the Assumption. The theory that any creature in human form, even the Blessed Virgin, could possibly ascend to heaven, is so preposterous that I could not accept it." I asked whether he did not unhesitatingly recite the Apostles' Creed and reminded him that this is practically word for word the same in all Trinitarian churches. "Why yes, of course I do," he replied. . . . "And every time you say it, you declare you believe that Christ ascended into heaven? If you can do that, conscientiously, why is it so hard for you to believe that it would be impossible for Christ to provide that His mother should reach celestial realms in the same way?" . . . "I don't know," the perplexed man answered. "I never thought of it in that light before. It shouldn't be so hard."[21]

I mention this episode merely by way of illustrating the point I am trying to make: that, if we can accept what we generally call the supernatural in one form, or in connection with one group or individual, it should not be too hard for us to do it in another. (If we cannot, that is, of course, something else again; but it would seem to me that readers who belong in that category will probably not be interested in the story of St. Teresa anyway!) In other words, if we accept as authentic the many examples of clairaudience and clairvoyance given in the Bible, the Old Testament as well as the New, not to mention the many others in the history of the Church, from its earliest times until the present day, then we should have no difficulty in accepting those which form such an integral part of St. Teresa's life. And I feel this should be all the easier for us because of her own attitude in regard to them, and her character and history as a whole. Far from making a show of her supernatural experiences, she never spoke of them if she could help it, and she begged all those who saw her in a trancelike state to keep as quiet about it as possible. It was only when she felt in duty bound, because she was talking with her confessor or some high ecclesiastical authority, that she mentioned them; and it was only those to whom she was closest, in a spiritual sense, that she permitted to share in her raptures. By and large, she lived a life remarkable for the high spirits, executive ability and endless energy which characterized it; and she was practical—even hardheaded—to a degree that we do not ordinarily connect with any visionary. Moreover, her supernatural experiences did not begin when she was an emotional and imaginative girl, in an almost constant state of nervous tension, but when she was a mature woman, experienced, sensible and worldly wise. That there were two sides to her nature, which almost certainly seem contradictory and which are very apt to seem incomprehensible, is undeniable; the mysticism of St. John of the Cross, whose life was eventually to become so interwoven with that of Teresa, is admittedly much easier to understand than hers, and to many of us it is more appealing. But history is adorned with the names of many mystics besides Teresa, who combined careers of great activity with periods of complete withdrawal from the world, both spiritual and physical. It would, perhaps, be more helpful to compare her with Catherine of Siena and Joan of Arc—one of the greatest politicians and one of the greatest warriors of the Middle Ages, besides being two of its greatest mystics—rather than with her own gentle and retiring fellow country-man. But whatever our standard of comparison, I do not see how we can avoid accepting the greater part of Teresa's story as historic. It is not shrouded in the mists of antiquity, like those of Avila's earliest saints, nor is it interwoven with fantastic legends. For instance, *according to tradition*, San Segundo was one of the seven disciples of St. James—who is the patron saint of Spain, where he is known as Santiago—and was sent forth by St. Peter himself, in conformity with Christ's command, "Go ye into all the world and preach the Gospel to all people." San Segundo is *credited* with having built the first Christian church in Castile, with having become the first Bishop of Avila, and with having suffered martyrdom under the Romans by being thrown from the city walls to the rocks beneath. The tomb in his hermitage, from which his remains were later transferred to the cathedral, does indeed bear an inscription in verse, composed by the noble knight, Suero del Aguila, which reads:

> *San Segundo fue el primero*
> *Obispo de esta Ciudad*
> *Que nos mostro la verdad*
> *del Trino Dios verdadero.*
>
> *Fue muy digno mensajero*
> *Del Apostol enviado,*
> *A sacarnos del pecado*
> *De que nos libro el Cordero.*[21-a]

But none of this is a matter of incontestable record; the skeptical could, if they wished, ask for proof of it and the most devout would have difficulty in supplying this. Skeptics would be in a still better position to jeer at the story of the huge serpent which coiled itself around the pitiful remains of Avila's next martyrs—Vicente and his young sisters, Sabina and Cristeta, who, *according to legend*, were not thrown from a great height down upon the rocks, but stoned to death by and among these. Was this so-called "serpent" some sort of an angelic being in disguise? We are not told. But we are told that the wealthy scoffer—for scoffers have existed in every age—who came to mock the youthful martyrs was convinced of his sacrilege by the serpent and converted on the spot; that, afterward, this man promised Christian burial to the innocent victims of wicked persecution and that the present magnificent Church of San Vicente was built by the convert and marks their burial place.

All this, as I have said, is in the realm of legend rather than in the realm of history. But we cannot place Teresa de Ahumada in the former realm. She belonged to one of the most prominent families of Spain, representatives of which are still living. Her godfather, Francisco Vela y Núñez was a brother of Don Blasco Núñez y Vela, the first Viceroy of Peru. The Captain General of the Netherlands, Fernando de Alvarez de Toledo and his wife—better known as the Duke and Duchess of Alba—were among her closest friends. All her brothers took a conspicuous part in the development of the New World and their valorous deeds are duly recorded. The places where she lived, studied and worked are still standing, many of them quite unchanged since the time she did so. Her writings are included in the classical literature of all civilized countries, Catholic and non-Catholic, and many of her contemporaries—not only St. John of the Cross, who is, of course, outstanding, but countless others—have left reliable accounts of her life and times. The Reformed Order which she founded continues to flourish and grow and has furnished us with many other notable figures, among them Ste. Thérèse of Lisieux, who is considered by many authorities the most conspicuous addition to the Calendar of Saints in modern times. All this being so, I think we are bound to accept Teresa de Ahumada as an important historical figure; and, having done this, I believe we should try to accept the mystery of her visions in the same spirit that we accept the mystery of her early attachments and of her strange illnesses, even if we can go no further than to say to ourselves, "I do not know it, but I believe it because I feel it."[21-b]

When we can do that, we may safely go on to the phenomenon of the transverberation, the most famous and specific, as well as the most disputed, of Teresa's mystical life. Every one of her biographers with whom I am familiar has included an account of this in his story about her and every one has let her tell it in her own words. I see no reason to depart from this practice:[22]

"I saw an angel close by me, on my left side, in bodily form. He was not large, but small of stature and most beautiful—his face burning, as if he were one of the highest angels, who seem to be all of fire. I saw in his hand a long spear of gold, and at the iron's point there seemed to be a little fire. He appeared to me to be thrusting it at times into my heart and to pierce my very entrails; when he drew it out, he seemed to draw them out also, and to leave me all on fire with a great love of God. The pain was so great that it made me moan; and yet so surpassing was the sweetness of this excessive pain that I could not wish to be rid of it. The soul is satisfied now with nothing less than God. . . ."

This visionary experience, as agonizing as it was exquisite, occurred not once but several times. At Encarnación, to this day, the privileged visitor may see two places where it occurred, according to documentation in the convent's archives. One of these places is in that part of the chapel now open to the public and plainly marked as the scene of the vision; the other is in a private oratory shown only under special conditions and with special permission. The same visitor, if he will take the pleasant ride from the city of Avila to the town of Alba de Tormes, and go to the Carmelite Church in the latter, may see in a reliquary beside the altar, the perfectly preserved heart of St. Teresa "pierced through the center exactly as if it had been stabbed by a dart. . . . In 1872 . . . three physicians, Professors of Medicine and Surgery at the University of Salamanca, made an examination of the holy relic at the request of the Prioress, and left an interesting affidavit. They measured the organ. They noted that it was of a bronzed red, and in a state of preservation not to be accounted for by any natural causes. They found the perforation (or as they called it, with super-scientific exactness, 'a cessation of continuity') on both sides of the heart, above the left and right auricles."[23]

It is quite possible that the heart in the reliquary may not be inspiring to all those who look at it; to many persons, even very devout persons, such sights are distressing rather than uplifting. It is also quite true that, to many others, the testimony of the three learned physicians from Salamanca may be unconvincing; from time immemorial, doctors have disagreed among themselves and, quite possibly, three others might hold a different opinion. Even more commonly, laymen have disagreed with doctors in general, and have set up their own views in opposition to those which, theoretically at least, should be more learned and more authentic. But I think it will be hard for any thoughtful person to disagree with the manner in which Sackville-West sums up the whole subject, in bringing to an end her comments about Teresa's account of the transverberation:

"The physical aspect of miracles may be negligible; unexplained, though capable of some perhaps quite simple explanation, so far, on our long journey, hidden from us; the occasional frauds contemptible, practised with the best intentions by the over-eager, over-reaching, avid, fanatical devout. The true miracle is that such intimations should exist in the soul, 'satisfied with nothing less than God.' "

8

Teresa did not misconstrue His Majesty's command that "henceforth she should converse not with men but with angels." She realized that it applied to the hours she had been idling away, pleasantly but futilely, in the parlor, not to the time she had spent in the company of men and women whose association with her formed an integral part of her spiritual development; and, indeed, complete isolation would have been almost impossible for her under any circumstances. Her family connections alone stretched far beyond the borders of Spain and embraced a large part of the New World. Her social standing was such that, even where no blood relationship existed, she was closely allied with the Spanish aristocracy, both at home and abroad; her great natural gift for friendship resulted in ties far beyond this exclusive circle; and her calling brought her into contact with ecclesiastical individuals and groups, in their various ramifications. She was completely at ease with all these different sets and they were with her; it would no more have occurred to her to speak discourteously or condescendingly to a shepherd or a servant than to a papal nuncio or a princess, for she was the personification of *noblesse oblige*. In consequence, welcome awaited her wherever she chose to go and a gracious reception was accorded all those who came to see her for good and sufficient reason.

One of the friends whose pious affection was such a "strong pillar of support" that it hardly seems sacrilegious to compare it to that given Teresa by mental prayer was a young widow by the name of

Doña Guiomar de Ulloa. The latter was the fortunate possessor of a beautiful and spacious house, actually a palace, which she generously put at the disposal of her friend. Here the woman who stood in such need of solitude and tranquillity could find the undisturbed quiet, the freedom from curiosity and criticism that were denied her at Encarnación; and here, when intervals of fellowship seemed to indicate more purpose and meaning to the periods of seclusion, she could find such fellowship in full measure, not only with Doña Guiomar herself, but with an extraordinary man and an extraordinary woman who were also habitués of her house.

The extraordinary man was Pedro Garavito, a native of Alcántara in the Province of Extremadura, who had studied at Salamanca, joined the Discalced Franciscan Reform and was now known as Fray Pedro de Alcántara. In pursuit of his calling, which included the foundation of many convents of the Strict Observance, he wandered on foot from one end of Spain—and of Italy, too, for that matter!—to the other and managed to come fairly frequently to Avila. His self-denial went to great extremes, even in the days when austerities which would seem to us exaggerated were regarded as indications of godliness; but his severity was directed toward himself rather than toward others. From the beginning of their acquaintance, Teresa found him the kindest, as well as the wisest, of counselors and, as time went on, one of her strongest advocates.

The extraordinary woman was María Díaz.[24] She was not an outsider, like Pedro de Alcántara, for her birthplace was Vita, a village in the Province of Avila, in fact, only a few leagues beyond the walls of the provincial capital. On the other hand, she was not a great lady, like Doña Guiomar and Teresa; she came of respectable farming folk, well-to-do (acomodados) according to village standards, though in relatively straitened circumstances compared to those of the Ahumadas, the Cepedas and the Ulloas. Certainly she had grown up in a family where hard work was taken as a matter of course, for her mother was so irritated because she spent more time in prayer than in labor that she once pushed her devout daughter out of the house with the angry admonition, "Very well, go to church and stay there all day. See if that will keep you fed!" María had three brothers but no sisters and when her parents died, she sold her share of their joint patrimony and went to the nearby city. Eventually, she lived alone in a cell-like structure which the Bishop permitted her to build beside the Church of San Millán; and this bare little room became not only a retreat for herself, but a humble center from which she could minister to the poor—for her sense of charity was as prodigal as her sense of self-denial was strict. But before she could put this plan into practice, Pedro de Alcántara had sought her out, with the help of her confessor, had grasped the bewilderment and lack of direction which made her seem like an eccentric, and had asked Doña Guiomar to receive her as a guest until her chosen path of penance, coupled with good deeds, should be less difficult for her to find and to follow. She lived for six years in that gracious lady's palace and this period coincided with the time that Teresa was also to find Doña Guiomar's house a refuge and a godsend.

On the face of it, Teresa benefited more by her intermittent stays there than María Díaz through her long sojourn. The former was honored, not only by the lady of the house, but by everyone in it, down to the humblest scullery maid; on the other hand, the servants lost no opportunity of letting the would-be hermit from Vita know that they considered themselves every bit as good as she was; they must have made life extremely unpleasant for her at times and she must have longed to escape from their mockery to the solitude of her envisioned cell. But, despite such discomfiture, she must also have realized that, if she had never gone to Doña Guiomar's palace, she would probably never have met Teresa de Ahumada; and when this meeting resulted in lasting friendship, her barren life was immeasurably enriched. Nor was this benefit one-sided; Teresa gained as much from the association as she did. Teresa had never before known intimately anyone like María Díaz, despite the sojourns at Castellanos and Becedas, for there she had lived apart from the peasants; the affectionate companionship between the cultured aristocrat, who was vouchsafed extraordinary visions for her guidance, and the unlettered girl, who had grown up on a farm and was groping her way heavenward through the mists of ignorance and bafflement, was to give Teresa sympathy with many other underprivileged women and enable her to understand and help them.[25]

Teresa's travels, like her visions, did not begin until she was well past middle age, and the first of these was undertaken not in behalf of her faith or of the poor, but at the instigation of the richest woman in Spain, Doña Luisa de la Cerda. By this time, Teresa had become a figure of considerable renown, not only in her native province but in many others, among them that of Toledo, which was where Doña

Luisa lived, in regal state. She, like Doña Guiomar, was a widow, but whereas Doña Guiomar had learned to find consolation in good works, Doña Luisa had not been able to find it in anything. Indeed, it is doubtful whether she tried very hard. She had not only been born with a golden spoon in her mouth, but she had taken it for granted that nothing except the greatest delicacies would be offered for her consumption and it had not occurred to her that anything unpleasant would ever happen to her. Her father had been the Duke of Medinaceli and, through him, she was descended from the royal houses of both Spain and France. Her husband, Antonio Arias Pardo de Saavedra, was the nephew of Cardinal Pardo de Tavera and himself the Marshal of Castile. When he died, she could not face such a harsh reality. She lay among the pillows emblazoned with coats-of-arms and wept and wept and wept. At last she stopped sobbing long enough to tell the relatives and priests and serving women who stood anxiously about, waiting for helpful suggestions, that, perhaps, she might find comfort in the presence of that strange *Avilesa* who came of a good family and was said to have visions. . . .

Doña Luisa had only to express a wish to have her word regarded as law. A message was immediately dispatched by the Carmelite Provincial to the Prioress at Encarnación, who, in turn, dispatched one to the Ulloa palace, where Teresa was staying: she must prepare to leave immediately for Toledo; another noble lady had far greater need of her than Doña Guiomar.

That the nature of this need was rather vague and that it was midwinter and bitterly cold seems to have made no difference to anyone. Teresa set out, accompanied by her faithful friend, Juana Suárez, and by her brother-in-law, Juan de Ovalle, the husband of Teresa's younger sister. When they finally arrived in Toledo, almost frozen to death, they were received and quartered in the regal fashion normal to Doña Luisa; and, throughout Teresa's six-months' stay, she continued to be treated in the same manner. Gradually, Doña Luisa was persuaded to take a more normal outlook on life and, undoubtedly, much, if not most, of the credit for this should go to Teresa, whose patience was often tried, but whose adaptability, like her tact, was extraordinary. As far as Teresa herself was concerned, the stay in Toledo had three very important results: among the new acquaintances she made was that of the Duchess of Alba, who was to remain her firm and lifelong friend; Fray Pedro de Alcántara came to visit her and brought with him, for her consideration, a set of rules for a project which both he and she had long had in mind; and she began work on her autobiography, the first of the books which were to bear evidence to her rare gifts as an author.

As was quite natural, the Duchess of Alba was among the many titled ladies who next offered hospitality to Teresa and, in due time, she was glad to take advantage of this more than once. Her younger sister, Juana—the one who married Juan de Ovalle—lived at Alba de Tormes, the ancestral seat of the great Duke whose name has come down in history as the Captain General of the Netherlands and who, like his wife, was to become Teresa's firm friend. Teresa was greatly attached to this younger sister, to Juana's husband and to their quiverful of attractive young children; and the Ovalles, like Pedro de Alcántara, had been very useful to her in helping her plan for the project which was so near her heart. She would have enjoyed going immediately to Alba de Tormes, so beautifully situated on the river which gives the town part of its name; it will be recalled that water, especially running water, had always been fascinating to Teresa, and she would have spent many happy hours looking out on the river Tormes, both from the windows of the Albas' palace and from those of the less pretentious house belonging to the Ovalles. But, for the time being, all her thoughts and all her hopes were centered on Avila. As soon as she learned that she was free to leave Toledo, as far as Luisa de la Cerda was concerned, she made ready for immediate departure. For it was in Avila that she meant to bring her plans to fruition and to make her hopes a reality.

9

The plans, which were for the foundation of a convent primitive in its simplicity, were of fairly recent date; the hope that such a community might come into existence went back a long way.

As a matter of fact, Teresa had probably begun to harbor such a hope from her early days at Encarnación, even though she was not actually conscious of this. It will be recalled that, from the first, she had been confused because a few of the many nuns there lived a life of great austerity while the majority did nothing of the sort; their interpretation of the Rule was far from rigid, even when they knew exactly what this was, which even Teresa did not for a long time; and the presence of the many secular guests, living under the same roof and under much the same conditions as the religious, certainly did nothing to create an atmosphere of greater tranquillity and recollection. Neither did the constant callers who were made so welcome in the parlor, the chitchat about this, that and the other thing, the music of tambourines and other instruments, the great and little feasts. As for the prolonged absences from the premises, whatever their purpose or alleged purpose—a lessening of financial strain for the convent, a better opportunity for convalescence than its infirmary afforded, a family crisis or merely a pleasant holiday—these absences inevitably acted as interruptions to a cloistral and contemplative life. The older and wiser she became, the more experienced in the practice of mental prayer, the more convinced Teresa became of this. Perhaps it would always be necessary for her, personally, to punctuate her devotions with other activities; but that was not her ideal, nor did she believe it should be the ideal of any consecrated Carmelite.

Concrete ideas for changes did not come suddenly or simultaneously. It was obvious that life in sixteenth-century Spain could not take exactly the same form, under any circumstances, as it had taken in the days of the biblical Carmel. But one of Teresa's first convictions was that Carmelite Convents should house only small groups, that the number of their visitors should likewise be strictly limited, that the only inmates should be nuns, and that only under the most exceptional circumstances should these emerge from the cloister. This would mean a degree of uniformity, of seclusion, of quietude and of contemplation that no place which harbored nearly two hundred women, free to receive as many callers as they chose and themselves free to come and go almost at will, could ever achieve. Teresa's next conviction was a natural sequel to the first: a Carmelite Convent should not only be small, but simple; there should be no more spacious private apartments, as richly decorated as taste dictated or as means allowed. The nuns should, indeed, have separate rooms; they should not be denied the instinctive need that a woman of refinement feels for privacy. Moreover, such privacy would facilitate the practice of mental prayer. But these separate rooms should be cells in the truest sense of the word, their white walls unadorned except for a single cross, their furnishings limited to the barest essentials—a bed, a bowl and pitcher, a candle. Their clothing, like their quarters, should reflect this ideal of simplicity; there should be no more rich fabrics, no more jewelry, no more artifices; just plain habits made of coarse materials, crucifixes, sandals. . . .

As these ideas gradually took form and substance in Teresa's mind, she began to voice them when she was with those nearest and dearest to her. It would appear that a favorite niece of hers, María de Ocampo, was the first to actually suggest, in so many words, such a foundation as Teresa had in mind, but that she did it more or less in jest.[26] When Teresa repeated the suggestion, however, to Doña Guiomar, that noblewoman responded with all seriousness.

"Found! I will help you."

After Teresa discovered that Doña Guiomar thought the idea was practical, she began to think so, too. And hardly had she started to do so, when a direct command came from His Majesty: she was to lay the plan, which was pleasing to Him, before her confessor. Somehow she could not bring herself to do this by word of mouth, but she did write to him on the subject; she was eloquent and persuasive when she spoke; she was even more so on paper. Without either encouraging or discouraging her, he, in turn, counseled her to make her request to the Carmelite Provincial, Padre Gregorio Fernández. It was not like Teresa to quail before anyone; but, probably, for the very reason that the project had by now assumed enormous proportions to her, she shrank from doing this. Doña Guiomar undertook to do it for her.

The result was, at first, a happy surprise: the Father Provincial made no objections whatsoever to the plan—in fact, he thought the whole idea was an excellent one, especially the provision that there should not be more than thirteen nuns in the Foundation; he would gladly give it his authorization. But, as soon as the news leaked out, all Avila was in an uproar, and at Encarnación the outburst was most violent of all. So this visionary was taking a "holier than thou" attitude, was she? Well, she had better be careful with her so-called reforms, which were nothing but an effort to disturb well-ordered lives. She had always been restless and rebellious. Those high spirits of hers would get her into trouble yet! The Inquisition knew how to deal with revolutionaries of such stripe. . . .

It was while this outcry was at its height that she took additional refuge in her Book of Hours. She had previously scribbled in it a few brief admonitions for self-guidance, which have since become as widely quoted as anything she ever said or wrote, and which are usually referred to as her "bookmark," perhaps because many persons use them for that purpose, to this very day. But, up to then, she had not really dwelt upon them. Now she did.

Let nothing disturb thee,
Nothing affright thee.
All things are passing,
God never changeth.
Patience gains all things.
Who hath God wanteth nothing.
Alone God sufficeth.

Certainly, she had need of what comfort these simple lines could give her. The Provincial, aghast at the storm which had been raised among the seats of the mighty, withdrew his promise of authorization for the convent. Teresa's confessor was likewise intimidated, and regretted that he had taken such a neutral attitude at the beginning; he now charged his penitent to give up her idea and told her the day would come when she would realize it was nothing but a fantasy. Even His Majesty did not help her in her extremity; He told her to obey her confessor and keep quiet. The modest house which was to serve as the convent dedicated to St. Joseph—San José—had already secretly been bought, thanks to the generosity of Doña Guiomar and María de Ocampo's promise of the legacy which she was expecting; now it appeared that the poor little convent was never to fulfill its destiny, after all! But in this dark hour, one of the most trying which Teresa was called upon to endure, she had one very powerful ally: Padre Pedro Ibáñez, a Dominican whom she had often gone to consult at his Monastery of Santo Tomás.

She now went to him again, accompanied by Doña Guiomar, who had also many times sought his advice. He listened to the two women attentively, and asked for time to think over everything they had said to him. A week later, he sent for them and advised them to go ahead with their project and that with all possible speed.

It would not be surprising if, in the face of so much contradictory advice and opinion, coupled with so much general uproar, Teresa and her faithful friend had become completely confused, as well as completely disheartened. It is greatly to their credit that, somehow, they found the adroitness, the wisdom and the courage to persevere. Teresa did not deliberately disobey her confessor; she made no further move to go on with the Foundation and she "kept quiet." However, with the knowledge and approval of Ibáñez, but otherwise with the greatest secrecy, Doña Guiomar wrote to Rome and asked for authorization to found a convent in accordance with the Primitive Rule of Carmel, which would be under the jurisdiction of the Bishop of Avila and not that of the Carmelite Provincial.

It was a long time before the answer came. Excitement gradually abated and opposition died down when there was no longer anything in evidence to oppose. To be sure, work was going forward at San José, but very few persons were aware of this. There was some slight surprise when it became common knowledge that Juan de Ovalle, Teresa's brother-in-law, was leaving his pleasant home in Alba de Tormes and establishing himself and his little family in Avila; but there were so many more interesting things to think about and talk about that the move caused hardly a flurry. Teresa spent a good deal of time with the Ovalles, but what was more natural than that? Apparently, she was getting cured of some of her strange ideas about the propriety of making visits, now that her sister was in town. It wasn't strange, either, that after awhile she wanted to get away from all those noisy children, and spend some time at Doña Guiomar's palace, which was nice and quiet. And, of course, when a summons came from Doña Luisa de la Cerda, that was something no one could refuse to heed!

Only the initiated few were aware that the house where the Ovalles were living was the future Convent of San José, with room for a chapel on the ground floor and thirteen cells above it, all surrounding a small but pleasant patio. Only the initiated few were aware that Lorenzo, Teresa's favorite brother, who was piling up a fortune in Ecuador, had supplemented the funds which Doña Guiomar had at her disposal. Only the initiated few were aware that, when Fray Pedro de Alcántara had visited Doña Luisa in Toledo, he had brought with him a set of rules for the new Foundation. Only the initiated few were aware that, on the very day Teresa returned to Avila, the long-awaited brief had arrived from Rome. . . .

The Ovalles went back to Alba de Tormes. Well, after all, there was nothing strange about that, either; their stay in Avila had probably been just the result of a whim and they had not had much of a house to live in. It might well stand empty for quite a while before anyone else would want it. And they had probably missed their close association with the great Duke and the charming Duchess. . . .

Then suddenly one morning the good people who lived in the vicinity of the poor little house which, apparently, had been deserted were awakened by the sound of an extra bell—not all the neighbors, to be sure, for there were so many bells in Avila that one more or less could very easily go unnoticed. But some of those persons who did hear the strange sound were sufficiently intrigued to go and see where it came from. And lo and behold! it came from a bell atop the house where the Ovalles had been living, and the door of the house was open and Mass was being celebrated inside. Some very prominent persons were attending this Mass, both clergy and laity; and four unfamiliar young women were being clothed by Teresa de Ahumada in habits made of coarse material. Something extraordinary had happened, after all. These good people realized that much. But there were many other things which they did not realize. Among these was the fact that, from that day on, they would begin to think of Teresa de Ahumada in a different way and call her by a different name. She had ceased to be a rebellious visionary to them now, just as, long before, she had ceased to be a girl who was too high spirited. She had become a Foundress.

10

In the course of the next twenty years, Teresa founded seventeen other convents, all in conformity with the Primitive Rule.[27]

There is no question that she firmly believed she was acting under orders from His Majesty in establishing these Foundations. When she first spoke to her nuns at San José about her conviction that she must go further afield and they begged her not to leave them, she reminded them that thirteen[28] was a very small number of women with which to accomplish a great reform and that this was the work to which she had been pledged ever since she recovered from her syncope. The Carmelite Nuns of the Primitive Rule, except for those called to help with the work of Foundation, could and must remain behind their heavy grilles leading lives consecrated to prayer; but she must see to it that they would have followers, in ever-increasing numbers, to carry on the work after she and those who had joined her were dead.

There can be no question, either, that, on the whole, she relished these excursions into the world and glowed with satisfaction as each new Foundation came into being. She was not lacking in the adventurous spirit that had driven all her brothers out into the New World; in fact, Rodrigo always maintained that it was she who had first tempted him to run away from home, when they were both children, for the alleged purpose of going to Africa and converting the Moors—an undertaking to which only the opportune, though unexpected, arrival of an uncle, who had appeared on the road they had taken when they began their flight, put an untimely end. She regarded obstacles not as stumbling blocks, but as stepping stones; she found fulfillment in achieving. But to believe that her life was an easy one, marked only by a long succession of triumphs, is to harbor a grave misconception. Travel, in itself, was an ordeal: riding in crude jolting carts over rough roads or tracts of land where there were no roads at all; fording rivers, floundering through snowdrifts; putting up for the night at filthy little inns and being overtaken by storm or darkness when even the meanest shelter was unavailable; catching such sleep as was possible in the open, both in the sweltering heat of summer and in the bitter cold of winter—these were the only conditions under which extensive travel was possible in those days, except for royalty and near-royalty. There were, to be sure, a few private coaches—not more than half a dozen in all Spain—and though these had splendid trappings and were richly emblazoned with heraldic designs, they were just as springless as the wagons. Moreover, Teresa had declined to ride in a coach ever since she had overheard some jeering remarks, when she had accepted a proffer of such transportation from the Princess of Eboli, about persons with pretensions to saintliness who, nevertheless, travelled like queens. In consequence of this persistent refusal, the physical strain of Teresa's journeys was terrific. She was nearly fifty when she began her life as a Foundress, and she was almost never free from digestive disorders, which, naturally, were complicated by miserable food or the entire lack of any nourishment at all, and by the hardships which she had to take in her stride whenever she set out on her travels. Terrific headaches, which may have been due to hunger, fatigue or tension, were also more and more frequent. Now, despite her inadequate fare, she grew increasingly heavy; added to her weight, a broken arm, badly set, and the prevalence of rheumatism made all her movements difficult. She grew dependent upon a stout stick of peculiar design which one of her brothers had sent her from the Indies and, eventually, she did not try to get along without it. Nor were her physical troubles all with which she had to contend; she could no longer be sure of a welcome everywhere. When she reached her destination, she might be royally received at a palace or she might find that her only shelter was as primitive as that she had found along her way; it depended on whether a great personage had sought the honor of her presence, or whether a hostile ecclesiastic and an angry citizenry were determined that she should not gain a foothold in the place—for, once she had a foothold, she was certain to create a permanent establishment. To the very end, she was obliged to struggle against opposition, some of it petty, some of it powerful, even though she was more and more widely recognized as a woman of resource, intelligence and learning and as a great organizer. Recognition of her as a great writer and a great mystic was slower in coming; eventually, it did come, too, but by that time she was old and weary.

It is interesting to note, in passing, that little things she said, as well as great things she did and wrote, came in for more and more general notice and have contributed in no small measure to her lasting fame. Some of these sayings had to do with her faith and the faith she wished to inspire in others; for instance:

"Sisters, to prayer, to prayer!" "And let every serious decision first form the subject of prayer!" "Let us listen to God as we do to our best friend. . . . When we set out to do His will we have nothing to fear. . . ." "He takes everything in hand." "Christ is a very good friend, for we can look upon Him as a man with His weaknesses and sufferings, and He becomes our companion. When we have acquired this habit, it is very easy for us to find Him by our side. . . ."

But many other sayings were less religious in tone. She left no one in doubt that she set great store by cheerfulness and good sense. Several times she expressed the hope that she and her associates might be delivered from gloomy saints; and once when a postulant was strongly recommended to her as being exceptionally devout, she inquired, "But has she brains? We can teach her to be devout, but we cannot teach her to think!" On another occasion, when a fanciful young nun became the prey to prolonged vapors and Teresa heard of it, she said tersely, "The girl had better eat meat!"

In telling the story of Isabel, as I visualized that it should be told by me, I said that I had purposely not tried to dwell on those periods of her life and those outstanding achievements of hers which countless great historians have retailed at length already. I can say the same of Teresa, with even more feeling, because those experiences and achievements are so wonderfully recorded in her autobiography and her other writings: *The Interior Castle, The Way of Perfection* and, by no means least of all, in the *Letters* which she wrote with such speed that she never even read them over, much less revised them, once they were written. Another reason for omitting a very important phase of her life from this sketch lies in the fact that it is so closely interwoven with the story of St. John of the Cross; and since their association was even more precious and more important to him than it was to her, I feel that it belongs in his biography, rather than hers, when both are to appear in the same book. Certainly I should not fail to remember, either, or to remind my readers that it is Avila, as interpreted through her stones and saints, that I am primarily trying to present, rather than any one of the people who have made her great, even if that one was the greatest of all.

We cannot, however, leave Teresa for good, in the little chapel of San José, when she is hearing Mass there for the first time and clothing her first fervent followers in their coarse habits. We must accompany her on a few of her wanderings—certainly those which took her to the palace of the King.

She was nearing the end of her life when this journey took place and, while starting out in response to the royal summons, it must have crossed her mind that she had waited a long long time to achieve a meeting which would, in some measure, compensate for the first bitter disappointment of her youth: that of being clapped into the Convent of Las Gracias by her troubled father, just a few weeks before the Empress Elizabeth, wife of Charles V, brought their little son, Don Felipe, to be clothed in his first "kingly breeches" at the Convent of Santa Ana. All Avila had been *en fête* for the occasion, and the sixteen-year-old Teresa would have been a ringleader in the festivities. Instead, thwarted and mutinous, she was the closely guarded charge of the Augustinian Nuns.

The young Don Felipe, who is known to posterity as Philip II, and who became King of Spain when his father, the Emperor Charles V, abdicated and retired to end his days at the Monastery of Yuste, had never entirely lost touch with Avila. This was not due to his actual presence there, for it is not a matter of record that he returned to the scenes so closely associated with his great-grandmother, with his father and with his own childhood. It is due to the Carmelite Master General, Juan Bautista Rubeo, whom he dispatched to investigate conditions at the Convent of San José; to Alonso Orozco, the remarkable monk who became his confessor, and to the many letters written him by Teresa. Of Rubeo, we have much to say elsewhere, in writing about St. John of the Cross; for the moment, it suffices to say that his report on San José was wholly favorable. Of Alonso Orozco, it seems better to interrupt our narrative about Teresa to say a little more.

He was not, strictly speaking, an *Avilés*, for he was not born in

Blessed Alonso Orozco from the steel engraving which forms the frontispiece of the book, *Vida y Escritos Del Beato Alonso de Orozco Del Orden de San Agustín Predicador de Felipe II*, by P. Fr. Tomás Camara.

that province, but in Oropesa, famous for the turreted castle of the Dukes of Frías, complete even to its own amphitheatre; but since Oropesa was, at that time, included in the Diocese of Avila, and since collateral descendants of his still live there, it has always been proud to claim Alonso Orozco as one of its own. He came of a noble family— his father was Governor of Castile and Warden of Torico—and, from early boyhood up to the age of fourteen, spent much of his time in Toledo as a *seise*—that is, one of six choir boys selected to sing and dance before the altar of certain cathedrals on great festivals.[28-a] He made a brilliant showing in theology and law as a student at Salamanca, where he spent eight years and was professed as an Augustinian Monk at the age of twenty-two. Upon his ordination, he was given the title of Preacher and was named Prior and Visitor to several houses and provinces. He greatly desired to go, as a missionary, to Mexico and even started on his way; but serious illness obliged him to turn back and he never succeeded in getting further from the mainland than the Canaries.[28-b] His disappointment was partly assuaged by a vision of the Blessed Virgin, in which she urged him to write, and several fine books were the result. The first of these was entitled, *Flower Garden of Prayer and Mount of Contemplation*, which went into many editions and was translated into both French and Italian; among the others was *Victoria de la Muerte—Victory of Death*. He founded several monasteries, including one in Talavera and one in Madrid; and, during the reign of Mary Tudor, was designated to recover and restore the convents of his Order in England, which had been confiscated or destroyed by her father, Henry VIII. Why he never fulfilled this mission is unknown. Over and over again, he was importuned to accept a bishopric, which he steadfastly declined to do. However, he could not decline to accept the official position of *Real Predicador*—Royal Preacher—first to Charles V and then to Philip II, and to act as confessor to Princess Juana, the sister of the latter. He preached not only in the royal chapel, but in the poorest churches and parishes, and visited jails, hospitals and slums, everywhere ministering to those in the greatest need. Philip II thought so highly of him that, when Orozco begged permission to retire to cloistral seclusion and spend the remainder of his days in one of the monasteries he had founded, the King, though habitually among the most meticulously courteous monarchs of his time, gave a rather curt answer.

"I cannot afford to let saints leave the court."[28-c]

Whereas the monarch could not afford to let saintly personages leave the Court, he could not only well afford to let them come there, but encouraged them to do so. He had a horror of heresy; indeed, he planned "to make the maintenance of religious unity in his realm his primary aim,"[28-d] and seldom lost sight of this purpose. It is therefore somewhat surprising that, when Teresa first went to Madrid, with a future Foundation in mind, he took no immediate steps to have her presented to him, though he received "respectfully" a message Teresa sent him through his sister, Juana, on whom Teresa had made a very favorable impression and though the message itself was not especially respectful. It purported to come from a still Higher Majesty and ended with the warning, "Remember Sire, that Saul too was anointed, and yet he was rejected."[28-e] After that, the Foundress wrote the King several letters, mostly about the quarrels between the Calced and the Discalced; to her distress, he left these letters unanswered. Perhaps he felt that even saints—for Teresa was already accepted as one in court circles and others—could presume too much. It is known that while the great Diego de Espinosa had the King's boundless confidence and was given almost unlimited power, Philip rebuked him one day with the reminder, "Cardinal, I am still the ruler of this kingdom." However, Philip evidently decided that perhaps he and Teresa could settle these moot questions better through conversation than through correspondence and he sent for her. Quite probably, the Duke of Alba had something to do with arranging the audience, for he whiled away much of his spare time, after returning from the Netherlands, in reading Teresa's *Autobiography*, with which he was much impressed; and Teresa's account of her meeting with the King was written to Doña Inés Nieto, the wife of the Duke's secretary, Albornoz.

It was not to Madrid, whither he had moved the Court, but to the still unfinished palace of San Lorenzo del Escorial that the Foundress was summoned. The only record of it still extant is in the letter[28-f] to Doña Inés, of which the first page is missing, and Teresa does not tell us in what part of the vast edifice the audience took place, whether much or little ceremony surrounded it or any of the other attendant circumstances. So we are free to form our own mental picture of the swift moving, slender monarch, whose black attire, as somber as it was elegant, was relieved only by the glittering Order of the Golden Fleece; whose piercing eyes missed nothing that came within their range of vision; and whose mentality grasped so much which he did not see that he could make good his boast of sitting quietly in his study and still ruling the world "on two inches of paper." We are also free to form our own mental picture of the clumsy, lame old woman, dressed in the patched habit and worn veil which she would not change for anyone, but who still had power to convince, to inspire and to charm anyone with whom she talked. And she *has* left us an account of the conversation which took place, doubtless in a huge apartment hung with allegorical tapestries and dark paintings of suffering martyrs, but unfurnished except for a *bargueño* and a chest or two and a few high-backed, carved chairs.

She began by saying, "Sire, you are thinking, 'I see before me this unquiet and restless woman, who goes about amusing herself with *devaneos* [idle pursuits] under pretext of religion.'" She spoke with downcast eyes; but when she raised them, she saw that the gaze meeting hers, though penetrating and direct, had no hostility in it. Without losing a moment, she began to plead her cause: the cessation of persecution by the Calced of the Discalced Order, for which she desperately needed his aid. The King heard her through without interruption. Then he asked, "Is that all you want?"

"I have asked a great deal."

"Then be at peace. All shall be as you wish."

She fell on her knees to thank him, but he told her to rise, bowed to her courteously, and gave her his hand to kiss. She left him with the praise of God in her heart and on her lips and, in concluding her letter to Doña Inés, she wrote, "As I left the other building where the duke was, your kind husband, to whom I owe so much, came up to me and told me that the King our Lord had ordered him to write down my petition so that my wishes might be carried out with the least possible delay. This was done: I dictated and Señor Albornoz noted down my words."[28-g]

She had won her point. The order she wanted went forth; and though it was not heeded, either as quickly or as universally as she might have wished, this journey of hers, like all the others, had accomplished its end.

Finally, we must go with her to Alba de Tormes, where she has been summoned, in a rather peremptory fashion, not because of any crisis which has arisen in the convent, but because an heir to the great house and the great name is expected and the Duchess of Alba feels that the presence of Teresa would help to insure a safe delivery to the Duchess of Huescar, the young wife of the Albas' son and heir. A magnificent coach is sent for her and, this time, she does not decline to ride in it. She is at Medina del Campo, where she has just been through a very unpleasant scene with the Prioress and she does not feel equal to any more argument. She is upset over this insubordination in one of her Foundations, and she has not slept all night or eaten all the morning. Nevertheless, when she discovers that Ana de San Bartolomé, the lay sister who accompanies her as her secretary, has forgotten to bring any provisions with them, she says and does nothing which might add to Ana's natural distress. She is very fond of Ana, who came to San José as a pitifully ignorant country girl, and who, through almost superhuman efforts, has qualified not only as Teresa's secretary, writing a beautiful hand and reading in a beautiful voice, but also as a practical nurse, with a real gift for making the aged, the infirm and the ill more comfortable. It is not like Ana to forget anything; she must be troubled, too. And they did get some dried figs in one village and some onions and herbs in another. It could have been much worse. Besides, she is not very hungry anyway. She seems to have a little fever and she is very, very tired.

A mounted messenger rides out to meet the coach. The Duchess of Huescar has already been safely delivered of a son; but, by then, it is too late to think of turning back. Teresa and Ana must go on to Alba de Tormes and spend the next night there at least. However, as Teresa is not really needed at the palace after all, she hopes the Duchess of Alba will excuse her if she stays at the convent instead. Privately, she has never greatly admired the furnishings of the palace; she has always thought there were too many knickknacks around, though of course she has never said so; she considers that Luisa de la Cerda has more elegant taste. But she does say now that she does not really feel equal to an official visit.

The Duchess is disappointed, but she understands; the next morning, she understands still better. Despite the tender care that has been given the Foundress by Ana and all her other spiritual daughters, she is still very tired and more than a little feverish; there have been hemorrhages, too. She has not tried to get up, but she has asked for the Sacraments. They are given her and she lapses into a peaceful state of unconsciousness from which she never wakens. However, just before this happens, she has been asked where she would like to be buried; does she wish to be taken back to the city of Avila? Her answer is characteristic: "Why, will they not give me a little earth here?"

The nuns prepare her body for burial—not the same ones who have done this before, of course, so many years earlier, when her father could hardly be persuaded to leave her, but persistently sat at her bedside, his fingers on her wrist. Nuns of the same Order, however, perform these last sad duties in the same simple way. They know that the Bishop of Salamanca is hastening to Alba de Tormes to officiate at the funeral, that the Duke of Huescar is only one of the great noblemen who will attend it. But they clothe her, as they know she would have wished to be clothed, in her old patched habit and her old threadbare veil. Then they help the workmen to prepare a place for the coffin by cutting a hole in the masonry of the chapel.

When everything else is in readiness, the Duchess herself comes forward to cover the humble bier. The pall she has selected is a magnificent length of cloth of gold.

11

The sequel to the story of the Girl with the Firm Mouth began, as I saw it, with her happy summers surrounded by her family, at the Palacio de Santo Tomás in Avila, and ended with her death at Medina del Campo. The sequel to the story of the Girl Who Was Too High Spirited is, as I see it, quite different, and divides logically in two separate parts. The story proper ends with the covering made from cloth of gold. Both parts of the sequel come long afterward.

I hope I have made it clear that Teresa was first, last and always an *Avilesa*. She was not only a product of that Land of Stones and Saints; she was an essential part of it. It belonged to her and she to it. She was also a Castilian, of course, but that was, in a sense, secondary. Like the immortal Passe Partout in Jules Verne's *Tour Du Monde en Quatre Vingt Jours* she could easily have made a remark equivalent to his observation that, if he had not been born a Parisian, he would have liked to be born a Frenchman—in fact, I would not be in the least surprised if future research should reveal that she had made just such a remark. But though, so far, none has come to light, at least as far as I know, she had her troubles in Avila, much as she loved it and sometimes they got the better of her temper. There was the resentment at Encarnación, on the part of the women who did not want to be deprived of their sweetmeats and—let us admit it—their sweethearts, and who bitterly opposed her reforms. There was the widespread indignation over the Foundation of San José. There were the threats from the Inquisition. There were the constant hints, often developing into outright accusations, concerning "a restless gadabout." Advancing years did not stop Teresa from being high spirited;

and one fine day she announced that she had had enough of Avila, of its carping criticisms and petty denunciations; she would shake its dust from her feet and betake herself to some place which was less narrow-minded, less provincial, less difficult to deal with, even—in the light of wider horizons—less difficult to understand.

It was the sort of declaration which the native of many a small and comparatively isolated place has made after becoming acquainted with a more tolerant world. It never should be taken too seriously. In Teresa's case, it should not have been taken seriously at all, though it was. For, in the very act of shaking Avila's dust from her well-worn sandals, she added that, of course, if she were ever *really* needed there, she would return. Return she did, over and over again, during her lifetime. And, according to many of her fellow *Avileses*, she has never ceased to do so.

The story they have told most often, in my hearing, is this: During the Civil War of 1936–1939, the Republican Army was very near Avila —in fact, as near as Sonsoles, which is on the road to Gredos, just beyond the River Adaja, only some six kilometres outside the walls. This is the site of several pleasant *fincas*, the summer residences of prominent Avila families, and it is also the site of a famous shrine from which it takes its name. There are several stories as to how it came by this. It is, undoubtedly, very old—indeed, certain signs indicate that it has existed ever since Apostolic times. According to one tradition, the body of San Zoilu lay in state at a primitive sanctuary there in the course of the journey which took the holy remains from Córdoba to Carrión de los Condes and it was first called San Zoles after him. According to another tradition, an image of the Virgin was already an object of great veneration at the time of the Moorish invasion, and this image was secreted in the craggy sierra to save it from destruction; later, when all danger was past, its hiding place was revealed to a simple shepherd who found it between two suns (*soles*). According to still another legend, a little girl was there vouchsafed a radiant vision, which she took to be the Blessed Virgin herself and, when asked to describe this glorious being, could only say, "Her eyes are twin suns!" (*son soles*). At all events, a small chapel has been built among the pleasant trees there and, in times of great need or danger, the image of Our Lady, which is its chief ornament, may be taken, given the approval of both the civil and ecclesiastical authorities, to the cathedral for a devout novena in her honor. At all times, the chapel is the object of widespread veneration and the scene of many reputed miracles. Its possible desecration or destruction, during the recent Civil War, was the cause of even more general alarm than the possible fate of the *fincas*.

At that period of the war, the Republican Army did not lack strength as a whole, but it was weak in one or two departments, notably that of Intelligence; therefore, it sought information when, where and whence it could be secured. Most persons fled at the approach of the troops. But a certain shabby old woman, dressed in rusty brown and wearing a ragged old black shawl over her head, who hobbled along with the help of a heavy stick of peculiar and unfamiliar formation, seemed to be continually hovering in their vicinity. For lack of anyone else to interrogate, the Secret Service questioned her: Had she been in the city lately? Had she seen many soldiers there? And what about the ancient fortifications? Were they well manned and supplied with guns?

The old woman answered readily enough and with more clarity and sagacity than her questioners would have expected. Yes, she had just come from the city, where she had long lived herself and had many children living; she was at Sonsoles only to pray at the shrine, according to her custom. Avila was full of Nationalist soldiers and more were pouring in all the time. The walls were bristling with them. They were fully armed and had cannon. Also more modern weapons of warfare which she believed were called machine guns. No one was in the least fearful that the population would not be protected or that it would fail to make trouble for the enemy. . . .

The officers who had consulted her took counsel among themselves. She continued to stand by and, when they asked her further questions, she answered with the same readiness and the same clarity she had displayed before and offered to go in search of other persons who would corroborate her story. The more she talked, the more convincing she became. It was at last decided that the wisest course would be to by-pass Avila.

Later, the decision was considered somewhat hasty and the officers decided to seek further information. None was available. The hobbling, shabby old woman, who had remained so close at hand until she told her tale, had disappeared, and it was now too late to take advantage of her offer to produce other persons who would corroborate her story. After considerable delay, the conclusion was reached that it would be best to abide by the original decision to by-pass the city.

Avila escaped entirely unscathed. But, as a matter of fact, it was practically undefended; it could easily have been reduced to rubble, with enormous loss of life. The only reason it was spared, so far as is known, was because the shabby old woman had said it was practically inviolable.

I do not ask that this story be accepted as factual, though I have told it exactly as it has been told to me by half a dozen reliable persons, among them the late Duke of Alba and the Count of Montefrío, and the episode is said to have occurred on the property of the latter's cousin. Moreover, I do feel it has a proper place among the legends of Avila and also, that it logically forms the first part of the sequel to Teresa's story. The second part of the sequel concerns the fiesta which bears her name and which takes place every year between the seventh and the fifteenth of October, inclusive.

Why this fiesta has not been more widely discovered and more generally attended is a mystery to me; for though, undeniably, it cannot compare in splendor with the Holy Week celebrations staged in several Spanish cities or with the *feria* of Seville, it certainly has many of the arresting features which have made these famous and the walled city of Avila gives it an incomparable setting. It is, by no means, wholly religious in character; it includes a carrousel, bullfights, bicycle races, roller-skating, dances in the plaza, football (*futbol*), chess tournaments, cavalcades, concerts, fireworks, *verbenas*,[29] expositions of paintings and the many types of handicraft in which the region excels. Festoons of colored lights are suspended from one side of every narrow street to the other, and the plazas, great and small, are brilliantly illuminated. Balconies are draped with tapestries, silks and velvets, with red and yellow—the Spanish colors—predominating; flags fly from all public buildings. The native population, so essentially averse to slumber, appears, throughout this particular week, to avoid going to bed altogether. Stores are completely closed on the twelfth, which, here, is considered less as Columbus Day than as one of St. Teresa's special days; they are also closed on the fifteenth and on any Sunday which falls within the octave; the hours at which they are open are conspicuously abbreviated on all other days.

The streets are thronged with pedestrians; less than ever are sidewalks regarded as the logical place for people to walk. In fact, the only show of violence, or even discourtesy, that I ever saw on the part of a Spaniard in the street occurred when a motorcar, which had only

Modern Fiesta of St. Teresa. From a photograph by Mayoral, Avila.

one way of reaching its destination—the home of its occupants, one
of them ill and elderly—attempted to go at snail's pace along the thor-
oughfare the celebrants had pre-empted, though it had not been officially closed by the police. Only the fact that the driver remained
level-headed and that one man's violence did not spread beyond his
immediate companions, prevented an incident which might have had
serious consequences.

However, riotous though the crowd may be, it is, on the whole, extremely good-natured; and, eventually, in the midst of the bullfights,
the *verbenas,* the races and the merry-go-rounds, the saint in whose
honor these events are staged makes her participation in them evident:
on the night of the twelfth, her statue, richly decked with flowers and
brilliantly illuminated, is taken from her church on a float, or *paso,*
and carried through the streets to the accompaniment of sweet singing by girls and women. And a gorgeous sight it presents. True, Teresa
is still clad in the white mantle and black veil of the Carmelites; but
the mantle is made of brocade and the veil of velvet and both are so
heavily encrusted with gold embroidery that their basic colors are almost lost to view. Around her throat, her wrists and her fingers are
priceless jewels, loaned especially for the occasion. Triumphantly she
progresses "along her accustomed route"—the official program does
not tell you what this is, for you are supposed to know. Then she
returns to her church.

This procession, impressive as it seems, is only the forerunner of
those yet to come, which are far more magnificent and symbolic. On
the fourteenth, she leaves her church again, and this time she is borne
on her *paso* straight to the cathedral and placed at the right of the
high altar, at the left of which is standing the statue of the Virgin of
Charity—*La Virgen de la Caritad*—who is, at all times, her patroness
and who now becomes her hostess as well. For, this time, St. Teresa
does not go back to her own church. She remains overnight at the
cathedral, as the guest of the Virgin.

On the fifteenth comes the grand finale. After a Solemn High Mass,
the two statues—St. Teresa and the Virgin of Charity—emerge from
the cathedral together to make "the accustomed round." The procession which, on the twelfth, was of relatively modest proportions, has
now swelled to formidable size. First come the *gigantes,* mammoth,
grotesque figures mounted on high poles, and carried by men concealed under the framework and draperies of these oversized images
of buffoonery, which are considered indispensable to any popular cele-

bration in Spain, however solemn its character may be otherwise. Then come the little girls from the different parochial schools, each group in charge of two nuns and each in distinctive uniforms: navy blue skirts and jumpers over white blouses, brown and tan plaid skirts and jumpers over cream-colored blouses, ensembles of pale blue. The nuns' habits are distinctive, too: the Spanish Sisters of Charity do not dress like the Sisters of St. Vincent de Paul, in blue, but in black, with sheer black veils over their white "wings." The nuns and their charges are followed by the seminarians, very slim and straight, their neat black cassocks brilliantly belted in red, their black birettas surmounted by red pompons; with them are the Dominican Fathers in black and white. All these precede the *pasos*. Directly behind the floats come the Bishop and Canons of the Cathedral, all in scarlet; and after them the Mayor, the Members of the City Council and other civic dignitaries, detachments of cavalry officers, superbly mounted, and infantry in dress uniform and, last of all, a military band.

The destination this time is not the cathedral, but St. Teresa's Church. The Virgin is going to return the saint's visit, as courtesy would require. It does not, however, require that this visit should be quite so long as the former one. The Virgin does not remain with the saint overnight. At seven in the evening, she is borne out of the church and taken to one corner of the plaza in front of it, which forms a triangle, with the church at its apex. Presently, the saint is borne out and placed in the opposite corner. Then her *paso* advances a few paces and the statue appears to curtsy, because the men who are carrying it on their shoulders lower it to the ground and bend over. This is the famous *despedida*, the leave-taking. Three times Teresa advances and, three times, she stops to incline with respect. All proper formalities have now been observed: a visit has been made and returned, farewells have been taken in due form. The Virgin goes back, rather unobtrusively, to the cathedral. The saint resumes her place of glory above the altar in the church which was built where her girlhood home once stood.

Now this sanctuary is her home. She has enjoyed the little jaunts around the city—was she ever one to hesitate at the prospect of an excursion? But at nightfall it is good to be back in her own quarters —for another year. Then she will come out again and once more, like everyone else, she will have a good time.

Who can doubt it? She lived three hundred years ago, but her high spirit still survives.

St. John of the Cross, from a steel engraving in the 1649 edition of his *Works*.

PART III

The Man Who Sang When He Suffered

(St. John of the Cross, 1542–1591)

1

A THIN, haggard woman, who was trudging wearily along the rough road between the poverty-stricken village of Fontiveros and the castellated town of Arévalo, drew her black shawl more closely around her with one cold, toilworn hand, and stretched out the other to keep her little son, Juan, from stumbling.

He was much too small and frail to endure the hardships of such a journey as she had undertaken. His brother, Francisco, who was older and stronger, was bearing up under it fairly well. But Catalina Alvarez could see that nothing except will-power was keeping the youngest boy on his feet, and fear that, at any moment, he might give out completely permeated her own fatigue. Yet there had seemed to be no choice left to her when she started out from her native village, taking her two children with her. She was a widow, for her husband, the *hidalgo* Francisco Gonzalo de Yepes, had died when Juan was a baby. His station in life was far higher than hers; he was the grandson of one of Juan II's men-at-arms, the nephew of an inquisitor at Toledo, and three of his other relatives were Cathedral Canons. Still others were prosperous merchants who sold their wares at Medina del Campo and he had met Catalina in the course of one of the trips which he made to the fairs in their behalf, for his route took him first through Escalona, the walled city pleasantly situated by a riverside, which had been one of those ceded to Isabel, and next, to Toros de Guisando, where the treaty had been signed and where there was now a *venta*, or roadside inn, similar to those in which Don Quixote was to take such delight, which was always the scene of good companionship. Then he went on through Cebreros, Avila, Madrigal and Fontiveros—the last another logical stopping place on a long journey and one which seemed more and more logical, the more deeply he fell in love. Unfortunately, he had been no richer than if he had come of peasant stock, as Catalina did, and he had left her almost penniless. His family had cast him off "with abhorrence" when he married her and, though he had done his best to earn his living as an artisan, he had no aptitude for it. Catalina had tried to support herself by cooking and cleaning and weaving for anyone who would hire such work done. But in Fontiveros everybody was poor. Even the pittance which was all she asked or expected was beyond the power of the most prosperous to pay; and there were very few in the village who wore silk, which she was especially skillful at weaving. She had tried to get some help from Francisco's relatives, the *Toledanos* whose circumstances were so much more comfortable than his had been, after he married the beautiful young peasant with whom he had fallen so deeply in love that he was willing to give up everything for her sake; but these hardhearted kinsfolk had turned a deaf ear to her entreaties.

She had been used, all her life, to plain fare. But when she was a girl, her people had kept pigs, so that now and then there had been pork to eat, and chickens, so that eggs were no great rarity, and there had always been a great steaming iron pot of porridge on the fire. Lately, however, there had been no *cocido*, no *tortilla*, no *gachas*;[1] and finally the day came when there was not even bread. It was then that she had decided to close the door of her miserable little house behind her and strike out for Arévalo. She had heard that life was not so hard or food so scarce there as in Fontiveros; surely someone would give her children and herself shelter, someone would share a loaf with them. If she could not find a willing welcome, she would go from door to door begging, until she found a grudging one. She could not sit still any longer, watching the boys die of slow starvation. It would not even be *slow* starvation much longer. Any morning she might wake up to find that Francisco or Juan had died from hunger during the night. This was what had already happened to Luis, her third little boy, the one who was younger than Francisco and older than Juan.[2]

She tightened her grasp on the littlest boy's hand and looked anxiously down at him. He had not stumbled, as she had feared he might; he was not even dragging his feet. Though he had to take short steps, because he was so small, he was keeping up with her just the same.

Both boys were undersized, from lack of nourishment; but Juan was even more so than Francisco. He was six years old,[3] but he could have easily been mistaken for three, as far as stature went. It was infantile rosiness, infantile chubbiness that were lacking. There was no color in his peaked little face, and his ragged garments hung on a tiny frame that was nothing but skin and bones. He looked more like a gnome than a child. Except when he smiled. Then he looked like one of the happy little angels in the paintings that hung in the parish church where he had been baptized, for his smile was sweet and sunny, just as theirs were. Catalina had noticed this when she glanced up from the font of dark, rough-hewn stone to the glowing pictures on the walls that surrounded it. But she had not thought about the resemblance for a long while. She had thought only that her little boy was getting thinner and paler every day and that, presently, he would die, just as his brother, Luis, had; and that though, of course, he would go to heaven and be an angel himself, it did not comfort her to believe this. She was beyond all comfort, or so it seemed to her, and it was very hard for her to keep back the tears.

But she was wrong in believing that she was beyond all comfort. As the little boy felt her hand tightening on his, he looked up at her and smiled. It was just such a smile as she had not thought of in a long while, sweet and sunny—and happy. Suddenly she realized that the long hard walk was not too much for him after all, that he was fully as equal to it as his brother, if not more so, because, somehow, he was sustained in a way that Francisco was not. For he was not only trudging along as sturdily as if he had been big and strong; he had begun to sing. It was a childish song, but it was a cheery one, and the tune was so simple that, presently, Francisco was whistling it. And soon, Catalina realized that she did not want to cry any more; she wanted to join in the song.

When they came in sight of the castle at Arévalo, where the widow of Juan de Castile—with whom the children's great-grandfather had fought—lived so long in the shadows, they were all singing; and their song was heard by a group of men and women who were gathered around the open door of their little white house. Savory smells were coming from the opening and, inside, a lamp was lighted and a table was already set for supper. Catalina paused, because she could not help it, but she did not have to beg. The boys had halted when she did and sniffed the good smell. And while Francisco looked hungrily at the lighted table, Juan went on smiling and singing, and one of the men came forward and put his hand on the little boy's shoulder.

"Stay and sing for us awhile," he said. "And share our supper with us. This is your house."[4]

2

Catalina and her children remained in Arévalo for three years and, during this time, they did not have to face actual starvation again, and Francisco, who was now old enough to help and who had inherited his mother's skill in weaving, found employment, too. But they were still in want much of the time, for work was scarce here, also, though not as scarce as in Fontiveros; and while they thankfully accepted an occasional helping hand, they had no mind to depend wholly on charity. Moreover, Francisco had fallen in with undesirable companions, who took advantage of his naturally jovial habits to lead him astray. He made a premature marriage, and though there was nothing against the girl, Ana Izquierdo, and she tried hard to carry her share of the family burden, actually she represented another problem. When Catalina heard that Medina del Campo offered better chances for earning a respectable livelihood than Arévalo, she followed the same course as when she had heard that Arévalo offered more than Fontiveros: she took to the road again with her two sons, this time with the addition of her daughter-in-law to the little party.

In Medina del Campo, they did indeed all readily find employment, for the great tri-yearly fairs, which had been such a lodestone for Isabel and Alfonso of Castile when they were children, still drew to it merchants from every part of Europe; millions of *maravedís* changed hands with resultant general prosperity and increase of permanent population. The city was, by now, one of some fifty thousand inhabitants, some of them really wealthy, many more of them well-to-do—a far cry from a village where even a few hundred souls had to fight for survival. It was able not only to attract and foster trade, but to make suitable provision to care for its people when they fell ill and to see that they did not grow up in ignorance. A wealthy and devout man by the name of Don Antonio de Alvarez[5] of Toledo founded a hospital and the new Order, known as the Society of Jesus, opened a school. Juan de Yepes, who had begun his education by attending the *Colegio de los Niños de la Doctrina*, and studying his lessons by the flame of one small candle while seated on a pile of wood, progressed to the benches provided by the Jesuits, which were somewhat better lighted; and in the intervals between classes, he worked in the hospital.

He showed such aptitude, both as an orderly and as a student, that he would have been warmly welcomed as a permanent fixture in either institution. Though his growth had been stunted by his early hardships, his appearance of frailty was deceptive; he had surprising endurance. Besides, he was not only strong and capable, he was extremely likable; he had very winning ways. When Don Antonio discovered that the boy wanted to become a priest, he encouraged his valuable helper by telling him that there would be a place for him at the hospital as a chaplain. The Jesuits were equally cordial; this boy would make a missionary after Loyola's own heart. Juan did not wish to seem ungrateful to his benefactors, and he was somewhat fearful lest this disinclination might make him susceptible to persuasion. But he had his own ideas about a vocation; and so unobtrusively that a certain secrecy surrounded his movements, he left the hospital in the dead of night, traversed the town and knocked at the entrance of the Carmelite Monastery of Santa Ana.

The summons was somewhat startling to the good Brothers, for they retired early; and the porter, roused from his rest, peered sleepily and apprehensively through a small, well-barred panel, which opened on hinges, before drawing back the bolts and turning the massive key in the lock of the door. But despite the unusual and somewhat dramatic manner of Juan's approach, there was no hesitation in admitting him to the community, once his purpose was explained. The Prior already knew a good deal about Juan and everything he knew was in the would-be postulant's favor. His novitiate was brief, for again he excelled in everything that was required of him, and again his singularly sunny disposition radiated happiness. Only a few months after his precipitate entrance into the monastery, he was clothed in a white woolen robe, received into the order, and given the name of Juan de San Matías.[6]

However, he remained less than a year in the cloister. The Prior, who had been so swift to recognize the boy's great natural endowments, knew that these should be further developed by study, and study under the greatest masters in the greatest institution of learning in all Spain, if not in all the world. Accordingly, young Juan de San Matías, who had still never called himself, or been called by others, Juan de la Cruz, was sent to Salamanca for a three years' course in the Arts, to be followed by a year's course in Theology.

3

From the beginning, Juan's life had been punctuated by abrupt and significant changes. The one which now took place was, perhaps, the most momentous of any.

He had grown used to a popular center, dominated by a hilltop castle and boasting a spacious plaza, an impressive town hall, several fine churches and a number of solid stone houses, belonging to prosperous burghers, besides a few establishments that were more pretentious, belonging to the nobility. But in Salamanca, he found a city that was all rose and gold, whose meanest buildings were beautiful in both form and color, whose massive cathedral was a scene of splendor and whose great university had both the majesty and the bloom of age. He had grown used to vast crowds, but these were mainly crowds of alien merchants, men much older than himself, who affected the life of the community without becoming a part of it, for their presence in Medina del Campo was limited to the duration of the tri-yearly fairs. Now he found himself one of a great company of fellow students, around whom the entire life of Salamanca revolved. True, by no means all of these ten thousand young men were Spaniards; they came pouring in from every part of Europe. But they had a common bond in their thirst for knowledge and in their love of learning. Juan had grown used to wealth, but hitherto it had been the wealth of trade, eagerly sought and reluctantly shared. Now he saw the palaces of great families used to provide cultural and social centers for their sons and the friends of these sons, whether the comrades in question were themselves rich or poor. A student like himself could and must live on next to nothing. However, he would still be entitled to wear a Bachelor's robe, to mingle as an equal with others so clad, not only in classrooms and college courtyards, in taverns and stalls on the *Rua* where books and parchment were bought and sold, but also in the hospitable halls of the nobles. Best of all, the richest and the poorest, those of low degree and those of high degree, had the same teachers and these, in both scholarship and saintliness, upheld the proud traditions of those two great sons of Salamanca, Domingo de Guzmán and Ignacio de Loyola.

Outstanding among such professors, at the time of Juan's entry, was Luis de León, an Augustinian from Cuenca, "a region where people are lovers of adventure . . . energetic, tenacious and keen." He had been born with a silver spoon in his mouth and had voluntarily turned his back on an income of four thousand ducats a year and a life of luxury and had gone to Salamanca some twenty years earlier, to study under such great theologians as Francisco de Vitoria, Melchor Cano and Domingo de Soto. Eventually, he had become a Professor of Theology himself. But though the Order to which he belonged was, theoretically, one of the strictest, "it offered delightful opportunities of amplitude, leisure and cultivated society, nor did it exclude its members from the great positions of power which were then open to the clergy. . . . Vitoria and Cano had been inspiring lecturers, but here was a speaker more personal, more poetical. Bracing, stimulating, lucid, and flashing with humour, his lectures gathered to him a crowd from the thousands of young men who flocked to Salamanca. For ten years he continued to nourish brilliant minds, and to startle dull and conventional ones by his novelty. Here was a Professor to stimulate the keen young Carmelite from Medina!"[7]

This stimulation, as a matter of course, was eventually in the field of Theology, and it did not fail to serve as an invigorating agent in that direction. But Juan had come to Salamanca as an *artista*; he was to spend three years in studying the Arts—Latin, Philosophy, Psychology, Poetry and allied subjects—before he concentrated on the one subject which was his ultimate goal. And fortunately for him, Luis de León was not only a Doctor of Divinity; he was also a student and a lover of poetry and he became a great poet himself. Indeed, he would be best remembered as a poet, were it not for the famous saying with which he greeted his pupils when he returned to his classroom after five years' incarceration by the Inquisition: "Well, gentlemen, as we were saying yesterday . . ." This remark has so captured the imagination of every succeeding generation, in the same way it did his own, that it has obscured more general recognition of his talents. But it was as a poet and not as the coiner of an epigram that "the keen young Carmelite from Medina" came to know him, and it was as a poet that he was to prove the source of the most important and lasting inspiration to his most famous disciple.

The poem which Luis de León was perusing with infinite absorption at the time was Solomon's *Song of Songs*; and "as he studied this famous classic of mysticism, he saw that behind all the allegorical interpretations which had been given to it, it was indeed a dramatic arrangement, telling a love story, and as a poem was sacred in its beauty." He translated it into Spanish and it was this very translation which was later to get him into trouble with the Inquisition, on the charge that his version belittled the authority of the Vulgate and that "to have that fervid poem at the disposal of the people might well provoke scandal."[8] But such trouble and such charges were all still fortunately in the future when Juan de San Matías came within Luis de León's brilliant and beneficent orbit. It was from this remarkable teacher that the earnest boy first glimpsed the meaning and the significance of mysticism, of which he himself was later to become such an ardent interpreter, and that he learned to recognize the many forms, none necessarily salacious, many sublime, some even sacred, which a song of love could take.

4

At the end of three years, having finished his course in the Arts, Juan returned to Medina del Campo to take his priest's orders.

He still had his year of theological study before him, but he already knew, or thought he knew, what he wanted to do next. He had derived enjoyment as well as enlightenment from mingling with many men and drawing on many minds, and the philosophy which he had learned so thoroughly was to characterize "the whole of his writings, giving them a granitelike solidity."[9]

However he had begun to feel the need of greater solitude, not only that he might assimilate, undistracted, what he had learned; but that he might devote himself more exclusively to the perusal of poetry and the theory of mysticism, both of which now meant to him more than the study of Logic and Latin; and that he might do this in natural surroundings which would serve to foster his yearning for a contemplative life. Just as young Francis of Assisi had felt more securely at home with gentle birds and friendly beasts, so young Juan de San Matías was happiest when he had for company only the books he really loved, and could read them while withdrawn in the depths of some remote wood or on some lonely mountainside.

He had therefore decided that the Order which would best suit his needs was the one which had its center at Grande Chartreuse, in Grenoble, and that rather than entering the Charter House near Burgos— the Cartuja de Miraflores, already famous as a royal pantheon—he would prefer the retreat of El Paular, near Segovia. This was located in the Valley of the Guadarrama, in a well-watered forest of oak and pine, hemmed in by mountain peaks; and here a small group of Contemplatives lived solitary lives, each inhabiting his own tiny hermitage, cultivating his own tiny garden, and meeting with his fellow Contemplatives only for union in prayer and worship. In this tranquil place, Juan would read the works of the great Spanish poets and of such prominent Belgian mystics as Denys, the Carthusian, who was then very highly regarded.

This was his plan; he would have said nothing could divert him from it. But he had hardly reached home when he received a totally unexpected summons. The Carmelite whose name in the world had been Teresa de Cepeda y Ahumada, and who was known in religion as Teresa de Jesús, had come to Medina del Campo for the purpose of founding a convent there, in addition to San José, the one she had established in her native city of Avila, after transferring from the Encarnación, where she had made her profession nearly twenty years earlier. He could not very well decline to answer the summons, though he had no idea what she wanted of him or how she had heard of him. But of course he had heard of her. Who, in the Province of Avila and the surroundings, had not? She came of a great family, she had been a beauty and a belle and, in speaking of her, people had said so often that it had become a byword, "Teresa de Ahumada? She will marry anyone she chooses!" But she had not chosen to marry anyone. From childhood, she had been headstrong; and despite her taste for finery, perfumes, romantic reading, romping with her cousins and participation in every sort of fiesta, her wilfulness had led her in the direction of a heavenly bridegroom instead of an earthly one. In addition to all her frivolous tastes, she had likewise always had a strong religious bent, inconsistent as this seemed. Even as a child of seven, she had run away from home with her brother, Rodrigo, on the announced pretext of setting sail for Africa and converting the Moors. (What a restless lot they were, these de Cepedas y Ahumadas! Rodrigo was only one of seven brothers who had gone streaking across the Atlantic![10] Perhaps it was no wonder that one female member of the family should also be so constantly on the go!) That time, she had, fortunately, been intercepted before she had led her little brother far astray and brought back to her father's handsome house. But the next time she escaped from the parental roof, she was already behind the grille of Encarnación before her angry father caught up with her; and devout gentleman though he was, he had raged at her stubborn refusal to return to the place where he felt she belonged. Once at the Encarnación, she had seemed quiescent enough for a time, but this quiesence was apparently largely the result of intermittent though serious illnesses. Once fully restored to health, she had begun to criticize the pleasant mode of life at the convent, intimating that its parlors were conducted more like those of a hospitable palace than like those of a cloistered Order; and when she could not prevail against the nuns who were agreeably ensconced there to change their ways, she had left it and surreptitiously arranged for the foundation of another convent in Avila, where the so-called reforms which she advocated were a matter of stern practice.

All this had been widely bruited about and Juan had heard Teresa de Jesús defined as a perverse opinionated woman, never satisfied with the existing order of things and arrogantly convinced that she could improve it. This, at least, was what most people said about her. There were some who said something else: that she was almost irresistibly beguiling, that she could charm a bird off a tree simply by looking at it, and that all this talk about setting her will and judgment against the will and judgment of others was sheer nonsense, because these others were left with neither will nor judgment of their own, once she had so witchingly and so wittily told them hers. And then there were a few—no less an authority than Fray Luis de León among them—who said something else again: that she was a great woman and a great writer and a great mystic, and that the reforms which she so ardently desired to bring about would take place to the lasting benefit not only of her Order, but to that of all Christendom, because she would bring to them vision and consecration, as well as boundless energy and generous purpose and intelligent action.

All in all, there was no doubt that never, since Isabel of Castile had died at Medina del Campo, had any other woman so stirred and shaken this mercantile city as this extraordinary and determined Carmelite did now. Even if Juan had felt that, with propriety, he could refuse her demand that he should wait upon her, he would not have wanted to do so. He could not help being curious to see for himself what she was like and to form his own opinion. He answered her summons promptly.

She elected to receive him in the gilded parlor of a prosperous merchant which had been put at her disposal, while the simple but solid house which was to serve as the second convent of her Foundation was made ready for occupancy. Juan had never before been invited to this pretentious residence and, even now, he did not see its proprietor.

Instead, he was ushered into the presence of a woman over fifty, thick-set and coarsely clad in a well-worn habit and a rusty veil. Her dark eyes were rather prominent, the brows above them heavy and black, and between her nose and her mouth were three small moles. If she had ever been a beauty, which Juan was inclined to doubt, it must have been long, long ago; if she had ever been an enchantress, which he doubted still more, the power to charm must have faded and died. And then the inevitable happened. He looked at her more closely and saw that her eyes sparkled and glowed, that her skin was fresh and rosy and unwrinkled, that her hands were small and white and lovely, and that her every movement, in spite of her size, was marked by distinction and grace. She spoke to him and he forgot her heaviness and her shabbiness, for her voice was like music. He listened to what she had to say, first with amazement, then with respect, then with admiration and, finally, with kindling response.

She told him she had received permission from Juan Bautista Rubeo, Vicar General[10-a] of the Order of Carmel, to found further convents for nuns under the conditions of Reform[10-b] which she had already put into effect at San José of Avila and which she was planning to put into effect at Medina del Campo. She was not sure yet where she would go next—very probably to Valladolid, though there were other possibilities, too. She said she also had permission to found two priories for men, likewise in conformity with the Primitive Rule. She told him that no less a person than Antonio de Heredia, the Prior of Santa Ana, had said he would gladly be the first to enter such an establishment. She wanted Juan to join him.

Juan was thunderstruck. The handsome, distinguished and learned man of whom she spoke had hitherto shown no particular leanings toward austerity and was known to have cherished the well-founded ambition of becoming the Provincial[10-c] of his Order. But even more amazing than the fact that Teresa had made such an impression on the Prior that he was ready and eager to leave everything he had so far gained and everything he was likely to gain, in the way of visible success, in order to follow her in an uncertain and humiliating undertaking, was the fact that she had selected him, Juan de San Matías, as the great Prior's companion. He thought he knew how he must look to her—undersized, insignificant, immature; he could not guess how much more she saw, how much more she had heard. She knew how beloved he was in Medina del Campo, how highly regarded in Salamanca. She knew the vast extent of his Scriptural and other reading,

the still vaster realms of his contemplation and prayer. She knew that
he had chosen a cell whose one small window looked out on the
Blessed Sacrament, so that he might always be supremely conscious of
its Presence. She knew that he and she would always speak the same
language, not only literally—the beautiful Castilian which was their
heritage and their birthright—but figuratively, because they were both
Avileses, children of that stern and stony land, whose motto was
Antes quebrar que doblar[11] and which brought forth no weaklings,
but men and women able no less than willing to become masters of
their fate and captains of their souls. In short, she knew this was the
man she wanted.

The words of which the lovely voice made music followed one another in melodious succession, at first persuasively, then impellingly.
When at last the woman whose beauty no longer seemed a thing of
the past and whose charm was very definitely a thing of the present
ceased to speak, the silence in the gilded room lasted only a moment.
Juan told her he must return to Salamanca to complete his studies
and take his degree in Theology—that much of his plan must remain
unchanged. He told her, too, of his yearning for the solitude of El
Paular and the reasons for it. But even as he did so, he knew that
El Paular was only a dream. Teresa of Avila had brought him back
to reality. He could not go wandering off in the shaded solitude of
those pleasant forests and their refreshing streams, under the shadow
of the snow-topped mountains which turned rosy in the glow of sunset.
He must follow the rough highroad that she was treading in her hemp-
shod feet. And he must do so with the same childlike and unquestion-
ing faith with which he had stumbled along beside his mother when
she had taken her desperate departure from Fontiveros.

5

As it turned out, Teresa's next Foundation was not at Valladolid
after all. At the insistence of Doña Luisa de la Cerda, a daughter of
the Duke of Medinaceli and a liberal patron of the Reform, it was
established at Malagón, a town not far from Toledo which belonged to
this noblewoman. Nevertheless, Teresa had already made her plans
for the establishment of a convent at Valladolid, since funds had
been provided for it by the will of Don Bernardino de Mendoza, a
brother of the Bishop of Avila; and she had also been given a "tumble-
down old place" at Duruelo, a village so far off the beaten track that

when she first went to visit it, she lost her way, accustomed as she was to the byways, as well as the highways, of the countryside. Though the house which her relative, Rafael Mejia, had offered her in this remote hamlet consisted only of a porch, a room with a loft and a lean-to, and a small kitchen, all in a state of almost indescribable disrepair and dirt, it was here that she determined to locate the first monastery of the Reform. With her usual prophetic perception, she visualized this hovel restored and cleaned, with the porch converted into a chapel, the lean-to into a choir and the one room into a dormitory. She lost no time in advising Antonio de Heredia and Juan de San Matías of her decision.

Neither one hesitated to accept her mandate. Juan, who had accompanied her to Valladolid, after finishing his course at Salamanca, went briefly to Medina to make the necessary preparations for permanent removal and, while he was there, Teresa handed the nuns at her convent some lengths of rough brown frieze; these were cut up and eventually took form as the habit of a Discalced Friar.[11-a] "The following day, the Mother Foundress, behind the parlor grille, in the presence of the nuns in their long white mantles as, lighted candle in hand, they sang the *Veni Creator Spiritus*, herself gave the habit to Juan de San Matías. He solemnly renounced the Mitigation, promising to live according to the Rule of Our Lady of Carmel, in obedience, chastity and poverty. And, barefooted, at long last slave only of his vows, at last free from the fetters of the world and material things, he who would in future be known as John of the Cross, wended his way to the *casita* of Duruelo. The prior Antonio de Heredia who was now Antonio de Jesús joined him there soon afterwards."[12]

A few months later, Teresa, who had set out for Toledo, but who was never averse to prolonging her jaunts, maneuvered her itinerary in such a way as to pass through Duruelo and make an unannounced visit at the new Priory. When she arrived, she found Antonio de Jesús industriously sweeping the porch; and when she had been proudly led inside, she saw that the dirty little hovel had been transfigured, exactly as she had foreseen. It was now spotlessly clean, its walls whitewashed inside as well as out, its floors polished. On the little wooden cross above the holy water basin was glued a small figure of Christ, which one of the monks had cut out of paper. On either side of the "chapel," Fray Antonio and Fray Juan had built hermitages, "so small that they could only sit or lie prostrate there"; and to these they retired to rapt devotion, often so absorbed in prayer that they were quite unconscious of the passage of time and, having withdrawn after Matins, remained secluded until Prime and came "into chapel . . . with their habits covered with snow without noticing it."[13]

Teresa was so impressed that she then and there christened the Priory "a veritable little stable of Bethlehem" and often referred to it afterward in that way. But Juan and his fellow friars by no means spent all their time either in the care and improvement of their Priory or in rapt seclusion, as she herself bore witness: "'They went,' she said, 'to preach at many of the villages round about which had no religious teaching, for which reason also I was glad the house had been founded in that spot; and since they told me that besides them they had no monastery near, neither was there any other place when it could be had, which was pitiful enough. Already in so short a time, so great was the credit they were held in that it gave me the greatest joy when I heard it. They went as I say to preach a league and a half, and two leagues away, barefoot—for at that time they did not wear *alpargatas* as afterwards they were ordered—and with much snow and cold: and after they had preached and confessed, they returned to the house very late to eat. Their contentment made everything seem little to them. As to food, they had enough and to spare, for the dwellers of the neighbouring townships provided them with more than they needed, and some gentlemen came to them to confession who lived in those towns, where they already offered them better sites and houses. Among those was Don Luis, lord of the Five Manors.'"[14]

The Don Luis to whom Teresa here referred was a rich nobleman, a cousin of the Duke of Alba, who had recently brought back to Spain from Flanders a primitive Madonna of great beauty, for which he decided to erect a suitable shrine. The place he chose for this was the village of Mancera, in the same locality as Duruelo, but a little nearer the mountains; and he was so impressed by what he had seen of the Carmelite Community's work that he offered to build a monastery as well, which would provide more appropriate accommodations than the first poor little Priory. Despite the seclusion in which they lived and the obscurity which they preferred, the fame of the good Brothers had spread; in ever increasing numbers, other men were coming to them, clamoring for the privilege of sharing their austere and charitable way of life. At the end of a year, they had fourteen novices and more were begging for admission. These claimants could not be denied, and there was no space for them in the one small room which served as a dormitory, even though Antonio de Jesús and Juan de la Cruz now used their respective hermitages for sleeping quarters.

The change was accordingly made, not without regret, especially on the part of Juan, who had been chosen as the new Prior. He had not missed the companionship of his fellow students at Salamanca or the guidance of his teachers, even such a teacher as Luis de León. He had not yearned for further glimpses of those attributes of gracious living with which he had become briefly acquainted at Valladolid, in the company of Teresa, who was still received as a great lady by the nobles who were her relatives, friends and patrons, rather than as a Carmelite nun. On the contrary, he had delighted in the very opportunities which he anticipated when he chose El Paular as his retreat, and which he thought he had lost in renouncing it to follow in Teresa's footsteps. He read little, for he had few books and less time; but this seemed no hardship, for he already knew a large portion of the Scriptures by heart, and could spend hours in reciting and reviewing them. He did no writing, for he had not yet begun to think of himself as an author; and, indeed, at no period of his life was he to set time expressly apart for the composition of those verses and essays which he visualized only as a means of guidance for his spiritual charges, without dreaming that they would survive the centuries and serve as models in mysticism for generations as yet unborn. But in his tireless mind were already germinating the "precepts" which, up to now, had taken no definite form; and he had achieved what he most wanted: "solitude and withdrawal from the world . . . a year fixed on far more direct intercourse of his spirit with the transcending Holiness than any he had yet known."[15] No wonder he had been conscious of abundant fulfillment.

True, the change from Duruelo to Mancera was not a great one, as far as the natural surroundings Juan so loved were concerned. In both places there was the same verdure which ample shade and forest streams assured, the same fields of golden wheat with open, rocky plains beyond them and, above all, the stark majesty of the great Sierra. But with the growth of the little community and the increase of his responsibilities, Juan found the complete isolation which was so precious to him hard to achieve; and he was not without forebodings that it would be harder still in the future. In the brief time since he had left Salamanca, Teresa had founded a convent there, after already establishing others at Toledo and Pastrana. Now she was about to found one at Alba de Tormes, which was important to her not only as the ancestral seat of her friend, the Duke of Alba, but as the home of her younger sister, Juana, who had lived with her as a guest at Encarnación for some time after the death of their father and who later married Juan de Ovalle "a noble and upright gentleman who had served with Charles V in the Flanders Wars." Both had been very helpful in the foundation of San José and Teresa was extremely fond of their five children, especially little Beatriz, who had been named for her grandmother and who was "pretty and gallant, very blond, with golden hair and a graceful figure." From an early age, she was a skillful musician and delighted her aunt with her music; later on she was to delight Teresa still more by becoming a devout nun; but, for the moment, she gave pleasure only as a charming and accomplished child. Fray Juan had a presentiment that Teresa might expect him to shift his sphere of influence to Alba de Tormes, where she was so happy and so much at home, and that, when he did, he would be on a scene of strife, instead of in a retreat of peace.

His forebodings proved all too true, though Alba de Tormes was not the primary scene of his labors. Teresa first summoned him to become the Superior of the new community at Pastrana, which owed its foundation less to her initiative than to the whim of the Princess of Eboli, the wife of the King's favorite, Ruy Gomez da Silva. This couple had recently taken possession of the town, made extensive changes and improvements in it, and decided that a convent and a monastery would supply the finishing touches to these undertakings. Da Silva was acquiescent, but the Princess moved like a whirlwind and it was almost impossible to withstand anything on which she had set her mind. Had it not been for the loss of one eye, over which she wore a black patch, she would have been the happy possessor of almost flawless beauty. Even with this blemish, she was irresistibly attractive to most men; whether rightly or wrongly she was very generally suspected of having been—or of still being—the mistress of more than one, including not only the King's secretary, but the King himself. The Carmelites could hardly have found a more disturbing element to their well-ordered lives. She expected to go in and out of their establishments at will and, when her husband died, to take up residence in the convent she had founded. Nominally, she actually entered the Order, but she was never anything other than a pseudo-Carmelite. She continued to dress conspicuously and extravagantly, and to exact all the homage due her rank in the world. Eventually, Teresa realized that the only way to rid her nuns and her friars of the discontent and disorder the Princess created was to withdraw altogether from Pastrana.

Meanwhile, however, Fray Juan had done his best to make a success of the new Foundation, a task which was none the easier because of the presence there of an excitable young novice from Medina del Campo by the name of Ana de Jesús.[16] Great was his relief when, after a month or so, he was permitted to return to Mancera. But his period of respite was brief. Successively, he was called upon to visit Alba de Tormes when the new convent there was inaugurated; to go as Rector to the College of the Reform at Alcalá de Henares; and to return to Pastrana and correct the unseemly modes of discipline which the new Master of Novices, Angel de San Gabriel, was putting into public practice.

This final experience was a harrowing one: it exhausted and disgusted the gentle little man to whom austerity had always seemed a primary virtue, but only if practiced without parade and without excess. He persevered in the revolting task thrust upon him by the melancholia of Angel, who sought release from his own mental sufferings by inflicting unnatural physical suffering on his helpless novices. When, at last, Juan was free to return to Alcalá de Henares, where his life and that of those who surrounded him was one of dignity and culture, if not of the seclusion for which he yearned, his sense of relief was so great that he could not believe it would be lasting.

Again, his presentiment proved all too true. He had hardly settled back into the scholarly routine of the university when he received another summons from Teresa. She had been ordered to the Encarnación of Avila, as its Prioress. The command was far from pleasing to her, for she had shaken its dust from her feet when she left it to found San José; and she knew that it would be equally displeasing to the nuns whom she had left behind on that occasion, and who were as critical of her as she was of them. In fact, the whole situation was far from being one of her choosing. But she had at least one choice —that of naming the Confessor for the convent. Her choice fell on Fray Juan de la Cruz.

She presented him to the rebellious nuns by saying, "Ladies, I am giving you as Confessor a Father who is a saint." It did not take much discernment on his part to realize that the ladies in question were far from regarding him as such, and certainly he did not think of himself in that light, either then or later. At the moment, it was also hard for him to think of Teresa as possessing singularly saintly qualities.

6

"When you make your confession, Mother, you have a fine way of excusing yourself."

It was not Fray Juan's way to speak severely, much less unjustly, to anyone; but he was pushed almost beyond endurance, and he betrayed this, even when speaking to Teresa. True, he had found both the hysterical nun and the wilful Princess at Pastrana very trying. However, trials, within reason, were not only to be expected but welcomed as a natural part of a life dedicated to the service of God. Juan could, he hoped and believed, deal with two difficult women simultaneously and still maintain his serenity of spirit. But when it came to dealing with a hundred and seventy . . . !

That was the number which now resided at Encarnación,[17] the greater part of them nuns, allegedly cloistered, though a few were gentlewomen who had never taken the veil, but enjoyed a quiet and secluded life, and were admitted as privileged paying guests, on condition that they would follow the general conventual pattern. Encarnación needed their money; in fact, it was the very scarcity of its funds which was responsible not only for the presence of these gentlewomen, but for various other departures from strict cloistral observance. Even the nuns who had taken their final vows, presumably committing them to lifelong enclosure, were allowed to make extended visits among their families and friends, for their absence meant fewer mouths to feed; and those who remained behind the grille were permitted to accept presents of food to supplement the sparse conventual fare. Fray Juan, though he could get along very well himself on a crust of bread and a sip of water, would not have looked askance at such supplements if they had taken the prescribed form, in accordance with the Carmelite rules, for he knew that some of these women were actually hungry; but it was an open secret that the private pantries of the nuns were supplied with many a delicacy which had no relation whatsoever to an abstemious diet. Fray Juan was supposed to confess every one of his hundred and seventy charges at least once a fortnight; he feared—indeed, he knew—that only a small proportion of them were admitting to the number of stolen sweets which they were enjoying.

Nor did these stolen sweets take only the form of edibles; the missives which went back and forth in the sliding drawer beneath the grille did not always deal with religious subjects, by any means; and the drawer was large enough to accommodate parcels as well as letters. It was pleasant to read romances while nibbling candy; it was pleasant to dance and sing during recreation; and the wherewithal for these diversions was not lacking; it was supplied by the generous visitors to the parlor. These visitors were, presumably, all relatives and quite possibly the presumption was, in a sense, well founded: the great families of Avila, and some not quite so great, had intermarried to such an extent that almost everyone was at least a distant cousin of everyone else; and the brother or father or uncle of one nun—who unquestionably had a right to visit her—might easily be the much more distant kinsman of another who was not forbidden to sit with the first behind the grille while such a call was taking place. Who could tell? She might very well be helping to save his soul.

Such was the argument presented to Fray Juan in defense of these visits; but it did not seem to him that the soul saving was a very active pursuit. Conversation during calling hours could take, as its topic, any that was most acceptable and agreeable to those engaging in it—local scandal, gossip from the Court, news from the *conquistadores*. What about this rumor that Diego de Espinosa had become so proud of his power and so independent in his use of it that the King had finally rebuked him by saying, "Cardinal, I am still the ruler of Spain"? And that then Espinosa had staggered away from the audience chamber in shame, and collapsed shortly thereafter, never to recover? Well, it was a true saying that pride came before a fall and a haughty spirit before destruction. But Espinosa had been a great man in his time and had added luster to the fame of the province as Professor at Salamanca, as President of the Council of Castile, as Inquisitor General and as Cardinal; and though he had ended by annoying the King because of his arrogance, Philip had certainly placed boundless confidence in him and given him to understand he could do pretty much as he pleased. The rebuke did not seem altogether justified. Anyway, now he had died and they must pray for his soul. . . . Speaking of the King, it seemed rather a pity that he had moved the Court to Madrid—could the Queen have been partly responsible? And he had sent Don Juan of Austria to Bizerta—he was always sending this half-brother of his off somewhere, when Don Juan would have been such an ornament at the palace—the handsomest man in Europe and the most irresistible, there was not the slightest doubt of it. . . . And speaking of the Inquisition, wasn't it terrible that Fray Luis de León, who had been Fray Juan's teacher, had been arrested and imprisoned because of the—well, the very *ardent* way he had interpreted the *Song of Songs?* . . . The latest news from Mother Teresa's brother, Lorenzo, was that he was more prosperous than ever and more and more disposed to help her with her foundations; his return from the Indies, laden with riches, could be expected almost any time now. But her brother, Pedro, was obviously much less successful. He sponged on Lorenzo, and cast a gloom on his surroundings, whatever they were and no matter how hard his family tried to please him. The *Madre* had no reason to feel set up about *him* and certainly she could not count on him for help, for he had never made any money. . . .

It was in ways such as these that tongues wagged on and on, rather than on sacred subjects; and though visiting hours were, allegedly, restricted, the portress knew how to stretch these, if it were made worth her while to do so. Fray Juan had reason to believe that, very often, this happened and that, moreover, the walled garden, no less than the parlor, was the scene of secret meetings, at which no serious subjects of any kind were discussed and at which no grille acted as a barrier to displays of affection which had very little to do with kinship.

Naturally, Fray Juan did not connect any of these misdoings with Teresa. Common sense, if nothing else, would have prevented such a connection. In the first place, her digestion had been delicate ever since her youth; no conventual rules were needed to make her cautious and abstemious in her diet. In the second place, she was now an elderly woman, long past the age when smuggled billets-doux and nocturnal assignations could possibly have held any attraction for her; but, even if this had not been the case, her essential integrity, quite apart from the serious view she took of her vows, would have effectually prevented her from resorting to any kind of surreptitious maneuvering. Fray Juan did know—as who did not?—that many years earlier, shortly after she was restored to glowing health following her long mysterious illness, and before the easy-going ways of Encarnación had begun to seem unwise to her, there had been one caller whom she favored above all others, among the many who were constantly clamoring to see her and whom she received with pleasure and without censure from her superiors: a handsome and charming man, well born, well bred and high principled, whose frequent visits were a source of undisguised joy to her. She had been encouraged to receive him, rather than discouraged from doing so. Everyone around her persuaded her—as if such persuasion were needed!—that her friendship with this young nobleman was as beneficial to her as it was to him. It was she who recognized the danger signals of a possible *amitié amoureuse* and of her own accord, if not of her own volition, brought their meetings, about which there had never been anything indiscreet or clandestine, to a tactful end.

All that was now ancient history, in any case. Music, Teresa did enjoy and she considered it fitting that it should give enjoyment to others. She still sometimes sang at recreation and she had been known to dance herself, in conventual privacy, to the delight of her daughters and in the same spirit that David had danced before the Lord and that the *seises* were still performed before the high altar of the cathedral in Seville. It also behooved her to keep in touch with what was going on in the world, both at home and abroad, and she welcomed tidings from her brothers and her friends. But there was never anything secret about the messages, as far as she was concerned; she was as candid in talking about them as she was in telling her confessor about the extraordinary experiences and visions she was having. While Fray Juan was worrying about what a hundred and sixty-nine other women were, or might be, concealing from him, he was also worried about what Teresa kept revealing.

He had never thought of her in connection with the supernatural. He had known her first as a woman of great charm and persuasiveness, to be sure, but above all as a woman of tremendous energy and purpose, bent on spreading the reforms of which not only the Carmelite Order, but all of Catholic Spain and, indeed, all of Christendom, stood in such crying need. The Catholic Kings had been only too well aware of this necessity. A hundred years earlier, Alonso Carrillo, Archbishop of Toledo, acting at their instigation, had issued an edict to the effect that priests must say Mass at least three times a year and bishops at least four; Mass as a daily requisite was not even envisioned! The way many clerics had been passing their time was only too clear from other provisions in the edict, which forbade them from dicing or otherwise "leading a riotous life," and enjoined them not to bear arms "except to take service with kings or other princes of the blood."[18] Even the great Cardinal, Mendoza, freely acknowledged at least one illegitimate son, and illicit relations between the clergy and the feminine members of their flock were by no means uncommon. Isabel had been dead only fifteen years when the German monk, Martin Luther, had broken with Rome, using depravity within the Church as his pretext, and he had stirred multitudes to similar action by his eloquence.

Ten years later, Henry VIII of England, who had gloried in the title, "Defender of the Faith," was deserting it, too, in a move made under even more disgraceful circumstances, and under conditions which caused special indignation in Spain because his wife, Catalina—or Catherine of Aragon, as the English called her—the youngest child of the Catholic Kings, was an innocent victim of his revolt. Thoughtful Catholics everywhere were roused to the realization that, if such apostasy was not to spread still further and faster, like wildfire, existent evils must be corrected from within the fold, rather than from without.

Recognizing all this, Fray Juan had entered heart and soul into Teresa's work of reform. He was more or less aware that when she had already been a nun for all of twenty years, in the course of which time her spiritual side had at no time shown predominance and at many periods had seemed actually dormant, she had been vouchsafed visions and other experiences which seemed like unusual and even extraordinary signs of Divine grace and favor. But it was not as a visionary that she had sent for him at Medina del Campo, or encouraged him and inspired him at Duruelo, Mancera and Pastrana; it was not as a visionary that he had thought of her at Alcalá de Henares. Now, though her energy was still boundless and her zeal for reform unabated, she had begun to reveal another side of her complex personality, and he was confused and troubled. On Palm Sunday, she was unable to swallow the Host when she went to Communion; apparently, she swooned at the very altar and, afterward, when she recovered consciousness, her mouth was overflowing with blood. For thirty years, it had been her custom to communicate on Palm Sunday, to take no food until midafternoon, and to give her normal portion to the poor. Now she explained her "rapture" by saying that Our Lord had spoken these words to her: "Daughter, I will that My blood be profitable to you. I shed it for you in great pain, make your greatest delight in it. This is My way of returning the invitation you have always made Me on this day."[19]

Fray Juan could not tell her that she had imagined that Our Lord had spoken to her. She was not a woman given to fantasies. Besides, he had witnessed both the fainting fit and the overflowing blood. But he wondered if Teresa should not, perhaps, be restrained in some way —a way that was not clear to him, though he vaguely connected it with the Eucharist. Hesitantly, because he could think of no other measure of wholesome humiliation, he broke the Host in two as he was administering Communion, and gave half of what would normally have been Teresa's portion to another nun. The result was even more disturbing than the occurrence on Palm Sunday: Teresa came to him with a story so extraordinary that it would have strained all his credulity if the candor and conviction with which it was related had not been so disarming and so uplifting.

"I thought you did it to mortify me," she said. "I had told you that I loved big Hosts, though I knew well enough that Our Lord was present, even in the smallest particle. Then His Majesty Himself spoke to me and said, 'Fear nothing, daughter, nothing can separate you from Me.' He made me understand that it did not matter. Then He appeared to me in an imaginary vision, as He had done before, but in the very depths of my being. He gave me His right hand and said to me: 'Look at this nail: it is the sign that from to-day you are My bride. Until now you had not merited that; in future you will be jealous for My honour not only because I am your Creator and your King, but as My true bride. My honour is yours: your honour is Mine.' "[20]

There was no doubt whatsoever that, from this day onward, Teresa dwelt more and more in realms of rapture; but Fray Juan was swift to see that the prolonged periods which she spent in a state of trance in no way impaired her efficiency in practical matters. Quite the contrary. The nuns who had hitherto remained unmoved by her appeals and his admonitions began, slowly but surely, to mend their ways. These women were not only awed by the marvels which were taking place at their convent; they were proud to feel that it had been singled out for such marks of favor and fearful lest these should be withdrawn, if the recipients were unworthy of them. So the nuns strove to deserve them, some so haphazardly or halfheartedly that there was not much merit, except in their own eyes, and no sacrifice at all; others more earnestly; a few with sincere and unremitting striving. The shabby little lies which had made the confessional a source of grief to Fray Juan were increasingly crowded out by faltering admissions of guilt; and the peccadillos which had been responsible for these untruths were less and less frequent. The pauses which marked complete omission of any avowal of downright sin grew shorter and, in their stead, came the healing flow of candid penitence and the petition for Divine pardon. The role of confessor to nearly two hundred women would never be a welcome one to a man whose love of solitude and nature came next to his love of God; but at least it ceased to be a

penance harsher than any haircloth he could have placed next to his
sensitive body. The little hermitage which had been built for him at
one end of the convent's enclosure, near the wall, did not give him
the sense of freedom which he enjoyed when he went singing along
a lonely road or sat all night before a forest stream, listening to the
sound of running water and looking up at the stars. It was neither as
isolated nor as primitive as he might have wished. He tried not to
dwell with envy on the cave where one of Avila's own saints, Pedro del
Barco, had lived in solitude for many years. Even as a youth, Pedro
had left his home for long periods and devoted himself entirely to
prayer and other pious exercises; and, after the loss of his parents, he
had withdrawn entirely to a rocky hollow on the bank of the River
Tormes, taking with him a few tools to till the nearby land for food,
but keeping no other worldly possessions. He found great spiritual
satisfaction in this lonely life, and its approaching end was announced
to him through heavenly revelation: when the water from the spring
where he drank turned to wine, he might know that his death was
near. Shortly thereafter, a young neighbor, whose friendly offices Pedro
could not decline to accept and who was his only companion, filled a
glass at this spring and brought it to the thirsty hermit, who quickly
noticed that it contained wine. He sent the boy back to the spring
and the miracle was repeated. So he knew that his hour was at hand;
and when it came, the bells in the churches of all the towns in the
Tormes Valley started to toll, though they were rung by no mortal
hand.

There was another legend about him, too: the chronicles of Pedro's
time—which was some four hundred years before the time of Fray
Juan—related that Barco and Avila disputed the possession of his holy
body and that the Bishop, Don Severo, decided that the controversy
should be settled by placing Pedro's mortal remains on the back of
a blindfolded mule. The animal travelled straight to Avila and went
directly to the Church of St. Vincent, and up to the sepulchre where
this noble martyr lies buried with his sisters, Cristeta and Sabina,
where it fell down dead. So that is where Pedro was buried. And why
should anyone doubt any part of this story, when the mark of the
mule's shoe can still be seen on the stone pavement, which was quickly
protected by a railing?

Teresa had learned this legend from her father, Don Alonso de
Cepeda, who spent much of his time reading the stories of saints with
devout avidity and acquainting his children with them; and Teresa

had made sure that Juan knew it, too. Perhaps she would not have done so if she had guessed how eagerly he would have exchanged the so-called hermitage in the garden of the Encarnación—really a very comfortable little pavilion—for a riverside cave such as Pedro del Barco had found. But this did not cross her mind. The pavilion was small and simple in comparison with the rooms occupied by the nuns, which bore little resemblance to cells, as we understand the term. Each comprised an antechamber large enough to serve as an oratory as well as a private parlor and an arched alcove for the bed; the nuns were permitted to relieve the bareness of these by paintings and other adornments, and a large window, looking out on a cloistered garden, afforded a pleasant view. When Teresa became Prioress, she had even more attractive quarters; her sleeping apartment led to her oratory by a small interior stairway, after the manner of a modern duplex, and both were spacious. Since she enjoyed such accommodations, it is not strange that she took it for granted Fray Juan enjoyed those provided for him and he did his best to suppress his longings for a cave. The pavilion might not be a real hermitage, but it was a refuge, it was a means of escape, and as often and for as long as his duties would permit, he retired to it.

His lessening sense of strain was facilitated by the fact that Teresa's supernatural powers, which at first he had regarded with normal concern, were showing results in more directions than one. Not only was her influence for good at Encarnación more and more manifest through its improved morale; she had begun to put her feelings, her ideals and her beliefs into a written form which she called, *Conceptos del Amor de Dios—Conceptions of the Love of God*. She wrote rapidly, eloquently and convincingly, as she spoke; and her written words had the same candor and the same persuasive charm as those which she pronounced aloud. She said, and she believed, that Christ Himself commanded and inspired her work and Fray Juan saw no reason why he should doubt it. She did not even qualify her statement by making one similar to that which he made somewhat later, in referring to his own work—"Sometimes I write by myself and sometimes Christ does it." As her confessor, he not only authorized her literary efforts, but approved them; and gradually he began to achieve clarity from confusion, light from darkness, hope from despair, joy from wretchedness. The mystic way was opening before him, too, and again he realized, with increasing force, that "God moves in a mysterious way His wonders to perform." He had thought to find fulfillment at

El Paular and, instead, he had been led unmistakably to Duruelo. He had left Duruelo with profound disappointment for Mancera, for Pastrana, Alcalá de Henares and Avila, in each place finding less and less of the solitude that he craved, less and less time for the contemplative life which, to him, had seemed the only possible approach to realms of mysticism. And now, in this crowded convent, amongst these troublesome and ubiquitous women, not only was his path suddenly illumined, but he learned that he, no less than Teresa, was to tread it in a manner that would often be inexplicable and sometimes abnormal.

There were many indications of this. The most striking occurred on the Feast of the Holy Trinity, when he and Teresa were conferring together, as they often did, in a small, bare, red-tiled parlor at Encarnación, where she sat on a chair inside the grille and he on a bench outside it. Suddenly their conversation, which had been on topics appropriate to the day, was engulfed in mutual ecstasy; and a nun, who was looking for the Prioress, was startled, first by the realization that neither Teresa nor Juan was aware of her presence, and then, by the sight of the latter, slowly leaving his bench as though through no volition of his own and gradually rising until his head touched the ceiling.

She fled, leaving him suspended there, and rushed to tell her fellow nuns what she had seen. All were excited and many were overwhelmed. A few tried to explain to her that she had witnessed the phenomenon of levitation.

7

At the end of three years, Teresa left Encarnación for good, and became Prioress at San José. In the meanwhile, she had been absent long enough to establish foundations at Salamanca and Segovia and to do some incidental travelling besides. Juan had accompanied her to Segovia, but had been gone, altogether, only about ten days. Except for this one short respite, he had not left Encarnación at all. When he did leave it, this was in a highly unorthodox fashion: he was twice kidnapped by the Calced Friars and imprisoned, the first time at Medina del Campo and the second, at Toledo.

The first of these two episodes, though certainly disgraceful enough, did no great or lasting harm to Fray Juan and had no remarkable results for either good or evil. The Calced Prior of the Avilese house had ordered that the poor little man should be forcibly taken to the Priory at Medina and kept there. But this unwise Prior had made the mistake of insisting that the abduction be public, the whole city had risen in an uproar of protest, and no less a personage than the Papal Nuncio, Ormaneto, had intervened: Fray Juan was to be immediately restored to Encarnación and the Calced Friars were to keep away from there. Unfortunately, this "sainted Nuncio," as Teresa called him, died shortly thereafter, and Jerónimo Tostado,[21] the Portuguese Vicar General of the Carmelites for Spain and Portugal, ordered Fray Juan and his companion at Encarnación, Fray Germán de San Matías— for there were now two confessors at the convent—to "return to one of their own houses." When they refused to do this, on the ground that the order which had sent them to Encarnación in the first place was still in force, they were abducted, with the aid of constables. After the episode at Medina del Campo, certain devoted friends, fearing the worst, had formed a voluntary guard around their tiny hermitage, and had kept watch there night and day. But when some time passed without any further untoward incident, they relaxed their vigilance, with disastrous results. Though Fray Juan, always the soul of gentleness, would never have resisted forcible arrest in any way, he was struck in the face before he was handcuffed and led off with the blood streaming down his cheeks; and, after being confined for several days at the Priory of the Observance in Avila, he was taken as a prisoner to the Priory of Toledo, through the connivance of its Prior, Maldonado. (Fray Germán was taken to La Moraleja and, after three months, escaped.)

Two charges were lodged against Juan, besides the one of disobedience to an authority which he felt he could not recognize, since the order, sending him to Encarnación, had never been revoked. The first of these was that he had "incited" the nuns to vote for Teresa's reelection as Prioress. Her three-year term had expired, and there was nothing on earth she wanted less than to have it renewed; Fray Juan realized this, and even if his own wishes had run contrary to hers— which they did not—he would have respected the latter. But fifty-five nuns had voted for her, and this represented a majority, for their number at Encarnación had been reduced to ninety-nine; now that she had left them, many had begun to realize what a treasure they had lost, and would almost have given their hope of heaven to have her back. The Provincial, who was acting under directions from Tostado, Teresa's implacable foe, excommunicated the rebellious nuns and would not permit them to hear Mass or even to go to the choir; he crushed the offending ballots underfoot, stamped on them, burned them and ordered another election. The nuns calmly replied that they had already voted and that there was no point in doing so over again. When they were forced to, the result was unchanged; and when the forty-four who had voted against Teresa in the first place did so again, the remaining fifty-five announced that they would obey her successor only as a vicar. Teresa, in writing about these unseemly proceedings to a friend, very naturally stated that she had no wish to be in the midst of such a Babylon and remained secluded at San José. Fray Juan withdrew, more resolutely than ever, to the precarious shelter of his hermitage. But his withdrawal did not save him from the wrath of Tostado; somebody had to be the nuns' whipping boy and the choice fell on their confessor.

The second charge against him was that he would not abjure the solemn oath he had taken as a member of the Reform. In some ways, the inhumanity with which he was treated seems even more terrible than the tortures to which the adherents of different forms of faith put each other, for his was essentially the same as that of his tormentors. They were all Catholics; they were all Carmelites; they said the same prayers and worshipped at the same shrines. The only difference in their way of life and of obedience was that the followers of the Reform strove, through intensified asceticism and sacrifice to correct the errors and erase the laxity that permeated the Order, and the example which they gave permitted no doubt as to the sincerity and fervor of this endeavor. But if Fray Juan had been convicted of some hideous crime, his abductors could not have shown him more cruelty. The cell in which he was imprisoned was a tiny chamber, lighted only through a grilled opening which looked out on a fortified passageway. He had only rags for a bed, only dry bread to eat. When this treatment did not break his spirit, he was taken from his cell and mercilessly flogged, night after night. He himself was characteristically silent as to the details of his terrible persecution; since it was his soul's sincere desire that he should follow as closely as possible in the footsteps of his Master, he could not possibly have disregarded the command, "Love your enemies, bless them that curse you, do good to them that hate you, and pray for them which despitefully use you and persecute you."[22] And it is possible that his distracted friends may have unconsciously magnified the tortures which he endured, especially since all their appeals in his behalf, even to the King, who had hitherto shown himself friendly to the Reform, went unanswered, and they became increasingly frantic over Fray Juan's imprisonment and the course it was taking. But even allowing for lurid exaggeration, in both contemporary and later accounts of Fray Juan's incarceration, there can unhappily be no doubt that they were based on very sad truth; they do not differ on any really important point and there is one detail which none omits and which is of extreme significance. Every night, after his "pitifully maltreated body . . . lay again in the dark hole of the cloistral wall, then suddenly another life arose in him which was not vulnerable to human hate. For it was a life that turned into song, into verse and stanza and the torment which he had suffered was changed into sweetness."[22-a]

The song was the *Spiritual Canticle* which has been defined as "the most sublime and at the same time the most passionate mystical hymn of Spanish literature—of the literature of the world."

8

As I have said, authorities differ regarding details of the severity— or rather, the inhumanity—of Fray Juan's imprisonment, though none deny that it lasted for many months and that it was characterized by extreme cruelty. In like measure, there is disagreement as to whether any, or all, of the *Spiritual Canticle* was put on paper before he was released and, also, as to the exact manner in which he was finally enabled to make his escape.

These differences of opinion do not seem to me extremely important. There is no doubt whatsoever that Fray Juan had a remarkable memory. It will be recalled that, during his stay at Duruelo, when he possessed practically no books, he spent night after night in reciting to himself long passages from the Scriptures; and the frequency of biblical allusions in his writings show that he could draw on his knowledge of it at will, without recourse to the written word. Moreover, many a far less gifted poet can compose and retain a clear mental picture of the composition for some time, without needing to write down a word of it. Therefore, it does not seem to me in the least incredible that Fray Juan never put pen to paper while he was in prison. But neither does it seem incredible that, eventually, the harshness of his treatment should have been somewhat relaxed, and that he may well have been permitted, either to have writing materials

in the cell which he usually occupied, or to have been taken, occasionally, to another where such commodities were available, especially as
there seems to be no doubt whatsoever that, during the latter part of
his incarceration, he had a jailer more humane than those who, at
first, had so terribly maltreated him.

It does not seem to me particularly important, either, whether Fray
Juan's eventual escape was due directly or indirectly to this jailer, Juan
de Santa María, or whether it should be attributed wholly to the
Blessed Virgin. Surely it constitutes no disbelief in Our Lady's powers
to suppose that she may have softened Juan de Santa María's heart,
so that he provided more light than usual to his prisoner and was
somewhat careless about bolting locks; or that she may have revealed
doors and windows to Fray Juan which were there all the time—
though he had not previously been aware of this—and suggested to
him how best to use these. Also, we may as well admit that, when
it came to finding a means of escape, Fray Juan showed himself
singularly resourceful. As a mere boy, when he decided that he should
leave the hospital where he was employed, and where he had every
prospect of profitable advancement, he had not waited to risk listening to any arguments which might cause him to change his mind; he
fled, in the dead of night, "by a ladder or secret stair," and presented
himself as a postulant to the astonished porter of Santa Ana's Convent
in Medina del Campo. Even after his second abduction at Encarnación, he had somehow managed to elude his jailers long enough to
return to his hermitage and destroy certain papers pertaining to the
Reform, the possession of which he felt would be dangerous in unfriendly hands; and though he had not quite finished his task of destruction before his pursuers caught up with him, he hastily tore into
bits and swallowed the documents that were left. His second flight
was therefore as successful as his first. Now he felt the time was ripe
to attempt a third one.

There may have been still another factor in his decision: night itself
had never held the terrors for him that it does for so many persons.
On the contrary, he had always felt that darkness was his friend; and it
was from the stars, not from the sun, that he derived the greatest
measure of comfort and inspiration. All this had been evident from
his earliest youth, both in his usual way of life and in his more precipitate actions; and, as he grew older, it was to become increasingly
apparent through his writings. The first five stanzas of the eight which
constitute *Dark Night*—the poem in which he epitomized "all the

doctrine he intended to treat"—in *The Ascent of Mount Carmel* make this feeling abundantly clear; and though the "Commentaries" on his treatise do not belong to the period of his imprisonment at Toledo, there is no doubt that *Dark Night* itself was composed then, as well as the poem in which each stanza is brought to an end with the line, "Although 'tis night!"[23]

All in all, it is quite evident that Fray Juan's mood was one which would predispose him to make an attempt at escape; and, this being the case, he would certainly not have resisted any loophole which his kindly jailer could give him, much less any phenomenon which might be interpreted as intervention in his behalf on the part of Our Lady. Choosing the Feast of the Assumption, so essentially associated with her, he knotted some of his rags together in a makeshift rope, located a possible egress, reached it without difficulty or interference and slid, unharmed, to the ground. He had no idea where he was or where to go next. For lack of any better guide, he followed a hungry dog who was prowling about, looking for food. And when this dog jumped over a wall, Fray Juan gathered up his tattered skirts and jumped, too. This time, he landed in a courtyard. It proved to be the patio of Teresa's convent in Toledo.

Within a matter of minutes, he was safe in the infirmary; within a matter of hours his hunger was stayed, his wounds dressed, his every physical and spiritual need receiving loving attention. Within a matter of days, he was taken to the hospitable home of Don Pedro González de Mendoza, a canon of the cathedral. Before he left there to attend a meeting of the Discalced Superiors in Almodóvar, at the request of his old friend, Antonio de Jesús, who had now become a personage of great power and prestige in the Reform, many stanzas[24] of the *Spiritual Canticle* and several other beautiful poems, among them the two to which I have referred, were on paper. All danger that they would be lost to the world was over.

9

When Fray Juan left Toledo for Almodóvar, he was still so weak that the kindly Canon insisted two of his own servants should attend the friar on his journey and remain with him until his strength was fully restored. They were still with him when, after a stormy meeting of the Discalced Superiors, which had no important results as far as he

was concerned, Fray Juan left for Beas, in the Province of Jaén, close
to the borderline between Castile and Andalucía. Teresa, whose foundations were constantly being located farther and farther afield, had
established a convent there and it seemed a logical stopping place
on the way to Escalona, his eventual destination. It proved to be
something far more significant than that. Its Prioress, Ana de Jesús,
was a very remarkable woman: a native of Medina del Campo, she
had taken the habit of the Reform at San José in Avila, and thence
had gone to Salamanca, where she was professed; she was one of the
first nuns sent to Beas and, from the outset, had made her mark there.
She and Fray Juan were already kindred spirits; now she proved herself his wise counselor as well, for it was due to her emphatic advice
that he was persuaded that he should write "Commentaries" on the
Spiritual Canticle and *The Ascent of Mount Carmel*. It is no exaggeration to say that, in a large measure, his permanent fame as a great
mystical writer rests with her, since, had it not been for her insistence,
he might very well have pursued his literary career no further. With
characteristic humility, he failed to recognize his great gifts and, for
the time being, he was spared the suffering which, in his case, gave
rise to such inimitable expression. But at Beas the process of putting
words on paper gradually became a habit with him; it was a habit by
which posterity has been greatly enriched.

From Beas, Fray Juan went to nearby El Calvario, where he had
been appointed temporary Vicar by the Chapter at Almodóvar; and
there he began the "Commentaries" on the *Spiritual Canticle* and *The
Ascent of Mount Carmel*, based on the poem, *Dark Night*. From a
present-day standpoint, this was certainly his most important achievement there; from the standpoint of the nuns at Beas, it was probably
far more important that, every Saturday, he interrupted his writing
and went—on foot—from El Calvario to Beas, in order to hear their
confessions. Far from hurrying them through these, as his predecessor had done, he stayed with them all that day and at least part of the
next, allowing them as much time as they wanted or needed to un-
burden their hearts to him in secret. But he did more than this: besides the hours he devoted to the confessional, he devoted many others
to making informal speeches, to reading his poems aloud, and to encouraging his charges to ask him questions. In a word, he was not
only their spiritual adviser; he was their teacher and their friend; and
far from finding this association an ordeal, as he had the one at En-

carnación, he was happy in it himself, while giving to others infinite joy.

It was with great regret that he left these quiet places to assume new duties which had been assigned him in the foundation of a college for Discalced Carmelites at Baeza. Granted that he was supremely well fitted for this task scholastically, with the background which Salamanca and Alcalá de Henares had given him; granted that he achieved tremendous success at the institution he established, the first of its kind in Andalucía; and granted that he found time, in the midst of his administrative and teaching duties, to continue his writing: nevertheless, the contemplative, rather than the active way of life, was his not only by predilection; it was his by supreme capacity for it. Whether he or Teresa were the greater mystic may be open to doubt; but there is no doubt whatsoever that his mysticism took a different form from hers. It had a more ethereal and, consequently, a more fragile quality. She could spend hours in a state of rapture, oblivious of everything that was taking place around her, and emerge from it to go over household accounts with a thoroughness and accuracy which would identify the expenditure of every penny; or, with equal ease, she could start off on a jaunt which would cover hundreds of miles; or, still with equal ease, she could enter into argument with some hostile churchman and keep on talking until she had worn him down and won her point. Fray Juan could do none of these things, and the very idea of attempting them was abhorrent to him. What was more, he had a very human dislike for the people in that part of Spain where Fate had now set him down. Teresa put the matter bluntly. "Fray Juan," she said, "cannot endure the Andalusians." She did not like them very well herself, and she not only understood his aversion to their languorous and luxurious ways, but shared this. From the first, she had known that one of their points of congeniality—and, consequently, of joint effectiveness—lay in the fact that they were not only both Castilians, but both *Avileses*; but since change of scene, turbulent activity, and toilsome travel were as meat and drink to her, she did not pine for her native province, when away from it, as he did.

It was two years before his exile ended, even briefly, and in the meantime he had filled a number of offices in various places, all efficiently, but all reluctantly, and he had suffered a great personal loss: his mother had died in the epidemic of influenza which was sweeping over Spain. It was as severe at Baeza as elsewhere and, for a time, the Carmelite College seemed more like the hospital where Fray Juan had worked as a boy than like the institution of learning of which he was the head. Again, he devoted himself to the care of the sick and dying, finding a certain amount of solace in this labor of love; but it was hard to think that none of this was of any benefit to the mother from whom he had been parted so long and from whom he had not been able to take even a last farewell. True, he knew that his brother, Francisco, and his sister-in-law, Ana, with whom Catalina Alvarez had continued to live, had done everything in their power for her; and the Carmelite nuns of Medina del Campo—Teresa's first foundation outside of Avila—offered their chapel for her burial and gave her a beautiful tomb. But the knowledge that his long separation from her was now final added to Fray Juan's general feeling of depression and nostalgia.

When he finally went back to Avila, the trip was a short one, as time was reckoned in those days, and was undertaken for a definite purpose, with the understanding that, when this had been accomplished, he was to go to Los Mártires, in Granada, where he had been appointed Prior, and to hold this office in conjunction with his rectorship at Baeza. A number of prominent families had united in a request that a convent of Carmelite Nuns should also be opened in Granada. Ana de Jesús was inclined to doubt the wisdom of such a move, because so many religious orders had been established there since the Conquest. But she had consulted Fray Juan, who was still her confessor and more than ever her friend, and he had shown himself favorably disposed toward the idea. So it was decided that he should make the journey to Avila, confer with Teresa, who was at San José, and, if possible, persuade her to return to Granada with him and establish the foundation.

He undertook the journey joyfully. Not only did he welcome the chance of getting back to Avila, however briefly, but the prospect of having Teresa near him again filled him with untold happiness. Ana de Jesús was, indeed, his valued friend; but Teresa was more than that: she was the mother from whom his vocation had parted him, the sweetheart he had never possessed, the associate whose companionship—unlike all others—brought him into close communion with God, instead of tending to separate him from the Divine Presence. He no longer thought of her as the aristocrat whose birth and breeding set her apart from a peasant like himself, the practical woman of affairs who was, naturally, impatient with a dreamer, the zealot whose fervor gave her too little time for reflection. It did not matter any more that she was a working and he a praying mystic; they were both mystics, each in a good way; moreover, they were both writers now and their writings, which would reach many people they did not meet in person, were a great responsibility. There was much they should discuss together, there was more that they should do. With Teresa beside him, the luxuriance of Andalucía would cease to seem more like a desert place than that rock-bound countryside from which they had both sprung. In common with many Spaniards, Fray Juan thought and spoke of his birthplace not as his country—*su patria*—but as his land—*su tierra*; in common with many others, he spoke of the town from which he came not as his village—*su aldea,* but as his people—*su pueblo.* Teresa and he belonged to the same *tierra,* the same *pueblo.* That was the common background which was part of their common bond. Their common goal, which was the other part of it, was that Mount of Perfection which they were trying to reach by treading the mystic way.

Fray Juan arrived in Avila, well equipped with mules and carts for the return journey to Andalucía, in time to be present at the profession of Ana de los Angeles, to whom Teresa generally referred as "the Flemish nun." After the ceremony was over, he and Teresa spent a long evening in conference together. During the course of this, she convinced him that she herself could not undertake a foundation at Granada just then, as she was already committed to Burgos for her next project; but she had made preparations for two of her "daughters" to accompany him, and they were to be joined at Beas by several others, including Ana de Jesús. She thought he had better be on his way early the next morning. . . .

It did not occur to her that Fray Juan was heartbroken until he had actually started. She had been glad to see him, but she had been preoccupied with the young nun who was just professed—another little white lamb brought into the fold of the Good Shepherd!—and with plans for the new convent in Burgos, where a warm welcome awaited her, instead of the doubtful one she would have had in Granada. Ana de Jesús, who was to be the first Prioress there, was quite capable of coping with that situation. And there was no reason why she should not do so. She was in the prime of life, able to bear the heat and burden of the day, whereas Teresa was growing old. She felt she was justified in thinking the time had come when she could take things a little more easily.

So she told herself, with no qualms of conscience. Then, as the creaking of the carts which were leaving San José died away in the distance, she heard another sound beside that and the clatter of the mules' hooves against the cobblestones. It was the sound of singing, and the voice was that of Fray Juan. She had known for a long time that it was his way to sing when he suffered and, all at once, she realized with a pang what this parting must have meant to him. The pang would have been even greater if she had also realized that she would never see him again.

10

Within two months after his final parting from Teresa, who died shortly thereafter, Fray Juan had taken office as the Prior of the Monastery of Los Mártires in Granada, and for the next six years it was to be his working center, though he was frequently expected to absent himself from it, in connection with this work.

He had begun it in sadness of spirit. But the new duties he was called upon to assume, and the surroundings in which most of these were performed, were not without their compensations. In the first place, the setting of Los Mártires was such that it could not fail to give him joy; the Priory was situated on a height which commanded an unobstructed view of a proud city, a countryside of unsurpassable fecundity and a majestic mountain range. Nearby were the Alhambra and the Generalife palaces, with their glittering fountains and flowering gardens; between these and the domes and turrets of Granada were fruitful orchards; and beyond was the Vega—the great plain with its winding rivers, its fields and vineyards, and its straight roads bordered by poplars; then, rising to meet the blue of the sky, the snows of the Sierras. A man to whom natural beauty was a never-failing source of both delight and inspiration could hardly have imagined, much less required, a scene more completely soul satisfying.

In the second place, Fray Juan was blessed from the beginning in his association with two women whose effect upon his later life, as a poet, as a priest and as a man, it is almost impossible to overestimate. His friend, Ana de Jesús, acting in Teresa's behalf, had arrived in Granada at the same time he did, bringing with her the nuns chosen to help her establish the foundation over which there had been so much controversy. At first, these pioneering women had not been able to obtain a house of their own which would serve as a convent; but

Reproduction of title page in 1649 edition of *The Works of St. John of the Cross.*

meanwhile they had been kindly received by Ana de Peñalosa, a wealthy widow, a Segovian by birth and background, who was living temporarily in Granada with her brother, Don Luis de Mercado, an auditor in the Chancery there. For seven months the nuns were the grateful recipients of the hospitality generously offered by these two; and during that interval Fray Juan was also their beneficiary. The friendship with Ana de Peñalosa, like that with Ana de Jesús, was destined to have results of far greater significance than any of those who formed the compact little circle could possibly have foreseen. Just as at El Calvario he had begun his "Commentaries" on *The Ascent of Mount Carmel* and the *Spiritual Canticle* because Ana de Jesús had been so insistent that he should do so, now—still urged on by her—Fray Juan finished *The Ascent of Mount Carmel* and the first redaction of the *Spiritual Canticle* and wrote *The Dark Night of the Soul*. This, perhaps, was not astonishing, granted her earlier evaluation of his writing, and the fact that her estimate of it was based less on its literary than on its spiritual importance. But that Ana de Peñalosa should have recognized both, and that her influence with him should have been strong enough to persuade him to compose *The Living Flame of Love*,[24-a] is nothing short of amazing.

For Ana de Peñalosa, though devout and intelligent, was not a nun, much less a mystic; she was very much a woman of the world, while Fray Juan was more and more a recluse and an ascetic by natural inclination. Yet such was the bond between them that, at her instigation, he wrote, in less than a fortnight, this poem, which has been called "the last and sublimest account which Fray Juan has given of life on the mystical height,"[25] and dedicated it to her. Even Teresa had never inspired such an outpouring of faith and fervor. Like many another man before and since, he had found that figuratively, even more than literally, the words graven on the façade of the great house of Dávila were true: "For every door that is closed, another one will open."[26]

But he had need of all the solace and support which he could derive from the contemplation of nature and the companionship of the two Anas. He still hated to travel almost as much as Teresa had enjoyed it; but with Granada as his center and his position as Prior there his paramount occupation, he was called upon to found convents and priories in Málaga, Córdoba, La Manchuela de Jaén and Caravaca; to attend Chapter meetings at Pastrana, Lisbon—where he was appointed Second Definitor and Vicar Provincial of Andalucía—Valladolid—where he was re-elected Prior of Los Mártires—and Madrid—where he was appointed a First Definitor and a *consilario*.[26-a] In between times, he visited Baeza, Beas, Ecija, Bujalance and Guadalcazar —where he fell gravely ill; presided at the re-election of Ana de Jesús as Prioress at Granada and conducted two elections for later prioresses there; and six years after becoming Prior at Los Mártires was permanently removed from Granada to assume the duties of Prior at Segovia.

This removal was not, as might well have been expected, in the nature of a well-deserved promotion and a promise of well-earned rest. It was a step deliberately taken to sidetrack and silence him; and though he was not physically maltreated in Segovia, as he had been in Toledo, and eventually not only resigned himself to his transfer, but rejoiced in it, he must have suffered great spiritual anguish when he first learned of it. For this time, not even dissension between two branches of the same Order—the Calced and Discalced Carmelites— could be held responsible for what had happened; it could be laid only to the mutual jealousy and mutual suspicion on the part of two of the most powerful clerics in Spain, *both* members of the Reform: the Castilian, Jerónimo de la Madre de Dios, better known as Gracián; and the Genoese, Nicolás de Jesús María, better known as Doria. This antagonism—in which different nationalities may well have played a part, for Spaniards and Italians frequently failed to see eye to eye— developed into an outright feud. Fray Juan was one of its innocent victims.

It is difficult to untwist the many tangled threads interwoven in the tortuous history of these two men and those who suffered because of their enmity. In order to explain, however inadequately, what happened to Fray Juan and why, it seems necessary to digress temporarily from his story and to trace first the story of Gracián and then the story of Doria, not from the time these began to affect the poor little Prior, but from their very beginning.

Gracián was a native of Valladolid and his parents were both persons of distinguished background. His mother, Juana Dantisco, was the daughter of the Polish Ambassador. His father, Diego Gracián de Alderete—the son of the Catholic Kings' chief armorer—had been secretary to Charles V. Two of his brothers were secretary to Philip II and a third secretary to the Queen Regent of Sicily; a similar position was open to still another member of the family, but this one apparently never considered any calling other than that of the priesthood. He was studying at the University of Alcalá de Henares when

Fray Juan arrived there, and long before he became personally acquainted with Teresa, he was a disciple of the Reform. While still a
novice himself, he was chosen as novice master and within four
months after making his profession, he was appointed Apostolic
Visitor to the Calced Carmelites of Andalucía. He had marked gifts
as a speaker and was imbued with great missionary fervor. Candid,
singlehearted, devout and gracious, it is not strange that he became
a very general favorite; and Teresa, who met him for the first time
at Beas, when she went there to establish the first foundation at any
distance from Avila, was so impressed by him from the moment of
their meeting that she made a voluntary vow of obedience to him.
As a matter of fact, however, she had singled him out, almost instantly, as her most promising partner in the Reform, and in this
partnership she meant to be the senior rather than the junior member.
"Although he was not of the first, he came at the right moment."
The "first" were, of course, Antonio de Jesús and Juan de la Cruz;
but "Antonio lacked common sense, he was touchy and given to
romancing; as to Fray Juan, the incomparable angel of *The Dark
Night*, he still sought to escape the all-absorbing effort which foundations meant, with their worldly contacts, business and diplomacy; it
was only much later that he adapted himself to all this. And then,
Teresa could not manage him as she pleased, even the most intelligent saint cannot manage an archangel. On the other hand, she could
manage Padre Jerónimo Gracián. . . . As quickly as possible, the
Foundress wrote to Philip II, begging him to divide the Mitigated and
Discalced Friars into separate provinces: she had at last found the
man who could assume responsibility for the Reformed Order."[27]

Her enthusiasm knew no bounds. Like most Spaniards, she was
addicted to the use of nicknames and she called Gracián "my Paul"—
because he was alternately so joyous and so depressed—and "my
Eliseus"—because his head was large and bald. She also referred to
him as an angel, and in many other terms scarcely less extravagant,
asserting that she would never spend happier days than those she had
spent with him. "Because he gave her a sense of security and peace,
he meant much to her and soon became indispensable. And then he
was not 'dour'; even in the first days of their acquaintance, he made
her laugh."[28] Teresa was always seeking security and peace and she
loved to laugh. She could not praise her new friend too highly, either
to his face or in speaking and writing about him to others, and she
did all three with frequency.

The enthusiasm was mutual. Gracián felt sure that Teresa was divinely inspired; he did not question her claim to deep spiritual intimacy with Our Lord, or the celestial origin of her voices and visions, whereas Fray Juan had never hesitated to say that he thought at least some of all this was the figment of a lively imagination. What was even more significant, practically speaking, was the fact that Gracián felt her so well qualified, in every way, to establish more foundations that he urged her to go still farther afield—namely, to Seville—and gave her the most glowing accounts of the city, its people, and its possibilities, as far as the Carmelite Order was concerned. When she hesitated, he reminded her that she had promised him obedience and said this was a command. After that, she hesitated no longer. She set out, accompanied by six other nuns, three friars and the inevitable muleteers and, after a terrible journey, reached Seville to find no one ready to welcome them with kindness and nothing but an unfurnished hovel offered them for their reception.

These handicaps were overcome in due course and did no lasting harm. But unfortunately, when Gracián insisted that Teresa should go to Seville, he had acted in defiance of a decision made by the Most Reverend Father, Juan Bautista Rubeo, Master General of the Carmelite Order, and it was not the first time that he had laid himself open to the charge of disobedience. Hitherto, he had escaped grave censure; now Rubeo was violently angry and the consequences were serious.

Gracián has been described as "impetuous rather than courageous"[29] and, as time went on, Teresa had more than one occasion to suffer from his errors in judgment. But to do him justice, he certainly had not been guided solely by impulse and intuition in this instance. On the contrary, he had powerful support, for both the Pope and the King had approved the new foundation, and the Nuncio, Ormaneto, had actually ordered it and confirmed his order. But Rubeo had not authorized it and this was another case where jealousy entered the picture; he considered that his authority was being flouted and he did not propose to permit this to happen, even though his opponents were at the head of church and state. His rage was not confined to Gracián, it included the saintly friar, Mariano de San Benito, who had accompanied Gracián to Andalucía, and Teresa herself. He prepared a brief of recall for the two friars, which he proposed to present at the forthcoming General Order of the Chapter; and though he had formerly been a good friend of Teresa and encouraged her to expand her foundations, he now left her letters of explanation and supplication unanswered and, through his lack of support, exposed her to the dangers of the Inquisition.

In time, Rubeo's wrath spent itself. Tostado, his Delegate to Spain —the same man who, shortly thereafter, was responsible for Fray Juan's imprisonment in Toledo—failed to wrest from Ormaneto "the desired permission to disturb the Reformed Convents" and left for Portugal "where it was hoped he might remain."[30] Though confusion and ill-feeling continued to prevail between the Calced and Discalced Carmelites, Mariano and Gracián were not officially recalled and went on with their work as best they could, while Teresa emerged unscathed from the Tribunal of the Inquisition. But the death of Ormaneto, the Nuncio who had been so friendly to the Reform, was a great blow to it; and his successor, Sega, sided with its enemies and detractors. While he did not withdraw Gracián's mandate as Visitor, he forbade the latter to exercise the duties and privileges of this office, even to the extent of going officially to a single convent. The King, who was not in the same accord with the new Nuncio as he had been with Sega's predecessor, and also the Council of Castile expressed the opinion that Gracián should be permitted to do so; but their support was couched in rather tepid terms. He withdrew, first to Alcalá and then to Pastrana and lived the retired life of a hermit, at first openly and then somewhat furtively. In the beginning this furtiveness was rather annoying to Teresa. ("Let your Paternity tell me where you are, for charity's sake, and not play the fool when I have something to inform you!" she wrote him.) And in the end it proved futile; the spies of Sega, who had excommunicated him, ferreted out the unfortunate man and, acting upon the Nuncio's orders, clapped him into a Madrid prison. Although he was tolerably well treated there, he did not accept his captivity with resignation, and again Teresa, who was slowly discovering that her idol had feet of clay, remonstrated with him, reminding him with what saintly patience Fray Juan had accepted not only incarceration, but horrible maltreatment. Probably the comparison was not especially pleasing to Gracián, though he did not need Teresa's reminder to recognize its truth. At all events, he continued his complaints until the King put an end to his imprisonment, not because of any greater sympathy for Gracián than for numerous other victims of Sega's wrath, but because the open dissension between the Calced and the Discalced had finally got on his nerves. He rapped out an order that it must cease and Sega dared not disobey. One after another, the Discalced Friars came out of their hiding places and their prisons and, within three years, Gracián had recovered enough of his lost standing to win the election for Discalced Provincial at the so-called "Separation" Chapter held at Alcalá de Henares. But this was by a very narrow margin; and though for the next four years, when he was succeeded as Provincial by Fray Nicolás de Jesús María—better known as Doria—his history was that of the Reform, he never entirely regained his prestige. Throughout the period of his trial and imprisonment, Doria himself had been mercilessly undermining this, despite the fact that he had taken the Discalced habit from Gracián's very hands.

As has already been pointed out, Doria was not a Spaniard, but an Italian, the scion of a noble Genoese family, and he continued to be called by the surname he had borne in the world, even after he entered the religious life, which he did not do until he had established an international reputation as a shrewd and skillful banker. It was in this capacity that he attracted the attention of King Philip II, who was nothing if not shrewd and skillful himself, and of Cristóbal de Rojas, Archbishop of Seville, who had allowed the financial affairs of the archdiocese to fall into some disorder. He had been made very welcome at Court and had enjoyed himself there. It was not until after Gracián's conflict with Sega had begun, when the former had already been a priest for seven years and an Apostolic Visitor for six, that Señor Nicolás Doria took the Discalced habit at Los Remedios from Gracián's hands; and he remained as useful and, consequently, as welcome at Court in his clerical as in his commercial guise and his advancement was rapid. At the "Separation" Chapter at which Gracián was elected Discalced Provincial by such a narrow majority, Doria was elected First Definitor, which put still more power into his hands; and when, four years later, he supplanted Gracián as Provincial, he did not rest until he had brought about the other's ruin. But long before that, he had been secretly undermining the man whose candor and singleheartedness made him slow to suspect the devious ways of others, and Doria was exceedingly adroit. "In the eyes of the Mitigated, he came to pass for an eccentric whose wits the yoke of the Reform had dulled, and when the Nuncio imprisoned those he felt most important among Discalced Friars, he left the 'good Nicolás' severely alone and free for any business that offered. He showed marvelous astuteness in living in the very monastery of the Calced Friars in Madrid. . . . He succeeded in concealing from the Mitigated Friars all his relations with the Spanish Court and with Rome, and the fact that he had the entrée to the King's person daily enabled him to set things in motion on behalf of the Reform."[31]

Teresa was only one of many who "never ceased to praise him." The credulous even went so far as to believe that the huge black and white Dane, which accompanied "this cunning Italian to the very doors of the great" and effectually intimidated them, had been miraculously provided by St. Dominic. In the early days of the Reform, Teresa had stopped at the cave where this saint had dwelt, midway between Segovia and Avila, and had begged him for his support, which he had promised, appearing to her in a vision. Since then, he had kept his promise in many different ways; and now, here was this great dog whose markings were in St. Dominic's colors! Nobody seemed to know where it had come from and, when there was no further need of intimidation, it disappeared. Was there not something supernaturally significant about this?

In time, these trusting souls changed their minds; for Doria "did not hesitate to scheme until he was governing the Councils of Spain in a way exactly opposite to Gracián's government and the Teresian tradition." Fray Juan was one of those who had "supported Gracián strongly against Doria's innovation." His removal from Los Mártires and his appointment as Prior of Segovia marked the beginning of his punishment for this.

He had not been unhappy in Granada. To a great degree, he had overcome his aversion to Andalucía by practicing what he preached: that if you offer love, you will receive it in return. ("Where there is no love, put love and you will draw forth love.") He had also learned to take travel in his stride, so to speak; he always managed to find time to look up at the stars and study the Scriptures, even when he was denied the seclusion that he considered ideal for his favorite pursuits; and though he had not achieved, at Los Mártires, the complete solitude for which he yearned, he had been able to order his life there, between trips, in such a way that there were many periods when he was relatively undisturbed, and therefore free for contemplation, in surroundings of natural beauty such as his soul craved; and he found release in his writing and joy in the friendship of the two Anas. Naturally, he was deeply disturbed by the dissension responsible for his removal, but, far from resenting the rebuke implied by his appointment to Segovia, it gave him some personal pleasure. It was not quite like going to Avila, which would have been going home. But it was the next best thing to this, for Avila was actually within walking distance, and the characteristics of the countryside and its inhabitants were much the same in the two provinces. Furthermore, he could still count on the largesse of the two Anas, both materially and spiritually: Ana de Peñalosa supplied him with funds for a new Priory and when she could not see him, she corresponded with him constantly. Ana de Jesús went still further; convinced that the action of Doria in dismissing Fray Juan as Prior at Los Mártires contravened the intentions of Teresa, she appealed to Rome in Fray Juan's behalf.

"Doria raged: then with resolute craft he made his plan. The Pope was ill, and it was managed to postpone action till he was actually dead. Doria had time to do his work. By treacherous translations, he succeeded in giving a false idea of the testament of Teresa. But this proved ineffective. In the meantime, he cut off all communications with the nuns, and refused to make arrangements for administering the convents. The nuns had asked to have Fray Juan as their visitor. He better than any other knew the mind of Teresa. It was also suspected that his advice was the motive power behind their successful appeal to Rome; and after fresh intrigues in various directions, a chapter of the order was convened at Madrid by Doria on May 30, 1591.

"It had some interesting business to discuss: what to do with the nuns, what to do with Gracián, and how to apply some three hundred new regulations worked out by Doria. The expedient of exile to Mexico, first devised for Gracián, was now applied to Juan de la Cruz.

" 'He saw,' says Mrs. Cunninghame Graham, 'the abyss into which Doria, blinded by his gigantic personal ambition, was bent on plunging not only himself but the order. He disapproved the constant and contradictory changes introduced into its constitution, subversive of all discipline and the origin of confusion. He pleaded—and we may judge (in spite of the carefully-worded and biassed words of the chronicler) that he pleaded ably and well—in favour of Gracián. Forecasting the future, he warned them against taking any cruel and hasty resolution which they must afterwards repent. He pleaded for the nuns, and deprecated the Vicar General's harshness in chastising all for the fault of one or two—if fault there was. His noble and dispassionate words produced no effect on the passionate and prejudiced audience around him; for since the Priors had been deprived of a seat in the chapters, Doria had no difficulty in filling it with his own creatures who owed all to him. Suspicious of Fray Juan's complicity in the action taken by Ana de Jesús, knowing that if the Bull granted by Sixtus V was confirmed the office of Commissary General of the nuns would naturally fall on one of the heads of the order (and who more likely than San Juan de la Cruz?) Doria hastened to annul his appointment to the Provincialate of the Indies, bestowed on him by that very chapter—an election which had already afforded a theme for murmuring tongues, so obviously was it an attempt to secure his absence from Spain.'

"Juan, therefore, was disgraced, was deprived of his offices, and made again a simple friar."[32]

If he grieved, if he felt dishonored and abased, nothing in his conduct or his writings betrayed this, and it is quite probable that, because of his essential humility, the letters which he wrote at this time are completely sincere. " 'Now that I am free,' he said, in one to Ana de Jesús, 'and no longer have charge of souls, I can, by Divine favour, if I so desire, enjoy peace, solitude, and the delectable fruits of forgetfulness of the self and of all things; and so for others, it is good for them also to be without me as they will then be free from the faults which they would have committed through my unworthiness.' "[33]

In this spirit, he went off to exile on the lonely rock of La Peñuela and there he "lived as he had always lived. In the earliest morning he rose to praise God in wild scenes: he spent much time alone: he knew that Doria had sent a friar to gather accusations against him, that every effort was being made to discredit him in order to expel him from the order, as Gracián was to be expelled and driven out of Spain. But he did not realize how far injustice could be pushed. 'They cannot take the habit from me,' he wrote, 'even for incorrigibility and disobedience, and I am quite prepared to amend my ways in all wherein I have strayed, and to be obedient, whatsoever penance they give me.' "[34]

There is a difference of opinion among authorities as to whether this was the last letter he ever wrote. Some believe it was written from La Peñuela, before he left on his final earthly journey, the one which took him to Ubeda; others that it was written after he reached there. A slight disparity of dates and scene does not matter very much, in my opinion; what really matters is that this letter shows the sublimity of his spirit, when he knew his life was drawing to an end—for that he did know this I cannot help believing, despite the cheerful tone of the letter. And what is even more significant—or it seems to me—

is the letter he wrote to Ana de Peñalosa just before he started on the last stretch of his rough road.

La Peñuela, September 21, 1591.

Jesus be in your soul, daughter. Here at La Peñuela I received the packet of letters which the servant brought me. I greatly appreciate the trouble you have taken. Tomorrow I go to Ubeda to cure a slight bout of fever, for I have been having attacks of it daily for over a week, and if it does not go I think I shall need medical aid; but I go with the intention of returning here again, for in truth I am deriving great good from this holy retreat; and thus, concerning your caution to me not to go with Fray Antonio, be assured that, both in this and in all the rest that you ask, I will act with all possible care.

I am delighted that Señor Don Luis is now a priest of the Lord. May this be so for many years and may His Majesty fulfil the desires of his heart! Oh, what a happy state it would be to leave behind one's anxieties and to enrich the soul speedily with Him! Give him my good wishes. I do not venture to ask him to remember me sometimes when he is at the Sacrifice; I myself, as his debtor, shall do this always for him; for although I am forgetful I could never fail to remember him, since he is so near to his sister, whom I have always in my memory.

Give my daughter Doña Inéz[35] my many greetings in the Lord and pray both of you that He may be pleased to prepare me to be taken to be with Him.

Now I can think of no more to say, and so, on account of the fever, I stop, though I would gladly go on.[36]

If there is a slight prevarication here, I think Fray Juan should be forgiven it. He was writing to a woman "whom he had always in his memory" and who, he knew, always had him in hers; he did not want her to be anxious on his account. But his "bout of fever" was by no means slight. He was a sick man when he left La Peñuela, a much sicker one when he arrived at Ubeda; and, instead of receiving the devoted care on which he had counted, he was the victim of the Prior of Ubeda, Francisco Crisóstomo, who had long nurtured a grudge against him because of a well-deserved reprimand, and who saw in Fray Juan's pitiable condition an opportunity for revenge. Until Fray Juan's old friend, Antonio de Jesús, now Provincial for Upper Andalucía, who felt concern about him, appeared on the scene and took charge of the situation, the dying man was lodged in the convent's meanest cell; and the physicians who were called upon to minister to him, far from relieving his pain, added to it by their harsh and ignorant treatment. After Antonio's arrival, and in no small measure due to this, Fray Juan's sufferings were mitigated and the stony-hearted Prior repented of his conduct and prayed for forgiveness. A well-meaning effort was even made to distract the sufferer by bringing in some musicians to sing to him.

But he did not want or need their songs. He had other music on which to draw. He quoted from the Sweet Singer of Israel: "I was glad when they said unto me we will go into the house of the Lord." And, as the hour of death drew nearer, he began to recite the rapturous words of the *Song of Songs*. A bell was tolling for midnight when he breathed his last words: "Unto Thy hands, O Lord, I commend my spirit."

There had not been a syllable of complaint, of recrimination or of despair. To the very end, he had sung when he suffered.[37]

María Vela with the Virgin and Child from a painting in the Convent
of Santa Ana, Avila. By special permission of the Prioress and Community
of Santa Ana.

PART IV

The Strong Woman of Santa Ana
(The Venerable María Vela, 1561—1617)

1

SHE HAD very beautiful hands—smooth, slim and translucently white, except for the tapering tips and the small oval nails, which were delicately rosy. Indeed, no one could fail to mark the loveliness of these hands, and María Vela was conscious of admiring glances, even when nothing was said, though comments were also frequent, more frequent perhaps than was altogether fitting in the Cistercian Convent of Santa Ana at Avila, where María Vela was a novice. She tried to pretend she did not hear the comments, and to discourage these in other ways, too, when that did not work; and, as far as possible, she ignored the glances, though they often brought a blush to her pale cheeks. Moreover, as much as she could, she concealed her hands under her scapular, as was prescribed by the Rule of the Order. But many of María Vela's duties required that they should be exposed. She was a skilled musician and, in addition to having a pleasant singing voice, learned with ease to play any available instrument; it was therefore natural that she should have been chosen as organist in the choir. She was also an accomplished needlewoman, and was called upon to embroider frontals for the altar, besides being in demand for many similar tasks of lesser importance; and she was an expert in the manufacture of those artificial flowers which were in constant demand for the adornment of all the statues and shrines in the convent, during the long cold winters when there was no natural bloom in Avila. So, all in all, her hands were exposed a large part of the time, and she could not help having them seen by others and seeing them herself.

Neither could she help knowing they were beautiful, even if she did not listen to the flattering comments or meet the admiring glances. Beauty was roundabout her in every imaginable form: in the winding

"The Gothic cathedral guarded by stone lions." From a photograph by Mayoral, Avila.

stream that flowed through the fields, in the open plazas shaded by splendid trees, in the narrow streets lined with noble houses, in the secret patios with their tiles and fountains, in the Gothic cathedral guarded by stone lions, in the Churches of San Vicente, San Pedro, Santo Tomás and a dozen others and, most of all, of course, in the great walls with their towering merlons and monumental gateways. Every one of these sights was permeated with beauty and every one had been familiar to her since childhood. To be sure, she did not see them any more, now that she was cloistered; but she could never forget them, and she was still conscious of beauty in many forms here at Santa Ana: in the shrines and statues which she helped to adorn, in the lofty rooms beamed with great rafters, such as the one Isabel of Castile had occupied when she was a young princess, in the brilliant sky framed by the arcades of the long corridors. And besides the beauty of these inanimate things, there was also the inescapable beauty of human beings. The Abbess was beautiful, in a stern remote way, and María Vela's closest confidante, Doña María de Avila, was beautiful in quite a different way. She was the daughter of a great family, niece of a cardinal and sister of an archdeacon, who had made her profession while María Vela herself was still a novice; and she had a singularly sunny disposition; she was always merry and friendly herself and her merriment and friendliness were contagious. Perhaps it was only this loving kindness of hers which produced an illusion of beauty. But, if that were the case, then the illusion seemed like a reality.

María Vela found it hard to believe that if beauty were in any way allied to wickedness Our Blessed Saviour would have created it and inspired men to create it in such abundance and in so many different forms; but since she had been taught that all vanity was a sin, and was fearful that the beauty of her hands might make her vain, she whipped them with cords, though such an action was no part of her prescribed penance; and when other novices mentioned this, she told them, almost fiercely, that she wanted her hands to look as they would after she was dead. There was something akin to anger in the way she lashed them, and she also had been taught that anger in itself was a sin and could not possibly lead to holiness of life. As a matter of fact, her hands did not really present a great temptation to her, for she did not want to be beautiful nearly as much as she wanted to be brave and strong; but all the beauty of Avila was inseparably allied with strength. According to legend, Hercules had founded it, giving it the name of Avila after one of his columns,[1] and Julius Caesar had made it a stronghold. There was an ancient rhyme, inscribed on the walls, which ran:

> *Hercules me edificó,*
> *Julio Cesar me cercó*
> *de muros y torres altas,*
> *y el rey Santo me ganó*
> *Con Garci Perez de Vargas.*[2]

María Vela had paused, many a time, to trace the words of this inscription with her beautiful fingers and to repeat the words which she knew how to decipher, thanks to the excellent education her mother had given her. She would have preferred to think that the origin of Avila was Christian—but then, since it had existed long before the birth of Our Lord, that was obviously impossible. There was another inscription on the walls which read:

> B.V.R.R.
> A.Q.LL.
> O.AB.S.M.F.

Though María Vela would not have been able to decipher this without assistance, her mother's confessor, who was also her own, had helped her to do so; he told her this stood for: *Bruto Valerio Rufo Romano, Aulus Quintilius Legislator Ordinis Abulense memoriam fecit,* and that this translated meant: *Aulus Quintilius Legislator of the Senatorial Order of Abula built this memorial to Brutus Rufus Roman.* He also told her other stories about Avila's early history. The one most generally accepted, it seemed, was that it had been founded not by Hercules himself, but by his son, Alcideus, some sixteen hundred years before Christ, and that Alcideus had named it in honor of his mother, who was called Avila from an African word that means a high place beaten by strong winds—which was certainly an appropriate designation in the case under discussion. According to this story, it was likewise Alcideus, and not Julius Caesar, who had encircled the high place beaten by strong winds with impregnable walls, who had erected beautiful strong buildings for the use of its inhabitants, and who had given them a beautiful strong government. In telling the story, the good priest always used the words beautiful and strong together and that was the way María Vela felt they should be used. She knew that the abundance of water not only made possible the innumerable fountains in both public and private places for which the city was famous: it provided for the great cistern underneath the cathedral, which, at any moment, could be used as a fortress, as well as a sanctuary. It watered the fields through which the Adaja wound and turned the wheels of the many grist mills and fulling mills which bordered this pleasant stream as it flowed toward the bridge that connected the city of Avila with the road to Salamanca. It nourished the cork oaks which bordered this road and kept from thirst the plentiful game that abounded throughout the locality and furnished much of its food. In short, she knew that water was a source of power, as well as a source of pleasure, and she learned that this was also true of many other elements.

Gradually she had come to feel that endurance under suffering was one of the ways she could test the strength and the courage which she wanted so much to attain; so she multiplied her mortifications. She not only whipped her beautiful hands, but when she went to bed she did so with her hands tied together and her feet, also. She was sure that, if this were done, she would be able to sleep only for short periods at a time and then she would devote the intervening periods to prayer.

Though her desire for valiance above all other qualities had become more poignant and more powerful during her novitiate, she had yearned for it all her life or, at least, ever since she could remember. Her grandmother, Doña María Vela, for whom she had been named, was a sister of Blasco Núñez Vela, Viceroy of Peru,[3] and her grandfather, Diego Alvarez de Areto, had accompanied him to his post in the New World as his admiral.[4] Among the cousins of her father, Diego Alvarez de Cueto, were Don Antonio Vela, the son of the Viceroy, Don Cristóbal Vela, the Archbishop of Burgos, and Don Juan de Acuña Vela, a Knight of Alcántara, a member of the war council and a general in the army of His Catholic Majesty, Philip II. Her mother, Doña Ana de Aguirre, likewise belonged to an illustrious family, and was herself noted for her courage: moreover, she was a woman of great comeliness and considerable culture. It was she who gave her children their lessons, not only in the rudiments of reading, writing and Christian Doctrine, but in the Arts. That she herself possessed sufficient education to do so set her apart from many aristocrats of the time, whose blood was blue but whose minds were uncultivated; and it was she who supplemented the book learning of her sons and daughters with stories of valorous actions, those of the past, as well as those of the present, and made both glow with reality and inspiration.

A story of her mother's, which María Vela had especially loved as a child, was the one about the defense of Avila by its women, after the invasion of Castile by the Moors. At this time, most of the male population had left the city and were striving to protect the frontiers of the province and repel the enemy hordes from the kingdom. To the King of Córdoba it seemed like a relatively safe and speedy undertaking to storm the walled stronghold, after laying siege to it; his troops numbered nine thousand and their leader was audacious and self-assured. It did not occur to either the King or his general that anything could go amiss with their plans; they felt confident that a rich prize was already well within their grasp. But they were thwarted, shamed and defeated by the strategy of one ingenious lady and the willingness of many brave females to follow her. The lady in question, Jimena Blásquez, arrayed herself in the trappings of a knight, gathered her four daughters around her, and summoned all the women of the city to arms, rallying them under the banner of her absent husband in the Plaza of San Juan. Then, led by her, they stole out to the city walls under cover of darkness and crowned all its merlons with hats; this done, they began to make a loud noise with bugles, trumpets and instruments of war. In the first dim light of dawn, the besieging army beheld all fortifications apparently well garrisoned, and were deafened by a din which suggested that reinforcements were plentiful. Startled from their sense of security, they abandoned their plan for storming the city, broke camp and retreated, to return no more. Avila was saved. The grateful populace marched in a solemn procession through the streets of the city and, as a token of thanksgiving, five hats—those of Doña Jimena and her daughters—were borne triumphantly aloft during this progress. From that day forward, hats simulating the ones they had worn were displayed on the family coat-of-arms;[4-a] and as a token of appreciation for their heroic action, Alfonso VIII, King of Castile, granted the women of Avila the right to vote and speak in the city council "the same as their husbands" and decreed that "they could not be denied admission therein."[5]

Over and over again, Doña Ana de Aguirre was importuned by her eldest daughter and María's brothers and sisters—Diego, Lorenzo, Jerónima and Isabel—to tell the story of Doña Jimena and her brave and resourceful defense of Avila; over and over again, the devoted mother complied. She was gratified by the impression made on all the children; but she could not help noticing that the story impressed María even more than it did the others. María, Doña Ana observed, was making Doña Jimena her ideal; and then another story, also a tale of courage, though courage of a different sort, captured the little girl's imagination to an even greater degree, perhaps because it was nearer in both time and space.

The family estate of Don Diego and Doña Ana was in the village of Cardeñosa, a few leagues from the provincial capital. It was unremarkable in itself—dozens of other Castilian *pueblos* consisted, as it did, principally of small one-story houses, bordering a single central street and clustering around a parish church. But it had been a favorite stopping place in the course of royal progresses between Avila and Madrigal and Avila and Arévalo, and it was there that the poor little "King of Avila," the great Isabel's brother, had died under highly suspicious circumstances; this tragic happening had brought it into the forefront of public consciousness. It had also been the birthplace and childhood home of Isabel de Santo Domingo, one of the most prominent followers of Teresa de Ahumada, who was still living, though now a very old woman, and who was, by many, already considered a saint.[6] Furthermore, it had been the birthplace and childhood home of a young woman who was now very generally known as Santa Barbada, though her claim to sanctity had not been officially authorized, and the recognition of the qualities which might entitle her to such authorization was both more local and more doubtful than that accorded to Teresa de Ahumada. Indeed, many of Santa Barbada's fellow villagers did not hesitate to say that the stories about her had no foundation whatsoever in fact, although a very noble lady had provided a tomb for her in the Hermitage of San Segundo, first Bishop and martyr of Avila, and caused it to be inscribed: *Esta rexa e retablo mando hacer la magnifica Señora Doña Isabel Rivera, hija del magnifico caballero Francisco de Valderrábano a honra de Santa Barbada Ano 1547.*[7]

María Vela was not among the villagers of Cardeñosa who doubted the authenticity of the story about Santa Barbada. She dwelt on it with the same faith with which she listened to the story of Doña Jimena and, as her mother observed, seemed to derive even more inspiration from it. According to this story, a young girl named Paula, of great beauty, though humble origin, was in the habit of going to the Shrine of San Segundo to pray, walking in alone from her native village to do so. Her visits attracted the attention of a young nobleman whose intentions were anything but honorable and he formed the habit of trying to detain her when she left the church. One day, realizing that she would not be able to escape him any longer, she prayed to San Segundo that some miracle might occur and immediately she was transformed into the semblance of an old woman, with a hideous growth of beard on her face. When she came out of the church, her would-be seducer did not recognize her and, after a long wait, went into the church intent on finding her, only to discover that it was completely empty and further search never revealed her whereabouts to him, though she left Cardeñosa and spent the rest of her life in a hermitage near the church.

It was not at all strange, María Vela maintained, that Paula should have formed the habit of going to San Segundo's Hermitage. The route she followed from Cardeñosa took her along the river bank of the Adaja—a lovely path shaded with leafy boughs during three of the seasons and glistening with snow of celestial purity during the fourth; and the hermitage itself, set in the midst of a green grove, was one of the most charming spots in all Avila. Neither was it strange that Paula should have chosen this place to pray; she was naturally devout, and probably she reasoned that she could worship there with fewer disturbances than in her parish church, where she was known to everyone. She could not have foreseen that she would so soon have an undesirable suitor. Yet, since she was so lovely to look at, that was not strange, either, was it? Had not beautiful young girls always attracted admirers? And if the girls were of humble origin and the admirers of high degree, were there not often difficulties in the way of honorable marriage? María Vela seemed to recall that the family of the *hidalgo*, Francisco Gonzalo de Yepes, had done everything possible to prevent his union with Catalina Alvarez of Fontiveros, though it would appear that their son, Fray Juan de la Cruz, now Confessor at the Carmelite Convent of Encarnación, was a very holy man, and that much of the credit for this should be given his mother, since he had been a mere toddler when his father died. Perhaps if Paula's admirer had only been brave enough to defy his family, her story might have had a different ending and a happier one. . . .

So far, it had to be admitted that María Vela reasoned logically. As to the beard, she went on, perhaps this did not appear quite as suddenly as the story said. Quite possibly, Paula had found some way of slipping out of a side door and hiding in a nearby house; that would explain the empty hermitage and the would-be seducer's fruitless search. Then, while she was still in hiding, hair might have begun to grow on her face. Some unfortunate women were afflicted with such a growth. Or was it really a misfortune—that is, always? In this case, had it not been a means of leading toward sanctity? Had Paula not been very very brave to bear with this disfigurement, so mortifying to normal feminine pride, when she could easily have drifted into a life of luxury and sin? And had it not also required courage to leave her home, her family and her friends and live out her life as a holy hermit? María Vela thought it had; she thought Paula, who had become Santa Barbada, was very valiant and she wished she could be as brave. . . . Years after she first heard this story, she looked down at her beautiful hands and resolved that at least she would try, that she would not let them lead to vainglory.

In the meanwhile, of course, many other things had happened. For the most part, her childhood had been uneventful but happy; she had been singularly free from strain and sorrow. She was born on Holy Saturday, when the bells were pealing for *Sábado de Gloria*, and it almost seemed as if this fortuitous timing was a symbol of the joy she would always find in religion and in the outward and visible signs of inward and spiritual grace. The loss of her father, when she was nine years old, was her first occasion of real grief; but her mother set her an example of such fortitude in their joint bereavement that the little girl could not fail to emulate it. Shortly after his death she made her First Holy Communion and formed the habit of communicating once a week—an unusual one for the time and place. Young as she was, the idea of entering a convent was already lying dormant in her mind; but she took no definite steps in the direction of the cloister, because she hesitated at the thought of leaving her widowed mother, whose once comfortable circumstances were now greatly reduced, and because she wondered, as nearly every normal girl inevitably does, whether sooner or later the "right man" would not appear and ask for her hand in marriage. Then, during a visit to the Shrine of Sonsoles,[8] she was taken suddenly ill and her illness lasted more than a year. This long period of enforced idleness gave her ample time for reflection and, also, ample opportunity for leisurely talks with her mother. Physically, there was a strong resemblance between the two; spiritually, they were in even closer harmony. Doña Ana did not use schoolbooks any more in the hours she devoted to her eldest daughter; neither did she continue to tell tales about valorous deeds nor discuss the plausibility of local legends. Instead, with gentleness and wisdom, she made it clear to María Vela that she had always hoped this beloved child of hers would follow what was so clearly her natural bent: that of accepting her Saviour as her Bridegroom and consecrating her life to His service.

Once convinced that her mother's viewpoint and her mother's wishes were the same as her own, María Vela did not hesitate any more. Indeed, her longing for the cloistral life had now reached a stage of such urgency that she felt she could not willingly wait until she had regained her health before embracing it, and she had no difficulty in choosing the cloister she desired to enter. Her father's sister, Doña Isabel de Cueto, was already a religious of the Cistercian Order at the Convent of Santa Ana, which had been founded by that good Bishop, Don Sancho Dávila, and of which the noble lady, Illana Muñoz, had been the first Abbess. It was suitably dowered, not only by Don Sancho, but also by King Alfonso VIII—the same King of Castile who had so richly rewarded the brave matrons of Avila by giving them civic rights equivalent to those enjoyed by their husbands. It had a yearly income of six thousand ducats and every *Avilés* farmer who owned a yoke of oxen and harvested as many as fifteen *fanegas* of wheat was required to deliver three *celemines* annually to Santa Ana; this portion was known as the *cuarilla* and assured its occupants of their daily bread.[9] A common dormitory was divided into semi-enclosed cells which provided a certain amount of privacy for the seventy nuns who made up the community and included some "of the second habit"—that is to say, lay sisters.[10] Three chaplains, one major and two minor, were provided for general spiritual guidance, and the nuns were, moreover, left free to choose their own confessors from among the regular and secular clergy of the city, so long as these were known to be men of integrity and outstanding piety. The atmosphere of the convent was one of great austerity, permeated with the spirit of prayer and penance; Matins were said at three in the morning and the entire Rule was one of rigid discipline and self-denial, scrupulously observed.

All this was, of course, well known to María Vela and to her mother, yet neither quailed nor even hesitated before such a prospect, any more than the Abbess of Santa Ana hesitated and quailed at the prospect of admitting to the community a very youthful postulant whose health left much to be desired. What is more, it did not deter Doña Ana's younger daughter, Jerónima, from deciding to enter the convent at the same time as her sister. María was very weak after her long illness and she still found it difficult to take more than a few steps at a time; but she found willingness to help her on every side. Strong men carried her in a chair all the way from Cardeñosa to Avila and across the city to the Convent of Santa Ana; her sister, Jerónima, accompanied her, walking sturdily beside the chair; their mother took leave of them without a tremor and, at the convent, their aunt, Doña Isabel, was waiting to welcome them warmly.

In a way, it was an occasion of great joy for her; but, as she looked at María Vela, her heart sank. Surely this fragile girl whose cloud of dark hair and translucent skin and beautiful hands all gave an impression of ethereality had come to the cloister only to die there—and she was barely fifteen years old! Doña Isabel turned to her other niece, who was even younger, and took courage; Jerónima fairly radiated good health and good spirits.

The great doors swung open on their iron hinges and closed again; the heavy bolts were drawn back and slid forward into place; the Abbess and other members of the community came forward to receive the postulants. Shortly thereafter, the two sisters took the habit together. Within eight years, Jerónima was dead, in the full bloom of her youthful loveliness. María Vela survived for more than forty years and, long before she died, she had realized her ideal: she had come to be designated as the Strong Woman of Santa Ana.

2

María Vela's novitiate lasted six years.

Just why it should have been so long is not clear to us. Certainly, from the beginning, she had always been adaptable to the Rule—in fact, she had carried austerity and discipline to far greater lengths than were required of her, though she went to no such extremes as her fellow religious, Petronilla Valdivieso, who had requested and received permission to wear garments made of Palencia—a cloth generally used only for blankets, even coarser than the usual habit—and to remove the *chapines*—a kind of overshoe, also made of coarse cloth—customarily worn over the sandals during the bitter winters as a protection against the cold. Neither had María Vela ever wavered in her faith; yet, for some reason, she hesitated to make her final vows. She dwelt on the "responsibilities" connected with these, reminding herself and others that there was more supervision in the novitiate than among the nuns who were perpetually pledged; she was uncertain whether she was prepared to do without such vigilant guidance. Apparently, at this stage, she lacked self-confidence, and also failed to put much reliance on the ability of other young persons to take full responsibility for their conduct and consecration, for she deplored the precipitancy of novices who acted like "thoughtless girls" in their haste to make their profession, though she was too charitable to criticize them openly. It seems strange that no one stepped forward to relieve her of her doubts; on the other hand, the extent of her deliberation may have been the best possible preparation for her future steadfastness.

One day when she had been a novice more than five years, word was brought to her that her beloved mother had died. High Mass was being celebrated at the time and, as usual, she was at the organ. Without any change of expression, she continued to play; her beautiful fingers did not tremble; they rested firmly on the keys and the sacred music swelled to splendid sound beneath her touch. Not until the final benediction had been pronounced and the choir nuns had filed out of the chapel with due ceremony did she leave her seat and go to the cell where her weeping sister and aunt were waiting for her to come and comfort them. Apparently, it did not occur to either one that she stood in need of comfort herself.

Though she was capable of such composure and self-control under shock, nothing seemed to alleviate her state of indecision. She continued to hesitate in the face of the "responsibilities" which would be hers if she became a professed nun; and the very fact that her aunt, Doña Isabel, and her elder brother, Diego, now tried to hurry her into taking the irrevocable step only served as another deterrent. Her second brother, Lorenzo, had become a Bernardine Monk and entered the Convent of La Espina; it would appear that, at this time, he took no part in the family arguments, though he was to play an important part in them later on. Her sister, Jerónima, was still with her and was also still a novice; María Vela's hesitation and the reasons for it had proved contagious. Their younger sister, Isabel, their aunt's namesake, was still at Cardeñosa; Diego felt he had quite enough to do, in looking after her and seeing her dowered and married, in a manner befitting the family prestige, which was still high, despite its fallen fortunes, without having María Vela and Jerónima on his hands again. It is to be feared that other factors, besides that of excessive piety, influenced his attitude. We may give Doña Isabel the benefit of doubt by assuming that she was more singlehearted; but, up to that time, she had proved a hindrance, rather than a help, to María Vela, by insisting that the girl should limit the severity of her discipline, the periods of her prayer and even the frequency of her Communion. Probably, Doña Isabel thought she was acting for the best; she had not forgotten the almost moribund state in which the fifteen-year-old girl had come to Santa Ana. However, though her concern for her niece's health might well account for anxiety regarding discipline and devotion, it certainly did not explain her insistence that María Vela should not have the solace and the inspiration of Holy Communion. It is to be feared that the aging nun was something of a martinet and even more of a busybody.

Fortunately, during these troublous times, there was one person to whom María Vela could turn with the assurance of sympathy, understanding and good counsel; this was her friend, María de Avila, long since a professed nun, but still spiritually as close to María Vela as when they had both been novices. María de Avila, whose own disposition was such a happy one that it triumphed over all doubts, succeeded in giving her friend exactly the kind of encouragement which was needed. She reminded María Vela that the latter's lifelong desire for perfection could certainly be attained more readily in the cloister than in the world; and that, as far as the "responsibility" of following the Rule unsupervised was concerned, how could she ask for better guidance than that of God, which she assuredly could trust Him to provide? It would appear that María de Avila hinted rather strongly that, as far as Doña Isabel was concerned, "the situation would change"—in other words, that this meddlesome aunt was getting on in years and that, after all, no one lived forever. Personally, I rather like to think that María Vela was human enough to be moved by this reminder almost as forcibly as she was by the others. At all events, her hesitation came to a sudden end and, with hers, Jerónima's ended, too. They made their profession together, as they had taken the habit together and, a few days later, their little sister, Isabel, fired by their example, joined them at the convent. Their brother, Diego, thus fortunately relieved from responsibility as far as all three were concerned, himself made a very advantageous marriage with a noble lady by the name of Ana María de Zuñiga.

3

María Vela had made her final vows on a Friday; every Friday there-after, as long as she lived, she renewed them. This was her way of reminding herself of the obligations they imposed upon her.

Two years after making her profession, she was relieved of her place at the organ and appointed assistant to the choir cantor. She entered into her new duties with great zest, and soon acquired a thorough knowledge of rubrics which was invaluable both to the community and to her personally. As an authority, she was frequently consulted on any and every difficulty which arose in connection with ceremonials, and these frequent consultations meant more companionship with her fellow nuns than she could normally have otherwise enjoyed. This companionship was doubly important to her because she had lost both her sisters. In one way, Jerónima's death was the harder to bear; they were very near of an age and had been close to each other always. As children, they had shared their lessons and their games; as young girls they had entered the convent together; they had taken the habit and made their final vows together. They had also shared the love of music; Jerónima had been of great assistance to María Vela in the choir, and her loss meant a terrible void, one that could never be filled. At the same time, there had been something peculiarly poign-ant about the death of little Isabel; she was still so very young, and she had come so trustfully and so joyfully to join her sisters because she wanted to share their vocation. And then she had lived less than a year. Her entry had severed María Vela's last close tie with the out-side world, for Lorenzo was absorbed in his own vocation and Diego in his delightful wife.

Under these conditions, it was natural that she should have placed great dependence on her confessor, and that his influence on her life should have become even more significant than was usual, even in an age which made this role one of supreme importance. She chose as her first one a certain Gaspar de Avila, a chaplain of the cathedral and "a clergyman of exemplary and spiritual life." He was also confessor to Doña Isabel, who probably had something to do with the choice; but he understood the young nun's problems and perplexities better than her aunt, and helped her to solve and overcome them. She made her first General Confession[11] to him, having first written it on a piece of paper, a practice she continued to follow whenever she gave her obedience to a new confessor; but, unlike many religious of the times, she did not change confessors frequently. On the contrary, Gaspar de Avila continued to give her spiritual guidance for fifteen years and probably would have gone on doing so indefinitely, if a paralytic attack had not incapacitated him. This seizure left him, for a time, without power of speech; and though eventually he regained this to a certain degree, his vocal chords remained twisted and his neck tilted to the left side, while his hands trembled almost uncontrollably. He lived twelve years longer, spending a great deal of time in prayer before a crucifix and, eventually, he was able to control the trembling of his hands enough to do some writing, though with great difficulty. But, obviously, he could not continue his strenuous activities as a chaplain and a confessor.

Gaspar's pitiable state was naturally a cause of great concern to all his charges, but probably none of them suffered, at the same time, so great a sense of personal loss as María Vela. This was not only because of the long and close connection between the two, or even because his disability deprived her of her most important association with any human being; it was also because she hesitated to entrust to another confessor the secrets she had shared with him about the mysterious "Mercies" she was receiving from the Lord. She was all too well aware that accounts of visions and "messages," supernatural in character, were received with caution and regarded with suspicion by most clerics. Gaspar de Avila was the happy exception to this rule. He had never doubted that she was telling him the truth, as she saw it, and had encouraged her confidences. She shrank from the prospect of disbelief and censure. It seemed to her that she could not face either the one or the other. At the same time, she did not see how she could be silent on the subjects which she had, for so long a time, freely discussed, partly because her failure to mention them would impair the value of her confessions, and partly because, despite her shyness, she was conscious that she could not long disregard the overwhelming need of imparting her precious secrets to someone who would give her enlightened guidance in regard to them.

She finally brought herself to consult her aunt and, between them, with the approval of the Abbess, they decided that she should make "ordinary" confessions to one of the chaplains of the convent, but that she should put her "extraordinary" confessions into writing and send them to Father Gaspar, who would reply to them in the same way, for, by this time, he had succeeded in partially controlling the trembling of his hands. It was necessary to enlist the services of a messenger for this interchange of confidential correspondence and Doña Isabel, who undertook the responsibility of finding one, selected an out-of-town boy who was studying at the Jesuit Grammar School. At that time, letters dispatched from and to the convent were not sealed with wax, as they were later on; they were rolled and tied with a cord. The messenger, whose studies apparently left him with plenty of time for other pursuits, whiled away some of this by going to the underground chapel of Our Lady of Soterraña, where he untied the cords and read the letters before delivering them. Either no one had ever told him that such a pastime would represent a breach of confidence, or else he did not care whether it did or not. Eventually, however, the still small voice of conscience began to whisper in his ear and he confessed what he had been doing. Coupled with the confession was the astonishing information that, whereas, he had never previously thought of becoming a priest, the letters had convinced him that he had a vocation.[12] Gratifying as this must have been, in one way, to Father Gaspar and his penitent, it was, in another very disturbing, especially to the latter, and they hit upon a different way of handling their correspondence: the rolls were placed in a small chest which was sent back and forth between them and to this each held a key; no one else could unlock it.

This arrangement continued, to the mutual satisfaction of Father Gaspar and María Vela, for several years. Apparently, it was the death of her aunt which caused the young nun to feel the need of a confessor who was closer at hand, and one with whom she could communicate directly. Domineering and interfering though Doña Isabel undoubtedly was, and ready as María Vela had been to circumvent her aunt—with her confessor's approval—on minor matters, the fact remained that she was now left without any member of her family to share with her the "responsibilities" of the Rule and that there had been a strong bond between the two women; when this was severed, María Vela felt more or less lost without the dominance and interference which, previously, she had so often resented. A new Abbess, Doña María de Mercado, the niece of the Bishop of Avila, had been elected only a short time before Doña Isabel's death; and with this change of authority had naturally come other changes, which added to the general atmosphere of unfamiliarity and instability. Not that the new Abbess wilfully upset the established order of things. On the contrary, she scrupulously observed all the customs of the convent, among them the one which demanded that, nine days after the death of a nun, she should enter the cell of the deceased, read aloud the list of the articles which the latter had been permitted to wear and to use, and then dispose of them as she thought best, always bearing in mind the sentimental value which they might have for some relative and the obligation to set aside some funds as suffrages for the soul in Purgatory. Courteously, the Abbess offered María Vela a suitable proportion of Doña Isabel's belongings; with equal courtesy, but in her most unwavering manner, María Vela declined to accept any of them. The Abbess was to dispose of them otherwise, in the way she saw fit; María Vela "reserved for herself only the obligation of offering her prayers and her sufferings for the repose of her aunt's soul."[13]

Having made this statement, she wrote to Father Gaspar with much less show of firmness. She was in a quandary. She had lost her immediate guide and adviser—her aunt—and she was confronted with many problems which her absorption with music did not help her to solve. For five years she had been communicating to Father Gaspar "the inner state of her spirit." But lately, God had been showing her even greater "Mercies" than ever before and she could not, or dared not, "write down everything her soul was experiencing." On the other hand, she could not consult with any other confessor unless and until she knew that he was "wholly satisfactory" and that such an arrangement would meet with Father Gaspar's approval. He himself was troubled. He replied that he would consider the question and let her know what he thought was best for her, but apparently it took him some time to reach a decision. Meanwhile, María Vela was "in extreme anguish"; God's "Mercies" continued to increase and she heard interior voices urging her to take a confessor near at hand, but she did not want to risk seeking one out of her own accord. At last, the long-awaited letter reached her: Father Gaspar agreed that she must have a second confessor, but he would help in selecting this priest and would continue his own general guidance as well. "The servant of God was greatly relieved with this decision and earnestly prayed to the Lord that He would enlighten them in making the right selection."[14]

The deliberate choice was of a teacher at the Jesuit College who later became its rector—Father Francisco de Salcedo, a nephew of Father Baltazar Alvarez, who had, at one time, been the confessor of Teresa de Ahumada, and who was well and favorably known in Avila. These two Jesuits, so closely related to each other, had many of the same characteristics, including tireless zeal and the ability to achieve a great deal of "ascendency" over their penitents, many of them persons with great spiritual gifts and considerable prestige. As soon as the selection had been made, María Vela sought permission from the Abbess to "take Salcedo for her confessor and obey him in all matters pertaining to her soul"—a petition which was, after all, more or less of a formality, as one of this sort had to be made every year, in conformity with the Rule, whether or not there had been any change of a spiritual director. Official approval was given to the choice of Father Salcedo and María Vela "made a General Confession to him and gave him a detailed account of the state of her soul and of the 'Mercies' God was showing her and of her aspirations toward perfection. . . . He told her to continue the same order of life and to put down in writing the supernatural 'Mercies' and revelations that God had made her and the ones she was to receive in the future."[15]

The Abbess' first expression of approval had been unqualified; soon, however, she was conscious of dissatisfaction with the appointment in the community. There was murmuring among the nuns that Salcedo, because of his youth—he was only thirty-four—did not have enough experience to guide souls, especially privileged souls like those of María Vela. Father Gaspar also made known his discontent; he found he did not always agree with this sprig of a Jesuit—his own protégé—who had supplanted him. Wisely, the Abbess did not interfere in this crisis; she was probably aware that jealousy, that "green-eyed monster," sometimes succeeded in slithering into as consecrated a place as a secluded cloister, or a chapel where a displeased and disabled priest prayed constantly before a crucifix. The poor penitent found herself torn between her loyalty to the unfortunate paralytic, who for so many years had been her kindest and most helpful counselor, and her growing conviction that his successor's advice was now wiser; for a time, her loyalty swayed her more strongly than her conviction and, again, she became the victim of unhappy indecision. In her misery, she besought the Lord to declare His Will and believed that He spoke to her reproachfully, saying, "Why do you want to know it, since knowing it, you will not follow it?" She accepted the rebuke with both humbleness and understanding; there was no longer any doubt in her mind what she should do. Sorrowfully, she decided that the moment of parting for good with Father Gaspar had come. Henceforth, for a long while, Salcedo was her only confessor.

4

Father Salcedo performed at least two great services for María Vela: he persuaded her to read the recently published works of Teresa de Ahumada, by then very generally called "*La Fundadora*—The Foundress" and "*La Madre*—The Mother," almost as if there were only one person entitled to such designations, and hardly less generally considered a saint, though actually her beatification did not take place until three years before María Vela died and her canonization several years afterward.[16] Salcedo also persuaded his penitent to record her own spiritual experiences freely, pointing out that, if it were right for the great Teresa to do this—as in his opinion it undoubtedly was—it would be right for the humble María Vela to follow in her footsteps, in this as in other ways. By this persuasion, he unconsciously performed signal services not only to María Vela, but to posterity; for her autobiography and the chronicles to which she gave no other title than "Mercies," recording the days of the week on which they were written, but not formally dividing them into chapters, offer incontestable proof that in the span of a little over a century—to be exact, 1515 to 1617—the small remote Province of Avila produced not only two mystics of extraordinary powers, as is generally known, but three, all of whom are likewise noteworthy for literary distinction. Granted that Teresa de Ahumada and Juan de la Cruz were the major figures on this scene and María Vela a minor one; nevertheless, her life and writings complement theirs and give entirety and finish to conditions and circumstances unique in the history of the world. Indeed, it is partly because María Vela was cloistered at so early an age, and lived and died in such obscurity, instead of traversing the length and breadth of Spain and mingling with all sorts of conditions of men and women who could thus come to know her well, that the importance of the role she played in the history of mysticism has so long been overlooked; it is even more surely so because her writings, instead of being published immediately, have, for three hundred and fifty years, been kept secreted in the archives of Santa Ana and only now released, that her God-given talents have not been more generally recognized.

It is certain that neither Father Salcedo nor María Vela realized that, by encouraging her to read great books and, in turn, by freeing her from extreme diffidence about speaking and writing of the supernatural herself, he was rendering her—and the world—his greatest service. There is nothing whatsoever to indicate that they attached more importance to this action of his than to any other aspect of his guidance—in fact, we are provided with more details about the various austerities she was permitted or advised to practice than we are about the cultivation of her mind and the release of her spiritual forces. The only seat in her cell was a *corcho*—literally a cork, not what we envision by that word (a stopper in a bottle) but a small round block, fashioned from the cork oak that grows so abundantly on the road to Salamanca. María Vela placed this *corcho* beside her bed in such a way that, if she were overcome with drowsiness while she was kneeling in prayer, she would fall over it and thus be startled into wakefulness. She did this every night before receiving Holy Communion and, as she was now permitted to communicate three times a week, her sleeping hours were drastically curtailed. At the same time, she began to be inspired "with vehement desire to keep the primitive vigorous fast of the Order, that is, never to eat meat[17] and on fast days to abstain from eggs and milk products."[18] Both her confessor and the Abbess gave her permission to fulfill this desire and thereafter, for a long while, she ate only bread and fruit on fast days. With characteristic shyness, she did not wish this extreme abstinence to be a matter of common knowledge in the community and, through the help of her faithful friend, María de Avila, she succeeded in keeping it a secret for a year and a half. They sat side by side in the refectory, where María Vela's fruit was concealed in a small bowl; to all appearances, the two Marías were eating their normally allotted food from the same plate, an arrangement no one apparently thought strange.

Meanwhile, María Vela was becoming increasingly meticulous in her interpretation of her vow of poverty. She declined to accept even the trifling presents which her well-fixed brother, Diego, wanted to make her from time to time and to which the Rule offered no impediment; and she took greater and greater refuge in silence. She read, she meditated, she prayed, she mortified the flesh; many of her fellow nuns began to find her complete withdrawal and her extremes of self-discipline annoying, and complained afresh that Father Salcedo was not the right confessor for her. Again, the Abbess listened calmly to complaints; by way of answering them, indirectly, she appointed María Vela sacristan. If the latter's detractors hoped she would not be able to fulfill her new and important duties, they were doomed to disappointment. "She was at home in the office, for she was very handy in things pertaining to the Divine Service and especially devoted to the Blessed Sacrament."[19]

Apparently, Salcedo was more concerned than the Abbess with the criticism he had aroused. At all events, he took a drastic step. He had already conferred with the chaplains of the convent about the advisability of counselling María Vela to record her spiritual experiences and they had all approved his course of action; but he wished to make assurance doubly sure. He gathered up her notes and took them to Salamanca, where he submitted them to José de Acosta, the regent of the Jesuit College. The regent was a busy man. He was glad to oblige his former student and willing to help in the guidance of so devout and humble a religious as this strange penitent seemed to be; but many other pressing matters demanded his attention and, moreover, he desired to confer on the subject under consideration with other teachers in the college. The report which he finally gave was favorable. He "approved the spirit of the servant of God and did not find in her revelations and exercises anything suspicious or subject to condemnation. Her doctrine was sane and sound. Some of the revelations did not come, perhaps, directly from God, but were rather mental images of her own creation. However, those in this category were only a few among many and in no way contradictory to the others."[20]

Overjoyed by this favorable report, Salcedo hastened back to Avila. It was high time; his penitent had suffered great humiliation in his absence. It is true that, to a certain degree, she had invited this: she had asked and secured permission from the Abbess to enumerate all the faults and failings of which she was conscious in the presence of the entire community when it foregathered in the Chapter; this done, she went from one nun to another and, bending low before each, kissed her feet. But the result of this candid recital and servile gesture was anything but fortunate. Many of the older nuns declared that they were scandalized. Nothing of the sort had ever been done at Santa Ana's before; they could not countenance such novelties. The younger nuns questioned the sincerity of María Vela's self-abasement; personally, they would never have dreamed of making such an exhibition of themselves. One and all declared it was evident that María Vela was ill advised. The triumphant return of Salcedo, bearing with him the glad tidings that, in the considered opinion of Salamanca's foremost professors, she was very well advised, and that her actions were a credit to her guidance, naturally put a stop to some of this gossip; but it was not until Salcedo had sought and secured a similar opinion from

Luis de la Puente of Valladolid, a cleric of exceptional authority and piety, that it was more or less effectually silenced.

There is a temptation to regard as slightly humorous, as well as more than slightly tragic, the fact that a provincial confessor should feel it necessary to go to seats and personages of learning, distant—as distance was reckoned then—from his normal sphere of action, in order to justify his methods of guiding one obscure nun and the manner of her response to this guidance. Actually, it shows that Salcedo recognized both the importance of his charge and the caliber of his penitent. Moreover, he was troubled because election time was drawing near, and he had reason to believe that the new Abbess would be less tolerant and understanding, as far as María Vela was concerned, than the one who had always so wisely befriended her. And it must be admitted that his penitent herself was failing to make matters any easier for him. Not content with her diet of bread and fruit, she now asked for permission to eat nothing at all on the days she communicated; and, as she was also clamoring for more and more frequent Communion, he was afraid she would soon waste away to a shadow, which would be bad enough in itself, but which, by impairing her health, would also seriously interfere with her duties in the choir and the sacristy, where her efficiency was a great asset to the community. She insisted that "the flavor of the Sacramental Species lingered in her mouth throughout the day, together with a consciousness of the Presence of Christ Our Lord"—but only if she took no ordinary food. When she did this, she was deprived of great favors and, moreover, she became ill. Though still beset with doubts, Salcedo finally consented to make a practical test "and to allow her to go without food on Communion days, even if they were successive, as on Saturday and Sunday."[21] She did this for one week and then another, while her friend, Doña María de Avila, and her confessor carefully observed her. All the while she did not miss any exercise or orison and attended to all her duties with a "buoyancy" which she could not explain; and all the while the external sign of the Sacramental Species did not fade away and she retained the consciousness of her Beloved's Presence in her soul.

Salcedo was impressed, but he was not satisfied; he sought learned and pious opinions from still other priests, among them Father Juan de Torres, "a grave religious of much experience and ability," Father Pedro Martínez, the confessor of the prospective Abbess, and Juan de Alarcón, Lector of Sacred Scripture at the Royal Convent of Santo

Tomás, "a very spiritual man, dedicated to prayer and to the guidance of souls, especially religious, but a deadly enemy of what he called 'devil's devotions' among nuns." Inevitably, Salcedo began to receive contradictory advice from sources that seemed to be equally enlightened and equally trustworthy. Some of the authorities consulted felt that María Vela might well be allowed to follow her instincts in regard to food and fasts, since her usefulness to the community was in no way impaired by such a course; others felt that she might be allowed a partial fast but not a complete one. She fainted several times and this, naturally, raised a hue and cry—she was starving herself to death! Then it was remarked that none of these periods of faintness coincided with her periods of fasting; when she abstained from food, she soon recovered her strength and sang in the choir and performed her other duties "as if she were sound and healthy." Father Alarcón then called attention to the fact that such singularity could not be approved, whether or not María Vela's fasts did her harm and even if they did her good; nuns were supposed to adhere to the prescribed pattern of the Order which they joined and any action which set them apart from their fellow religious was improper.[22] The prospective Abbess, at the time the cellarist, upon hearing this dictum did not fail to point out that María Vela was, indeed, making herself conspicuous by her absence from the refectory at regular mealtimes and her failure to eat normally when she did go there. Father Alarcón agreed with the Abbess; considering the views he already held about devil's devotions, it is needless to say that his disapproval of María Vela was now unqualified.

Again, there is a temptation to regard as serio-comic and somewhat tedious all this turmoil about when, what and how much a simple nun should eat if, for all her humbleness, she failed to fit unobtrusively into the pattern of her Order. In this day and age, it might be just that, for the physician, like the confessor, now has recognized responsibilities to cloistered nuns, no less than for lay women and his advice is sought and followed in matters of diet and others pertaining to health. But this was not the case in the age under consideration; and in our effort to understand and appraise María Vela, we must not fail in our endeavor to understand and appraise her era. At a period more enlightened about such matters, there would probably have been a realization that the ability to go without food for unusually long periods, or to thrive on comparatively little and that of a type not generally accepted as nourishing, varies greatly, not only with individuals, their personal habits and mode of life, but with localities, with climatic conditions and with contemporary beliefs and practices. All these, as we now know, enter into the picture; so do certain allergies and predilections. There are countless authoritative cases on record of explorers and victims of major disasters, such as fire, flood and shipwreck, who have survived near-starvation without permanent ill results; even more frequent are the cases of pregnant women whose morning sickness developed into pernicious vomiting and who received practically no nourishment for months, until methods of intravenous feeding were discovered; yet, though they lost weight, they usually not only survived themselves, but brought healthy babies into the world. One of Abraham Lincoln's best-known maxims began with the advice to eat "three square meals a day"; and that was the general practice of everyone who could afford it, in the United States, a century ago. Now, except in the case of those who perform hard physical labor, the practice has generally been reduced to one hearty meal, and physicians are constantly urging that even the menu for this one should be much less extensive than is the general habit of all persons who are not already dieting to reduce weight or blood pressure or to control diabetes. Moreover, most American physicians regard rice as one of the most fattening of foods and curtail or forbid its use to persons who are overweight; yet the nationals of countries like Japan and China, where it is the main staple, are lean and sinewy and almost never fat. Tomatoes were once considered a source of deadly poison; now the juice, if not the vegetable, is on almost every prescribed diet. Babies born fifty years ago were fed on practically nothing but milk and it was given them every few hours; now they begin to have strained vegetables at a remarkably early age and are soon limited to three meals a day. Similar examples of changes in medical opinion are too numerous to mention. Rural regional cooking in the Near East is actually repulsive to many Europeans and Americans; in like measure, many of the dishes we enjoy are repulsive to Arabs and Persians. Numerous Asiatic peoples are prohibited, by their religion, from eating meat or drinking alcohol in any form. Orthodox Jews have dietary laws which do not prevail among Christians, among them the rigid rule which prevents them from eating flesh products and dairy products at the same meal; and in many countries where food is abundant and great importance attached to cuisine, the latter are used very sparingly, in others hardly at all. China is an outstanding example of this. In Spain, even today, there are only a few native cheeses, butter is not used for cooking or shortening, and milk and cream are neither pasteurized nor plentiful. Foreigners, especially Americans, feel the lack of these and frequently suffer digestive upsets until they become adjusted to it; but Spaniards thrive on their accustomed fare.

Taking all this into consideration, it seems quite likely that María Vela was getting all the nourishment she needed from bread, fruit and vegetables, and that the meat and eggs forced upon her, sometimes with kind and sometimes with unkind motives, actually disagreed with her. (In saying this, I am casting no doubts on the sincerity of her belief that she was receiving supernatural guidance in regard to her diet—indeed, it seems to me entirely credible that, since she needed such guidance, in the face of all the opposition she was enduring, Our Lord supplied it.) But no one in sixteenth-century Avila realized this nor can we expect that they would have done so. The unfortunate dissension went on and on and, meanwhile, though María Vela wept and wrung her beautiful hands in the solitude of her cell, she maintained her serene silence in the presence of everyone except her confessor, to whom she kept reiterating that she was sure she was acting according to the wishes of her Saviour and that He was giving her the strength to do without food. It does not seem to have occurred to her, or to those with whom she was connected, that she was showing herself strong in other ways: through her calmness in the midst of tumult; through her refusal to be drawn into bickering and argument; through her quiet pursuit of the duties and accomplishments in which she excelled; and, most of all, through her unwavering faith in Divine Guidance. But there was no question in her mind or that of anyone else that, physically, she had extraordinary powers of endurance; and since strength was what she had craved above everything else, the form it took and the conditions under which she achieved it were unimportant to her. The point was that she had it. This being the case, she persisted in her stubbornness, as well as her silence, until a dramatic episode suddenly turned the tide of events.

One morning, toward the end of Lent, as she was approaching the grille at early-morning Mass, she had a seizure whose symptoms strongly resembled lockjaw. Her teeth and jaws became clamped together "as if they were fastened with screws." This alarming condition remained unchanged until dinner time; then, just as suddenly as they had tightened, her jaws loosened. "The fact that the attack had come just before Holy Communion—which, of course, she could not receive

—and was gone when the refectory bell was ringing caused great surprise to some nuns and scandal to others. They sent word to the Fathers; Salcedo and Torres arrived first and found the convent much upset, but the patient calm and serene. Alarcón and Martínez tried to inform themselves, but the reports were contradictory. Some said it was a natural sickness; others that it was the result of the rigorous fast; a few that María Vela feigned it and the most prudent that they could not understand it."[23] Father Torres was the first to suggest that the malady might be caused by the devil, to hinder her from receiving Communion; but he did so without a "firm conviction" and nobody paid much attention to him. The Dominicans who were consulted insisted that the fasts should not continue and advised that María Vela should become a daily communicant, provided she ate something. The Jesuits held a contrary opinion.

Meanwhile, the seizure was repeated every day. During the early part of Holy Week there was no change; every time María Vela approached the grille the same thing happened. By Maundy Thursday, the convent was in an uproar and matters had come to such a pass that the controversy was a matter of public knowledge; almost everyone in the city, whether qualified or not, was taking sides in the dispute which was now raging between the Jesuits and the Dominicans. "In the midst of this confusion and bewilderment, Divine Providence ordained that there should drop into town Father Gonzalo de Avila, S.J., brother of the Abbess [this was the former cellarist, now newly appointed] and of Don Rodrigo de Aguila, Knight of Calatrava, chief steward of the empress and founder of the Convent of San Antonio of Discalced Franciscans in this city [Avila]. He was the Provincial of New Castile, a man of great authority in his Order, not only because of his nobility and amiability, but also because of his virtues and holiness. Father Salcedo hastened to inform him of what was going on at Santa Ana and asked him to speak to Doña María. She gave him a detailed account of her life, answering fully all the doubts and questions he put forth. He also listened to the arguments of her opponents and, after mature deliberation, voted decidedly in favor of the penitent. He convinced his sister, the Abbess, that she should give María Vela all necessary permission to carry out her penitential discipline. The Provincial was astonished to witness the sudden recovery of the sick nun with this change of treatment, and went on his journey, remaining a great admirer of his new friend."[24]

5

It is unfortunate that this distinguished peacemaker could not have prolonged his stay, for apparently he was unable to exert his influence over his sister at a distance. Indeed, he was hardly out of sight and hearing when the Abbess changed her mind, and began to try out "new ways and theories" at María Vela's expense. By this time, Salcedo's patience was exhausted, and his superiors realized that his efforts at Santa Ana were worse than unappreciated; they were futile. He called on the Abbess and, in the presence of his penitent, told her he was tired of torturing the latter with so many experiments and had no more courage to make her suffer and go against what was evidently God's Will; therefore, he would be greatly pleased if the Abbess would find another confessor who would understand María Vela better. The Abbess, thinking that this was a good way to pacify the community, was secretly glad that the suggestion for a separation came from him, as she looked with disfavor on his methods of guiding his penitent. She turned to María Vela and awaited her comments.

None were forthcoming. She remained silent and apparently as tranquil as if the matter did not concern her at all, though, as a matter of fact, Salcedo was her only support, both within and without the convent. He enjoined her to make her ordinary confession with the chief chaplain and to report special experiences to the Abbess. This was a "crushing mortification," for she knew her superior would never understand these and she was extremely reluctant to reveal them to such persons. But, still outwardly unruffled and serene, she bowed her head and bade him farewell.

"Where men's judgments come to an end, God's judgments begin." The nuns thought that the difficulties with María Vela would end with the departure of Father Salcedo, since they blamed him for aiding and abetting her in her strange ways or, at least, consenting that she should follow them. The very opposite happened. Contrary to their expectations, María Vela now became seriously ill; the unsympathetic nuns were obliged to carry her to her cell and care for her there, while expecting her to die at any moment. The Abbess, who was annoyed as well as confused, decided to wash her hands of the whole problem by selecting a new confessor for María Vela who would assume entire responsibility for her behavior—that is, if she lived.

This time, the choice was as unfortunate in its consequences as it had been felicitous in the case of Salcedo. It fell upon Julián de Avila, a cleric of great learning and distinction, who, at one time, had been Teresa's confessor and who had been of invaluable assistance to her in the foundation of San José. But he was an even greater enemy of the so-called "devil's devotions" than Juan de Alarcón and he had a special aversion to seeing one of his penitents make a record of supernatural experiences. He had actually rebuked Teresa for doing this and, with an abruptness and lack of courtesy which were far from characteristic, she had disrespectfully replied, "Hold your peace, Father. What I am doing will be of great service to God's church." She was right and she spoke with the courage of her convictions. But María Vela, though she was valiant in so many other ways, did not have this kind of courage. When Julián de Avila ordered her to eat meat and to receive Communion only three times a week, she obeyed; when he told her that her visions were a deceit and that she must withstand the interior voices, she did her best to believe him and to comply. But she did not succeed in either of these ways. In her desolation she had recourse only to the Lord and "with tears and supplications she begged Him to shed His light on her confessor and herself, so that both would know the truth. He told her that she had never been so pleasing in His sight. This was the real test: whether she could be faithful to His teachings when no one believed in her and even her confessor would not help her."[25] Julián's retort to this "message" was short and angry: to say that God wished to direct her Himself, taking her out of the common rule, was equivalent to admitting that she knew nothing about real spiritual life, but was allowing herself to be guided by demons. She renewed her efforts to placate him, but now, in addition to hearing voices and seeing visions, she began to go into trances, exactly as Teresa and Juan de la Cruz had so often done. This seemed to Julián like insult added to injury, as far as his teachings were concerned. The strain between priest and penitent grew greater and greater; at the end of only two months, he told her tersely that she had better look for another confessor.

If the question of what constitutes proper diet is a moot one, the question of what assures Divine origin to clairvoyance and clairaudience is open to even more heated argument. It always has been and it probably always will be. Of course, there are many persons, as I have already said in writing of Teresa, who categorically assert that both are either fictional or the product of diseased and unbalanced minds; there is absolutely no use in trying to discuss the matter as far as these individuals are concerned. Others, more open to persuasion, may perhaps properly be reminded again that some of history's greatest mystics, like Joan of Arc, Catherine of Siena and Teresa of Avila—all of whom I have mentioned before—have been persons who also excelled in many mundane pursuits, such as warfare, politics and construction. Others, like St. John of the Cross, while admittedly less practical minded, have left the literature of the world enriched in a way which never could have been done by anyone who was a congenital liar or possessed of an unsound mind. It is even more noteworthy that the Scriptures, from the earliest chapters of Genesis to the final chapters of Revelations, are replete with accounts of visions and voices of supernatural origin. Adam and Eve "heard the voice of the Lord God walking in the garden in the cool of the day"; Jacob dreamed and beheld "a ladder set up on the earth . . . and the angels of God ascending and descending on it and behold the Lord stood above it"; Joseph's dreams were manifold and led to the deliverance of the Israelites from the Egyptians; the Ten Commandments were written down by Moses as he heard them from the voice of God and all the directions for building the Ark of the Covenant were of Divine origin. The Archangel Gabriel was the first to say, "Hail Mary," and it was through dreams that Joseph was reassured about taking her for his wife and warned that "the Young Child and His Mother" must be hurried out of Bethlehem. The heavens opened before Saul when he was on the road to Damascus and there he heard the question, "Why persecuteth thou Me?" that changed his life and the course of history. St. John the Divine brought his record to an end by saying that Jesus had sent His angel to testify unto him.

Many who accept all this unhesitatingly cannot seem to do the same in the case of revelations which do not have a biblical source, even though their Divine origin seems quite apparent to the persons with whom the skeptics are taking issue. Furthermore, skepticism about a mystic's experiences is always more widespread among his contemporaries than it is among scholars and clerics of a later age. Joan of Arc's belief in her voices and her conduct as a result of this belief led to her death at the stake; but they also led to her canonization. Similarly, the ecstasies of Teresa were a source of scoffing and led to her investigation by the Inquisition; but they did not prevent her from founding nearly a score of convents, under almost insuperable difficulties, during her lifetime, and they have given her lasting fame, as well as lasting glory. María Vela's role in the realms of mysticism was a humbler one. But her experiences had ample precedent and I see no reason to question that they should be respectfully and even reverently regarded.

Julián de Avila, however, did not argue this way. "Such was his nature that once he apprehended something, nobody could make him change."[25-a] The Abbess did not know whom else to suggest and, by this time, María Vela had begun to feel "as if she were drifting like a rudderless ship in the midst of so many contradictions."[26] It was a long while since she had held any direct communication with the remaining members of her family; but in her painful perplexity, she finally decided to appeal to her brother, Diego, and he came to the convent with exemplary promptness. It was, of course, necessary that he should first be received by the Abbess; and after talking with her only fifteen minutes, he told her he would think over what she had said and then call upon her again. Consultation with various leading citizens of Avila did not do much to reassure him; the general opinion seemed to be that María Vela was crazy. Far from being convinced, he was deeply resentful and voiced this resentment as abruptly as Teresa had done when she told Julián to hold his peace about her writings. "Everyone is welcome to feel about my sister's affairs as he pleases," Diego said shortly. "But I know she has been a saint from her childhood and I trust to God that, in due time, He will take her out of the craggy road which He is now causing her to tread."[27]

Diego was not the only member of the family now roused. María Vela's other brother, Father Lorenzo of the Bernardine Order, came to town and had a long talk with his sister. At the end of it, she handed him a report that had been written by "a certain religious, condemning her spirit" and asked him to tell her frankly what he thought of it. Lorenzo had hardly begun it, when he found a statement which convinced him that most of the assertions in it were probably groundless; the writer freely admitted that everything he had put down was based on hearsay. Lorenzo was no less indignant than Diego had been and he put his reasons for indignation into writing "with conclusive arguments." The resultant thesis carried great weight, even at the time, and eventually became a document of priceless value.

Emboldened by these virile, confident and learned expressions of brotherly opinion, María Vela went to the Abbess with renewed courage and asked for permission to order the rest of her daily life in accordance with her profound belief and her soul's sincere desire. Hesitantly, permission was given; results were astonishing, both to the

Abbess and to the community: María Vela's precarious health immediately improved. She was able to fulfill all her duties in the sacristy and the choir with her former regularity and with greater efficiency than ever before. To be sure, these duties were sometimes interrupted by the trances which were becoming more and more frequent and María Vela felt the same shyness about these that she did about everything else; she hoped and prayed that she might be forewarned of their coming, so that she could retire to her cell and remain there in seclusion until she had regained normal consciousness. But, very often, the ecstasies occurred in the midst of a service or while she was engaged in registering the choir. She earnestly requested María de Avila to draw her veil down over her face when this happened, so that no one could observe her expression when she was in this state; but María de Avila was reluctant to do this because "on such occasions María Vela became very beautiful." It enraptured the entire community, much of it hitherto so skeptical, censorious or downright hostile, to gaze at her. Ordinarily, María Vela, who had been comely like her mother, as a child, and who had become lovely in a rather ethereal way, had no special claims to any real beauty except that of her hands; but now that she was at last following the mystic way, unforbidden and unimpeded, a change had taken place. The members of the community wanted nothing to hide from their awed and admiring eyes this new beauty, which, at last, they recognized as God's gift.[27-a]

6

The Abbess, like other nuns in the community, had now been won over; not only did she herself sponsor María Vela's course of action; she suggested that Salcedo might be recalled to his former post of usefulness, though, wisely, she did not at once bruit her decision abroad. Gradually, however, it became known and this without resentment. Very probably, he would have continued the service he resumed of acting as María Vela's immediate spiritual adviser, until either he or she died, had not his term as rector of the college in Avila ended. This was a signal for his transfer to Valladolid. It was then arranged, as it had been so long before in the case of Gaspar de Avila, that he and his most prominent penitent should correspond and that, as far as possible, he would direct her in this way, though she would make her General Confessions to the chief chaplain at the convent.

A few days before his departure, and with his knowledge and consent, another religious of Avila sent her a note, beseeching her to recommend to the Lord a matter which was of great importance to the city. He stressed the fact that the Divine favors she received and the raptures she experienced had now become the subject of public knowledge, and that she was very generally regarded as a saint whose intercession would be invaluable. This was a decided change from the attitude expressed, only a comparatively short time earlier, to her brother, Diego; the tide of popular opinion had turned in her favor, just as the general feeling of the convent had done.

Not that this approval was universal or unqualified—after all, that would have been too much to hope. When the Abbess decided to give her more responsibility and show her greater honor by appointing her Mistress of Novices, there was some murmuring. But this was based mainly on the fact that, according to custom, only a very old nun was chosen for this position and, at Santa Ana, a nun was not considered very old until she was about seventy, whereas María Vela was not yet forty! However, this objection was overruled and, again, she showed signal talent in the fulfillment of important duties, as she had in the choir and the sacristy. "The novices she brought up showed the prudence and discretion she possessed, for she came to know the disposition of each . . . as well as the nature of her vocation. This is one of the things that must be examined carefully, since not all the postulants come with an efficacious calling and it is of utmost importance to scrutinize the talents of each one, because a discontented nun is an occasion of much uneasiness and, if the discontent persists, she may become the spirit of contradiction for all virtue and observance. Doña María's prudence was of the highest degree; she was very gentle in her commands, but rather severe in reprehending, more with her look than with words. She humbled herself to shame her novices, saying that if they did not amend their faults it was because they saw so many in her.

"In the first place, she tried to instill into their hearts a deep devotion to the Blessed Virgin and, among other practices, she taught them to recite three 'Salves' when coming out of the choir: one after Prime, asking for humility and patience; another after None, asking for mortification and purity of heart; the third after Compline, asking for obedience and silence. . . . She also wrote some notes for them on how to keep the Rule of the Order more perfectly; these are so well arranged that grave men who have seen them are short of words in their praise. [Do not know how to praise them sufficiently.] Her own example was the best teacher on how to practice mortification and keep the composure that they [the novices] should observe when going from one place to another. She had instructed them on how to make a signal to advert one another when any of them was caught speaking loudly or was otherwise distracted, and she ordered them to give the same signal to her when she overlooked or forgot something. As her foremost exterior virtue was obedience, she taught them how to obey and behave in the presence of their superiors.

"During her office as Mistress, she was criticized because she did not correct her novices whenever they made any mistake, especially in choir. If her critics judged by what they saw, they were right, because her attention and devotion at the Divine Office were such as can be seen only very rarely. She loved more than she prayed, and a proof of this is that she received the greatest favors from the Lord while saying the Office in choir. There was nothing that disgusted her more than the distractions of the nuns in choir; and this was the reason why she did not want to reprehend her novices there, thinking that this would cause more distractions; she preferred to keep the reprehension for the novitiate, where she called attention to mistakes. . . . To forestall any such mistakes, she adverted the novices the night before about everything they had to do the following day. Against this criticism the novices themselves defended her cause, revealing how she corrected them. She scolded them because they excused her, teaching them not to give excuses.

"She said her Office privately in the same way that she did in choir. She contemplated the scenes of the Passion of Christ our Redeemer by following some notes she had written in her breviary for each Hour; before beginning its recitation, she was recollected with the meditation of each scene, so that she contemplated rather than prayed. She taught this method to her novices and provided them with some verses of David, short prayers or ejaculations to help them recollect themselves whenever they were distracted. She taught them the exercise of mental prayer, each one according to her ability, and how to overcome the difficulties they would find at the beginning. She told them: 'Your singing must be like that of the nightingale, more spiritual than bodily.' "[28]

This account of María Vela's methods of dealing with her novices seems to me so charming that I have quoted it almost word for word, without even trying to make the translation idiomatic rather than literal. I find especially touching the statement that "she loved more than she prayed," for, as we know, she prayed a great deal; so, by this time, her very being must have been permeated with love, both for God and for the eager and devout young girls entrusted to her charge. It is evident that they loved her in return and that, through her, they learned to love God with a greater spirit of dedication than they could have done without her help. It is also evident that by providing them with "some verses of David, short prayers or ejaculations," she was constantly increasing the scope of her own reading, which, at first, had been largely confined to the works of St. Teresa. Indeed, we are told by the same faithful chronicler to whom we owe so much that "in her longing for perfection, she was greatly aided by reading spiritual books, to which she was devoted all her life." He adds that he wishes all would imitate her manner of reading and goes on to describe it: "On taking up a book, she lifted her spirit, concentrated her mind, and placed herself in the Presence of Christ Our Lord, who was to be the true teacher of the doctrine contained in that book and to bring forth the wisdom she was to acquire. She advised everyone to do some spiritual reading every day, not by greedily going over many pages, for that is merely turning leaves without permitting the soul to get any nourishment, but by pondering on what we read."[29]

María Vela also found time for attention to such matters as those of dress. It will be remembered that, when she herself was a novice, she had not followed the example of Petronilla Valdivieso, who substituted the coarse cloth called Palencia for the material of which the nuns' habits were generally made—though this was coarse enough to suit almost everyone—and gave up wearing the warm overshoes called *chapines* in addition to her sandals, though she was entitled to do this in cold weather. But, apparently, during the intervening years, María Vela had been giving thought to these measures, for she now decided to take similar ones herself and hoped that her novices would be permitted to do likewise. It was not a question of fabric that interested her as much as a question of cut; she wanted to return to the *aljuba*, which was the primitive habit of the Order, a garment whose shape, like its name, was of Moorish origin—that is, it hung in loose folds instead of being trimly divided into waist and skirt. Just why she wanted to wear this is not clear—perhaps it took less time to adjust than the more formal garments which had come into general conventual use and, therefore, might allow more time for prayer and meditation; or perhaps it was suggestive of the hermitical mode of life, which she admired and followed as far as possible. At all events, she asked her superior to allow her to don the *aljuba* and, at the same time, to give up her *chapines*.

Shortly after María Vela became Mistress of Novices, a new Abbess, an aunt of María de Avila, had succeeded the one who, for so long a time, had shown herself both irresolute and harsh, though she ended by greatly admiring the most outstanding member of her community. This new Abbess was, fortunately, "of very mild disposition and noble condition, very religious and virtuous." Though she hesitated a little over the primitive habit, it is obvious she did not actually forbid it, for on St. Francis Day, María Vela appeared at chapel without the *chapines* and wearing the *aljuba*, to which she had added the cowl of thick serge made after the fashion of the Recollect Mothers of the Order. "Everyone looked at her and some, with sour faces, began to criticize her; others to mock her or to joke about her dress. The servant of God paid no attention to their gossip and jests, bearing these silently and gladly and saying: 'They will tire of gossiping if I do not tire of suffering.' . . . Her good example was so powerful that some of the young religious were moved by it and began discussing among themselves and with the servant of God how to adopt the new habit, one of them being a grave nun who became the Abbess within a few years. As they sought only greater perfection, they asked permission from the Prelate, who gladly granted it. So one morning they appeared all dressed in the said fashion. The scandal and the outcry of the nuns against the Prelate for having authorized it and against María Vela for having initiated it was such that they at once sent notice to the Dominican Fathers. The Prior of their convent came to Santa Ana, sent for the Prelate and for other grave nuns who disapproved the innovation, and told them his opinion, making them, particularly the Abbess, responsible for consenting to those singularities and enjoining her to order the reformers to give up the new clothing. The Prelate gave this command to the others, but not to Doña María, saying that she had been wearing the changed dress for many days already. This action on the part of the Abbess served as a pretext for the devil to spread lies against her outside of the convent: he hinted that the others had obeyed and that she did not want to. Things came to such a pass that the Abbess sent word to María Vela, informing her of what was going on and telling her that she would better take off the *'aljuba.'* The servant of God, who was then preparing for Communion, at once retired to her cell, put on the old habit and the *chapines* and returned promptly and calmly to communicate. The Prelate then compromised by letting her take off the *chapines* and make a skirt out of the *'aljuba.'* In this fashion, she dressed the rest of her life."[30]

Shortly before María Vela's advancement to the position of Novice Mistress, the convent was favored by a royal visit. It will be recalled that Isabel of Castile had spent some time there during her girlhood, as a student, and that it was there she was first offered the crown. Later, after she had become Queen, she visited Santa Ana, with her husband, King Fernando; and her grandson, Emperor Charles V, not only favored it in the same way, but selected it as the *mise en scène* for the ceremony at which his son, the future Philip II, under the supervision of his mother, the Empress Isabel, was "dressed in shorts with a sword" by the nuns themselves. "Avila glistened with gay tapestries and bright-coloured hangings that sparkled against the granite and was completely invaded by the court. Its sombre streets came to life with gay processions, in the squares tourney followed joust and there was a continual but pleasant hubbub intermingled with the sound of music and the clash of bells."[30-a] Such regal ceremonies were by way of becoming traditional in both city and convent, for Philip III and his wife, Doña Margarita of Austria, were the next monarchs to honor Avila with a visit. On this occasion, the Church of San Gil, connected with the Jesuit College, was decorated with precious and embroidered hangings; and, in its nave, was placed a galleon that had been built, in 1594, for the transfer of San Segundo's remains, complete with all its riggings, masts, cannons and standards in perfect arrangement, and adorned with written inscriptions and many ingenious poems alluding to the coming of Their Majesties, in whose royal presence some of the students presented a play. One of the boys, chosen to recite a poem, was dressed as a lady (representing the city with its coat-of-arms) and the festival closed with a graceful dance which the monarchs received with enthusiasm.[30-b]

Santa Ana was also favored with a visit in the course of this royal progress and though, unfortunately, we have no such detailed record of it as we have of the celebration at San Gil, we know that it also took a splendid form and that María Vela, like the rest of the community, was privileged to have a part in the proceedings. Doubtless, she prayed more fervently than ever for humbleness under these circumstances; nevertheless, a later visit was to afford her still more personal joy.

This was the one made her by her two brothers at the same time, after she became Mistress of Novices. Both Diego and Lorenzo had her physical, as well as her spiritual well-being at heart; and, ever since his earlier visit, when he had defended her so wholeheartedly, Diego had been somewhat concerned about the former and, periodically, had protested that he thought she was not treated with as much consideration, understanding and sympathy as she should be. He conferred with Juan de Alarcón and Fray Gerónimo de San Eliseo, a Carmelite who had recently come to town, and who had been acting as María Vela's confessor part of the time since her unhappy experience and definite break with Julián de Avila. "They answered him satisfactorily that they had never doubted the sincerity of María Vela's virtues, but found great difficulty in admitting all her strange ways, and that they blamed mainly her confessors for having made public her revelations which were the occasion of disturbances in the convent; that they knew his sister was very obedient and willing to be unknown and unseen and her confessors should have kept her experiences in secret as was her wish. After long discussions, they convinced him that he should send for his brother, Father Lorenzo de Cueto, who then was residing in a convent in the hills and might guide their sister, as a learned and spiritual man, until they found another director, since the door was closed to the Discalced Carmelites. Don Diego was pleased with the plan; but, when he went to Santa Ana to propose it to his sister, he learned that the Abbess had been trying to obtain permission of the superiors to let Father Gerónimo come and hear the confession of María Vela every fortnight. She was glad to hear that the latter's brother, Lorenzo, might be sent here, wrote letters and helped Don Diego obtain the permit. Father Lorenzo was given a long leave and, after a hard journey, arrived in the middle of winter; the three had a happy family reunion and were greatly comforted."[31]

As time went on, the memory of this visit became one which María Vela cherished increasingly, for it was the last that the three had together. Not long afterward, "while the servant of God was enjoying some peace and quietude, her elder brother, Don Diego Alvarez de Cueto, who was a very discreet knight and good Christian, fell mortally ill. As soon as she heard it, she hastened to the Lord, begging Him to spare her brother. His Majesty revealed to her that it was convenient for him to die of that illness. She resigned herself to the Divine Will, and though she still prayed for her brother's health, she also prayed the Lord to give him the right disposition to die."[32] Then she told her confessor about the situation and asked him to visit her brother and inform himself on Diego's condition.

Happily, she had at last acquired one whom she could not only trust with such a mission, but upon whom she could rely for guidance and support in her every temporal and spiritual need. Though Fray Gerónimo had finally been granted permission to minister to her as often as was necessary, these ministrations had lasted only from Twelfth Night to Easter. Then he came to tell her that he had been ordered to leave Spain, that he had no hope of returning to his native land, and that he hoped she would "pray for the success of the important business entrusted to him"—the nature of which he did not divulge. He added that he left her in the hands of her brother, Lorenzo. As usual, such a haphazard arrangement did not prove satisfactory; Father Lorenzo's cloister was in the hills and his sister's in the city; though he could leave his, under special conditions and with special permission, she could not leave hers. The conferences which they could hold face to face were, consequently, strictly limited; and María Vela had taken no steps "to find a fixed confessor, because of the many trials she had suffered under previous ones"—a negligence for which, under the circumstances, we can hardly find it in our hearts to blame her! But this seems to have been another of those cases where the judgment of God began where the judgment of man ended.

There was in the city, at this time, a certain secular priest by the name of Miguel González Vaquero; his name is always preceded by the title of Doctor, which was not the general custom; we may safely assume that he had acquired a doctorate in either Philosophy or Divinity, or both, probably at Salamanca. In his writings, he never refers to himself except as a native of Avila and María Vela's confessor, but he was also the Chaplain of the Hospital of Mosén Rubin, which is now the Dominican Convent. His curiosity, like that of many other persons, was roused on the subject of María Vela and he somehow managed to meet María de Avila, who had no fixed confessor, either, and convince her that she should send for him to hear her confession; under that pretext, he could also speak to María Vela. He was still without any intention of serving her permanently; however, in writing about this first encounter afterward, he said, "I have counseled some very superior souls, but none has impressed me as much for her humility and sincerity and the fullness of her love of God."

This good opinion was not based entirely on one meeting. Dr. Vaquero had already heard a great deal about María Vela from one Ana de los Reyes, "a woman old in age as well as in the practice of all virtues," and a disciple of María Diaz, the farmer's daughter from Vita, who had become a friend of Teresa de Ahumada when both were house guests of Doña Guiomar de Ulloa, and who spent the latter part of her life as so holy a hermit that she was declared Venerable by popular acclamation. There was a very close bond between the two women. Indeed, it was said that, one day when María Diaz was examining her conscience to find if she was overattached to any of the persons who were in contact with her, she said of Ana de los Reyes, "This one, Lord, is indeed inside my heart; but You must leave her to me, for I have brought her up for You."

Not unnaturally, Dr. Vaquero set great store by the views of Doña Ana de los Reyes; and since his own impressions immediately confirmed these, an arrangement was quickly made by which he could see María Vela frequently. At first, he did not do this officially or openly, but through the intervention of María de Avila. Apparently, such expedients were not considered deceitful, in an evil sense, but merely useful methods of avoiding futile arguments, until matters of importance were definitely settled. At all events, we hear of them rather often, not only in the records of María Vela's life, but in the records of others whose standards of integrity we cannot question. For three months, Vaquero was in secret communication with María Vela under the pretext of going to hear the confession of her friend. "This was not difficult," he writes, "for the nuns preferred her to deal only with her brother and she seldom went down to the confessional and then she consulted me only about special matters, without placing herself under my obedience. As she was going through a period of religious fervor and was receiving great supernatural favors, she was satisfied with this arrangement, though the Lord was making known to her His Will to take me as her permanent confessor. Finally, a confirmation of the Divine disposition came when Father Lorenzo was ordered by the General of his Order to return to his monastery. She [María Vela] told me she was going to ask leave from her Prelate to obey me. I said that she knew I had placed myself under the obedience of Father Julián de Avila, who was one of the greatest opponents to her ways, and so I believed that he would refuse to allow me to take care of her soul, as he knew my shortcomings and was in the habit of mortifying me; nevertheless, I thought we should commend this matter to Our Lord, Who alone could smooth all the difficulties. We agreed that she should speak to Father Julián and place herself in his hands, saying that she was without a fixed confessor, and asking him to have the kindness of proposing the one she should choose, as he was acquainted with everyone. The saintly man was greatly pleased to hear that and said at once that he would take charge of commanding me to hear her confessions, at the same time warning her that, if I took care of her, she should refrain from going to others, for he always thought that sharing her experiences with so many, who then made them public, had done her great harm. She promised, and was greatly consoled and confirmed in her opinion that this was God's Will. As soon as I learned this decision, I went to see the Father and found him greatly changed in regard to his opinion of Doña María. When he told me to take charge of her, I discussed with him my difficulties, which were not few: there were her extraordinary ways, which so many learned, spiritual and prudent men had judged differently—how could I cope with her problems, since I was lacking in everything that those men had had in abundance? He listened to me very patiently and said: 'Well, go and do as you are told and obedience will take care of everything.' It was settled that, with the penitent's leave, I should give him an account of her affairs, so that we both would be under his obedience. The saintly nun was greatly pleased with this arrangement and I told her that my first and foremost desire was to keep all her experiences in strict secrecy, for I was convinced that it was a mistaken policy to make those affairs, especially of women, known, for, if God wishes that they be known and broadcasted, He will take upon Himself to shelter and defend them, as He did with St. Catherine of Siena and other saints. 'Blessed be Thou, O Lord,' she exclaimed on hearing this, 'Thou hast accomplished what so often I have begged Thee: that Thou givest me a confessor who would bury me alive.' She already had leave from her Prelate to obey me, as Father Julián had spoken to her; and so she readily gave me obedience."[33]

It is extremely hard for us, in our time and our country, to judge how important a turning point this marked in María Vela's life, or how great Dr. Vaquero's responsibility became. The contacts of the average American lay person with his confessor are apt to be limited to a recital of sins, mostly venial, which he has committed within a given length of time—sometimes as long as a year, since Easter Duty is all that the Church actually requires. Quite frequently, this recital is hurried, because the layman is one of a long line waiting to enter the confessional, and he hesitates to waste the time of an overburdened priest, or to delay unduly the confession of others who have come to the church for the same purpose that he has, and who may have done so at considerable inconvenience, or because their consciences are more overburdened than his. If he is a person whose work requires that he should travel a great deal, he may know nothing whatsoever about the unseen priest to whom he is talking; even if he lives a settled life, it is doubtful whether he knows his pastor well personally. With the present shortage of priests in many dioceses, it is absolutely impossible for them to make parochial calls, unless summoned in some grave emergency, in which case, of course, they somehow manage to respond. Recently, I heard a priest quoted as saying that, in southwestern Louisiana, which is predominantly Catholic, there is only one priest to every six hundred persons and that, in his parish, there were only three clergymen available for ministry to eight thousand persons; if he called on four families every day in the year, he still would not be able to visit each one. I myself have lived for years on end in cities where I have attended church regularly, unless prevented by illness, without making the acquaintance of a single priest, nor do I resent this. I know that the clergy simply cannot cope with the situation.

In view of all this, I think it is important to stress the difference in the role played by a Spanish confessor, not only to a cloistered nun but to any practicing Catholic, and not only hundreds of years ago, but to this very day. The relation of a confessor to his penitent was, and is, as personal as the relation of a physician to his patient, probably more so. Many Spanish country seats of spacious, but by no means regal, proportions still have their own chapels and their resident chaplains; all ships in the Spanish Merchant Marine number a priest, often one of high rank, among their officers. (The same is true of Italian ships and, I believe, to a certain degree, of Italian country seats, though, since I am not as familiar with the latter as those in Spain, I cannot speak with as much authority on the subject.) In the smallest Spanish village, the one priest is the figure most familiar to everybody; with every increase in population, there is a corresponding increase in the number of clergy and the relationship with the inhabitants is correspondingly close. At the era under consideration in our story, the proportion of clergy to laity was very large—in fact, according to some statistics, one out of every four Spaniards in the sixteenth century was vowed to a religious life in some form. I cannot vouch for the complete authenticity of these figures, but they are certainly not far from accurate. A confessor, therefore, had plenty of time to give his penitents, because he had only a few of them; and it was taken for granted, both by him and by them, that he would do so. Besides the hours that he spent in their presence, he spent many more in considering their problems and, in confidence, consulting others about these. We have seen that Salcedo undertook wearisome journeys to Salamanca and that the most prominent professors there gave the questions submitted to them careful consideration. We have seen that Luis de la Puente came all the way from Valladolid to Avila in order to be helpful, and that Lorenzo, the Bernardine Monk, was granted leave of absence from his cloister for the same purpose. None of this struck anyone connected with María Vela as strange; what they would have thought strange would have been any failure or refusal to do so.

Vaquero, as it turned out, did even more than any of the others: he guided María Vela kindly and wisely for fifteen long years—that is, until her death. He discovered that, in addition to her other attainments—literary, musical and spiritual—she had the gift of prophecy. He encouraged her, as Salcedo had done, to write; and though he admonished her to keep these writings secret, he preserved them with the utmost care and, shortly after her death, caused one copy of them to be made at the convent, lest such a valuable record be lost. (A second was made in 1744.) At the same time, while everything he knew about her was still fresh and vivid in his mind, and while he could confer with numerous other persons who had known her in the flesh, he wrote a biography of her which is a minor masterpiece. Though he might not have succeeded in doing so much, it is almost certain that he would have tried. He would have considered the lack of such an effort a serious omission in the line of duty.

When she asked him to visit her sick brother, Diego, at Cardeñosa, her own last illness was, fortunately, far in the future. Vaquero undertook the commission as a matter of course, and he did so with the more willingness because he had reason to believe that Don Diego's wife, Doña Ana María de Zuñiga, was the victim of chicanery. "There was at that time in the monastery here one of those brethren who go about dressed as postulants, and try to imitate in their language a holy man called Brother Francisco de Alcalá—it would be better if they imitated his sincerity and virtues as well," he tells us. "This Brother began to give great demonstrations of prayer, especially at Mass, where he said the raptures he appeared to have came more easily to him. Don Diego's wife, a very pious woman, was so impressed by these demonstrations that she asked for permission to have the Brother at her home during her husband's sickness. The pseudo-postulant spoke to her reassuringly, saying, 'Do not weep, my good sister; our brother will not die,' and then and there fell into a trancelike state. The patient, as a sensible man, did not feel easy in his mind about this; but in order not to disquiet his wife, he said nothing."

Of course, it is cases of impostors like this that make the Church cautious about pronouncing visions and voices to be of Divine origin, and that cause skepticism and ridicule among the laity. "When I came to see Don Diego, his illness was getting worse," Vaquero went on. "But the postulant was very confident and the good lady was complaining about her sister-in-law who, she thought, was not praying for the health of her brother as she should, for he was not improving. I tried to console Don Diego's wife and told her to write, in her affliction, to the saintly nun. I then took the letter to Doña María myself. She would have preferred not to answer—she had not done so in similar cases when friends and relatives of a certain religious and a certain young gentleman had come to her, asking her to pray for the recovery of their loved ones, nor had she revealed, except to her confessor, that she knew these sick persons were going to die. I told her that this case was different and ordered her to answer the letter. She did it very prudently, telling her sister-in-law how important it was to be resigned to God's Will and asking that her brother should be told to commend himself to God. . . . The discreet gentleman, on hearing the letter read, understood its message and said to his wife, 'Answer my sister to the effect that I have been consoled by her message, and since her prayers will not avail to preserve my life, ask her to pray that they may avail me to have a good death.' He at once began to prepare for this and died on December 9th, in as Christian a way as he had lived. Doña María Vela received the news when she was about to communicate and, appealing to God, she said, 'Thou knowest, my Lord, that I have placed all the satisfaction of my works and troubles in Thy hands, in favor of the souls in Purgatory. I entreat Thy infinite goodness that, if these are of any value in Thy eyes, they may now be applied in favor of my brother's soul.' "[34]

Vaquero adds that she said this prayer every day for the rest of her life. In passing, he also remarks that her sister-in-law, Doña Ana María de Zuñiga, though grief stricken, was "disabused of the sayings and doings of the lay brother." Evidently, he thought there was no great loss without some small gain.

7

"By this time," Dr. Vaquero writes, with the wisdom of experience, "I was convinced of the truth of that saying by St. John Chrysostom that the Merciful God does not permit the tribulations of the saints to be continuous, nor the consolations, either, but with prosperity and adversity He weaves a fabric of wonderful and exquisite variety. During the ten years that this servant of God suffered interior tribulations, they were not uninterrupted, but intermixed at different intervals with periods of peaceful relief; and her patience and silence were such that only her confessor knew her trials. Her friend, María de Avila, came to surmise some of them, but she was not acquainted with the essential or main troubles."

This statement summarizes, so skillfully, the general tenor of María Vela's life, as it drew toward its end, that the modern chronicler is tempted not to enlarge on it, for fear that details might seem superfluous. Yet, incontestably, certain examples of the alternating "prosperity and adversity" that are woven into that "fabric of wonderful and exquisite variety" belong in the narrative to make it complete.

A strange accident was the occasion for one of these periods of adversity. A certain day, after Meditation, as the nuns were leaving the choir, the heavy silver crozier of the Abbess, which was not in use at the time, was suddenly dislodged from the place where it was standing; and, as it toppled over, it hit María Vela on the head with such violence that she was badly hurt and blood began to gush from the wound. One of the nuns, contrite and alarmed, maintained that she had inadvertently knocked it down as she was passing by it; but María Vela was sure that this accident was the work of the devil, exactly as Teresa had been certain it was Satan who had caused her to fall downstairs and break her arm. Indeed, for the first time, María Vela insisted she had seen the devil; and since, up to that time, she had been equally insistent that she never had, though she had been aware of his presence and his evil designs on her, it is not astonishing that her words carried weight. Vaquero, with commendable impartiality, gives both versions of the possible cause of the accident; but his recital of what happened next presents this mishap and its consequences as factual: "The anxious nuns took her to her cell and sent for a famous surgeon from Salamanca who chanced to be in town and who was a great servant of God. As soon as he had examined her wound, he asked if she loved God very much and when her companions inquired why he said that, he answered, 'She will need all that love to stand the pain she is going to suffer.' He cut the skin over the whole scalp in the form of a cross, to see if the skull was cleft and found that it was not, though badly bruised. At this moment, I came in [having expected] to hear María Vela's confession, and when the surgeon finished, I drew him into the corridor and he told me that the damage was serious and that he would have to work on it for several days. That night, María Vela placed a rosary on her head and invoked the Blessed Virgin. When the surgeon returned in the morning, he found the wound healed, except for a little pimple, which he did not mind. The nuns began to publish this happening as a miracle, and the person most astonished of all was the surgeon, who said it could not be explained otherwise. To hush all comments, I told María Vela to remain in bed, as if she were really sick, and asked the doctor to treat the little pimple in spite of his assurance that she did not need his services."[34-a]

Some time after this occurrence, a siege of pneumonia seemed destined to bring María Vela's life to an end, but was followed by one of those periods of "peaceful relief" which enabled her to resume all her normal occupations in the usual way; and throughout her illness she insisted that "Our Lord had made her understand she would not die of it, but that she would get well by means of obedience." She had always been swift and eager to obey; unlike many nuns who fulfill their vows of poverty and chastity without undue difficulty, but chafe under the pledge of obedience, she dwelt on the promise she had found in Proverbs: "An obedient man shall speak of victory" (21:28). Now she told Vaquero about her "understanding"; however, as he felt very strongly that spiritual directors should not be guided by revelations and supernatural manifestations without being sure they were true, he at first received this confession without any undue show of interest, but "waited to see how God would dispose events." The illness grew worse and the patient revealed her great faith that, if Vaquero would order her to get well, she would do so; still he hesitated, though he could see "she was bent on it." At last, on the twentieth day of her illness, the attending physicians became so alarmed over her "debility and exhaustion" that Vaquero finally yielded. He "sent her a command in virtue of holy obedience to dress, go to Holy Communion and attend to her other duties. She obeyed at once and came downstairs for confession and Communion. When the doctors arrived and found her singing at Mass, they were speechless and the nuns did not know what to say, either. From the choir, she went to the refectory and waited on table."[35]

Vaquero himself makes no further comment on this extraordinary performance. In the light of modern medical knowledge, it seems probable that, by the twentieth day, the crisis had already long since passed, and that the debility and exhaustion which so alarmed María Vela's physicians were merely symptoms quite usual in the aftermath of a serious illness such as pneumonia. Given her great desire to prove she was going to get well, it is not astonishing that she could summon enough strength for a supreme effort to show that she was right; and, personally, I am very pleased that she was human enough to say, in effect, "I told you so!" to Vaquero, even if she collapsed afterward, though we are not told that she did. Obviously, however, she harbored no resentment because he had been slow to accept her understanding of Our Lord's message as true, for she herself later recorded her "firm conviction" that spiritual directors should "exhaust all possible means of investigation that human prudence dictates" before accepting alleged superhuman experiences as authentic; and it was by her leave that Vaquero "took counsel with many learned men whenever the occasion was propitious."[36] In other words, it would seem that, whereas she did not doubt the Divine source of her revelations, she did not wish that there should be the slightest doubt of this elsewhere—an attitude which shows amazingly good sense. And after all, she had learned this lesson in a hard way, through the exposure of a pseudo-postulant, who had preyed upon her sister-in-law, Doña Ana María de Zuñiga.

It would appear that, usually, María Vela accepted the "messages" she received as clear and direct, and that the interpretation of the "visions" she had was not difficult for her, either; occasionally, however, we find a record of one that puzzles her. "The Lord showed her a big fire in the midst of which arose a very high and dry pole; around this, a rope was twisted twice; and on top of it was perched a snow-white dove, with fiery beak and feet, and with many spots of the same fire all over its body. She was told to look closely and to ponder how white the little dove remained on the high dry pole, in spite of the fire below and the smoke around it. The servant of God gave me an account of it, imagining that it might mean the Lord was to fulfill the great desire she had harbored for so many years—martyrdom for the Holy Faith. As I have so little knowledge of these supernatural favors, I told her we should not weary our minds trying to find an explanation for this, but leave it for God to declare if such were His pleasure. An artist was, at that time, painting some decorations inside the convent, and I told María Vela to ask him to picture on a cross this vision and three others she had had; they might come true in the future and I wished to keep a record of them. I still have this cross with these representations, in case Our Lord is pleased to reveal their meaning."[37]

Whether the meaning of the "three others" was ever revealed directly to Vaquero, we are not told; but he does tell us that María Vela herself was vouchsafed an explanation of the dove's significance. "The great fire that she saw represented the exterior and interior martyrdom she had suffered; the dry pole the utter abandonment and helplessness in which she found herself; the rope twisted twice around it, the snares of the devil, which threatened both the life of the body and the life of the soul; the little white dove, the soul itself, which would be preserved through Divine Grace without being touched or soiled by the fire and smoke, but rather grow in Sublime Love through its trials, as indicated by the fire on the feet and bill of the dove and by the spots strewn all over its body. She at once informed me of her relief in learning the meaning of the vision, and she accepted this interpretation of it with complete resignation to God's Will, and with readiness to accept every hardship for his love, so long as he did not let her fall into sin."[38]

María Vela was reading more and more and writing more and more all the time. She describes at length—and so does Vaquero in quoting her—what she calls "piercing charity," and the word piercing is used almost literally, rather than in the more figurative manner that has come into general modern use. "This ardent love leaves in the soul three wounds," we are told. "The first is the inability to remove all faults and imperfections which, while we are on earth, will always exist. . . . The second wound is the memory of past offences; though she was pure and blameless, she always felt in her heart sorrow for her sins, real or imaginary. . . . The third wound is sorrow for sins committed in the world; this is one of the deepest and most constant pains that afflict her heart."[39]

A comparison between these "wounds" and the one inflicted on St.

Teresa by the fiery dart, during the phenomenon of transverberation, comes almost instantly to mind; and, over and over again, there are passages in María Vela's *Autobiography* which recall the principles, the convictions and the sayings of her great predecessor. Their feeling in regard to Our Lord's actual Presence, even their manner of referring to Him—usually as His Majesty—are strikingly similar, as are many other aspects of their writings. Not that María Vela was consciously trying to copy St. Teresa's style or that she could have done so if that had been her wish or intention; the former was merely, in a restricted way, following in the latter's footsteps. María Vela lacked many of the advantages which the other possessed: her people were gentle, rather than distinguished; her upbringing secluded, rather than social; her education thorough, rather than advanced; her talents limited, rather than varied; her vocation instinctive, rather than inspired. Inevitably, she had to tread what, centuries later, was to become famous as the Little Way of Thérèse of Lisieux, rather than achieving such a *Way of Perfection* as Teresa of Avila visualized and described, though María Vela longed for this, too. ("After I made a General Confession the year I entered the convent—thirty-one years ago, at the age of fifteen, on the Feast of the Presentation of Our Lady—Our Lord in His great goodness began to give me longings for perfection," she tells us in beginning the chronicle which she wrote "under express obedience" to her confessor.) But the Little Way has proved the path to salvation to many simple souls and María Vela's words and acts of guidance toward it, though, for centuries, unrecognized, can no longer be overlooked or underestimated.

All in all, though more details are lacking, it appears that prosperity, rather than adversity, marked María Vela's later years, when her sphere of usefulness was expanded to include the duties of an infirmarian. In 1617, His Holiness, Paul V, announced the granting of a Plenary Indulgence to all Christendom and, in Avila, the proclamation of this was made in mid-September. At the time, María Vela was caring, with great love and diligence, for a former novice of hers, who was gravely ill; and, when Vaquero visited the two in the infirmary, María Vela expressed the hope that she herself might be able to fulfill the prescribed devotions in connection with obtaining this indulgence; if she could, it would seem to her like the one mercy which was still lacking after all the others she had received from Our Lord. However, she added, with quick and customary docility, "His Will, not mine, be done."

Just why she should have felt doubtful—for her words certainly imply doubt—as to whether this hope could be fulfilled is not clear, since, obviously, she was in good health at the time or she would not have been caring for another nun who was ill; but that very night she was stricken with severe pain—a *dolor de costado*—which was probably pleurisy, and it was soon evident that her condition was serious. According to the medical practices of the day, she was bled and her blood-stained clothing was not changed;[40] and, in accordance with the Rules of the Order, the Abbess was summoned into the cell of the sick nun before the latter received the Viaticum, in order that she might bequeath her belongings to the convent. In this case, they consisted of nothing more than her clothing and the bed on which she lay, for, as we have already noted, she took her vow of poverty very literally. Physically, she must have been in considerable pain. But there were no "piercing wounds" of a mental or spiritual nature, nor any of the interior turmoil and anguish which had so often tormented her—needlessly, or so it would seem to us. She was wholly serene. When her confessor asked her whether she was disturbed or distressed by anything, she shook her head and said, with a smile, "I am already surrounded by complete peace and quietude." Then she went on to describe a crown, richly encrusted with jewels, which His Majesty Himself had placed on her unworthy head. The experience had seemed to her so vivid that she could hardly believe it was only a vision.

She received "with the utmost tranquillity" the entire community which—again, according to custom—filed in to see her and she sent affectionate and encouraging messages to her former novice and patient, bidding the latter to be of good cheer and to hold fast to the Faith. But, at the end, it was only María de Avila, her most loyal and best-beloved friend, whom she wanted with her, and who came—and stayed, holding her fast in strong and gentle arms until she no longer needed support from anyone on earth.

Hardly had the news of María Vela's death spread through the city when the convent was besieged with crowds, clamoring to pay her their final tribute and to seek relics of her. The community would have preferred that no outsider should approach the bier until after a suitable interval; but the clamor became so great that the nuns were not able to withstand it. The people were shouting the word, "Saint," and raising an outcry: Vaquero must show himself and talk to them about her; they must be permitted to have locks of her hair, scraps of her veil, fragments of her scapular. Not unnaturally, the nuns desired such relics themselves; and, since Vaquero advised them that the crowds should be permitted to enter the courtyard, as long as they did so "with faith and devotion," the convent resorted to one of those minor acts of deception which, apparently, at that period, seemed untouched by evil: namely, María Vela's clothes were changed for those of another nun and the garments of the woman whose sanctity was already a byword were kept for the community.

By order of the Bishop, Don Francisco de Gamarra, burial was not to take place in the communal cloister as usual, but at the foot of the altar in the Chapel of Our Lady of the Sun, to whom María Vela had shown great devotion; and it was the Bishop who presided at her funeral, accompanied by the canons of the cathedral, the nobles and the gentry of Avila and followed by an immense throng of humbler folk. As many as possible mounted beforehand to see her in her cell, where she lay crowned with flowers and holding a palm between the beautiful hands which had so long been active and which were now so peacefully folded. Then, after the Office of the Dead had been devoutly recited, she was placed in a casket, something never before done at Santa Ana, and carried to the chapel, where, the next day, the Funeral Mass was held; and, at the request of her sister-in-law, Doña Ana María de Zuñiga, that further honors should be shown her, this was followed by a Requiem Mass under the auspices of the Discalced Carmelites, at which the oration was given by a very famous preacher, Fray Gregorio de Sotomayor.

During the course of the next six years, numerous miracles were attributed to María Vela, who had been declared a Venerable by acclamation. At the end of this time, her casket was transferred, upon order from the same Bishop who had officiated at her funeral, to a magnificent tomb, adorned with a gilded grille and noble pedestals, which was located between the two choirs. On this tomb, the following inscription was carved:

"Aqui yace el Cuerpo de la Venerable Mujer Fuerte Doña María Vela, Monja de esta santa Casa y natural de esta ciudad: murió a 24 de Septiembre de 1617 y de su primer sepulcro le trasladaron a este el Señor d. Francisco de Gamarra, Obispo de Avila, que primero fué de Cartagena, con auerdo del Claustro de Teologia de la Universidad de Salamanca en 5 de Agosto de 1623, siendo Pontifice Urbano VIII y Rey de España Don Felipe IIII y Corregidor de esta Ciudad Don

Juan de Beaumont y Navarra y Abadesa de este Convento Doña María Dávila."[41]

At the time of this transfer—the first of several which eventually took place—the casket was opened in the presence of many dignitaries who issued an official report on their findings. This report is so lengthy and detailed that it seems out of place to quote it in full; but one outstanding phenomenon must certainly be noted: the corpse was in a remarkable state of preservation, with all its members in much the same condition as when burial had taken place, of course without embalmment. In short, María Vela proved to have what is technically known as an "incorruptible body."[42] The report speaks of her face, her lips, her teeth—and then of her crossed hands "supple and covered with flesh and skin." But, this time, the reference to them does not include any mention of beauty. They must, at last, have been as she herself had visualized, when she first entered the convent—preferring, in her humility, that they should not appear so lovely that everyone involuntarily gazed at them—and earnestly told her fellow novices she wanted her hands to look as they would after she was dead.[43]

San Pedro Bautista. From the statue in the Hermitage at San Esteban del Valle.

PART V

His Excellency, the Ambassador
of Spain to Japan

(San Pedro Bautista, 1545¹ — 1597)

1

IT IS NOT easy, in the Land of Stones and Saints, to find a section which belies its name, and the more searchingly and frequently it is traversed, the more apt the designation seems to become. But tucked away between the Pico de Gredos and Arenas de San Pedro—where Pedro de Alcántara died—is a little dale or glen, one of the counterforts that came down from the sierra, or mountain range, which shelters it. In the heart of this glen nestles the tiny town of San Esteban del Valle. It hardly seems part of the same world as the rest of the region where windswept stretches of arid rock-strewn land are broken only by gaunt gray hills. It is verdant, luxuriant even, shaded by an abundance of fruit trees and watered by innumerable streams; and in its beneficent climate vegetables and fruits grow exuberantly. Its kitchen gardens flourish; its vineyards are laden with grapes; its groves are silvery with olive branches and golden with the glow of oranges. It is often called the Andalucía of Avila. The grinding poverty of Fontiveros and other similar villages of the province has never touched it; its people have only to look to the land for everything they need. Therefore, when we first make the acquaintance of the child, Pedro Blasques Villacastín, it is in a very different way from that in which we first made the acquaintance of Juan de Yepes. We do not find a poor hungry little boy being led by his desperate mother away from the place where one of her children had already starved to death; we find a very healthy happy one, surrounded by a family circle of parents and four sisters, whose comfortable home is in the center of a pleasant and prosperous place and whose background is one of culture, as well as Christianity.

There is nothing to indicate that Pedro was handicapped by actual precocity; on the other hand, the brilliance of his mind and the natural piety of his habits were certainly evident from a very early age. He learned the usual lessons and played the usual games with the small boys who were his neighbors; but he showed extraordinary ease in mastering the equivalent of the three R's; and he made small crosses out of the little sticks of wood which he and his companions picked up, and marched through the streets, leading the singing of *Gloria Patri*, as well as the jubilant processions. Music was always a source of delight to him and he was to reveal his aptitude for it and his enjoyment of it in countless ways during the course of his life; but his first achievements, after he had passed beyond the rudiments of primary education, were in Latin and Cosmography, which he studied at Mombeltrán, where his father sent him to school at a very early age, because it was evident he had already outstripped all the facilities which San Esteban del Valle could offer for more advanced learning. At Mombeltrán, Pedro seized upon the advantages offered by an exceptionally fine teacher. From there, he was sent first to the Jesuit School in Oropesa and then to the city of Avila, where he began to study plain chant and organ music in earnest, first while serving as either an acolyte or a choir boy—possibly both—at the cathedral and then while teaching beginners himself.

With these preparations and these predilections, the next step was almost inevitable: he went to Salamanca to study Philosophy and Theology. Like María Vela, he took no irrevocable step for six years; then he was ordained a deacon in the Cathedral of Avila by the Bishop, Don Alvaro de Mendoza. But, also like her, he obviously delayed making any further definite decision about a vocation, not because he was unwilling or unready for it, but because he feared he might be unworthy. His humility, despite his remarkable attainments, was very genuine. If any proof of this were needed, it could be easily found in the fact that it was the Franciscan Order, founded by the gentle and lowly saint of Assisi, which drew him to its self-denying and consecrated way of life. After prolonged thought and prayer, he went to his father and told the latter that it was his soul's sincere desire to become a friar.

We cannot blame the elder Blasques for being somewhat disappointed by this announcement, as he must have been by the first step —that of the boy's ordination as a deacon—which had led to it. Pedro was an only son, whose brilliant mind, fine physique and exemplary character were all exceptionally well suited for the perpetuation of the family. Moreover, so long a time had passed after he began his studies at the university, it had been logical to assume that the cultivation of minds, rather than the care of souls, was likely to be his permanent preoccupation. Without putting any real opposition in his way, his father asked him to think the next step over for a few more months.

He did this, willingly and pleasantly. Then he wrote to the Provincial, asking for permission to join the Order. This was readily granted and, early one morning, he left the parental roof on foot and took the road which ends in the pine grove of La Cuesta de la Parra, where the Franciscan Convent of San Andrés was located. Although he did this "secretly," in the sense that he did not say good-bye to his family, it would seem that this omission of farewells was due to the desire of avoiding pain on both sides, rather than of causing it to anyone, much less of acting with deliberate deceit. Pedro's parents were devout Christians, and he knew that once they had become accustomed to the idea that their son wanted to be a priest, rather than a professor, they would accept this without grief. Moreover, since their four attractive daughters—María, Inés, Francisca and Catalina—did not lack suitors, they would realize that, sooner or later, some of these girls would marry, and that there would eventually be grandchildren who could carry on the family name, since, in Spain, this is not necessarily done only through a male descendant. Certainly Pedro must have believed himself justified in such arguments; otherwise, he could hardly have started so buoyantly.

Local legend still insists that his journey was not without alarming incident—on the contrary, that his way through the woods was blocked by a fierce demon who sought to check him by obstructing his path and to terrorize him first by loud roars and then by terrible visions; and, to this day, on his fiesta, an hour before the celebration begins, the church bells ring out to commemorate the *alborada*, or battle at dawn, which was won by the valiant young deacon while fighting against the powers of darkness. The road leading to San Andrés was, undoubtedly, a rough one and the latter part of it, just as undoubtedly, penetrated to the depths of a dark forest where it would be easy to imagine that almost anything might happen. However, Pedro arrived at his destination, certainly uninjured and, apparently, unperturbed. Indeed, he could hardly have been in a more salutary state. The crystalline air, for which the region is renowned, was scented with the fragrance of pines, and Pedro must have taken deep drafts of it with ever-increasing delight; and he probably paused in the clearing around the convent, to inspect its flourishing kitchen garden, which gave assurance of ample and wholesome nourishment, and to examine the famous blackberry bushes with which this was surrounded, and which were thornless—or so he had been told—ever since Pedro de Alcántara had used them for discipline and endowed them with miraculous attributes. At all events, he finally knocked at the great door which opened wide to receive him and was warmly greeted by the Guardian,[2] who was waiting to welcome him. Less than a month later, he took the habit; and, a year afterward, when his novitiate ended and he made his profession, he changed his name from Pedro Blasques Villacastín to Pedro Bautista.

2

The Convent of San Andrés had been founded by Pedro de Alcántara, the great friend and counselor of St. Teresa, and was chosen for his burial place; it still exists and now bears his name. Its extreme simplicity, its complete isolation enhance rather than lessen its atmosphere of consecration to an ideal which, in the person of the Order's founder, combined happiness with humbleness and, thereby, led to holiness. At the time of Pedro Bautista's novitiate, the memory of the great Spanish Franciscan was still fresh and vivid in the minds of men who had either known him in the flesh themselves, or who were acquainted with older persons who had firsthand knowledge of him. His example and his teachings were even closer to his disciples than those of St. Francis of Assisi. Inevitably, they made a profound impression upon Pedro Bautista, though, in emulating the austerities of the one, he never forgot the loving kindness of the other. His natural eloquence was already so exceptional that he was soon sent out to preach in the general neighborhood; then he was ordered farther afield: to the Convent of Peñaranda in Salamanca, where he taught Philosophy, and to the Convent of Cardillejo, near Fontiveros, where he became Guardian. In both regions, he also preached widely throughout the vicinity, always with increasingly successful results;

and, from Fontiveros, he went, as Official Preacher, to the Franciscan Convent in Toledo and thence, as Guardian, to the one in Mérida.

By this time, he had covered a good deal of ground, both figuratively and literally, for a comparatively young man, since he was still only a little over thirty. But he already had his eyes fixed on more distant horizons, and there were now no family ties to bind him to the lovely valley where he was born. His parents had both died shortly after he made his profession, within a year of each other; so had his sister Francisca, who had become locally renowned as a *Beata*[3] prior to her early death. María and Inés were both happily married and—as he had foreseen—were the mothers of numerous children; one of these was his namesake and the line was in no danger of extinction. Only Catalina remained to cause him possible concern and, unfortunately, details about her life are lacking; but we do know the date of her death: this took place a year before he actually set sail for the Indies, though perhaps not before he had applied for permission to do so. Having heard that "goodly numbers" of Franciscan Friars were to be dispatched first to Mexico and, later on, to the Philippines, he expressed a fervent wish to be included among them and his petition was granted. In April of 1581, the thirty who had been chosen assembled at the Convent of San Bernardino in Madrid, where the papal nuncio, Monsignor Felipo Lego, celebrated a Pontifical Mass and blessed the recruits in the name of His Holiness, Gregory XIII. Shortly thereafter, they left, in a body, for Seville, where they embarked, reaching Mexico about the end of July.

We cannot help regretting that Pedro's years of service there began more than thirty years after those of Juan de Zumárraga, first Bishop and Archbishop of Mexico, had been ended by death. Certainly the two men would have been kindred spirits, not only because they were both scholars, Franciscans and missionary zealots, but because they both had such strong ties with Avila. Zumárraga, though a Basque by birth, had held the important position as Guardian of its Convent of San Francisco; Pedro Bautista, a native of the province's most beautiful and benign section, had spent two of his most formative years as an acolyte or choir boy, possibly both, in Avila's cathedral and had been ordained as a deacon in that same severe but splendid setting. All this would surely have given them congenial tastes and interests and would have created bonds of strength between them, which would have resulted in great benefit for the furtherance of faith. Neither can we help wishing that Pedro Bautista had recorded his experiences among the Indians with the same amplitude that marked the writings of St. Teresa and María Vela, for certainly they would have made exciting reading. But, at the same time, we cannot fail to admire him as a man of action rather than of words. He remained in Mexico three years, and his contemporary, Marcelo de Ribadeneira, who afterward worked with him in Japan, tells us that, during Pedro's Mexican sojourn, "in order to sow the Divine seed in as many places as possible, the Lord directed him to take a long journey to Mechuacán, on foot and barefoot." This he unhesitatingly did. Moreover, "moved by fervor and trusting in the Lord, he ventured to enter the land of the Chichimecos, a fierce and barbarous tribe, that committed many cruelties on the men they captured."[4]

Pedro Bautista was not captured, nor was he called upon, at the time, to endure any cruelties. Apparently, this wise and kindly man had the same gift in dealing with savages that St. Francis had in dealing with wild beasts. Instead of antagonizing or angering the fierce and barbarous tribe in any way, Pedro made them his friends and became their welcome guest. In due time, he effected numerous conversions; it is doubtless because he did not try to force this issue that he was so successful in the end. All too often, though undertaken with the best intentions, hasty and peremptory methods had no lasting results; it was the missionaries whose own example was gentle and Christlike who endeared themselves personally to their charges and who made their message ring true.

Personally, as I have just said, I should like very much to read Pedro's own account of these long journeys which he undertook on foot, moved by fervor and trusting in the Lord, to see through his eyes the landscape, so rich in contrast of lush vegetation and snow-capped volcanoes, and the strange barbaric people, who had a pageantry and a splendor all their own, despite the contempt in which most Spaniards held them. But apparently he found little time for writing at this period, though he did some with great effect later on. His superiors always found him so invaluable that he was hardly well under way with his work in one place before they decided he would be of even more inestimable service in another. Instead of being dispatched to take more long journeys in Mexico, on foot, he was sent, in a ship, to the Philippines, embarking from Acapulco, with the entire Pacific Ocean between himself and his next destination. And, this time, his position was no longer that of a simple missionary, like that of his companions. He had been given the high-ranking office of *Comisario Visitador de la Custodia de San Gregorio*.

3

Pedro's new position carried with it great responsibilities,[5] for a *Comisario* was the official representative of a Provincial—that is, of a superior of a region which normally contained at least ten convents. However, a *Custodia*—that is, a region which contained fewer than this—could be raised to the higher category of a *Provincia* at the discretion of a Pope. Either this was the immediate intention of the Pontiff or else he hopefully assumed that the *Custodia de San Gregorio* would become a *Provincia* as soon as Pedro Bautista had been set to work establishing extra convents.

The missionaries were warmly welcomed to the Philippines by Fray Juan de Plasencia, Custodian of San Gregorio, and the sight of its principal port must have stirred nostalgic longings in the heart of Pedro Bautista. True, less than a hundred Spanish families made up the population of Manila; but it was already a walled city, with both a resident bishop and a resident governor; three religious communities —Augustinian, Franciscan and Jesuit—were established in it and about two hundred soldiers were stationed there. True, the walls did not resemble those of Avila—were there any in the wide world which would or could? The cathedral had none of the splendors which permeated the very stones of Salamanca's. The residences set apart for the Bishop and the Governor were palaces in name only and there were no others which, by any stretch of the imagination, could have merited such a designation. The convents were devoid of that restful isolation, that austere dignity, of all those in Spain to which he had been accustomed. But here again were the kind of culture, the level of society, even the type of architecture, albeit in embryo, of which he had been deprived during his long journeys through the wilds of Mexico. Pedro Bautista would have been less than human if he had not enjoyed these amenities and he was, fortunately, a very human sort of person. He entered upon his new duties with a happy heart.

These new duties were by no means light. In his capacity of *Comisario*, and with the authority vested in him through this office, he visited the flocks of which the Franciscans were in charge, that is to say, both those of the Spaniards who lived in the walled city and those of the Tagalog Indians who lived outside it and who were far more numerous. He confirmed the legality of the elections held in the Chapter the previous year, taught the children in the school which had been founded by Juan de Plasencia, preached the Gospel, heard confessions and learned the language of the Tagalogs.

Persons addicted to numerology would certainly be tempted to feel that it played a part in Pedro Bautista's life for, over and over again, his different spheres of activity and usefulness seem to be divided into three-year periods. Of course, this is actually a matter of coincidence or the result of prescribed terms of service. It was three years after the death of his father that he was sent from San Andrés to Peñaranda; his missionary work in Mexico lasted three years; and three years after his arrival in Manila, he was elected Custodian of San Gregorio. Very shortly thereafter, he added two other responsibilities to those he had already undertaken.

The first of these was instigated by the interest which had been aroused by a young man named Gonzalo Garcia, recently admitted to the Franciscan Order. Gonzalo's parents, natives of Portugal itself, had settled in the Portuguese colony of Goa, on the Arabian Sea, where their son was born; but he had spent nine years in Japan with the Jesuits, who were already entrenched in that country, and spoke the Japanese language fluently. There were a good many Japanese nationals in Manila, mostly merchants who came and went. Some were already Christians before they arrived there; others were converted through the preaching and example of the missionaries. With the co-operation of Gonzalo, Pedro Bautista met some of these Japanese and was able to talk with them freely because the young Portuguese lay brother was such an excellent interpreter. Soon, the *Comisario* came to believe that many of them had need of more spiritual guidance and material comforts than they had so far obtained in the Philippines; and, characteristically, he offered to take charge of both, and founded a parish especially for their benefit at Dilao, a suburb of Manila.

His labors in behalf of his new parishioners were hardly under way when the first Dominicans arrived on the islands and, as they lacked any sort of headquarters, he offered them the hospitality of his, which he had named the Convent of Santa María de los Angeles. By this time, however, it was evident that he needed more help if he were to continue expanding his sphere of usefulness and, without wasting time or energy in approaching persons with less power to help him, he wrote directly to the King of Spain, Philip II.

Fortunately, this letter is one of Pedro Bautista's writings which has survived and is carefully preserved in the Archives of the Indies at Seville, that treasure house of riches for the historian.[5-a] I cannot hope to do justice to its tactful text and accomplished wording and, indeed, anything written in one language inevitably suffers by its translation into another, no matter how skilled and enlightened the treatment. But, at least, I can give some idea of its contents and purpose:

May Jesus ever abide in the soul of Your Majesty:

There is no place in the world where children can find a more sympathetic understanding of their needs than in the hearts of their fathers, and Your Majesty is *our* father, as well as our patron and our defender and, as such, we appeal to you, confident that we will find help. Since Your Majesty is already informed of the progress our religious have made in saving souls, I shall not dwell on that; but because this progress depends on those who are converted, and because I desire there may be no loss in what we have already gained and that our holy work may proceed rapidly, I humbly beg Your Majesty to send us friars from our Province of San José; and if they come from others, which are Recollect, then let them be vigilant in maintaining our ideals of perfection and sufficiently learned [to carry on our work]. This is what our brothers desire and what I beg of Your Majesty, in their name, for the furtherance of our holy religion and this new church, since, for lack of more friars of such qualities as I have described, those who are here are greatly discouraged. They do not have as much help as they require, but they could not leave the work without the loss of many souls. Last year, two of our brothers were sent to us, but hardly anyone comes here to whom it is possible to give the habit with the conversion of souls in view.

May our Saviour keep Your Majesty.

Given in Luzon at the Convent of Santa María de los Angeles at Manila. June 27, 1588.

Fr. Pedro Bautista, Custodian.

"From this letter," Robles Dégano sagely observes, "it is easy to see what kind of friars Pedro Bautista wanted—that is to say, men who were both saintly and wise." It is indeed. It also shows that his memories of his own earthly father, who had been so swift to recognize Pedro's great spiritual and mental gifts, and to give him every opportunity of developing and revealing these, were permeated with lasting appreciation and affection.

4

The plea for friars, which Pedro made to the King, did not go unheeded, though it was not effectively answered until three years later,
when seventeen more Franciscans arrived in the Philippines. Meanwhile, many other things had happened.

Pedro founded a second monastery, the Convent of San Francisco
del Monte, in a secluded place about a league from Manila; a little
hospital near the Laguna de Bay at the base of some thermal springs
which he had discovered while making parochial calls in the vicinity;
and another hospital in the seaport of Cavite, which he opened at the
request of the people living there. His nostalgic longing for Avila was
fast waning because, here in Manila, he was helping to create the atmosphere and the architecture and to observe the amenities which had
meant so much to him there. At the end of his term as Custodian at
San Gregorio, he was re-elected to this office and, shortly thereafter,
arrived the long-awaited Brief from His Holiness, Sixtus V, elevating
the *Custodia* to the rank of *Provincia*. The Chapter was again convoked, a Catalan—Pablo de Jesús—was elected Provincial and Pedro
stayed on as Guardian and Preacher, but only for a year and a half,
because of developments along entirely different lines.

The islands had acquired a new governor, a Galician by the name
of Don Pedro Gómez Pérez das Marinas, who had come accompanied
by his son, Don Luis. A page to the latter was so moved by the eloquence of Pedro that he dropped everything and scurried off to join
the Franciscans as a postulant—a rash act which angered the Governor
and his son to such a degree that they tried to remove the truant by
main force. They were pacified by the "sound reasoning" of Pedro
and persuaded to leave the boy where he was; but the Governor's
wrath was again roused when the Franciscan, who had several times
appealed privately and without results to His Excellency, concerning
the oppression of the Indians by the Spaniards, made the abuse in
question the subject of a sermon. This time, the Governor, in his rage,
immediately instigated legal proceedings. However, his ruffled feelings
were soothed by "prudent persons" who succeeded in persuading him
that everything Pedro said had been justified; and certainly it would
appear that his animosity must indeed have been short-lived and that
all idea of suing the friar must have been quickly dismissed; for a little
less than a year after the public rebuke he had received, the Governor's

choice, when suddenly called upon to appoint an ambassador to Japan, fell upon Pedro Bautista.

True, Gonzalo Garcia must be credited with partial responsibility for this; the entrance of the young Portuguese into the Franciscan Order and the part he had played by arousing his superior's interest in the Japanese merchants who frequented Manila, had certainly not escaped official notice. Neither had the subsequent establishment of the parish at Dilao. But even after taking all this and the good opinion of many prudent persons into consideration, Don Pedro Gómez would certainly not have given such an important appointment to a man whom he either disliked or distrusted. The mission was a dangerous, as well as a delicate one; it involved not only the emergency of a moment, but the lasting prestige of the Spanish Empire. It would be necessary for both the Governor and his emissary to act with the greatest caution.

The complicated situation appears to have been precipitated some years earlier by a certain Fajiba, a Japanese of humble birth, once a woodcutter and street sweeper, who had risen to the rank of general and who, at the death of Nobunanga, the *togo* or ruler of some thirty of the sixty-six provinces into which Japan was then divided, had taken forcible possession of his late master's dominions. At first, he had not shown himself unfriendly to the Christian religion, and conversions had been steadily increasing until the Jesuits—who, as we have noted, were already well entrenched in Japan—angered him on "certain occasions which they had given him or which he had seized upon," as Pedro Bautista sized the matter up in a letter—the second of which we shall hear more—that he wrote to King Philip II and that the Bishop of Manila took with him when he left the Philippines for Spain. Fajiba, who had now changed his name to Cambacu or Cambacundono, made these "occasions," whatever they were,[6] a pretext for prohibiting the further teaching of Christianity and for issuing an edict of banishment, directed against all missionaries.

Three or four Jesuits left Japan at once; others remained there in hiding, mostly in Nagasaki or its vicinity. It would appear that the native *bonzes*, or Buddhist priests, who apparently bore them no ill will, actually helped to conceal them on condition that they would maintain a discreet silence. But such concealment and silence meant that many converts were either completely without a pastor or inadequately attended, for there was hardly anyone left who dared preach openly or administer the Sacraments and not a few Japanese "returned to their idolatries." This state of things lasted for three years.[7]

It is very hard for a modern person to interpret, with impartiality and wisdom, the reasons why the Society of Jesus has aroused so much antagonism, not only in Japan, but in many other countries throughout the years since its establishment early in the sixteenth century. Iñigo de Loyola, its founder, more generally known as St. Ignatius Loyola, was a brave soldier and a distinguished scholar before he became a militant Christian; his first and most famous follower, Francis Xavier, whose acquaintance he made while they were fellow students at the University of Paris, was equally courageous and cultured; and his zeal as a great missionary, whose labors and accomplishments embraced a vast territory, have seldom, if ever, been equalled and certainly never surpassed. Their followers, to whose customary monastic vows of poverty, chastity and obedience is added a fourth of special obedience to the Holy See to go wherever sent on missions, have maintained, from the beginning, the high standards which their founder set. They have established schools, as well as churches, all over the world and not a few have suffered martyrdom for their faith and have achieved canonization, among them the North American Martyrs, Isaac Jogues, John de Brébeuf, Anthony Daniel, Gabriel Lalemant, Charles Garnier and Noël Chabanel. Yet, over and over again, they have been suppressed or exiled from the scene of their valiant labors, sometimes on the charge of disturbing the public peace; and the term "Jesuit" has even been used—in my opinion, most unjustly—to describe any "crafty, intriguing or equivocating person (in allusion to the methods ascribed to the order by its opponents)."[8] The Jesuits whom I have known personally have commanded my respectful admiration, and I have borne and can bear witness to the importance of the work they have done and are still doing, and to the mental and spiritual ruin that has often followed their expulsion.[9] Exactly what happened in Japan, to antagonize Cambacu, we shall probably never know, and it seems far more likely that he was looking for a pretext to get rid of the Jesuits—in other words, that he "seized upon an occasion" than that they gave him any just cause for complaint.

We should, moreover, remember that another important factor in the situation lay in the strained relations, not only between the Japanese and the Jesuits, but between the Portuguese and the Spaniards. After the discovery of the New World by Columbus, the rulers of Spain and Portugal, under the direction of the Pope, had agreed on a certain meridian line, thirty-six degrees of latitude west of Lisbon, which should divide their future possessions and, in the Western Hemisphere, the demarcation was very clear from the beginning; no Spaniard, for instance, tried to lay claim to Brazil; no Portuguese tried to lay claim to Peru.[10] But, in the Eastern Hemisphere, the line was considerably more vague. We now know that this should have passed through the middle of Japan near Akashi, west of Asaka. However, at the period under consideration, no one knew for certain which part of Japan Spain could rightfully claim and which part Portugal, or indeed, whether one of these countries could claim all of it—which was what Portugal was trying hard to do. The Jesuits in Japan were Portuguese in their sympathies, which was not unnatural, as most of them were Portuguese by either birth or inheritance; they wished to close the door on both Spanish merchants and Spanish missionaries. Therefore, they petitioned Pope Gregory XIII to prohibit entry into Japan by any Order other than that of the Jesuits and, since these were sent out from the mission in Goa, this was practically equivalent to saying any except Portuguese Jesuits. The petition was granted by Brief; but this did not arrive in Japan until four years after it had been requested; and, in those four years, it had become obvious that there had been such an expansion of interest in Christianity that thirty Jesuits, more or less, did not suffice to bring in as many sheaves as the rich harvest of souls provided. During this same period,[11] a ship which happened to have among its passengers two Franciscans had put into the Port of Firando in distress. It was two months before the friars found means of leaving and, in the meantime, they made many friends. As a result of these chance encounters, the Governor and the Bishop of Manila and the Custodian of the Franciscans began to receive letters from "many Christian gentlemen in Japan"; they also received one from Gaspar Coelho,[12] the Portuguese who had been St. Francis Xavier's host when the latter visited the Shrine of the Apostle St. Thomas, near modern Madras, and who was, by now, Vice Provincial of the mission in Goa, which had been founded by Francis. These letters unanimously asked that more Franciscans should be sent to help the Jesuits in Japan and the favorable response which they received is clearly set forth in three communications to King Philip II, the first from Padre Plasencia, former Custodian of San Gregorio, the second from a certain Don Santiago de Vera and the third from Pedro Bautista, which was the one the Bishop took with him to deliver in person when he left for Spain. However, the notification of the Papal Brief, giving the Portuguese Jesuits the monopoly they desired, which reached the Philippines a year later than it reached Japan —that is to say, six years after the petition responsible for it had been dispatched—naturally brought to an abrupt end all preparations to send out Franciscans. This was unfortunate, for the want of protection which the Japanese Christians had suffered through the decree of Cambacu, banishing the Jesuits, had intensified the desire and the need for other missionaries and more and more letters and verbal messages were brought to Manila by Japanese merchants, begging for friars.

Finally, the Japanese Christians who lived in Manila applied to the Bishop, beseeching him to make provision for the dispatch of the Franciscans and arguing that the suppression of the Jesuits had made this a positive necessity. The Bishop then called a meeting, to which all the religious of the city were summoned; and the consensus of opinion was that, when the welfare of so many souls was at stake, there was no real obstacle to granting the appeal, since the Brief had been issued under the impression that the Jesuits enjoyed every liberty in Japan. The Governor, Don Pedro Gómez, whose ire Pedro Bautista was so often to arouse, had then only just arrived at his post and announced that he was not prepared to take any action in the matter. The leader among the Franciscans had no such scruples. He seized his pen and dashed off the famous letter to the King which the Bishop carried to Spain. In this, Pedro Bautista told everything that had occurred and besought His Majesty to ask the Pope for a revision of the Brief. He did not hesitate to say that he considered His Holiness had been "very ill informed" and that the reasons for granting the document were "trifling and quite without cogency." Then he wound up his remarks by saying that it was one of "destruction and not of edification."

This was a bold way for a comparatively obscure Franciscan friar to address his sovereign in referring to an edict from His Holiness; and its contents must have caused amazement, to say the least, among those who had hitherto regarded Pedro Bautista as efficient and devout, but gently and quietly persuasive rather than abruptly outspoken. That he was impelled to write as he did because he had the courage of his convictions there can be no doubt; and that his convictions were founded on more than courage was evident when Sixtus V, the successor of Gregory XIII, duly revoked the Brief some years later.

The receipt of an official document of this character was absolutely necessary to move the meticulous Portuguese Jesuits from their position; but Pedro Bautista was in no wise intimidated by the delay. He had not been an honor student at the University of Salamanca, and Guardian, Custodian and *Comisario* of various monasteries for nothing. Theoretically, law might not be his forte; but actually he was as well acquainted with it and as adroit in finding ways to interpret it as almost any legal authority. He forthwith called attention to the fact that the Brief of Gregory XIII was already revoked *by implication*, since the Brief of Sixtus V, in which the *Custodia* of San Gregorio was raised to the rank of a province, authorized the Franciscans to found convents and preach the Gospel throughout "all those regions [in the Indies] except Malacca, Cochinchina and Siam"; and that, furthermore, this implication was confirmed by a Bull from Paul III, authorizing the Franciscans to preach *"in all parts of the world."*[13]

Meanwhile, the bandit Cambacu, elated by his easy triumphs in Japan, was now looking for fresh fields to conquer and first turned covetous eyes on Korea, where he sent a sizable army. Then, having been told that it would be a simple matter to turn the Philippines into tributary territory, he ordered a Japanese by the name of Faranda to take a letter to Gómez. Faranda, however, had not been given ambassadorial credentials and was, therefore, afraid to go to Manila in person; so he secretly sent in his stead a Christian nephew, Gaspar, while he himself remained safely hidden in a Japanese port. Upon Gaspar's arrival in Manila, this unwilling pawn entrusted his letter to Fray Gonzalo for translation and then presented it to the Governor. Its contents revealed demands which were extravagant, to say the least, and menacing to say the worst: it gave orders that Cambacu should be recognized as the ruler of the Philippines, and went on to state that, if such recognition were not immediately forthcoming, the despot's army would be sent to pillage and destroy.

When the news of this arrogant communication leaked out, Manila was in an uproar and Don Pedro Gómez was distracted. Eventually, he decided it would be best to send the Dominican, Juan Cobo, to Japan with a guarded and respectful reply, offering friendship and favorable conditions for trade, but saying nothing whatsoever about submission or recognition. A prominent layman, Lope de Llano, was designated to accompany Cobo, and Gaspar remained timorously in Manila, spending much of his time in trips to the Mission of San Francisco, where he repeatedly begged that friars should be sent to Japan.

(The impression made by the two shipwrecked Franciscans ten years earlier had certainly been not only favorable, but lasting!) In due course of time, Cobo and de Llano arrived in Japan and, accompanied by Faranda, who neglected to say that he had never left its shores, presented themselves to Cambacu, who had changed his name again, and was now known as Taicosama. He received the emissaries, with tolerable politeness, at the Fortress of Nagoya, where he had gone to keep closer watch of the progress made in Korea, meanwhile leaving his nephew, Hidelsugu, to act as Regent at his capital of Meaco.[14] The mission was explained and the Governor's letter delivered without unpleasant consequences, according to a communication written by Cobo, in which he also asked—speaking for the Japanese Christians —that ten Franciscans should be sent to Japan at once, with Pedro Bautista at their head. This letter arrived safely in Manila; the emissaries themselves, and any communications which Taicosama may have entrusted to them, disappeared without a trace!

In April of the following year, Faranda, whose fears had now obviously been overcome in some mysterious way, turned up in Manila, calmly announcing that he was Taicosama's Ambassador, and that the documents testifying to this must, undoubtedly, have been carried by Cobo, whose disappearance he seemed to accept with imperturbability. Again, Manila was roused to a state of frenzy; but Faranda, still completely calm, presented a petition to the Governor in which he repeated the request made in Cobo's letter: that ten Franciscans should be sent to Japan. He gave as his reasons, first, that Japan was greatly in need of missionaries and second, that it would give Taicosama much pleasure to meet men who lived a life of such austerity. Then he added, "In the name of my King, I promise that they will be well received and kindly treated, and that they will not be harmed in any way."

It was certainly true that Japan lacked active missionaries; it is equally certain that, aside from this statement, Faranda's veracity was open to doubt. At the same time, it was necessary for Gómez to find some means of accounting officially, if he could, for the disappearance of Cobo and Lope de Llano and, apparently, the only possible way of doing this would be through the good offices of some other Spaniard.[15] The Governor gave the matter a good deal of anxious thought, as well he might, and conferred at length with the Provincial Pablo de Jesús. This time, he decided to send Pedro Bautista with the rank of ambassador, and to give him as companions Fray Padre Bartolomé

Ruiz, Fray Francisco de la Parilla and, as interpreter, the lay brother, Gonzalo. To the new Ambassador the Governor entrusted a letter which he was instructed to present with his credentials. In this letter, after referring to the previous mission, the Governor added, "Now, to eliminate all doubt and confusion, I am sending you Fray Padre Bautista, who is a very important priest of great substance and quality, one with whom I take counsel concerning matters of moment to my King and who is beloved and respected throughout this commonwealth. He goes with my authority to accept and confirm the peace and friendship besought of me in your royal name by Faranda, with every assurance of security, and will remain until my King is advised of this move and orders what next shall be done. I hope that everything will meet with such success that it will be pleasing to you and I will endeavor to procure everything that is in my power to give you."

Hardly had the Rector of the Jesuit Convent in Manila, Antonio Sedeño, heard of the appointment and of the letter that had been written, than he presented a protest, based on Gregory's Brief, and furthermore claiming that Cobo's embassy had been responsible for the destruction of a church and houses which the Jesuits maintained in Nagasaki. The Governor sought information about this, presumably from Faranda, and learned that Taicosama and not Cobo had been responsible for such destruction. Then, three days later, in the Convent of St. Augustine, Gómez convoked a general meeting of all religious and civil authorities in Manila. At this meeting, it was resolved, after careful examination of all documents, that the mission of Pedro Bautista and his friars to Japan was legal and fitting, notwithstanding Gregory's Brief and the rights of monopoly claimed by the Portuguese and the Jesuits; also, that the new Ambassador should be on his way to his post as soon as was feasible.

It seems obvious that Pedro Bautista did not doubt for a moment that his credentials as Ambassador to Japan were authoritative and, since then, his opinion has been confirmed by many theologians and by Pius IX in the bill for Pedro's canonization. There has been a further claim that the Brief of Gregory XIII had been revoked by natural law in view of the dire necessity of the Christians in Japan and the impossibility that the Jesuits should minister to them openly after the edict of Cambacu which ordered their exile and effected their suppression. But let us give Antonio Sedeño the benefit of the doubt and assume that he, no less than Pedro Bautista, was acting in accordance with his conscience and his convictions. Surely, he would not lightly have defied the Governor, risked the anger of the King and put himself on record as differing in a matter of law and propriety with every other religious and every civil authority in the Philippine Islands. The story of Pedro Bautista is strange and tragic enough, in its known facts, without adding anything to these which may be based only on supposition.

5

The galleons which were to carry the new mission to Japan finally weighed anchor on the fifteenth of May, 1593. Pedro Bautista and Bartolomé Ruiz sailed on a Portuguese frigate captained by Pedro Gonzalez de Carvahal; Gonzalo and Francisco, on a Japanese frigate. The former arrived at Firando the eighth of July; the latter, at Nagasaki, ten days later.

Pedro Gomez,[15-a] the Vice Provincial of the Jesuits, sent a message of welcome to Pedro Bautista as soon as he was informed of the mission's arrival, together with gifts of poultry, bread and fruit. Quite obviously, he had never taken the edict of exile seriously and if he had ever gone into hiding, he must long since have emerged from this, or he would not have been able to act so openly. His offerings were gratefully acknowledged by Pedro Bautista, who added that he would be glad to go and pay his respects to the Jesuits, but that, until he had been received by the King, etiquette forbade him from making any other visits.

Taicosama, who was still in Nagoya, sent his majordomo, Fungen, with two frigates, to convey the mission thither; but after Pedro and Bartolomé reached there, they were kept in confinement for a month, while awaiting Gonzalo and Francisco. When the latter arrived, too, the gifts they had brought—a horse, two civet cats, a mirror, various articles of clothing and some swords of Toledo steel—were duly offered to Taicosama; but, in making the presentation, Faranda and Fungen were careful to say that these were mere trifles, and that an offering of a thousand *pesos* in gold would soon be added to them. Pedro refused to confirm this message, because he did not wish to present anything that might be termed tribute money; but, in spite of his objections, the two Japanese, wishing to have the embassy make a certain show of gratitude for its reception, arranged for the presentation of a tray laden with two hundred or more *escudos*.

Upon reaching the royal residence for their reception, the mission found that the presents were already in place and—contrary to the wishes of Pedro—a Japanese interpreter was in attendance. Taicosama had now appropriated the title of Emperor; he was seated, magnificently dressed, on a low throne with a background of scrolls and screens, and the members of the mission, clad in their coarse brown robes, approached one by one, each making a respectful reverence as he did so. After Pedro had delivered the Governor's letter, they moved backward, still continuing to face the Emperor, and took their places, cross-legged, on straw mats, according to the custom of the country. Taicosama, without reading the letter from Gómez, abruptly began a conversation by saying that the emissaries from the Island of Luzon would do whatever he required of them; otherwise, he would send his army to Manila. The interpreter, who had been on his knees while listening to the Emperor, reared up in fright and, turning to the missionaries, cried out, "Obey! Obey! Obey!" Quite unperturbed, Pedro, who had been well prepared in advance by Gonzalo, requested the lay brother to step forward with him and ask for permission to speak. When this was given, he did so with so much tact that Taicosama was very quickly appeased. Pedro said, among other things, that Faranda had told them, in Manila, that His Highness was asking for friendship, not obedience, and that they had come to offer this and would keep their pledge; in proof of it, the four religious now assembled before him would remain in his kingdom and regard him as their father. As for obedience, however, they owed that only to God and their own King.

Again, Pedro had acted with a boldness which, a few years earlier, would have seemed out of character and he had certainly spoken tongue in cheek; Faranda—or rather, the latter's nephew acting in his behalf—had unquestionably made the same threats that Taicosama was making now. But the Emperor took both the new Ambassador's manner and his words in good part. After declaring himself very much pleased, he said that of course he wanted to be on friendly terms with the Spaniards and asked the friars whether they would care to partake of some refreshment. When they had adjourned, under suitable guidance, to another richly adorned apartment where they were served tea and cakes, Taicosama joined them; he playfully twisted the cord with which Pedro's habit was belted around his hand, and talked with Gonzalo, whom he knew already, asking him numerous questions about the other friars and also about the King of Spain. Then, bidding his guests good-bye, he took his departure, seemingly in the best of spirits.

The next message that came from Taicosama was to the effect that Fungen should take the mission to Meaco and show them every courtesy there. These instructions were followed to the letter, for the majordomo installed them in his own house. Here, in due course, they were visited by the Regent, Hidelsugu, who invited the friars to dine with him and "by many other Lords and some of the Christians who lived in the vicinity."

It would appear from all this that an *entente cordiale* had been very quickly established. In any event, it was not long before two very important results of Pedro's mission took concrete form. The first of these was embodied in a letter to his Provincial, which stated that the Franciscans had been very warmly welcomed by the Japanese Christians; the second, in a letter to Gómez, bearing the important tidings that the edict of banishment against the Jesuits had been revoked through the good offices of the Franciscans. No less than eight Jesuits —none of them Spaniards—confirmed this statement. Among those doing so was a certain Pablo Ungasavara, "a fervent Christian and the grandson of the first Japanese baptized by St. Francis Xavier."[16] . . . . "The Franciscans have made peace and brought about friendship between the Emperor and the Company of Jesus," he wrote, "and the churches which had fallen down or been demolished are being raised and repaired and new ones are being built. If they [the friars] leave Japan, it is certain that the Emperor would return to his old ways of persecuting the Christians. This is the testimony of one who has seen with his own eyes."

The charitable spirit shown by Pedro to the Jesuits is all the more praiseworthy because his mission had been so strenuously opposed in Manila by Antonio Sedeño. In his letter to the Governor, he goes on to say, "Everything that I can tell you about them [the Jesuits] is good. . . . It would give me great pain if I thought any harm could come to them."[17]

In the Fall of 1593, Taicosama returned from Nagoya to Meaco and Pedro greatly desired to send Captain Carvahal to Manila with a report. This was not possible because there was no present to give the Emperor and it was contrary to precedent to speak to him without offering one. Therefore, application was made to the Viceroy, Guenifoin, who, according to Pedro was not only a courteous man, but "very charming." After many importunities, the letter from the Emperor was finally received and with this and several others entrusted to him by Pedro, Carvahal left for Manila where "the whole city was overjoyed with the good news from the embassy."

6

Fungen continued to entertain the friars in his own house as best he could, feeding them from such funds as were put at his disposal for this purpose by Taicosama. But this residence was not suited for living in conformity to Franciscan Rule or for proselyting and the friars greatly desired to have a convent and church of their own. They had still not learned what plans the Emperor might have made for their disposition, nor had they been granted another audience with him; and, eventually, they boldly decided to attempt speaking to him in the street some day when he was coming out of his palace. Accordingly, Pedro, Gonzalo and León Karatsuma, the first and most prominent of their converts up to this time, stationed themselves at a point he was almost certain to pass and—doubtless somewhat to their surprise and certainly to their relief—he received them benevolently, listened to their petition, granted it graciously and dismissed them with expressions of warm friendliness. The same day, he ordered the Viceroy, Guenifoin, to give them a place which would be pleasing to Pedro, who chose one called Foricava, on the site of a former Buddhist Monastery.

With alms provided not only by leading converts, but also by non-Christians, work was immediately begun and both church and convent were started "in the Spanish style" and finished in time to dedicate on October fourth (the Feast of St. Francis) as the friars had hoped; but meanwhile three additional friars had been sent to Japan, at Pedro's request, by the Provincial, Pablo de Jesús, and the provisional Governor of the Philippines, Don Luis Pérez las Marinas, had entrusted to them a letter for Taicosama, together with the long-awaited present. The friars, Agustín Rodríguez, Marcelo de Ribadeneira and Jerónimo de Jesús did not arrive until the thirtieth of September and, of course, it was unthinkable that there should be any delay in delivering the letter and the present from Manila; therefore, Pedro contented himself with arranging to have the church blessed by Fray Bartolomé in his absence, and with Gonzalo, León and the three newly arrived friars, set out for Fujimi, where Taicosama was occupied in building a new palace. As the Emperor's pride forbade him from receiving the delegation in a half-finished apartment, he kept the friars waiting several days; and it was not until the eleventh that they were able to return to Meaco and hold the celebration on which they had set their hearts. However, the account which Pedro was able to send the Governor concerning both the building and the expedition must have represented a very real compensation for the delay: "We already have a modest convent of wood and clay and bamboo, with its church, here in Meaco, on a fine site which the King has given us," he wrote. "We want to build a hospital next to our house, where we can train others to help us care for those who are sick in body or soul. The King has told us that he is the friend of the poor and that it would please him very much for us to have such a hospital. We are also told it would be very effective in helping to bring about conversions. We have been given permission to baptize the sick and poor, provided we do it privately, a thing which is entirely possible."

As soon as the convent was finished, the friars resumed their monastic way of life. "So long as this King lives, we shall have security," Pedro wrote next. "For he acts like a father to us, gives us food as to the poor and grants permission to administer our convent and church, recite our Divine Office as if we were in Spain, ring bells, sing Mass and say other services aloud and undertake campaigns for conversion without interference. We have already enjoyed some very special favors from this same Emperor and his nephew."

He had started his church and convent "in the Spanish style"; he had obtained permission to sing Mass "as if he were in Spain." In Japan, no less than in the Philippines, Spain set his standards and inspired his ideals; and that these were high standards and beautiful ideals is evident from the fact that interference with the friars in Meaco came from only three persons: Organtino, an Italian; Juan Rodriguez, a Portuguese who was there to serve as interpreter for Taicosama in matters relating to the Jesuits; and Pedro Ramon, also a Portuguese. They did not have a church for public worship, but an oratory where they said Mass and administered the Sacraments privately. The methods of the Franciscans, so different from those of the Jesuits, seemed wrong to the latter, and they began to disturb the friars with complaints and warnings. Armed with their famous Brief, which they insisted was still in force, they would not allow themselves to be persuaded that Pedro could legally found convents or preach sermons or administer Baptism or even so much as live in Japan. He, on the other hand, never interfered with the Jesuits in any way; he neither complained about them nor gave them unwelcome advice; he wanted only that they should be persuaded to leave him in peace. With this end in view, it was necessary for him to confer with the Jesuit Vice Provincial before anyone else; it was also advisable to consult this functionary before attempting to establish a center for the Franciscans in Nagasaki—a project which Pedro was especially eager to effect, partly because this was the normal trading center between Manila and Japan, and partly because communication between Manila and Meaco was so difficult. Therefore, about the first of December, Pedro took his departure from his first church, accompanied by Fray Jerónimo, leaving Fray Marcelo de Ribadeneira as Superior of the convent in Meaco, Gonzalo and León in charge of the hospital, and—at their earnest request—establishing the Third Order of St. Francis among the Christian laymen who were his friends.

7

Fray Jerónimo says, in referring to this mission on which he accompanied Pedro Bautista and to the proposed new foundation in Nagasaki: "The Portuguese who lived there asked for it themselves and came to Meaco to bring us there by force. [They claimed] they had been vouchsafed a heavenly vision of [a monk in] the habit of San Francisco in Nagasaki." This was the same habit as that worn by their fellow countryman, known as San Antonio de Padua, who was a native of Lisbon, and who was and still is greatly venerated by the whole world. Furthermore, they were eager to satisfy their desire for public worship, which the friars hoped to give them and which the Jesuits were not permitted to do, despite the fact that there were now several thousand Christians in the locality.

Before his departure from Meaco, Pedro went to see the Viceroy Guenifoin, since no ambassador was supposed to leave the capital and the Court without saying a suitable farewell. He took this occasion to ask for a letter to Terezava, the Governor of Nagasaki, in order that the latter might not hinder work on the proposed foundation; for while Taicosama had given Pedro permission to live in any part of Japan that he chose, this permission had been given only verbally, albeit in the presence of many persons. Upon arrival in Nagasaki,

Pedro and Jerónimo were hospitably received and lodged in the Jesuit headquarters and Pedro took counsel with the Vice Provincial as to what might properly be done. According to de Ribadeneira, work proceeded in conformity with what the Vice Provincial said, both in conversation and in writing, and as was commanded by the holy *Comisario*. But we should remember that de Ribadeneira had been left behind in Meaco and, therefore, did not speak as an eyewitness. Obviously, Gomez considered that Pedro's credentials were valid; however, not all of those associated with him shared his opinion. Some were determined to prevent the Spanish friars from establishing a foundation and again the famous Brief of Gregory XIII was used as an argument against this. Next, Pedro's antagonists succeeded in arousing the interest of Governor Terezava "with petitions and gifts, as they had been accustomed to doing in other cases" and no site for a foundation was forthcoming. However, with Terezava's acquiesence, the approbation of the Vice Provincial, and the permission of the Portuguese, at whose expense the Hospital of San Lázaro had been built on the outskirts of the city, the friars went there to live, and began their ministry in its little chapel. Every night during Lent large numbers of Portuguese came to hear Pedro preach, and every day the friars went to the hospital to help feed the sick and assist in their general care. However, after Easter, which came early that year, the Portuguese veered in quite another direction from the one they had previously pursued; they came in a body and told Pedro that he and his companion must leave the premises. Instead of doing this, Pedro immediately took pen in hand and wrote a letter of protest to the Vice Provincial, couched in even bolder terms than any he had used before.

Very Reverend Father in Christ:
    The virtue and holiness of Your Paternity are such that I cannot believe you are aware of all the affronts and insults which my companion and I have suffered in this hospital. And though hitherto I have kept silent, I cannot do so now, because the behavior of those who wish to drive us away from the hospital— a place which, throughout the world, belongs to the poor—is such that it would cause gratification to the heathen.
    Let it be known to Your Paternity that I am in Japan with the permission of God and the Pope, with that of King Philip of Spain, of Taicosama, Emperor of Japan, and of Guenifoin, Governor of Meaco. Let these unjust disturbances against our religion [i.e., the Franciscan Order] cease. If they do not, Let Your

Paternity be advised that I shall either have to go in person or send to the King and the Pope and give an account of what is happening in Japan. And furthermore, Let Your Paternity consider what will happen when it is known that unbelievers give us support and shelter and that the faithful, the servants of God, will not so much as let us stay in a hospital, which, all over the world, is the home of the poor.

No more to Your Paternity, except the prayer that our Saviour will protect you.

Fray Pedro Bautista.

The Vice Provincial to whom this letter was addressed was the same who had welcomed Pedro two years earlier with fruit and fowl and bread; but there seems to be no evidence that he now even sent a direct reply; and a few days later, the friars were ejected from the hospital by order of Terezava, who, not daring to drive them away altogether from Nagasaki, instructed them to retire to the outskirts of the city on its other side. A Christian friend offered them the use of his home and some devout Portuguese raised the money to buy it, whereupon the friars settled themselves in it as well as they could. But their enemies persisted in demanding their removal and, eventually, Terezava ordered them to leave Nagasaki altogether and forbade them to establish a foundation anywhere in the territory under his jurisdiction.

Rather tardily, Gomez expressed sympathy for them, offered to let them stay in his house until they could find a way of getting back to Meaco and took them to see the Seminary of Arima and the College of Amakusa. On their return from this expedition, they found Terezava's attitude somewhat more conciliatory. Fearing, no doubt, that the Emperor would blame him for not having received an ambassador properly in his territory, he told Pedro and Jerónimo, after excusing himself for his previous conduct as well as he could, that they could continue to live in the city until he himself could go to Meaco, where he would inform himself what he ought to do under the circumstances. After hearing this, Pedro felt so confident that the dispute would be settled in a way favorable to the Franciscans that he decided he should return to Meaco, in order to be there at the time of Terezava's visit, and sent for Bartolomé Ruiz to keep Jerónimo company.

Meantime, his mind was at rest. While awaiting a ship, he often walked to a hill at the north of the city, where he spent many peaceful hours gazing out at the sea, or absorbed in meditation and prayer. This was the place where he had hoped to build his convent and where he still believed he might be able to do so. It proved to be the place where, a year and a half later, he was crucified.

8

There were no immediate danger signals to warn Pedro of defeat and disaster. True, he had suffered great humiliation at Nagasaki. But though it was his duty, *as an ambassador*, to insist that the dignity and importance of the *office* be properly recognized, it was part of his creed, *as a Franciscan*, to accept such mortification with Christlike meekness. Besides, he was baffled, rather than discouraged; and on his return to Meaco, he found things going so well that, inevitably, his fallen spirits must have soared. A lay brother, Juan Pobre de Zamora, who apparently was permitted to remain there unmolested, had been sent to Nagasaki by the Father Provincial in Manila, Juan de Garrovillas, to inform himself how things were going there and elsewhere in Japan; and, in a letter written while Juan Pobre was still in Nagasaki, Pedro told the new arrival that the friars already had, in Meaco, "a hospital housing so many poor that there is not even standing room for them. . . . We minister to them in both body and soul," the letter went on to state. "We preach publicly without interference from anyone. Many unbelievers come to see what we are doing and are greatly astonished . . . and many are converted as a consequence of what they see."

Since there was not even standing room in this hospital, where the Japanese disciples, León Karatsuma and his wife were in charge, and which the friars had named Santa Ana, they now began to build another. They called the second one San José, and placed in it, as infirmarians, Pablo Susuki and his wife who, like the Karatsumas, were among the Franciscans' earliest converts. These four Japanese were assisted in their works of healing and mercy by numerous other native Christians; and as Pedro wished to have comments on the work from Japanese as well as foreigners, he asked the patients to express themselves, as a group, on paper. This letter, signed by eighty persons, is certainly unqualified in its praise:

"The year following their arrival in Japan, the Franciscan friars saw us roving through the streets and huddled against the walls—cripples and lepers, men, women and children, some of whom were dying without any kind of physical or spiritual succor, others without any shelter from wind, rain or snow. They had compassion on us and built us two hospitals, with wards for both men and women; they ministered to our bodies by visiting us, bathing us and burying our dead, and to our souls by baptizing us and teaching us Christian doctrine. Everyone who sees this is astonished and exclaims, 'In Japan, nothing like this has ever been done previously, either by children for their parents or by parents for their children.' Heretofore, when a person was ill for any length of time, he was either stabbed in the stomach or thrown into the river. Therefore, we pray, with tears in our eyes, not only that the friars who are already here may remain, but that their number may increase for our benefit."

Shortly after this letter was written, Juan Pobre, who had now come to Meaco, reports in the *Informe* which he had been instructed to prepare, that Pablo Susuki's wife was delivered of a girl child, who died soon after being baptized. "And then"—the report continues— "the friars went out and found another [still living] near the river, among those who are often cast away there; and they rescued her and baptized her and gave her the name of Lucía, and the wife of Pablo received this baby for her own and took her to nurse. Of such abandoned children, both boys and girls, they found many, some alive and well, some on the point of death, and such as they could they baptized; and the wives of other Christians raised them like their own children. . . .

"A school was built near the convent for the male children," the report goes on, "where the teacher, who had been a doctor, now ministers to their souls and minds, as well as their bodies. The school was constructed in the hope of getting these little boys away from the *bonzes*, who had misled them, as the Brothers found out from some who had left the monastery."

The *bonzes* were recognized as proper teachers for all male children in Japan and there was so much opposition to the new school that the friars thought it would be wise to close it, at least temporarily. However, the teacher, Francisco, had previously been baptized by Marcelo de Ribadeneira, and remained with the friars, consecrating his life to serving the sick in the hospital and to teaching the catechism. He was only one of the many persons, representing all ages and stations in life, who were now flocking fast to the friars and remaining attached to them. We have already mentioned León Karat-

suma, who, in his youth, had been a *bonze* and who is described as a
learned and courageous man "without fear of the world." He had
brought into the fold his elder brother, Pablo Ibarki, by occupation
a cooper, and his friend, Pablo Susuki, whom we have also mentioned
already, and who is often confused with León's brother because their
first names were the same. We are not informed concerning Susuki's
profession or trade; we are only told that, before his conversion, he had
"a very quarrelsome nature."

All these men had Christian wives and proved honest, industrious
and faithful; however, from the viewpoint of prestige and financial
assistance, two others were to prove even more helpful: Cosme Joyo,
the secretary of the Regent Hidelsugo—Taicosama's nephew—and
Gabriel Duisko, the sixteen-year-old scion of a wealthy family who,
upon the death of his father, had become the page of a great war
lord. Even Gabriel was not the youngest of the new flock; three years
his junior was Antonio, who had come to Meaco with two young
friars newly sent out from Manila, Martín de la Ascensión and Francisco Blanco; and Luisito, the nephew of León, who had been entrusted to his uncle for care and education, and who was only eleven.
Between all these, in both age and experience, were Ventura, a young
man of twenty-five, who had been orphaned at an early age and
brought up in a Buddhist Monastery, but who suddenly remembered
that, before his parents' death, he had been baptized and hastened off
to join the friars; Francisco Cayo, a carpenter who lived near the
hospital at Meaco and put himself at the disposal of the friars; Tomé,
an apothecary of forty, who had observed Pedro's kindness to the sick
in a small village near Meaco and, in consequence, offered his services
at the hospital as an assistant to Dr. Francisco; and Juan, a former
weaver, whose brother was the *demandadero* who carried messages
and did errands for the hospital, and whose tragic loss of his wife and
children within a week of each other had caused him such desperate
grief that he was on the verge of suicide when he was rescued and
given the same useful work to do.

This, in itself, seems quite an imposing list, but it is by no means
comprehensive. From the time that the Franciscan Convent was established in Meaco, not a day passed without one or more baptisms;
and when Juan Pobre left there in the Spring of 1596 over five hundred persons had been newly received into the Church, while the
number of apostates and renegades who had returned to it was much
greater still. It is almost impossible to estimate how many Catholics

had fallen away after the persecution of '87, some from fear, and others for lack of instruction and of ministers to vitalize and maintain the Faith. But, according to Gonzalo, it was common knowledge that at least three thousand returned to the fold during the first year after the arrival of the Franciscans and, as time went on, there were, of course, many more.[18]

Neither the new converts nor those who had been restored to the Faith were by any means persons who confined themselves to lip service; they were sincere and loyal, as they were to prove over and over again when the persecution of the Christians began with fresh fury. "So many come to gather up the precious manna of the Holy Evangel which my Brothers scatter, even more with words than with deeds, that I can say the whole country is populated with those who are trying to cast out darkness and let in the light of heaven," Fray Juan tells us. "And with our coming many Jesuits, who had been frightened and had gone into hiding, have taken fresh courage and gone out into the villages, though since they must still do so without the knowledge of the King, they dress like the Japanese." When Juan returned to Manila in April, he must have intuitively felt disaster was coming, for he adds, in his report to the Provincial, "If the Lord permits persecution, His Majesty will have many thousands of Christians who will face the *bonzes* with the truth; and while, in the previous one, there were few who would confess to the Faith, this time there are many who desire to bear witness to it. I give thanks that the Saviour can see in how short a time there has been a great change and how much courage and fortitude the goodness and constancy of our poor and simple friars have given to the people."

As far as Pedro was concerned, the storm signals were still lacking or, if he saw them, he ignored their elements of danger. Early in 1596, he had decided that it would be wise to establish a foundation in Osaka, forty kilometres south of Meaco and, with this in view, sent there Marcelo de Ribadeneira, Gonzalo and León. Two Jesuits, Francisco Pérez and Pedro Morejón, the latter a native of Medina del Campo, were there before them and were ministering, as well as the limitations put upon them would permit, to the Christians in the city, but this ministration, through no fault of theirs, was inadequate. No quarters which would serve for a Franciscan foundation were immediately available, so Marcelo and Gonzalo went on to the suburb of Sacay to search further; but while they were gone León, who had been left behind, found "a small mean house" whose general undesirability was the greater because the building itself belonged to one person and the land on which it stood to another, whose wife wished him to have nothing to do with the friars. However, when Pedro came down from Meaco to look over the situation, he succeeded, with his usual persuasiveness, in straightening out matters and the little house soon became the shrine for an altar, surmounted by a statue of the Child Jesus with a cross and nails in His hands. To honor this statue, the place was given the name of Belén—the Spanish word for Bethlehem—and Mass was soon said there regularly. Agustín Rodríguez, whose health had been poor in Meaco, was put in charge of the foundation and a little boy by the name of Tomé Kosak came with him to serve as acolyte. The infant Foundation also acquired a cook, a native Osakan, who had been baptized by Pablo Susuki during a serious illness and given the name of Joachím; like Susuki, he had allegedly been very quarrelsome before his conversion, but after it became "mild and humble."

Modest though it was, everything about the atmosphere of the new Foundation was pleasant and promising. Pedro had reason to be confident of its success and, reassured as to this, he no longer entertained fears as to the wisdom of the boldest step he had so far taken, namely that of reserving the Holy Sacrament in the church at Meaco. He had decided to do this shortly after his return from Nagasaki, partly at the earnest request of his five friars and partly because he believed it would be a source of great spiritual comfort not only to them, but to all the Christians in the city. The day when the Holy Sacrament was placed in the tabernacle, Pedro himself carried it in the procession and Juan acted as censer bearer.[18-a]

Among those present on this occasion were some who insisted that they heard celestial voices in the church and others who were so conscious of the Divine Presence that they felt it to be visible in various forms. Who will deny the possibility of such miracles? Certainly not I. But the great miracle to me lies not in what was seen and heard by others on this day of days, but in the dauntless courage and unswerving faith of the man who made possible the Reservation.

9

On the twelfth of July, 1596, a splendid galleon, the *San Felipe,* left the Philippines for Mexico. It carried two hundred and thirty

passengers, among them many noblemen, a detachment of artillery
and seven religious: one Dominican, four Augustinians and two Franciscans, Felipe de Jesús and Juan Pobre, the latter already known to
us. It presented a brave sight as it left the harbor, its golden prow
cleaving the blue waters, its great white sails billowing in the wind.
But it was hardly well under way when giant waves began to sweep
over it and vicious hurricanes tore its beautiful sails to pieces. Three
months after its triumphant departure from Manila, it came limping
into the port of Urando on the southern coast of Shikoku. With the
hope of saving the rich cargo of silk which the vessel was carrying,
the hatchways were hurriedly opened and the precious freight thrown
out on the beach. Immediately thereafter, the *San Felipe* sank without
a trace.

Acting on the advice of Chosokabe, the territorial Governor, who
received the victims of the shipwreck with apparent sympathy, the
captain of the galleon, Don Matías de Landecho, dispatched five of
its passengers to Fujimi with a fine present for Taicosama and letters
for the Spanish Ambassador, Fray Pedro Bautista. The latter was done
in order that, in his official capacity, he might ask the Emperor to
put another ship at the disposal of the captain and to give orders that
the cargo might be removed, undamaged, from the beach and stored
in a safe place until it could be taken on its way again. With the three
laymen chosen for this mission were sent Fray Juan Pobre and Fray
Felipe de Jesús. As he speeded them on their way, Chosokabe
charged them to leave everything in the hands of his great friend,
Masuda, Governor of Upper Meaco; this, he assured them, would
bring about results which would give them not only relief, but the
utmost satisfaction.

After a wearisome journey, they arrived, ten days later, at Osaka,
where Pedro happened to be temporarily. He immediately offered to
go with them to Fujimi and sent a note of reassurance to Landecho,
telling him to be of good cheer, "because the King promised me three
years ago that all Spaniards who came to his realm, either by land
or by sea, would have safe conduct and would never be harmed in
any way." Next, in his capacity of ambassador and in a suitably diplomatic manner, he charged Landecho to thank Chosokabe in his name
—that is to say, in the name of Spain—for the kind reception given
the shipwrecked Spaniards.

Pedro would greatly have preferred to deal with the Viceroy, who
had always shown himself so favorable to the friars; but he realized

this would upset the two governors concerned, since they already had negotiations under way, and he therefore consented to treat with Masuda, in accordance with the instructions from Chosokabe. He wisely took the precaution of sending an unofficial message to the secretaries of Guenifoin, asking them to let their master know why he had not approached the Viceroy direct, and saying that, as soon as possible, he, Pedro, would wait upon Guenifoin and take him a present. This done, the Ambassador went with the Spaniards to Masuda, who received them courteously, invited them to dine, told them to be of good cheer, and said he would advise them when they could present themselves to the Emperor. Two days later, they received a message to the effect that Taicosama wished to receive neither the Spaniards nor their present and, shortly thereafter, they heard he had given orders that Masuda should proceed at once to Urando and confiscate the goods which had been in the ship; at the same time, it was unmistakably indicated that the very lives of the Spaniards were in danger.

Realizing that the situation was critical, Pedro immediately sent Juan Pobre back to Urando with Cristóbal de Mercado, one of the three laymen who had accompanied the priests on their mission, while he himself hurried back to Meaco in the desperate hope that it might not be too late for the transaction of business with Guenifoin. The hope was vain. Masuda had already arrived in Urando and begun an inventory of the cargo, which, a few days later, he removed to Fujimi, leaving the poor Spaniards without goods, without money, almost destitute of clothing and under arrest. The traitor, Chosokabe, had acted with great swiftness; he had sent his secretary to Masuda with instructions to advise the governor that the artillerymen and the additional religious who had been on the galleon represented a great threat to Japan. Masuda, who was equally traitorous, had promptly reported this to Taicosama.

The moment was propitious for quickening the cupidity and credulity of the tyrant. A series of earthquakes, some very severe, had completely destroyed his newly-built palace and ruined everything in it; the arrival of a precious cargo, which might well serve to refurbish a new palace, could not have been more opportune. Nevertheless, he hesitated to take forcible possession of the Spaniards' belongings, in view of the guarantees he had given Pedro three years earlier. At this stage, Masuda concluded that he should be somewhat more insistent; he hoped to have a share in the booty and realized that he would not get it unless the Emperor gave orders that it should be appropriated. He continued his importunities and won his point.

Landecho was helpless to prevent the removal of the cargo from the beach, but at least he could protest against it and his remonstrances were answered in a way that was as insulting as it was amazing to him. It had been reliably reported to them, so the minions of Masuda maintained, as they continued to haul away their loot, that the *San Felipe* was a pirate ship, that the wreck was a hoax, and that it was the purpose of the captain and his crew to overrun the country and turn it into a Spanish colony, subjugating the Japanese and making away with their ruler. It was well known to Taicosama, these men went on, that when the Spaniards wanted to take possession of a kingdom, they first brought or sent friars to Christianize it—wasn't this what had been done in both New Spain and the Philippines? Then they added, with apparent irrelevance, that the Portuguese were not subjects of the Spanish King.

The last of these misstatements seems to give authenticity to the declaration later made by Andrés Zuazola, the clerk of the galleon, to the effect that the Portuguese living in Japan had a hand in the seizure, if not directly, then at least indirectly; certainly, they did nothing to prevent it or to help the unfortunate Spaniards in any way. News indeed travelled slowly in those days; but Philip II had been King of Portugal as well as Spain since 1581—fifteen years earlier; and however much they may have resented this—and resent it they certainly did—it seems incredible that the Portuguese in Japan would not have known it by this time. If they did know it, they could not deny the fact that, through the lack of any other lawful heir to the Portuguese throne, Philip had acquired title to it through his mother, the Empress Isabella—that same royal lady who had taken him, as a child, to Avila for investiture in his royal breeches.[19] We cannot help believing, therefore, that there must have been wilful misrepresentation —misrepresentation which Taicosama was only too glad to accept as factual, of course, just as he willingly swallowed the suggestion that the *San Felipe* was a pirate ship instead of a merchant vessel in honorable standing. I do not know of any cases where the friars preceded the original explorers;[20] but that Spaniards made a practice of taking their priests with them on their voyages of discovery is true enough and, sometimes, priests furthered the work of discovery already begun. It always has been and still is the firmly established custom of Spaniards to carry chaplains, with the rank of officers, on their ships; and when the *conquistadores* were pursuing their discoveries, they did not leave their chaplains behind. It is also true that, in many cases, the clerics achieved as much fame as their military contemporaries—witness Zumárraga and Cortés in Mexico and De Soto and Junípero Serra in what is now the United States; and it is further true that terrible tales have come down to us of cruelty during the course of conquest —tales which modern Spanish scholars are at some pains to disprove and about which North Americans find it hard to argue effectually when the former point to the immense surviving Indian population of Mexico, Central and South America, and ask what has become of our Indians. In any case, during the period under discussion, cruelty to the conquered was taken almost as a matter of course, not only by Spaniards, but by every other so-called civilized nation, including the Portuguese. The outraged captain of the *San Felipe* was justified in feeling strongly and saying hotly that all three items of information passed on to him were calumnies.

How far Portuguese priests, as well as Portuguese merchants, were involved in these calumnies, it is difficult to say and, certainly, they should be given the benefit of all possible doubt. Of the forty Portuguese Jesuits who were then in Japan, some were fond of the friars and treated all Spaniards like brothers; others, especially those who lived in the villages, kept apart and meddled in nothing. But five or six Portuguese priests who lived in Nagasaki and Meaco could not bring themselves to countenance anything the Spaniards did. They interfered with the friars because they were Spanish; in as far as possible, they prevented trade with the merchants who were Spanish; they hated King Philip because he was Spanish. As far back as 1572, when San Francisco de Borja died, the Jesuits in Portugal begged that no other Spaniard should ever be elected General of the Order. Then in 1581—the very year when Philip ascended the throne of Spain—for fear that the Pope would appoint a Spaniard, it had been resolved at a clerical council meeting in Nagasaki that there should not be a bishop in Japan. Probably as a result of this, no episcopal appointee was sent there until August of 1596, when Don Pedro Martinez, a native of Coimbra and a deadly enemy of everything Spanish, arrived in Nagasaki. He had been in the Portuguese Island of Macao for two years before coming to Japan and, during this time, had not hesitated to say that he wanted to find no friars when he reached there himself. He had gone farther than this: he had written a long letter to Pedro Bautista, telling him to go back to Manila, because Japan was Portuguese by right of conquest. Pedro had answered this letter "very prudently"—but had stayed on. He must have been even more bewildered than had been San Juan de la Cruz when that gentle saint received contradictory orders from his Provincial, his Bishop and the papal nuncio, since, in the latter case, both ecclesiastical and royal authority were involved. Pedro was in Japan by order of his Provincial and of his King. He was a missionary, but he was also an ambassador. He felt he had no choice but to remain at his post until he was officially relieved.

This, however, was not the viewpoint of Don Pedro Martinez. He had hardly arrived in Nagasaki when he preached a sermon in the Jesuit church, forbidding all Christians to hear Mass and go to confession in the little sanctuary still maintained there by the friars, despite the previous orders for their suppression. This order was now renewed, coupled with instructions for an immediate return to Manila. The three who had been left in charge—Fray Jerónimo, Fray Bartolomé and Fray Marcelo—after having tried in vain to soften the Bishop's heart, sent an account of what had happened to Pedro Bautista, who gave an order, in the name of Holy Obedience, that each one separately should record his experience in writing and send these accounts to him. Having received these, he signed and sealed them and sent them to Fray Agustín, with an outline of the proceedings, and instructions that Marcelo de Ribadeneira, whose health had been poor all the time he was in Japan, should take it to the Provincial in Manila, and that Fray Jerónimo should go to Osaka, where Fray Martín, who knew very little Japanese, was all alone.

The Bishop's next move took the form of a pastoral visit to Meaco, where he promptly summoned Pedro Bautista into his presence and began the audience by announcing that he was willing to give the Ambassador and the friars his protection. This announcement, however, was coupled with a condition, namely that his representative should approach the Emperor and present him with gifts in behalf of the shipwrecked Spaniards, but that Pedro Bautista should take no part in the mission. This was, of course, equivalent to saying that his official status would not be recognized and nothing would move the Bishop from this position. Several interviews took place between the two with increasingly disagreeable results which were productive of nothing but further friction; and finally, the Bishop decided to make an end of what he considered Pedro's insubordination by bringing about the expulsion of the friars not through his order, but through one from the

Emperor. Taicosama's co-operation, at the moment, was easy enough to secure; he had turned against the Spaniards as he had previously turned against the Portuguese, only later on to forget, to all intents and purposes, that he had done so. Now his dislike for the friars was fanned into enmity by his physician, Jacuin, a *bonze* who had long hated them and been seeking a pretext to get rid of them. The whispering campaign about alleged pirates and their purposes furnished this all too effectively; his evil insinuations resulted in an order very different from the one for which the Jesuits had been hoping and expecting.

The edict that Taicosama decided to send out was not one for banishment of the friars; it was for crucifixion of all Christians.

10

Dates are dull items in any narrative. But occasionally they are necessary to serve as guideposts in obscure, confusing or unfamiliar territory. Such guideposts seem to be essential in order to clarify the Way of the Cross which Pedro Bautista and his faithful followers trod during the last weeks of their lives.

On the third of December, 1596, Masuda and Chosokabe arrived at Fujimi, taking to Taicosama the rich prize he was awaiting and the misinformation they wanted to give him and that he wanted to hear: namely, that the refugees were very suspicious characters. Taicosama, in a fresh access of fury, declared it was intolerable that Christianity should be preached in Japan, that he had been right in suppressing it formerly, and wrong only in failing to enforce both suppression and banishment. After some give and take with the war lords who were present, who pretended they were trying to calm him and who declared that, after all, banishment would be sufficient punishment, he ordered that all priests should be arrested and that guards should be put at their houses, so that they could not escape. This must have happened about the fifth or sixth of December. The Bishop, apparently aware of the coming storm, left Meaco the seventh for Osaka, and went from there, via Sacay, to Nagasaki, taking with him Juan Rodríguez and an Italian priest, Francisco Pasio.

There were two houses of religious in Osaka, one Jesuit, the other Franciscan. Taicosama did not know there were Jesuits in Osaka and, therefore, only ordered guards "for the religious." But the local judge, in order to carry out the order more faithfully, according to his lights, placed guards at both houses on the eighth of December—the great feast of the Immaculate Conception. In the little Convent of Belén were Fray Martín, the cook Joachím, the little acolyte, Tomé, and Cosme Takeya, who usually served in the hospitals of Meaco, but who happened to be temporarily in Osaka. In the house of the Jesuits, the judge found only a lay preacher, Pablo Miki, a catechist, Juan de Goto, nineteen years old, and an old servant, Diego Kisay.

Jibunoyo, Governor of Lower Meaco, where the Convent of San Francisco was located, was in Fujimi at the moment; and as he was interested in freeing the Jesuits, and as he knew the wrath of Taicosama was mainly directed against the Franciscans, he ordered one of his men to arrest only the friars, which was done on the same day. That evening, the rumor began to spread that all religious and Christians were to be beheaded, and Cosme Joya told this to Pedro Bautista. The news had hardly been brought to him when many Christians of Meaco, eager to share in the martyrdom of their beloved friars, began rushing to the convent and, as they found it locked, with guards at the doors, they stormed the walls of the kitchen garden and more than three hundred succeeded in entering.

In the light of everything that was happening, Pedro Bautista decided that it would be best to have the Sacrament of Baptism administered to all those in the hospitals who had not yet received it, but were willing to do so; and the two lay brothers, Gonzalo and Francisco, took charge of doing this. Meanwhile, Pedro heard as many confessions as possible in the church; and, in a letter written to Fray Martín a few days later, he said, "One hour before dawn, I celebrated Mass and administered Communion to all our brothers, both friars and members of the Third Order and, also, to many other Christians who had come to confession that night. And I ordered Gonzalo to talk to those about him in a way which would encourage them not to turn back, but to prepare themselves to suffer for Christ. To which they all replied they only wished they had a hundred lives to give for Him, Who had offered His on the cross for them."

After Mass, Pedro Bautista ordered the laymen to go to their homes, but more than two hundred remained in the enclosure just the same. "The following morning"—says Cosme Joya—"came three magistrates with all their henchmen, and cleared the premises of all Japanese Christians, so that no one remained inside but the friars and their catechist and servants, while guards continued to remain. And the magistrates took from the convent, as prisoners, León and the lay preachers, Pablo Susuki, Ventura, Tomé Danki and Gabriel Duisko, who continued to preach with great spirit and fortitude as they went along, and wrote me a letter from prison, saying that, without doubt, they would lose their heads because they were Christians, but that they would be glad to suffer this and other tortures. And I replied that Our Lord, for Whom they would endure all this, would help them to fight the good fight."

On the tenth of December, Jibunoyo, fearing that Taicosama would be angry if he knew the Jesuits of Meaco had not been arrested, ordered guards to be put at the house of the *Compañía*, where the Ministers of Justice found only a lay brother and two servants, its other usual inmates having prudently hidden in another place. At the same time, the Governor began to feel it would be wise to attempt dissuading Taicosama from carrying out the edict as he had originally planned. This was partly because so many thousands of men, women and children, far from dreading martyrdom, actually seemed to hope for it, since they hastened to inscribe their names on the lists which Taicosama had commanded should be made of all Christians; it was also because, among those so inscribed, were the sons of the Viceroy and others of almost equally high rank and it was obvious that it would be very poor policy to make away with them. Probably Taicosama had never heard the famous saying of Julian the Apostate that it was not wise to issue a public edict for the persecution of Christians, because they flew to martyrdom like bees to a hive; nevertheless, he began to realize that such was the case and, little by little, his fury spent itself.

First, he was found open to persuasion by the Governor who, for one reason or another, did not wish to have all the Jesuits included in the edict of extermination. Then, the judge who had been charged with pronouncing the death sentence on all Christians, neglected to put this into writing and, until he did so, the order could not be carried out. It became increasingly evident that it probably never would be, less for reasons of mercy than for reasons of prudence. Simultaneously, the people, thus spared, began to believe, or at least to hope, that, though the friars might temporarily be banished, they would not be executed, and Pedro Bautista apparently shared this hope, for, in a letter written on the eighteenth of December, he said, "The rumor now is that we will *either* be put to death or sent back to Luzon."

Meanwhile, the victims of the shipwreck were still imprisoned at Urando, where Juan Pobre had rejoined them; but before Chosokabe and Masuda left there, carrying away the booty, Landecho had asked for permission to appear personally before Taicosama and thus to have an opportunity of denying the charges made against the Spaniards and of begging for restitution of their rights. After some hesitation, Masuda gave the requested permission on one condition: that Landecho should not take his departure until eight days after the Governor's, thus giving them time to reach the Emperor first with their story and their booty.

Landecho accepted the condition and kept his promise; as a matter of fact, Chosokabe and Masuda arrived in Fujimi a day before the captain and his companions so much as left Urando; for, owing to inclement weather, a voyage, which normally would have taken only five days, took nineteen; and as the poor excuse for a boat which was all the refugees could secure did not prove sufficiently seaworthy to risk continued overloading, Landecho put briefly into port and secured a small supplementary bark which was called a *funea*, in which he dispatched Juan Pobre ahead with a native interpreter, Antonio, while he continued on his way with Diego de Guevara, an Augustinian; the clerk, Zuazola; the first mate, Francisco de Olandia; the ensign, Pedro Cotelo; and two lay passengers, Diego de Valdés and Bartolomé Rodríguez Rangél.

Juan Pobre and Antonio arrived in Osaka on the sixteenth; and, as the convent was under guard and Fray Martín a prisoner, Juan took refuge in the home of a friendly Christian and sent the interpreter to Meaco with letters from the captain and himself, together with a petition designed for the Emperor which he asked to have translated into Japanese. A week later, Juan received a reply from Pedro Bautista, telling him that the petition and the letter from Landecho were already translated and giving directions as to how the captain should present himself to the Emperor, though, at the same time, he made it clear that there was now very little hope that such a presentation would bring about good results. This was all too true. Juan was not even able to transmit Pedro Bautista's instructions to Landecho when he and his six companions finally arrived in Osaka, exhausted and half frozen. They had been told beforehand that they were to seek lodging in a house belonging to Chosokabe and they did so, still unaware that the friars had been imprisoned; but shortly after their arrival, the Governor's majordomo advised them that it was useless to depend on Pedro Bautista's services, as Taicosama intended to keep them imprisoned and, in due course, to crucify them. By way of adding insult to injury, he moved them from the house to a stable on the property, placed them under guard, and told them that they were there to await the decision of the Emperor.

It so happened that this same day—December twenty-third—another Spaniard, Jerónimo de Jesús, with whom we are already acquainted, arrived in Osaka to become Superior at Belén. In the course of his voyage from Nagasaki, he had learned something of what was occurring and, before he disembarked, had sent a message to Pedro Bautista, asking for instructions. Fray Martín was able to give him these in behalf of his Superior: he was to hide in the house of some Christian until receiving further orders. On the night of the twenty-fourth, however, he was able to go to the convent by stealth and there a happy reunion took place with Fray Martín, for they celebrated the Vigil of Christmas together; and afterward, many Christians managed to come for confession and Communion at Midnight Mass, since the guards permitted almost anyone to enter "for a consideration." A similar "consideration" was shown to Landecho and his companions, though they were marched to the convent with an escort of Japanese soldiers and returned to their prison the day after Christmas; but, meanwhile, something had been done to assuage the anguish they had felt upon arriving at Osaka to plead a lost cause, and to find that the friars were condemned to death and that they themselves were in danger of being so.

To me, there is something infinitely moving in the visualization of these unfortunate people who, in the midst of their cruel uncertainty, still had the calmness and the courage to observe Christmas in their customary way. It was the founder of the Franciscans, the gentle saint of Assisi, who had first conceived the idea of reproducing the immortal scene at Bethlehem by peopling a primitive stable with reverent human beings and docile animals. His disciples had continued to carry out the original ideal as completely as they could, wherever they were and whatever the means they possessed or lacked. In Osaka, the Brothers and their fellow Christians, including the captain and five fellow victims of a shipwreck, managed to hold a celebration at a "poor mean house" which had, symbolically, been given the name of Bethlehem. In Meaco, the Spanish friars, who did not know from one hour to another whether the next would be their last, still had a *nacimiento* and the image of the Infant Jesus which was placed in their makeshift manger that year is reverently treasured in Spain to this day, as well it may be.[21] As usual, the friars intoned Vespers and burned incense.

They could not accommodate, in their little church, all who wanted to worship with them, whatever the danger of doing so might be; but they invited these loyal followers to come into the enclosure of the convent and there these people stayed, throughout a night of bitter cold, and listened not only to Vespers and Midnight Mass, but to Matins. More than this: they begged for another Mass at dawn, and the friars chanted this also, erecting an altar in their simple portal and singing songs, "according to their custom."

It was still "according to their custom" to give Glory to God in the Highest and pray that there should be "peace to men of good will."

11

Landecho wanted Fray Jerónimo to go to Nagasaki to intercede for the Spaniards with Ruy Mendez de Figueredo, the captain of a Portuguese ship which was anchored off there, who enjoyed easy access to Taicosama, so the Spanish captain consulted Pedro Bautista by letter and the latter replied, on December twenty-eighth, "Since the Captain General asks it, Fray Jerónimo may go to Nagasaki, though I think it would be proper to delay the departure until after receiving a dispatch from the King. However, if he wishes to go at once, let him do so with God's blessing and mine, and let him stay there until I give notice what is to be next, unless they crucify us first, which is what I desire for love of Christ." In the same letter, he adds, "Have Fray Jerónimo go back to Manila and inform our Provincial what is happening here. . . . They [the magistrates] wish to eject the poor from the hospitals and I do not know how we are going to feed them, in any case, if our imprisonment lasts. It does not trouble me because I do not have a good bowl of rice, except that I have none to share; and, thanks be to God, the Christians have, so far, given us more alms for the hospital than ever before. . . . Commend us to God, as we in turn commend all and especially the poor sufferers of the shipwreck, saying the Litany every day. May Our Saviour shed His Holy Spirit upon them."

To the very end, Pedro Bautista continued to work, both for his poor and sick and for the victims of the shipwreck, trying to do all he could for them. As late as the thirtieth of December, he wrote a letter to Landecho, in which he said, "It would make me very happy if the King would allow Gonzalo and myself to talk with him in the presence of Your Honor. But I have heard that he does not wish this because the truth has been kept from him. So may the Saviour grant that Your Honor shall have a good reception."

Pedro Bautista may have had some slight stirrings of hope, since Taicosama seemed in no hurry to pronounce the death sentence on the friars and Christians who were in prison. Jibunoya was even less so. But the arrival of Landecho and his companions in Osaka brought matters to a head. Jacuin, seeing that the Emperor had pardoned the Jesuits, and fearing that the liberation of the friars might follow the audience of the Spanish captain with the Emperor, renewed his persuasive arguments that the Franciscans should be put to death; and it was as a result of the *bonze's* representations that the Emperor decided to give no audience to the shipwrecked Spaniards and to do away with the friars. Therefore, on the twenty-ninth of December he pronounced sentence: the friars and the Christians associated with them were to have their ears and noses cut off and, after having had their shame paraded through all the principal cities in the vicinity, were to be taken to Nagasaki for death on the cross. The prisoners in Osaka were to be taken to Meaco and included in this sentence.

Two days after pronouncing it, the Emperor himself went from Fujimi to Osaka, where he was building a new palace for his only son, Hideyori, a child five years old, who was the apple of his eye, and whom he had rescued at the time of the earthquake by escaping from the tottering ruins with the little boy in his arms. His presence in Osaka was probably responsible for the fact that the Jesuits who had been found in the house of the *Compañía* at the time of the first arrest—Pablo Miki, the lay preacher, Juan de Goto, the old catechist, and Diego Kisay, the old servant—did not escape the general amnesty to their Order. The Governor had never given instructions to remove their guard, and the appeals of the Spanish Jesuit, Morejón, in their behalf, were unavailing;[22] they, as well as the friars, were forcibly removed from their house to prison on the night of January first and, the next day, taken on horseback to Meaco. That same afternoon, during Vespers, the magistrates of the city arrived at the Convent of San Francisco. Pedro Bautista, realizing who had come, reached for a small crucifix which was in the choir, thrust it inside his robe and signalled to the friars that they should kneel before the altar and sing the *Te Deum*. Then he brought the services to an end, and ordered all who were in the church and the house to give themselves up without resistance.

The magistrates read aloud a list of the alleged offenders: first, the five friars, Pedro Bautista, Francisco Blanco, Gonzalo Garcia, Francisco de San Miguel and Felipe de Jesús. Pedro Bautista was careful to tell the two magistrates that Felipe de Jesús was not a member of their mission; but they declined to pardon him, because he had been aboard the *San Felipe*. The others enrolled were the two children, Antonio and Luis; Pablo Ibarki; Miguel Kosaki; Matías the cook; Juan Kizua, the messenger; and Francisco Cayo, the carpenter. This last was not in the convent that day, and as there was no response when his name was called, another man who was in attendance spoke up readily, saying, "I am Francisco Kichi." It was the consecrated physician. The magistrates, without making any more inquiries, took him away with the others.

They were marched out of the church, handcuffed, between two lines of soldiery and, as they went, the friars sang the hymn, O *Gloriosa Virginum*. A bystander outside ran back into the church and fetched a cross, which he raised in front of the procession, saying that as this was the object the Christians adored, it should go before them. Many others who were in the crowd came rushing up to the friars, trying to force their way through the guard and protesting that they wanted to accompany the Brothers on their way, wherever they were going. These impetuous volunteers were clubbed back and the men and boys who had been arrested were taken to the public prison called Michiu, where five lay preachers had already been confined. The same evening, the six prisoners from Osaka were brought in.

The next day all twenty-four were taken, with their hands tied behind them, to a plaza in Upper Meaco, where the common executioner cut off half the left ear of each one, in the presence of a great multitude which "stood amazed at the fortitude of the martyrs." Immediately thereafter, they were placed by threes in open oxcarts. In the first were Pedro Bautista and the two friars most closely associated with him; in the second, the two boys, Luis and Antonio, together with Tomé, the little acolyte from Osaka. This arrangement is understandable. Pedro Bautista was, of course, presented as the leader of the offenders; the little boys, to show that even children could not escape the righteous wrath of the Emperor; but, just why the three Jesuits were chosen to bring up the rear of the sad procession is less understandable. Each cart was flanked by spear-bearing soldiers, and behind them walked the magistrates and the deputies, while a soldier read aloud from the sentence which was borne aloft on a tablet.

Thus the mutilated prisoners were taken through the streets of Meaco as if they were common malefactors, purposely exposed to the mockery of the crowd—an outrage which could hardly have occurred without the instigation of the Emperor, for even the infidels in Meaco very generally respected the friars. And gradually the jeering ceased. The people realized more and more keenly how little the Brothers and their followers deserved such treatment and began to bewail their disgrace; not a few of them tardily burst into tears, and others actually tried to climb into the carts, to show that they were willing to share the enforced humiliation. In fact, it was the multitude, rather than the martyrs, that was oppressed by the sense of this. On the contrary, the three children burst into song and did not stop singing until they were returned to their prison; and Pedro Bautista continually turned around, with a smile, so that those behind him might be encouraged by the sight of the cross which he took from the folds of his robe. A few days later, as the prisoners were being taken from the city for good, he chanced to see Cosme Joya, the Viceroy's secretary, in the crowd and, leaning over, gave him the crucifix. It might get broken, he said, or the soldiers might force him to give it up. It would be safer in the keeping of his friend.[22-a]

From Meaco, the prisoners were taken on horseback, with their hands tied behind them, to Sacay, where they were housed in a Buddhist Monastery and permitted to receive visits from their converts, and to Osaka, where they were again put in prison. In both places, they were subjected to the same humiliating experience which they had already suffered in Meaco, of being paraded through the streets like criminals; and, in Osaka, where Landecho and his companions were still confined, the two groups of prisoners were not allowed to meet, despite the captain's entreaties. In fact, at that time, the refugees were still in considerable peril; Taicosama was not so preoccupied with the new palace which he was building for his little son and adorning with the silks from the *San Felipe* that he had forgotten them; his latest whim had taken the form of an idea that perhaps it would be just as well to have them beheaded; but Chosokabe, who had given his word that they should come to no harm, was now moved to one of those tardy acts of compassion which seemed to be fairly general: he asked that their lives should be spared and, after due consideration, Taicosama relented to the extent of ordering that they should all be sent to Nagasaki, but again with the provision that their departure should be delayed; he did not wish to have them arrive there until after the crucifixion of the condemned and, as far as these were concerned, he had not changed his mind regarding an execution, though his ministers had serious doubts as to its advisability. "'Sire, we have already cut off the ears of the friars and their Japanese friends, twenty-four in all. What shall we do with them now? It would be a good thing to send them to Manila with the captain of the galleon which is here in Usaca.' But the King replied, 'It is not to be thus, they are to be crucified in Nagasaki, so that there will be no more Christians. It is necessary to inspire fear there, for that is where all the ships come from China and the Philippines.'"

This, at least, is Fray Jerónimo's version of what happened, and as he was successfully hiding in Osaka at the time, he was doubtless in a position to know. He managed to get a letter to Pedro Bautista, asking for permission to come out in the open, to join his fellow Franciscans and to share their fate. The Superior refused to allow this. "We are condemned to death on the cross because we have preached the Holy Gospel," Pedro Bautista replied. "Our ears have been partially cut off and we are told that our noses will be cut off as well. I pray you stay hidden, so you may later console such Christians as remain and provide that our Order may not be wiped out in Japan. For this I give you my authority."

There can be no doubt either that Jerónimo was sincere in his expression of a desire to join his fellow Franciscans, or that Pedro Bautista showed good judgment in ordering otherwise. For Jerónimo lived to bear witness to the truth that was in him, not only to his own generation, but to all that have come since, including our own.

12

"The martyrdom of our saints," declares our faithful chronicler, Fray Jerónimo, who already regarded in this light the Brothers whose fate he had not been allowed to share, "is the most celebrated that has occurred in centuries; for, from Meaco to Nagasaki, which is more than a hundred leagues, they were continually tortured."

This martyrdom, as I have said before, has never been as widely heralded as might be expected; therefore, a modern writer can hardly refer to it, with accuracy, as celebrated, though there can be no doubt that Jerónimo thought it would be; and, indeed, he had every reason to hold such an opinion, for it is certainly true that the next stage of the friars' journey was both tragic and terrible. After they had been insulted, imprisoned and mutilated in Meaco, Sacay and Osaka, they and their associates were marched, in midwinter, for twenty-seven days, through rain and wind, snow and ice, going without shelter during the day, and spending the nights either in the open or in stables and filthy prisons. Their food, when they had any, was scanty and wretched; the road was so rough that their feet bled continually; and they were subjected to cruel treatment by their jailers, who often beat them, and to further abuse from anyone standing by the roadside who chose to attack them. Crowds gathered everywhere to watch the sad progress of the condemned; and while some individuals among these were Christians and friendly infidels, eager to show their sympathy, there were, inevitably, others who shouted invectives and threw loaded snowballs and sharp stones. As the leader of the band, Pedro Bautista did everything in his power to comfort and cheer his charges; and not once did any of them waver or complain; even the children showed almost superhuman courage and fortitude. As a result, this journey of the martyrs was like a cry in the wilderness. "Our death march was one of impressive solemnity," Fray Martín declared in a letter, "because in every village through which we passed, the Holy Name of Jesus was exalted." True, this could not be done with words to any great extent; but it was accomplished through the noble examples of patience, constancy and joy on the part of the condemned. The multitudes were so often moved by these great qualities that one exasperated *bonze* exclaimed, "It looks as though the King, through his sentence, had actually ordered the Christian religion to be preached throughout his realm!" Indeed, all of the Christians who heard of the edict, whether or not they actually saw the victims of the Emperor's wrath, resolved anew to remain steadfast in the Faith; not a single case of apostasy is on record.

By the first of February, the martyrs had reached Facada, whence they were taken by sea to Karatsu in the Province of Figen, where Nagasaki was located. The Governor of this province was Terezava, of whose enmity to the friars we have already heard; but as he was now fighting in Korea, his brother, Fazamburo, was serving as Regent in his stead, and it was this brother that Taicosama charged to carry out the wholesale execution. This notification reached Nagasaki the middle of January and Fazamburo acted promptly: he imprisoned the three friars who had continued to live there, Fray Bartolomé, Fray Agustín and Fray Marcelo, choosing for their confinement the Portuguese vessel still anchored in port and commanded by Ruy Mendez, who was given strict orders not to let the Brothers escape; then, when the martyrs arrived at Karatsu, the Regent ordered the chief jailer to turn them over to his own henchmen and took charge of them himself.

Because he acted so swiftly, we do not know exactly when or on whose authority Francisco Cayo and Pedro Sukeshiro were included in the list of prisoners or where they joined the others, though the fact remains that Fazamburo took twenty-six persons into custody, instead of the twenty-four who had originally been sentenced. We are also told that when he went to see the prisoners, Fazamburo was immediately attracted by Luisito. There was something very appealing about the little boy, still so sturdy and cheerful despite his long and terrible march—and so completely unabashed in the presence of the Regent. Fixing his eyes on the child, Fazamburo said, "If you would care to come and serve me, I will save you."

Luisito turned to Pedro Bautista and looked trustfully at him. "I will do whatever the Superior directs," he said. Pedro, whose heart must have been wrung every time he looked at his small disciple or thought of him, answered without hesitation, "Tell him that you will be glad to go to him, if he will let you continue to live as a Christian." Fazamburo shook his head; Luisito would have to renounce his religion. As unhesitatingly as his leader, the child shook his head, too. "Then I don't want to stay," he said firmly. "It wouldn't be sensible to give up eternal life for the sake of one that wouldn't last."

On this note, Fazamburo shrugged his shoulders and left them; there was something fantastic about these Christians. Here he would have made the boy his personal page, lapped him in luxury, given him a fine education; and he chose to stay with a poor Franciscan friar and be crucified! Fazamburo could not fathom it.[23] But, having seen how harshly the condemned, among them Pablo Miki, an old acquaintance of his, were being handled, he had sufficient compassion on them to order that they should be better treated, though they had still made no complaint—in fact, when Fazamburo expressed his astonishment at this, Pedro Bautista replied, much as Luisito had done, "Sir, what we are facing is only a temporary death; what we are gaining through our suffering will be immortal life." Then, seeing that the Regent apparently felt some sympathy for them, he asked two favors: first, that the execution might be delayed until the seventh, which was a Friday; second, that before they were crucified they should be given time to communicate.

Fazamburo promised that both favors would be granted; the promise was not kept in respect to either one.

13

At the same time that the chief jailer turned his prisoners over to Fazamburo, he delivered an official letter from Taicosama, again instructing the Regent to carry out the death sentence without fail; and at almost the same time that the latter was expressing his sympathy with the prisoners, he sent an order to Nagasaki for fifty crosses—a number which has never been explained. However, when the news of this order leaked out, many Christians inferred that the number had been augmented to include them. Far from taking fright at the prospect, they welcomed it eagerly.

The fourth of February was, apparently, the day appointed for the two groups of foreigners to arrive in Sonogi. Since early morning, Fazamburo had been awaiting the martyrs there with fifty armed men; but it was Landecho and his companions who arrived first, about nine. They presented the passports which Taicosama had given them and asked if there were no way in which the friars could be saved. Fazamburo replied that the edict of Taicosama must be obeyed; that he greatly regretted the necessity of being their executioner, because he knew they were good men, totally undeserving the death to which they had been condemned; but they were awaiting it and would be crucified the following morning.

Seeing that nothing could be done by dealing with Fazamburo directly, Landecho and his companions decided to press on to Nagasaki and see if they could not effect a ransom from the Portuguese. Accordingly, they hurried down to the beach to look for a boat, and there they met Father Pasio and Father Rodríguez, who had arrived with a message that they were to say Mass and give Communion to the prisoners; the Provincial, Pedro Gomez, had sent them, in accordance with the request of Pedro Bautista. Landecho spoke to them also on the subject of a ransom and they made the same reply as Fazamburo: all further efforts in behalf of the friars were useless. They did not offer their boat to the captain and, as no other was available, he and his companions proceeded on foot around the harbor of Omura and arrived that same night at Tokitsu—which was separated from Sonogi only by a short canal—where they found lodging at an inn. Their hasty departure had convinced the Regent that, in spite of all that had been said to discourage them, these stubborn men still intended to attempt the rescue of the friars, and it seemed to him entirely possible that, among the Spaniards in Nagasaki, they might find some who would help in such a desperate attempt. He, therefore, decided to crucify the Franciscans as soon as they arrived in Nagasaki and not to wait until Friday as he had promised. With the same haste that had marked the departure of the Spanish captain, he set off to give the necessary directions for the execution, leaving orders with the commander of the troops that, as soon as the friars arrived at Sonogi, they were to be shipped off to Tokitsu.

Father Pasio and Father Rodríguez remained to await the coming of the prisoners, which was not until midafternoon, at which time—according to Canon Law as it then existed—it was not possible to say Mass. Therefore, after a brief exchange of greetings, Father Rodríguez told Pedro that he, Rodríguez, and Pasio would return to Nagasaki and see if they could not persuade Fazamburo at least to put at their disposal a place where the prisoners could communicate. Without losing time, they left by the bark in which they had come, and arrived home about ten at night. Evidently, they were not wholly unwilling to be helpful in regard to that last desperate attempt which they, like Fazamburo, suspected Landecho intended to make, for they quickly sent servants out with horses, so that the captain and his companions could take a midnight ride and still arrive in Nagasaki before the time set for the execution.

Since they had not been led to expect any such dramatic assistance, the Spaniards had gone to bed at the Tokitsu inn and were soundly sleeping when they were awakened by a considerable commotion which they learned was caused by the fact that the prisoners, now in chains, had just come in. Since again all pleas that they might be allowed to talk with the friars were denied, they decided, on their own initiative, to start for Nagasaki on foot, leaving behind only Rangél, to watch over the remnants of their pitiful belongings. It was a terribly cold night, but there was a moon, so they were not forced to stumble along in the dark over an unknown road; and they had not gone more than a league when they were met by the servants and the horses sent out by the Jesuits. They galloped off, made good time, and by three in the morning were in Nagasaki, where they immediately began the search for the ransom which they had never given up hope of obtaining. Now they found that their cause was, indeed, a lost one; no one would risk incurring the Emperor's wrath, and continued efforts to soften the hard hearts of those they approached would only mean that they, too, would lose their lives.

No better results were obtained by the priests who had hurried back from Sonogi to ask for a place where they could hear the confessions of all the prisoners and give them all Communion and, at the same time, afford the three Jesuits among them a chance to renew their vows. They found awaiting them a message from Fazamburo, telling them to call on him at once. When they arrived at his house, he informed them that it would not be possible, after all, to delay the execution long enough for confessions and Mass; the most he would grant was permission for a stop at Urakami, two or three kilometres out of Nagasaki, long enough to permit the three Jesuits to confess; he also agreed to send an officer with the two priests, so that the guards in charge of the prisoners would not try to prevent this halt.

The three left together and, when they reached Urakami, the officer and Father Pasio remained there and Father Rodríguez went forward to meet the prisoners and tell them about this latest decision. Meanwhile, Fazamburo issued a public proclamation which prohibited anyone else from going out of the city to meet them, and ordered the immediate erection of twenty-six crosses on the usual place of execution outside the city on the right of the road between there and Urakami, whence the prisoners would be coming. He was still assailed with fears that some last-minute intervention might take place and, at midmorning, he took the mace which was his badge of office and went himself to oversee the final preparations.

Rangél, the only Spaniard who managed to see and speak with Pedro Bautista on the day of execution, has left us a record of this meeting which is all the more important because there is no other so personal. Somehow, he wheedled the guards into giving him permission for such a meeting and talked with the Superior before either left Tokitsu; and the impression made upon him by this conversation was so profound that he decided it was far more important to remain with the friars as long as he could than to stay on and look after a few mean bundles of clothing. "I found the Brothers all mutilated, but very happy and ready to suffer martyrdom," he said in his declaration. "And I left in company of the said friars for Nagasaki and was with them for some time and saw how they were maltreated. They walked barefoot, their hands tied behind them; and their hardships were all the greater because, at this season, there was so much ice and snow and very little shelter; and, as the prisoners could not go as fast as the Japanese guard desired, he kept beating them, with no other result than making them fall; several times this witness helped Pedro Bautista to rise. About a league out of Nagasaki, Pedro Bautista told this witness not to continue with them to the place where they were going to die, because they did not wish him to come to any harm; and the Superior gave this witness a letter for the priests of the ship and asked him to give affectionate greetings to the captain and his companions, and to tell them the friars were consoled because they had received permission to celebrate Mass and to communicate. And this witness remained where the friars commanded and they passed in front of him and walked away from him."

None of them had received Communion since the second and they were all eagerly awaiting it and, therefore, fasting. But soon after the parting from Rangél, they were met by Rodríguez, who told them there would be no chance for this, since they were to be crucified immediately. By this time, they had arrived at Urakami, where there was a small hermitage; and Pasio took the three Jesuits inside, to hear their confessions and the renewal of their vows. All the others remained outdoors, despite the bad weather, and the three friars heard the confessions of the others and prayed with them and encouraged them. While they were there a few Portuguese from Nagasaki, defying the orders of the Governor, came bringing them a little food and wine; and although all the condemned seemed very serene, the Portuguese could not help weeping with compassion, at seeing them thus disgraced, maltreated and brought close to death. It was they who ended by consoling their visitors with the reminder that they themselves would soon be in heaven, where all who had been kind to them would be remembered and commended to God. As for the others, it was hoped they would ask only that the martyrs' death might find favor in His sight.

When Father Pasio had completed his duties in Urakami, or rather, all those which he had been allowed to perform, he went quickly to the place of execution and made one more appeal: was it not possible that the two supernumeraries, Pedro Sukeshiro and Francisco Cayo, might be liberated, since Taicosama had condemned only twenty-four to death? Fazamburo gave several reasons for refusing to do this;

grudgingly, however, he said that Rodríguez might be present at the execution and, shortly thereafter, he granted a second petition. This one came from the Portuguese who had gone out from Nagasaki with food and drink for the prisoners and who had seen the crosses at the place where, normally, justice was meted out only to malefactors. Humbly they asked that the crosses might be placed on the other side of the road, so that, in time, a church might be built there. "This request was courteously granted," we are told by Bernardino de Avila, one of the few Spaniards who was living in Nagasaki at that time, who saw the execution, and whose thorough knowledge of the Japanese language enabled him to inform himself concerning many aspects of the sad situation. "By doing this, Fazamburo gave pleasure to the Portuguese in a matter which seemed to him of little importance, but which he thought might prevent the disturbance which he had continued to dread." Bernardino does not add, as well he might have, that by their very act in asking for the removal of the crosses from one place to another, the Portuguese were tacitly admitting that the friars and their associates were not criminals, but victims; and though the petitioners could not have foreseen this as certain, a church did rise and still endures on the site which Pedro Bautista had chosen for his Foundation, which was indeed established, though not in the manner he had visualized it, on the place of his martyrdom.

14

When the news spread through the city that the martyrs were near at hand, both Portuguese and Japanese, disregarding Fazamburo's proclamation, began to surge out in such numbers that the roads were blocked. Landecho and the men who were with him did not mingle among these crowds, but remained in strict seclusion at the lodging to which they had finally retired. The explanation he afterward gave for this course of conduct was that he had only four Spaniards with him—Rangél still not having rejoined him—and that to watch such an injustice, while they could not prevent it, would be a further insult to Spain. In one way, his reasoning may have been sound. In another, it does seem as if the mere presence of compatriots might have afforded some comfort to the dying friars in their darkest hour.

The martyrs arrived at the place of execution about eleven in the morning, coming two by two, with their hands bound and halters encircling their necks. Each was placarded with a notice bearing his name and was surrounded by armed men; in front of all, the declaration of the death sentence was hoisted on a pole. One of the first to arrive was Gonzalo; one of the last, Pedro Bautista, who was still walking sturdily and giving no sign of depression. The soldiers forced a path through the multitudes and led their victims to the new Calvary, which Fazamburo had ordered enclosed by further forces of armed men. The prisoners entered this enclosure, singing, *Benedictus, Dominus, Deus Israel.* "It was a sight to see the people assembled to view an action that had never before been taken in Japan—that is, to kill strangers who were, moreover, religious," Bernardino de Avila writes. "Some spectators even tried to force their way along by beating others out of the way with cudgels and poles. In the windows, on the balconies and on the roofs of the houses were also many, many people, stationed where they could see the Calvary, which was about six hundred feet distant from the city." Among those who, unlike Landecho and his companions, stood by to the last were the father of Juan de Goto; the wife of Cosme with their ten-year-old son, Máximo, who had followed him from Osaka; and also the parents of the child, Antonio, who came to meet him crying bitterly and begging that his life might be spared. As this was not possible without renunciation of the Faith, the child consoled them as well as he could, took off the little coat which he had worn until then and, tossing it toward them for a souvenir, ran toward his cross, threw his arms around it, kissed it and began to sing the *Te Deum.*

"After the pits had been dug," continues Bernardino de Avila, "a cross was placed in front of each one. This done, the saints were led to their crosses," and, as they were separated, they bade each other farewell and the Japanese kissed Pedro Bautista's hand. Afterward, each embraced the cross assigned to him and stood beside it, awaiting crucifixion. "At this time, there was such a sound of weeping, sobbing and lamentations from all those present that it could be heard far away and many went to the saints, begging for blessings and commendation to God."

The crosses were formed with two bars, a long one for the arms and another, shorter, for the ankles. Three or four executioners were provided for each victim and, therefore, in a very short time all were fastened in place. Nails were not used for this purpose, but heavy iron rings: one at the neck, one at each wrist and one at each ankle. This method of crucifixion was not designed to kill, but to confine until the victims were speared to death. All the crosses were raised almost simultaneously, whereat the outcry of the multitude was so great that "it seemed as though the heavens were falling and though I was witnessing this spectacle from a far-off window, the clamor of this outcry affected and moved me not a little." This comment from the Bishop, who had done nothing whatsoever to prevent the catastrophe, is, undoubtedly, one of the most appalling in all history. But it must, in very truth, have been a spectacle of terrible grandeur, this long line of crosses, and raised on them, with arms outstretched, twenty-six heroes, all completely calm and, apparently, as joyful as if they were already beholding the open gates of Paradise.[24]

Four thousand persons had gathered around the Calvary. Inside it, at six paces in front of the crosses, was the tall shaft placarded with the death warrant. Beside this stood Fazamburo with his staff of office, giving orders. Near the crosses, Pasio and Rodríguez were exhorting first one and then another of the martyrs, and close beside them stood the executioners with their spears. Some of the crucified prayed silently, others aloud; among them were not a few who asked that the Emperor and the executioners might be pardoned. ("Father, forgive them for they know not what they do.") Some, using the cross as a pulpit, preached to those before them. Some sang hymns and psalms. The child, Antonio, who was at the side of Pedro Bautista, surprised because the saint had said nothing to him nor asked him to sing *Laudate Pueri Dominum*, as they had been in the habit of doing, turned toward him, as well as he could and asked, "Father, shan't we say our psalms?" When he received no answer, he realized this was because Pedro Bautista was absorbed in prayer and contemplation and the little boy began to intone alone. Soon Luisito, who was at his left, started to sing with him. They went on doing so until they were killed.

The iron which bound the throat of Felipe de Jesús had been so unskillfully fastened that he was in the position of being suspended from it and Fazamburo, seeing that he was on the point of choking, ordered that he should be speared first. After this had been done, the executioners began to dispatch the Japanese, first at the right and then at the left, two by two. Then they speared the friars in the same way. Last of all, they came to Pedro Bautista. He did not seem to notice them. He still seemed transported and absorbed.

He probably was unconscious of what was going on. He had fought the good fight, he had finished the course, he had kept the Faith. The fight had been bitter and the course had been hard, but he had never fled from the forces of evil or ceased to press on and he had never wavered in his Faith. To be sure, he had not won the fight. But the great Apostle on whose "large, divine and comfortable words" Pedro was now dwelling had not specified winning among the requirements; he had only specified perseverance; and his faithful follower had persevered. Pedro could not help remembering, with a pang of sorrow, the poor and sick with whom, toward the end, he had not even had a good bowl of rice to share and who no longer had as much as that; but at least he had preached the Gospel to them and given them the Sacraments. Their lives and the lives of others would be spiritually nourished because of this. He could rejoice on that account. . . .

He could also rejoice because he was fast reaching the realms where there would be no more question as to whom he owed obedience, whether to his kind Provincial in Manila or to the unfriendly Bishop in Nagasaki or to the great King and still greater Pope so far away; he would not have to think any longer whether he was primarily a missionary or primarily an ambassador. A fortnight or so earlier, he had written to Don Pedro Martinez and expressed the hope that the condemned might receive an episcopal benediction before they died. The Bishop had sent this benediction by messenger to the Calvary and Pedro Bautista had acknowledged it by asking that Don Pedro be thanked for it and by begging forgiveness if he, Pedro Bautista, had failed in any way. He knew that his apparent insubordination had been held against him and, perhaps, the stand he had taken had been wrong. But he had done what he thought was right and now, though he hoped and believed there would be many provincials and bishops and popes in the place where he was going, there would be only one King and it was to Him and Him alone that Pedro Bautista would owe allegiance. . . .

The celestial realm where this King reigned would, of course, be much more beautiful than any earthly Paradise. But even so, as the vision of it came to Pedro Bautista, it reminded him of a place where he had been before and which he had not seen in many years: a place in which there were flowing streams and green mountainsides and glowing fruits and beautiful flowers—the place where his father's house had stood in San Esteban del Valle. Well, he was on his way to the house of his Father now—his King who was also his Father. It did not seem confusing to him that the one King should also be his Father and that he should have two of these, one earthly and one heavenly, any more than it seemed confusing that this place to which he was going was not unlike San Esteban del Valle, as he saw it in his vision, except that it was so much more beautiful. . . .

He had often heard his native Province of Avila called the Land of Stones and Saints, without any reference to its beauties. Well, of course, there had been many saints there, beginning with San Segundo, including the Great Saint Teresa, and ending, as far as he knew, with Juan de la Cruz. But perhaps, in time to come, there might be more saints from Avila. As for stones, of course they were there, too. However, stones were a source of strength. Had not Christ said, "Thou art Peter and *on this rock,* I will build my Church"? Avila had helped to strengthen that Church with its stones, as well as through its saints. Perhaps there was some connection between the two. Perhaps it was natural and fitting for the land which produced the stones to produce saints, also. . . . This barren place, this Calvary where he was now, and which he was so soon to leave, was a place of stones. Could it not also become a place of saints, through the infinite mercy of God the Father, of Christ the King? . . .

The first spear thrust given him did not kill the saint. It was at the moment that the second thrust was given him that Rangél galloped up to the Calvary. He had stayed behind when he was first asked to do so, but there had come a moment when he could not bear to do so any longer. He dismounted quickly and ran to the cross to find that Pedro Bautista was already dead. But blood was still gushing from his side. Rangél caught it up in his handkerchief and stumbled away, sobbing. But there was still no visible change in Pedro Bautista. "He had yielded up his soul to his Saviour with his face turned toward heaven" and his serenity was sublime.

15

And afterward?

Afterward, Fazamburo placed a heavy guard around the Calvary and gave strict orders that no one should be allowed to enter the enclosure. Despite the guard and the order, a few persons somehow managed to penetrate to it, even before blood had ceased to flow from the dead bodies of the martyrs, and many more persons reached there in time to tear off clothing for relics. The Bishop became so fearful lest the corpses themselves should be stolen that he threatened excommunication to anyone who had taken the least part of these. Nevertheless, parts did, mysteriously, disappear.

Whether the Japanese of this period had acquired the habit of tardy changes of heart from the Bishop, or whether he had acquired it from them, I do not know. But the fact remains that, a few days after the crucifixion, Martinez visited the Calvary and declared, standing with uncovered head before the crosses of those whose death sentence he had not attempted to have set aside, "Those are martyrs, like San Lorenzo. Let us commend ourselves to them, saying, 'Holy martyrs, pray for us.'" Three days later, he repeated his visit and, on his return to the episcopal palace, said to one of his retainers, "Go and see those servants of God and you will behold something miraculous; they seem to be clothed in glory." The following Sunday, he preached about the martyrs in his cathedral, and announced his intention of building a hermitage at the Calvary which should be called Santa María de los Mártires. Shortly thereafter, however, he was recalled to Macao, did not return to Japan, and never did anything about a hermitage. But when, later the same year, he was summoned to give testimony regarding the aftermath of the execution, he said, "The expression of the martyrs' faces remained so sublime that they appeared to be peacefully sleeping or lost in contemplation, rather than dead. I saw the Portuguese and other Christian people treating the garments of the crucified as if these were relics, and multitudes came from far and wide, over a long period, to venerate their remains. All this testified to the sanctity of their death. . . . Without doubt, they died for our Holy Catholic Faith like brave and valiant soldiers of Christ."

Long before this testimony—which does not sound reluctant—was given, many signs and wonders were reported: every Friday night, or so it was rumored, a line of luminescence, such as might come from a great candlelight procession, was seen to stretch from the Calvary to the Hospital of the Lázaros. Eventually, Landecho, who was still in Nagasaki, was at last persuaded to go out to the Calvary and see a still more remarkable sight—three great columns of radiance which hovered over it and then streamed away toward the city; Rangél, who went with him, insisted that this was true. There were stories of fresh blood which still flowed from time to time, on certain special occasions, and various beholders corroborated what the Bishop had said about the appearance of Pedro Bautista: that his countenance continued to be beautiful and that he looked as if he were peacefully sleeping. They added that his body was now largely uncovered, because so much of his raiment had been removed for relics, and that the skin on the parts exposed had a fresh and rosy tinge. One charming story related that, every now and then, Fray Pedro Bautista would appear to say Mass at his little church in Nagasaki, that, when he did so, he was always served by the small boy, Antonio, as an acolyte, and that celestial voices were heard, though no angels were actually seen, whereas Pedro Bautista and Antonio were clearly visible. When the process of beatification began, one of the witnesses, Rodríguez Curial, added further details to his testimony: he said that, having seen Pedro Bautista at the altar, he hurriedly left in the middle of Mass and went out to the Calvary, where he saw that the saint's cross was vacant. He spoke to the guards, who told him this had happened on several occasions. He hurried back to the church, but Mass was over; then he returned to the Calvary and saw Pedro Bautista again hanging on his cross.

We are, of course, at liberty to believe or disbelieve any or all of these stories as we prefer. According to Robles Dégano, the Sacred Roman Rota, which is certainly not given to unfounded credulity, has approved them in several cases. At all events, there can be no question that the number of miracles attributed to Pedro Bautista was sufficient to assure his beatification and, more than two centuries later, his canonization. But that part of the story belongs to another era. For the moment, we must stay in the one where we left him.

A few at a time, the Spaniards that had been most closely associated with him left Japan. The friars who had been imprisoned on the Portuguese galleon, commanded by Ruy Mendez de Figueredo, and who had remained unharmed throughout the course of their captivity, were taken to Macao at the same time as the Bishop—that is, in March of 1597. Landecho and about half of his passengers and crew succeeded in getting back to Manila in May, and the rest of the passengers and crew were able to follow a month later; no further charges of piracy were ever brought against any of them. Soon after their arrival, by order of the new Governor, Don Francisco Tello, a solemn procession was held, in connection with a Mass and sermon at the Convent of San Francisco, "to thank God for the triumph of the holy martyrs"; and this was followed by two court inquiries, one held in Manila and the other in Macao, for the purpose of defending Pedro Bautista against any baseless accusations in connection with the shipwreck. The first of July, two galleons leaving for Spain, via Mexico, took the sad news of his death; and later that same month the Governor sent another ambassador to Japan. This time, it was not a Franciscan friar, sworn to humility; it was a bold captain of infantry, Don Luis Navarrete. He promptly demanded satisfaction for the martyrdom and authority to remove the bodies from alien soil in order to give them decent Christian burial elsewhere.

Of course, there was no real way in which he could get "satisfaction" and Don Luis was aware of this. But Taicosama knew better than to tamper with the infantry; this time, he himself might well have been the victim of wrath far more righteous than his had been. He gave the indicated orders without argument.

By now, relics, rather than bodies recognizable as such, were naturally all that remained to remove. Even the crosses had disappeared from the Calvary, not because there had been wilful desecration—and this seems a miracle in itself—but because so many fervent Christians, according to the custom of the times, had possessed themselves of whatever they could for sacred souvenirs. Fray Jerónimo, who had —and this was certainly another miracle!—remained unharmed in Japan until then, succeeded in joining the other friars in Macao, taking with him a certain number of these relics, among them the cross that Pedro Bautista had removed from the folds of his robe and given to Cosme Joya at the gate of the city. From Macao, Fray Jerónimo, Fray Marcelo, Fray Juan Pobre and Fray Matías left for Manila and went from there to Spain, with all the proofs necessary to warrant beatification, the process for which began in 1620. In 1862, the magificent ceremony of canonization took place in St. Peter's in Rome in the presence of two hundred and sixteen cardinals, archbishops and bishops, besides that of a vast multitude, and with Pope Pius IX presiding.

And is that the end of Pedro Bautista's story? Not quite, I think. As a matter of fact, I do not think the end can be told, even now, and perhaps never, though the town of Paracuellos and the city of Manila have taken him for their patron, and the house where he was born has become a shrine, and altars in his honor have been raised in the Convent of Arenas and in several nearby towns. To be sure, there is none in the cathedral at Avila, where he served as an acolyte, which seems strange to an outsider. But perhaps there is some good reason for it and, in any case, he does not really need it. Altars have been raised elsewhere, in different ways, just as the Foundation he hoped to establish in Nagasaki has taken a different form from the one he planned and expected.

After his martyrdom, the number of Christians in Japan increased by leaps and bounds. Within a month of his death, the Jesuit, Gregorio de Céspedes, wrote from Shimabara, "Here we all have new strength and courage, and even the Christians who were wavering have been fortified afresh." Sixty-three years later, the last priest was banished from Japan and, this time, the banishment was real; the countryside was scoured until not a single one remained, and many other death sentences were imposed and carried out before total exile was an accomplished fact. But after the ports of Japan were opened to American trade by Admiral Matthew Perry, and the clergy followed the navy into the country, it was discovered that somehow—unrecognized, undirected, unfostered—Christianity had survived for two hundred years.

What greater tribute could be paid, anywhere in the world, to Pedro Bautista, Franciscan friar and Ambassador of Spain—a native of the Province of Avila, otherwise known as the Land of Stones and Saints?

NOTES FOR PROLOGUE

1 The French original was published in 1950 under the title, *La Vie de Sainte Thérèse D'Avila* by Editions du Seuil, Paris. The English translation was made by Kathleen Pond and the book was published in the United States by Pantheon (1953).

2 A complete list of the names on St. Teresa's statue follows herewith:

SAINTS	MILITARY
San Segundo	Gil González Dávila
Santa Barbada	Alonso Dávila Alvarado
San Vicente	Sancho Dávila
Santa Sabina	Fernán Gómez Dávila
Santa Cristeta	Alonso Dávila Guzmán
San Pedro del Barco	Pedro Dávila
San Juan de la Cruz	Antonio Dávila y Toledo
Blessed Alonso de Orozco	
Venerable Mari Díaz	
Venerable Mariá Vela	

POLITICAL	ARTISTS AND WRITERS
Isabel I of Castile	El Tostado
Pedro Sánchez Zurraquín	Juan Sedeño
Sancho Dávila	Alonso Díaz de Montalvo
Pedro de la Gasca	Juan Díaz Rengifo
Diego Espinosa	Luis Dávila
Diego de Guzmán	Sebastián Vivanco
Enrique Dávila Guzmán	Nicolás García
Diego Mexía de Velázquez	Gil González Dávila

As the reader will see by consulting the Table of Contents, the main part of this book is devoted to biographical sketches of Isabel of Castile, Teresa of Avila, San Juan de la Cruz, Venerable María Vela and San Pedro Bautista, whose name, for some inexplicable reason, is not included among those on the statue. (I thoroughly agree with the opening lines in the Prologue to Felipe Robles Dégano's *Vida y Martirio de San Pedro Bautista*, in which he says, "An illustrious martyr and leader of martyrs; a doctor of the church, mystic and ecstatic; a virgin and author without peer, that is to say, Pedro Bautista, John of the Cross, Teresa of Jesus. Here are three of the great glories of sanctity, the three saints already canonized who saw the light of day in this Diocese of Avila, which is very logically envied by the entire world. But how many people know who San Pedro Bautista was? The glory of Avila is not centered solely in Teresa of Jesus and John of the Cross, nor did theirs exceed that of Pedro Bautista who, however, unfortunately, is very little known.")

Shorter sketches will be found of the following persons, beginning on the following pages: San Segundo (p. 97); San Vicente, Santa Sabina and Santa Cristeta (p. 98); San Pedro del Barco (p. 150); Blessed Alonso Orozco (p. 112); Venerable María Díaz (p. 101); Santa Barbada (p. 183); the two Sancho Dávilas (pp. 12 and 294); Diego Espinosa (pp. 115 and 145); and El Tostado (p. 320). There is also incidental mention of them elsewhere in the text, as listed in the Index.

Careful research concerning the others has resulted only in very fragmentary information up to the time this book has gone to press. The following items, however, certainly give rise to hopes that more may be obtainable, as, in almost every case, they seem to me extremely interesting.

Gil González Dávila. While still very young, Gil González Dávila went to the Indies with Pedro Arias Dávila and served under Hernán Cortez in the conquest of Mexico and Yucatan. He died in 1541 in Mexico City, where he lived in a beautiful house in which he fed and sheltered many men less fortunate than himself. This house was known as the "Hospital de los Buenos"—meaning men who were poor but healthy—to distinguish it from the "Hospital de los Enfermos," which means one for the sick.

Alonso Dávila Alvarado. He was a Spanish explorer and conquistador of the first half of the sixteenth century. He landed in Yucatan in 1528. At the head of fifty footmen and sixteen cavalrymen, he explored the coast of Chelqual, founded the town of Villa Real and performed many heroic deeds. Continuously harassed by the Indians, he went to Mexico City to secure reinforcements. Unable to obtain them, he returned to Spain in 1533.

Fernán Gómez Dávila. He was chief superintendent in the household of the Catholic Kings. I am especially disappointed that I have been able to find out nothing more about his achievements in this capacity. However, I have learned that he took part in the War of the Comuneros, a party that rose in rebellion against the encroachments of Charles V when the latter imposed heavy taxes upon the Castilian cities at the beginning of his reign. Then he led the Abulense troops that took part in the reconquest of Navarre from the French—the war in which St. Ignatius of Loyola was wounded during the siege of Pamplona in 1521.

Alonso Dávila Guzmán. He was either a son or a brother of Gil González Dávila (historians are not in accord) and accompanied this near relative when the latter took part in the Conquest of Mexico. He was at the Battle of Otumba where he distinguished himself by his bravery. He escorted the treasure of Montezuma when it was being taken to Spain, but the French pirate, Juan Fleury, captured the ship and Alonso Dávila was thrown into the prison at Rochelle. Many years later, he was liberated by Charles V.

Pedro Dávila. He was Captain General and Governor of the "Terceras" Islands, the designation given by the Spaniards to all the Azores, though the Portuguese call only one of these Terceira. These islands belonged to Spain when Portugal was annexed by Philip II and remained united to Spain until 1640.

Antonio Dávila y Toledo. He was Marqués of Velada and belonged to one of the noblest and oldest families of Avila. Their descendants claimed to be related to the Ahumadas and probably were. They were great benefactors of Santa Ana's Convent, which they endowed with a number of bushels of wheat every year. Antonio was born in Avila in 1590 and distinguished himself in the Wars of Flanders against the rebellious Dutch, in Germany against the Protestants, and in northern Italy when Milan and other towns were under Spanish rule. He was Governor of Flanders and Milan and, for a few years, Ambassador to England. He was also at the head of a fleet assembled to chase the Dutch and English pirates, who preyed on the Spanish galleons which brought gold and goods from the New World, and succeeded in capturing a number of Dutch ships.

Pedro Sánchez Zurraquín. He was the first Bishop of Avila after the reconquest of the city from the Moors, around the year 1100, and the confidential adviser of Count Don Ramón, who was responsible for a large part of this victory and for the future development of the city.

Pedro de la Gasca. He was born in Avila in 1485 and died in Valladolid in 1567. At the age of sixty, he was appointed by Emperor Charles V, President of the Royal Audiencia of Peru, to overcome the rebellion of Gonzalo Pizarro. He led the campaign, in which St. Teresa's brothers took part, with great ability and courage and defeated the rebellious forces and condemned Pizarro to death. He reorganized the administration and finances of the Vice-royalty and promoted the wealth of the country so successfully that he was given the title of "Restorer and Pacifier." On his return to Spain, he was made Bishop of Palencia.

Diego de Guzmán. He rose to high positions from the chaplaincy of Kings Philip III and IV. He was made President of the Council of the Indies, appointed Archbishop of Seville and created Cardinal by Urban VIII.

Enrique Dávila Guzmán. He was born in Avila and was captain of the Spanish "Tercios"—infantry regiments famous for their bravery and the battles they won in the Low Countries and Italy—in Flanders. Later, as President of the Military Orders and Viceroy of Valencia, he showed a shrewd diplomatic tact and an energetic military character. He distinguished himself for his honesty and austerity toward those who were plundering the public finances and misappropriating the gold brought by the galleons from America. His policy was praised by King Philip III and he was made Marqués of Povar.

Diego Mexía de Velázquez. He was the Marqués of Leganés and, as Governor of Milan, began his campaigns in Italy by winning several victories, defeating Victor Amadeo and capturing Nice, Brema and Vercelli (1636 and 1637). He besieged the city of Casal (1640) and was acclaimed as their liberator by Arti, Saluzes, Coni and other towns. In Cataluña, he was unsuccessful in the Battle of Horcas and was confined to Ocaña. Reinstated to his rank, he was named Captain General and Viceroy of Cataluña in 1645. In his campaigns in Portugal, he took several towns. In 1647, he saved Lérida (in Cataluña) from the siege that the French had laid to it and put them to flight.

Juan Sedeño. He belonged to one of the first five families of Arévalo, where he was born. He went as a soldier to Italy, where he translated several works, among them Tasso's *Jerusalem Libertada* and Tansillo's *The Tears of St. Peter.* Back in Spain, he became an historian and a playwright. He printed, in his home town, *La Suma de Varones Ilustres* (date unknown) which was reprinted in Toledo in 1590. He wrote the tragi-comedy, *Calixto and Melibea* (Salamanca, 1540). His prolificacy and erudition were praised by Hieronimo Chilino in his *Theater of Literary Men.* He was buried in Arévalo, in a chapel of the Church of San Juan.

Alonso Díaz de Montalvo. He was a jurist and compiler of the Royal Ordinances of Alcalá. He was held in high esteem by the Catholic Kings, who entrusted important commissions to him. The exact dates of his birth and death are unknown, but he must have died after 1492, as this was when he published his Ordinances.

Juan Díaz Rengifo. It is generally believed that this was the pen name of Father Diego García Rengifo, a learned Jesuit, Professor of Humanities in Avila, who, in 1592, published in Salamanca his *Arte Poética Española*, which acquired extraordinary renown. As a didactic work, it was widely used in schools. He was also a poet of note.

Luis Dávila. His full name is given in the special number of *El Diario de Avila* as Luis Dávila y Zuñiga and his title as Marqués of Mirabel. He was a General in the Cavalry of Lorena and, in 1544, wrote the celebrated Commentaries on the Campaigns of Charles V in Africa. He was an ambassador in the Council convoked at Trent by the Pope and wrote the equally celebrated Commentaries on the War in Germany.

Sebastián Vivanco. He was a Professor of Music at the University of Salamanca and published two volumes of music for Solemn Masses, as well as motets.

Nicolás García. He was a miniature painter of the first half of the nineteenth century who did many portraits of the nobles and kings of his time. He was considered the best in his line and some of his miniatures may be found in the collections of the Marquéses of Toca and of Somio.

Gil González Dávila. This is the second instance where two men by the same name are commemorated, but, as a matter of fact, it is merely a coincidence. The achievements of the military man have already been noted. The historian —born in 1578, died in 1658—was official chronicler of Kings Philip III and IV and wrote many volumes on history, the best known being *Teatro Eclesiástico de Las Ciudades y Iglesias Catedrales de España*, which was a classical book on Spanish Church history. He was considered a great authority on the history of many cities of Spain and of their leading figures. In his Church history he says: "That great Captain, the Duke of Alba, had such a high opinion of the sons of my fatherland [Avila] that when anyone applied to him for admission in the army in Flanders where the Duke was Governor and Captain General and showed that he was from my native city [Avila], he immediately promoted him in rank, saying: 'It is not that I am partial; no one has failed me so far.' "

3 Hutton, Edward. *The Cities of Spain.* Page 319.

NOTES FOR PART I

[1] I have been puzzled at finding no references to this part of her education in any of the biographies of Isabella that I have read, but it is not only a matter of proud tradition with the nuns at Santa Ana. It is commemorated by a tablet on the outer wall of their convent, which reads as follows:

EN ESTE MONASTERIO ESTA ENSALZADO EL OBISPO DON SANCHO DAVILA MAESTRO DEL NIÑO REY ALFONSO XI, SALIDO DE AVILA PARA SER LA MAJESTAD CATOLICA FORJADOR DE LA GRAN CASTILLA.

EN ESTE MONASTERIO SE INSTRUYO EDUCÓ LA NIÑA PRINCESA ISABEL SALIDA DE AVILA PARA SER LA MAJESTAD CATOLICA FORJADORA DE LA GRAN ESPAÑA.

EN ESTE MONASTERIO SE VISTIO POR VEZ PRIMERA DE HOMBRE EL MONARCA DEL GRAN IMPERIO ESPAÑOL MAJESTAD CATOLICA FELIPE II.

TRILOGIA DE GRANDEZA PATRIA,
EL AYUNTAMIENTO DE AVILA LA PERPETUA
EN HONRA A LA HISTORIA DE LA CIUDAD.

AVILA-MAYO-1941

Freely translated, this reads:

IN THIS MONASTERY WAS EXALTED THE BISHOP DON SANCHO DAVILA TUTOR OF THE CHILD KING ALFONSO XI, WHO LEFT AVILA TO BECOME THE CATHOLIC MAJESTY, FORGER OF GRAND CASTILE.

IN THIS MONASTERY WAS EDUCATED THE YOUNG PRINCESS ISABEL WHO WENT OUT FROM AVILA TO BECOME THE CATHOLIC MAJESTY, FORGER OF GREAT SPAIN.

IN THIS MONASTERY HIS CATHOLIC MAJESTY PHILIP II, SOVEREIGN RULER OF THE GREAT SPANISH EMPIRE DONNED MAN'S ATTIRE FOR THE FIRST TIME. (The so-called breeching of a man child, particularly one of noble or royal birth, was accompanied by a great ceremony. Until he was three or four years old, he wore the same kind of clothes as a girl. The change into breeches or trunks was considered a great step forward.)

TO HONOR THE HISTORY OF THE CITY
THE MUNICIPALITY OF AVILA PERPETUATES
THIS TRILOGY OF THE GRANDEUR OF SPAIN.

AVILA-MAY-1941

In the April, 1954, number of *The Cisterium*, a periodical published by the Cistercians of Spain, there is a very fine article, entitled *Real Monasterio de Santa Ana de Avila* (*Royal Monastery of Saint Anne of Avila*) which refers at some length to Isabella's education and to numerous other facts relating to her. Quotations from this article will appear in a later note.

[2] One of the missals she illuminated is still carefully preserved in Granada; another in the British Museum in London.

[8] In his book, *Isabella of Spain*, Walsh states that they were summoned to the Court at Madrid; but it was not until the time of Philip II that Madrid became the official residence of the Court and in the time of Isabella, it was still a very small place. The *Diccionario de la Historia de España*. *Revista de Occidente* states that Enrique lived mostly at Segovia, either at the Alcázar or at the hunting lodge which is now the Convent of San Antonio el Real, and that it was here he summoned his half-brother and half-sister. This statement is corroborated by other sources.

[4] Walsh, William Thomas. *Isabella of Spain*. Page 70.

[4-a] Archbishop Carrillo's full name was Alonso Carrillo de Acuña; it cannot properly be separated into its component parts, just as Alvarez de Toledo and Lope de Vega cannot be separated. Besides, there was another, and very famous, Archbishop of Toledo called Carrillo—Cardinal Gil Alvarez Carrillo de Albornoz, who flourished in the XIVth century. Once this has been noted, Carrillo de Acuña may be called Carrillo for the sake of brevity, since he is the only one who appears in this narrative.

[4-b] The coat of arms of the city, to this day, represents the King of Avila in this way.

[5] Dávila—which is, of course, a contraction of de Avila—is one of the greatest names of the province and we find it recurring over and over again in history, often with Christian names as well as surnames the same. The Sancho Dávila who was Bishop of Avila for more than fifty years, and who built both the Convent of Santa Ana and the one at Guisando—also so closely connected with Isabel's story—should not be confused with the great Captain General who is buried in the parochial church of San Juan at Avila, where St. Teresa was christened, and whose epitaph reads:

Aquí yace el noble y valeroso Cavallero Sancho Davila Capitán General de la costa del Reino de Granada Fundador de esta capilla: comenzó a servir en la guerra de Alemania, Lombardia, el Piamonte, Nápoles, toma de Africa. Fué Castellano de Pavia, Capitán de cavallos en Flandes y Capitán de la guarda del Duque de Alba, Castellano de Amberes, Almirante de la mar. Desvarató los rebeldes cerca de Dalem, socorrió a Maderburg Wal Krem, ganó a Ramua, venció la famosa batalla de Mo Kem, siendo cabeza del ejercito, a 14 de Abril de 1574 a donde fué muerto el Conde Ludovico y se tomaron 36 banderas y tres estandartes, con que aseguró los Estados de Flandes a su Magestad. Fué Maestre de Campo general de la conquista del Reino de Portugal, badeó a Duero, recobró a Oporto, desbarató al enemigo, ganó todo el Reino con gran gloria de la nacion Española y de su patria. Murió en Lisboa a 8 de Junio de 1583 a los 59 de su edad.

Freely translated, this reads:

Here lies the noble and valiant knight, Sancho Dávila, Captain General [Civil and Military Commander] of the Coast of the Kingdom of Granada, Founder of this chapel. He began his military career in the war of Germany, Lombardy, Piedmont, Naples, capture of Africa. He was *castellan* [Lord] of Pavia, Cavalry Captain in Flanders and Captain of the Guard of the Duke of Alba, *castellan* of Antwerp, Admiral of the Sea. He routed the rebels near Dalem. He gave succor to Maderburg Wal Krem, conquered Ramua, won the famous battle of Mo Kem, at the head of his army, on April 14, 1574, when Count Ludwig was killed, taking from him 36 banners and three standards; with this victory he assured the estates of Flanders for His Majesty. He was Grand Field-Master in the conquest of Portugal; he waded the Duero River, recovered Oporto, routed the enemy, won the whole kingdom with great glory to the Spanish nation and his country. He died in Lisbon on June 8, 1583, at the age of 59.

Brantomê places Sancho Dávila among the great captains of his time. He was aide-de-camp of the Duke of Alba in his campaigns in Flanders and his right hand. He won many battles and was celebrated for his courage and military ability. In the conquest of Portugal, he was chief of staff of the Duke and died in Lisbon from the kick of his horse. (The information about this Sancho Dávila is culled from the writings of Pierre de Bourdeilles, Lord of Brantomê, a French writer, who was born in Perigord in 1540 and died in 1614, and who fought in the Armies of France and Spain. According to the authorities I have consulted, "he is a chronicler, rather than a historian, but very keen and accurate in his observations." He wrote various works, among them *Vies des Grande Capitaines Etrangers*, which is where he speaks of Sancho Dávila, who was known as *Rayo de la Guerra*—Thunderbolt of War.)

6 These verses read:

DON SANCHO OBISPO DE AVILA COMO SENNOR HONRADO
DIO MUY BUEN EXEMPLO COMO FUE BUEN PRELADO
FIZO ESTE MONASTERIO DE SANTO BENITO LLAMADO
E DIOLE MUY GRANDES ALGOS POR DO ES SUSTENTADO.
PUSO Y MUCHAS DUENAS ET DE MUY SANTA VIDA
DIOLAS SU ABADESA ENTENDIDA ET SABIDA
DE LIBROS Y VESTIMENTAS LA IGLESIA MUY CUMPLIDA
E DE MUCHAS OTRAS JOYAS LA FIZ O ENRIQUECIDA.
PUSO HI CAPELLANES QUE CADA DIA REZASEN
ET LAS HORAS DEL DIA TODAS MUY BIEN CANTASEN
ET POR TODOS LOS FINADOS A DIO SANTO ROGASEN
CA DIOLES BUENAS RENTAS CON QUE BIEN LO PASASEN.
E PORQUE ESTE MONASTERIO FUESE MEJOR GUARDADO
ET EN TODOS SUS ALGOS FUESE BIEN AMPARADO
DIO LA VISITACION A CUALQUIER QUE FUES PRELADO
OBISPO QUE FUES DE AVILA E NO DE OTRO REGULADO
ANDABA ENTONCES EL ERA CUANDO EL FUE ACABADO
EN MIL E CCC ANOS SEGUN DIZ EL DICTADO
ET MAS LXXXVIII POR MEJOR SER REMEMBRADO
ET DIO GRACIAS A DIOS EL OBISPO MUCHO ONRADO.

Freely translated, this reads:

Don Sancho Bishop of Avila was honored as an upright master and was a worthy prelate who gave a good example. He built this monastery, which is called San Benito, and bestowed on it the large sums whereby it is supported. He placed here many ladies of holy life and gave them as Abbess a learned and prudent woman. The church has been well supplied with books and vestments and enriched with many other treasures. He placed here chaplains who would

EN ESTE LUGAR
FUE JURADA DOÑA ISABEL LA CATOLICA
POR PRINCESA Y LEGITIMA HEREDERA
DE LOS REINOS DE CASTILLA Y DE LEON
EL 19 DE SEPTIEMBRE DE 1468

HIZO PONER ESTA INSCRIP
CION EN EL AÑO 1921 DOÑA
MARIA D LA PUENTE Y SOTO
MARQUESA DE CASTANIZA

"In this place Doña Isabel the Catholic was declared the Princess and legitimate heiress of the King-doms of Castile and León. September 19, 1468. This inscription was placed here in 1921 upon order of Doña María la Fuente y Soto, Marquesa de Castanza." From a photograph by Mayoral, Avila.

pray every day for both the living and the dead and who were well qualified to chant the Offices and gave them incomes on which they could live well. And in order that this monastery might be safeguarded and its funds well protected, he entrusted its visitation to no less a prelate than a Bishop of Avila. It was finished in 1388 and the Bishop gave thanks to God.

7 Walsh, whose biography of Isabella I have so greatly enjoyed and admired and whom I have found almost invariably accurate, in comparing him with other authorities, gives a different account of this audience. He says, "One after another [the grandees] knelt before her and kissed her hand." The nuns at the Convent of Santa Ana, however, are very insistent in saying that this is a mistake, and that Isabella remained behind the grille with the Abbess, throughout the interview. Their archives support their version of the story and it had the approval of the late Agustín de Amezua, one of Spain's most prominent modern historians, with whom I discussed the question. Therefore, I have not hesitated to abide by local tradition.

8 The translation of the document on page 296 follows the form used by Walsh. *Isabella of Spain*. Pages 81 and 82. (Walsh, however, refers to Buete, instead of Huete, which, obviously, is a typographical error, since there is no town by the name of Buete in Spain. However, the present Duke of Huete says that his family possesses no record showing that this city was ever part of Isabella's dowry.)

9 The Cortes, or National Parliament of Castile, consisted of three estates: the nobles, the clergy and the commons, thus bearing a general resemblance to the Parliament of Great Britain. Unlike this, however, it did not always meet in the capital city or even always in the same city. When a question of great importance arose, such as a question of succession, like the present one, the three estates would meet together in whatever town the King happened to be staying.

10 The *maestresala* was the chief server and taster at a royal table or that of any great nobleman. As he was entrusted with the task of detecting poisons in the food, his position was one of great importance and trust.

11 Walsh, William Thomas. *Isabella of Spain*. Pages 85 and 86.

11-a Palencia achieved distinction in another way also; he became one of the period's most reliable chroniclers and, except for Pulgar who was equally reliable, is the one most frequently relied upon by modern writers, as he was a witness to everything he described.

12 Juan II of Aragon had married twice: first, Blanche, Queen of Navarre, by whom he had three children, Charles, Blanche and Eleanor; and second, Juana Enriquez, by whom he had two children, Fernando, who married Isabel, and Juana, who became Queen of Naples. Juana Enriquez' family tree was quite as intriguing as that of her predecessor, Blanche. Her grandfather, Alfonso Enriquez, had, like her father, Fadrique Enriquez, been an admiral, though his title was *Almirante de la Mar* instead of *Almirante de Castilla*; and Alfonso Enriquez was the bastard son of still another Don Fadrique, Master of Santiago and twin brother of King Enrique II of the House of Trastamara, both bastards. The first Don Fadrique was one of the many children born to King Alfonso II of Castile by his beautiful mistress,

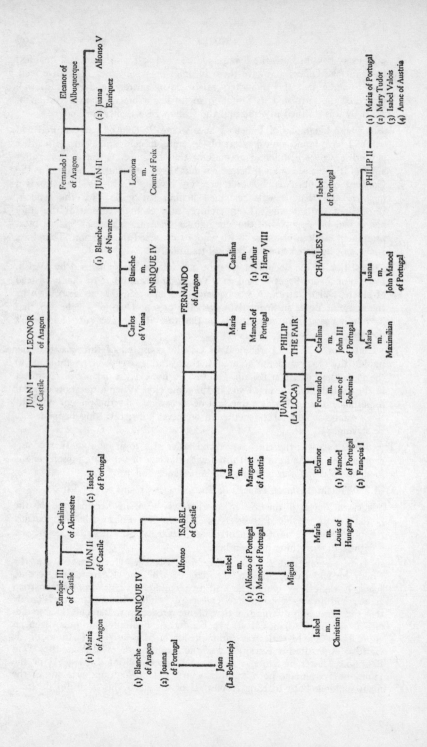

Doña Leonor de Guzmán. Juana Enriquez, therefore, had not only noble but royal blood in her veins and was far more conscious of this than of the double bar sinister that went with it. Her determination that her only son, Fernando, should marry Isabel, Princess of Castile, was based not only on the obvious material advantages of such a match, but on Juana's proud conviction that Fernando was Isabel's equal in birth and breeding.

12-a "Flowers of Aragon
are inside Castille!
Standard of Aragon!
Standard of Aragon!"

13 The genealogical chart on page 298 is offered solely for the purpose of clarifying this relationship and those which followed shortly thereafter. It has seemed to the author that a complete chart of generation after generation would only confuse the average reader in connection with this particular story.

14 Most authorities seem to agree that it was a forgery and some even maintain that the Archbishop himself had connived with Juan of Aragon in producing it. At all events, Isabel, who gradually became less trustful, though no less loving, later took the precaution of securing a second dispensation, signed by Sixtus IV, which declared her marriage legalized, her child legitimate and her rights of inheritance secure.

15 Walsh, William Thomas. *Isabella of Spain.* Page 99.

16 Authorities differ as to the duration of Fernando's absence. Walsh, generally so dependable, says (p. 136), "The news of Enrique's death and Isabel's coronation had reached him in Perpignan, where he had gone early in the autumn [that is, the autumn of 1474] to answer a desperate appeal from his father." (The italics are mine.) Plunket, however, places his departure in the autumn of 1470 (p. 82) and speaks of Fernando's brief return in 1473 (p. 86). Christopher Hare tells the story in much the same way and at greater length. Referring to the autumn of 1470, he says:

"The Infanta Isabel had a time of dark anxiety and suspense to endure, and for many months the issue was doubtful. Her young husband, at the head of a company of Castilian horse, had joined his father the King of Aragon in his war with France for the possession of Roussillon and Cerdagne, while anarchy reigned through all the land which owned the sway of King Enrique. The nobles fought against each other from their walled fortresses, and one town was at feud with another, while the land lay desolate. For a while the adherents of the child Juana appear to have gained ground, and Isabel held her simple Court in the quiet town of Dueñas, where her eldest daughter, who received her name of Isabel, was born on October 1, 1470. . . . Some time after this, there was a brief truce between Enrique IV and his sister, who had a friendly interview at Segovia, where Fernando also arrived to join in the festivities held on the occasion." (Pp. 82 and 83.)

Later, Hare, writing of the coronation (p. 84), says, "Her husband [Isabel's] the Prince of Aragon, was not present on this occasion as he had again been summoned to help his father in the war with France." (The italics are mine.) I have followed this latter version for several reasons: the demonstrations at Sepúlveda, Agreda and Aranda de Duero, according to reliable accounts, were all made in favor of Isabel alone, not in favor of Isabel and Fernando; if husband and wife had been together, he surely would have come in for his share of the tribute. Moreover, throughout this entire period—1470 to 1474—no children were born to the couple, nor is there any record—that I have seen—of a miscarriage until the one at Tordesillas in 1475—that is, within a reasonably short time after the reunion that followed Isabel's coronation.

[17] The translation follows the form used by Walsh. *Isabella of Spain.* Page 140.

[18] They rule with equal rights and both excel
Isabel as Fernando, Fernando as Isabel.

[19] One of Fernando's illegitimate daughters, Doña Juana, made a brilliant marriage: she became the wife of the *Condestable* of Castile, Bernardino de Velasco. The other two daughters, both named María, both became Prioresses at the Convent of Santa Clara in Madrigal—Isabel's birthplace—where their portraits are carefully preserved and greatly treasured. The son, known as Don Alonzo of Aragon, became Archbishop of Saragossa at an early age. When Mendoza was known to be dying, Fernando unwisely promised Alonzo that he should be the great cardinal's successor. Isabel blocked the appointment, again reminding her husband of the provision in their marriage settlement, to the effect that all such benefices should be hers to bestow. She won her point, and her Confessor, the humble Ximénez, was unwillingly elevated to the proud position which carried with it more power and prestige than any in the kingdom except that of royalty itself. This disagreement about Don Alonzo is, apparently, the only one which occurred between the royal pair, after Isabel's unequivocal stand at the time of her coronation.

[20] Isabel's unfortunate daughter, Juana la Loca—Joan the Mad—was kept in confinement there for nearly forty years by order of her son, Charles V.

[21] Walsh, William Thomas. *Isabella of Spain.* Page 156. Taken from Pulgar's *Crónica de los Reyes Católicos.*

[22] Walsh, William Thomas. *Isabella of Spain.* Pages 185 and 186. Taken from Pulgar's *Crónica de los Reyes Católicos.*

[23] Walsh, William Thomas. *Isabella of Spain.* Pages 187 and 188.

[24] It may, however, not be amiss to mention, in passing, the *Ordenanzas de Avila,* issued in 1485, because of its laws relating to hygiene, far too often overlooked entirely in that day and age and very seldom treated as having real importance. From the time these *Ordenanzas* were put into effect, Avila ceased to be a typical medieval town "unhealthful and disordered, with stinking streets where chickens and pigs roamed freely." It was prohibited to do any washing in the River Adaja "from the fisheries of the mill on the bridge of Alonzo Dávila upwards" and in the fountains and watering troughs; also, to throw rubbish anywhere "in the city and its vicinity except in the places designated . . . and if anyone does throw it, he shall forfeit the pail, basket or bag in which he carries it; a severe punishment shall be inflicted on whomsoever casts manure, refuse or sweepings in the streets or plazas of the city or its suburbs, if a witness testifies to this." Market men had to

pitch their tents in the streets near the market places. One of these was the
Calle Andrin which is now the Calle de los Reyes Católicos. (Fr. Efren, 1.c.
Nos. 34, 35, 37. Arch. Cons. Avila, S, 1.8, n.13.)

25 Fray Hernando de Talavera later became Archbishop of Granada.

26 María was a twin; the other twin had died at birth.

27 Juan II of Aragon died in 1479 and Fernando succeeded him, without dispute,
to the throne. León had already been united to Castile during the reign of
Ferdinand III (13th century); the Infanta Petronila of Aragon married
Ramón Berenguer IV, Margrave of Barcelona and Catalonia, and the former
ceded her rights to their son, Alfonso II (1162–1196); Sicily had been united
to Aragon through the marriage of Constance, great-granddaughter of the last
King of Sicily, to Pedro III of Aragon (1276–1285). Fernando himself
conquered Navarre in 1515. The Infante Juan was acknowledged heir to
Aragon in 1481.

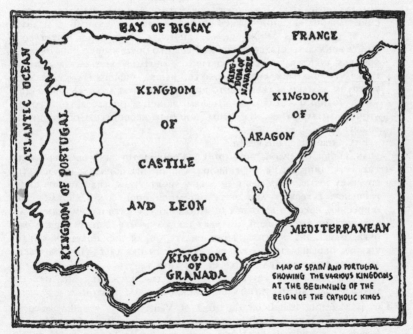

Map of Spain and Portugal showing the various kingdoms at the beginning of the reign of the Catholic Kings.

28 Pietro Martire was generally known in history as Peter Martyr, but in Spain as
Pedro Martir.

29 Juan Dávila and his wife are buried in Santo Tomás at Avila in a tomb no less
splendid than the Infante's own.
   It bears the inscription:

Los Senores Juan Davila y Doña Juana de Velazquez de la Torre su mujer, amos del muy alto y muy poderoso Principe Don Juan. Finaron el Sr. Juan Davila ano de 1487 y la Sra. Doña Juana ano de 1504.

Freely translated, this reads:

The Lord Juan Dávila and the Lady Juana Dávila de Velázquez de la Torre his wife, tutors of the very high and mighty Prince Don Juan. Lord Juan Dávila died in the year 1487 and Lady Juana in 1504.

The present Prior at the Convent of Santo Tomás has given me this notation in connection with it:

Perpetual care was arranged by Prince Juan and his parents for the chapel where his teachers are buried. Juan Velazquez, the son of these teachers and, in turn, the bosom friend and treasurer of Don Juan, was responsible for all the charges for this sepulchre in the same way that he was for that of the Prince's.

The Infante's own tomb bears the inscription:

JOANNES, HISPANIARUM PRINCEPS, VIRTUTUM OMNIUM, BONARUM ARTIUM CHRISTIANAQUE RELIGIONIS VERUS CULTOR, PATRIAE PARENTUMQUE AMANTISSIMUS, QUI PAUCIS ANNIS MAGNA PRUDENTIA, PROBITATE, PIETATAEQUE MULTA BONA CONFECIT, CONDITUR HOC TUMULO QUEM FERDINANDUS CATHOLICUS, REX INVICTUS, ECCLESIAE DEFENSOR, OPTIMUS, PIUS PATER CONDERE IMPERAVIT. GENITRIX VERO ELISABETH, REGINA PUDICISSIMA ET OMNIUM VIRTUTUM ARMARIUM TESTAMENTO FIERI JUSSIT. VIVIT ANNIS 19. OBIIT 1497.

PER JOANNEM VELAZQUEZ, EJUSDEM PRINCIPIS QUAESTOREM AERARIUM ATQUE FAMILIAREM AMANTISSIMUM, HOC OPUS PROCURATUM OPEREQUE EST COMPLETUM.

Freely translated, this reads:

JUAN, PRINCE OF SPAIN, ADORNED BY ALL THE VIRTUES AND LEARNED IN ALL THE ARTS, TRUE LOVER OF RELIGION AND OF HIS COUNTRY AND GREATLY LOVED BY HIS PARENTS, WHO, IN A FEW SHORT YEARS, THROUGH HIS GREAT PRUDENCE, INTEGRITY AND PIETY DID MUCH GOOD, RESTS BENEATH THIS SEPULCHRE, ERECTED BY ORDER OF FERNANDO THE CATHOLIC, VALIANT KING, DEFENDER OF THE CHURCH, HIS VERY GOOD AND MERCIFUL FATHER. MOREOVER, ISABEL HIS MOTHER, MOST CHASTE QUEEN AND GUARDIAN OF ALL VIRTUES, ORDERED ITS IMMEDIATE ERECTION IN HER LAST WILL AND TESTAMENT. HE LIVED 19 YEARS. DIED IN THE YEAR 1497.

IT WAS RAISED TO ITS PERFECTION BY THE TREASURER AND GREATLY LOVED BOSOM FRIEND OF THE SAID PRINCE, DON JUAN VELAZQUEZ.

[30] This is Margarita Island, off the coast of Venezuela. It was discovered by Columbus in 1498 and still bears the name he gave it. Pearls from Margarita Island are considered, by Venezuelans, as superior to any found in the Orient and I can personally bear witness to the fact that they are, indeed, very beautiful.

[31] The translation follows the form used by Dennis. *Seek the Darkness*. Page 45.

[32] The translation is the author's own, approved by the Prior of the Convent of Santo Tomás. In Spanish, it reads:

"Venerable Deán y Cabildo de la Iglesia de Salamanca:

Nos enviamos a Juan Velazquez para que traiga el cuerpo del ilustrísimo

Don Juan nuestro fijo, que santa gloria haya. Encargámosvos que se lo entregueis luego, y dedes fe y creencia a todo lo que el dicho Juan Velazquez os dirá de nuestra parte, y lo que os escribiere el Obispo de Salamanca nuestro confesor, como si nos vos lo escribiésamos.

Yo el Rey—Yo la Reyna
De Avila 2 de Noviembre de 97 años."

32-a This is a kind of coarse ticking which was used in ancient times for deep mourning.

32-b From time immemorial, there have been two market places in Avila: the one where horses, mules, donkeys, cows, calves and sheep are sold or bartered; and the one where vegetables, poultry and game—including rabbits and squirrels, as well as the partridge for which Avila is famous—are the stock in trade. The former is, therefore, known as the Market of Great Animals and the latter as the Market of Small Animals. Friday is the traditional market day and then people come from all over the province, and beyond it, to be present.

32-c In concluding his comments on Prince Juan's death, in *A Stranger in Spain*, H. V. Morton says: "If this young man had lived and had carried on his line, Spanish history, incredible to think of, would have lacked the reigns of Charles V and Philip II. The Prince was also the brother of Catherine of Aragon, and had he become King of Spain, perhaps Henry VIII might not have found him easy to deal with when he wished to divorce her for Ana

Tomb of Prince Juan in Chapel of Convent of Santo Tomás. From a photograph by Mayoral, Avila.

Bolena. History has many a question mark, and this tomb in Santo Tomé
is one of them." (I have never before heard this particular point raised. To
me it is an extremely interesting one.)

[33] Walsh, William Thomas. *Isabella of Spain.* Page 592.

[34] Walsh, William Thomas. *Isabella of Spain.* Page 594.

[35] 1502.

[36] Dennis, Amarie. *Seek the Darkness.* Page 82.

[37] Dennis, Amarie. *Seek the Darkness.* Page 95.

[38] A great controversy has long raged concerning the exact place where Isabel
died. There is no question that her death took place at Medina del Campo,
but, according to some authorities, she left the royal castle when she knew
she was dying and moved to a house on the plaza which had belonged to
some of her ancestors. As the sources for both statements seem to be equally
authoritative, the reader may, presumably, be entitled to make his own
choice. The present author feels only that the controversy should be mentioned in the interests of comprehensive study.

[38-a] Prescott tells us that: "A short time before her death, she received a visit
from the distinguished officer, Prospero Colonna. The Italian noble, on
being presented to King Ferdinand, told him, that 'he had come to Castile
to behold the woman, who from her sick bed ruled the world'; 'ver una
señora que desde la cama mandava al mundo.'" *History of the Reign of
Ferdinand and Isabella.* Volume III, Page 173.

This seems almost prophetic of the claim made by Isabella's great-grand-
son, Philip II, that, from the tiny cabinet where he was confined by mortal
illness, he could still rule the world "on two inches of paper."

[39] A tax of 10% on the sale price of all goods.

[40] Plunket, Ierne. *Isabel of Castile and the Making of the Spanish Nation.* Pages
383 and 384.

[41] Walsh, William Thomas. *Isabella of Spain.* Page 603.

[42] Walsh, William Thomas. *Isabella of Spain.* Page 604.

[43] 1504.

[44] Dennis, Amarie. *Seek the Darkness.* Page 107.

NOTES FOR PART II

1 Auclair, Marcelle. *Teresa of Avila*. Page 23.

1-a The personal appearance of Teresa, as outlined here, is based on the description given by her contemporaries, María de San José, an intimate friend and an assiduous correspondent of Teresa's, and Diego de Yepes, an Hieronymite Monk, who became Prior of several houses and confessor to Philip II and Philip III and, eventually, Bishop of Tarazona, quoted (in Spanish) by her later biographer, the Reverend Father Efrén de la Madre de Dios, O.C.D.

2 Auclair, Marcelle. *Teresa of Avila*. Page 24.

3 Auclair, Marcelle. *Teresa of Avila*. Page 28.

4 Auclair, Marcelle. *Teresa of Avila*. Page 20.

5 No aspect of Teresa's life, not even those connected with her mysterious illnesses, her still more mysterious visions, and the phenomenon of her transverberation, has been the subject of more heated dispute than this phase of her life. Walsh does not even mention the possibility of an indiscreet love affair; indeed, he goes even further and states his belief that Teresa never contemplated marriage—that she was probably the confidante of some older girl who was considering it and who told Teresa "more than she could comprehend and so disturbed a lively imagination and a sensitive conscience with fears and scruples that assumed an importance out of proportion to their actuality." Then he goes on to say that any evidence of a possibility that she was considering it herself, "is of the flimsiest." (I may as well admit, here and now, that it does not seem so to me!) He continues, as in justice bound, that "this is possible of course, and would detract in no degree from her honor or her sanctity"; and reminds us that the Catholic Church ". . . has officially declared after the usual investigations that she lived in a state of 'angelic purity of heart and body' throughout her life."

Sackville-West, who is not herself a Catholic, but whose work is rightly regarded by many eminent churchmen and Catholic historians whom I have consulted as both reverent and authentic, takes exactly the opposite view: "Teresa at fourteen was unregenerate. She would be cautious, certainly, for she greatly feared disgrace and her own nature would prevent her from failing in the honour of the world, but within those limits she would enjoy life; and, she adds, 'I was very adroit in doing anything that was wrong.' The picture she draws is extremely vivid: a band of young cousins, boys, all round about her own age, some a little older, who were always with her and had a great affection for her. It was she who kept the conversation alive in everything that gave them pleasure, their loves and their follies; and it is indicated that her sister Maria, a quiet and sober young woman, much older than herself, stood quite outside this gay circle with no influence upon Teresa. The influence came, instead, from one of the cousins, a girl whom Teresa's mother had so greatly mistrusted that she had taken great pains to keep her away but, owing to the kinship and the many reasons for her coming, she could not actually be forbidden the house. Don Alonso and Maria, equally distressed by this friendship, were likewise handicapped, and Teresa continued to enjoy the gossip, the recital of affairs and vanities, and, clearly, profited by the part of go-between that this unclean and parasitical tempter was willing to play. The servants, too, she found 'ready enough for all evil.' This is where it becomes difficult to determine what Teresa really did. It is clear that she blames herself bitterly for something; she uses strong words, 'mortal sin,' 'blinded by passion'; and insists that the fear of God had utterly departed from her though the fear of dishonour remained, a torment in all she did. However scrupulous her conscience in retrospect, this is scarcely the language she would have used, even allowing for the excessive rigour of the Spanish code, even allowing for the degree of sanctity she had attained by the time she wrote this account, in referring to some boy-and-girl cousinly flirtation or to a temporary relish for the salacious conversation of older girls. Whatever her apologists may say, for three months something very dark was taking place in Teresa's life; something so dark according to her views that she never brought herself to be explicit on paper. It concerns the girl cousin and 'another who was given to the same kind of pastimes' (*otra que tenia la misma manera de pasatiempos*). It is to be noted that this 'other,' so ambiguous in English, appears in the feminine in the Spanish original; and, since few things are more distasteful than veiled hints, it may also be outspokenly noted that in her own country the name of Teresa has been associated with that of Sappho." (I hasten to add that I do not agree with this viewpoint, either; while it is quite true that "otra" is the feminine form of "other," it is commonly used as an abbreviation for "otra persona"—another person—and *persona* is invariably a feminine noun, whether it refers to a man or a woman. It is my firm conviction that Teresa was here referring to the former.)

Other biographers, including those who were her contemporaries or lived shortly after she did—the Jesuit, Ribera, for instance—take a middle course; so do those two great modern French writers, Louis Bertrand and Marcelle Auclair, who, it seems to me, treat this delicate and debatable subject in the most human and rational way of any authorities I have consulted. Walsh gives it as his considered opinion that every writer who has grappled with it has found in it "the reflection of his own spirit." . . . . "On the one hand, sinners have imputed serious sin to a woman canonized by the Church," he states. "At the other extreme are those pious souls who like to think of saints as almost bloodless abstractions, without the faults and passions of ordinary human beings." One does not have to be a sinner—except in as far as we are all sinners—to attribute—I believe that is a better word than "impute"—serious sin to a woman canonized by the Church. There is no lack, on the Calendar of Saints, of those who have committed serious sins and who have repented of them; the most famous are probably St. Mary Magdalene and St. Augustine, though there are many others. However, in the case of Teresa, she is definitely listed as a virgin, and the Papal pronouncements in regard to her, as well as the definitions in the missal, make this listing official. The confessor who is quoted as saying he believed she was taking her indiscretions too seriously and that, as far as he could see, she had done nothing "that could not have a happy issue by way of marriage" cannot, of course, be quoted more extensively because he could not have said anything more than that to anyone—he was bound by the seal of the confessional; and it is impossible for an author, bound by limitations of space, to quote Teresa more extensively on this subject than I have already done. However, any reader who wishes to know everything that she herself has said on the subject can easily fulfill this desire by reading her Autobiography of which there are many excellent translations in numerous languages. My own opinion as to her innocence, in the sense that lack of innocence is interpreted to mean illicit sexual relations, I have tried to make abundantly clear in the body of this book; but I will epitomize it in a sentence: I do not believe she was guilty of any such sin, either at the period under discussion or later; and my belief is founded not only on the pronouncements of the Church, made after the usual careful investigations, but on such knowledge of human nature as I have acquired in a long and by no means secluded life. I think Marcelle Auclair was absolutely right when she said:

"Teresa was not afraid, but she would not have allowed the finger of scorn to be pointed at her, nor was she the kind of girl to get married because honour dictated it. If she had to defend herself from audacious overtures, she did so through a twofold instinct for purity; purity of body in the first place and then care for her reputation. *It is too often forgotten that if sexual attraction is a natural instinct, virginity's defence is just as instinctive.*" (The italics are mine.)

6 This house is still standing, and the sculptured coat-of-arms over its front door and fine façade have traces of great beauty.

7 Auclair, Marcelle. *Teresa of Avila*. Page 45.

8 Auclair, Marcelle. *Teresa of Avila*. Page 49. (The italics are mine.)

9 Auclair, Marcelle. *Teresa of Avila*. Page 51.

10 Translation is that used by Marcelle Auclair.

10-a Translation is that used by Marcelle Auclair.

11 Auclair, Marcelle. *Teresa of Avila*. Page 60.

12 Auclair, Marcelle. *Teresa of Avila*. Page 58. (The italics are mine.)

13 A lighted room where a dead body lies in state.

14 Ana de Jesús as quoted by Marcelle Auclair. *Teresa of Avila*. Page 67.

15 Auclair, Marcelle. *Teresa of Avila*. Page 67.

16 Padre Silverio de Santa Teresa as quoted by Marcelle Auclair. *Teresa of Avila*. Page 73.

17 Padre Silverio de Santa Teresa as quoted by Marcelle Auclair from the shorter edition of *Her Works*. *Teresa of Avila*. Page 78.

18 Sackville-West, V. *The Eagle and the Dove*. Page 44. (The author should add: it is very important to remember that the word, imaginary, as used in this sense, does not mean fancied—something unreal. It means something that forms an image, that is, a definite impression or picture.)

[19] Padre Silverio de Santa Teresa as quoted by Marcelle Auclair. *Teresa of Avila.* Page 95.

[20] Auclair, Marcelle. *Teresa of Avila.*

[21] I might, of course, have gone all the way back to the Old Testament (2 Kings 2:11) and reminded him of Elijah, who was taken up to heaven in "a chariot of fire." This story is accepted as authentic Scriptural reading in all Protestant churches with which I am familiar and, as I grew up in exceptionally devout Protestant surroundings, I am familiar with a good many.

[21-a] Freely translated, this reads:

San Segundo was the first
Bishop of this city
Who showed us the truth
Of the true Trine God.

He was a worthy messenger
The Apostle sent
To free us from sin
From which the Lamb had liberated us.

[21-b] I have been extremely interested to note, in recently re-reading Agnes Repplier's *Mère Marie of the Ursulines*, that this thoughtful, distinguished and observant writer, certainly one of the greatest essayists of our times, calls St. Teresa "a model of all nuns" and makes frequent comments along the same lines that I had made them before the renewal of my acquaintance with Miss Repplier's work. In connection with the foregoing paragraphs, it may not be amiss to quote some of these comments: ". . . mysticism was to the Eighteenth Century a delusion and a snare. We are more receptive to-day because more familiar with scholastic philosophy which offers an avenue of approach. William Penn was a mystic [this I never knew before] and so was Jeanne d'Arc, and Saint Catherine of Siena, and *that capable woman, Saint Theresa.* All experienced their first revelations at an early age. . . . Mère Marie considered with Saint Theresa that acute physical discomfort was incompatible with absorption in prayer. . . . Saint Theresa is one of the high lights of hagiography. Her field was wider than Mère Marie's, her task harder, her mind keener, her personality more magnetic. She has stamped herself upon the history of her church. The work of reformation was her work. She did not destroy what she undertook to reform, which is always an easy thing to do. She preserved it, bettered and purified, which is exceedingly difficult. Her figure attracts and holds attention because of her vivifying and cleansing blitheness of spirit. She possessed the quality of distinction which Matthew Arnold says 'corrects the world's blunders, and fixes the world's ideals.'

"One may be a great poet without nearing Shakespeare, and a great statesman without rivaling Pitt. Mère Marie resembled Saint Theresa inasmuch as her piety was equalled by her capacity for work. She had the same talent for administration, albeit it was exercised within narrower bounds. Her outward life was normal, and was regulated by the rules of her order. Her inner life, noble and sustained, bore fruit in her steadfast perseverance, and in her cheerful acceptance of circumstance." (The italics are mine.)

A quotation from *A Stranger in Spain*, by H. V. Morton, also seems in

NOTES 309

order here: "Of all the saints in heaven, she is surely the most friendly, the most humorous, and the most understanding. As a woman she is related to all the capable and gallant women one has ever known, who go through life putting things in order; as a saint she travelled into regions where only another saint could follow her. That amazing self-revelation, her *Life*, and her other writings, almost persuade us that we too could become, if not saints, at least honourable travellers along that high and lonely road.

"She is fascinating, also, as proof of the toughness and resiliency of the human body when powered by a strong spiritual force. To have seen her at the age of twenty-four, crawling about on her hands and knees, after a cataleptic seizure, during which she was nearly buried alive, would have been to deny the possibility that she could become the indomitable, middle-aged woman who rode all over Spain, sleeping in flea-bitten inns and on the boards of empty houses as she founded her reformed Carmelite convents.

"Of her mystical experiences it is not possible to write here, but readers of her books will know that she accepted the raptures of the spiritual life as something which any sufficiently devout, and devoted person might achieve. It was typical of her that the strange phenomenon of levitation, which most of us experience only in dreams, dismayed and embarrassed her. She would hold on to anything in order not to be lifted off her feet. She considered levitation 'a most extraordinary thing, which would occasion much talk,' and commanded her nuns never to mention the subject. When she felt she was losing weight and was about to be lifted into the air, she would throw herself on the ground and beg the nuns to hold her down."

Still another quotation seems indicated here—one from Sackville-West on the subject of levitation: "In whatever position she [Teresa] was when the rapture overcame her, in that position did she continue until she regained command of her senses, sitting, standing, or kneeling; the body lost its natural warmth; and the hands became as hard as pieces of wood. One of her nuns, finding her alone in this condition in the garden of the convent, re-monstrated with her for endangering her life by undergoing such trials, only to be met with the tart rejoinder, 'Hold your peace, child; do you think that this depends upon myself?' Indeed it did not. Nor did that strange phenom-enon known as levitation, to which she was most liable and which seems to have alarmed her more than anything else. Her body would then become buoyant, as if all weight had departed from it; a great force beneath her feet lifted her up, and she could clearly be seen to leave the ground. She would do everything in her power to prevent this from happening, for she thought it 'a most extraordinary thing, which would occasion much talk,' and com-manded her nuns never to speak of it, but conceal it from them she could not. Sometimes she threw herself on the ground to avert the happening and they would cluster round her to hold her down; at other times she would clutch with both hands at an iron grating. It was bad enough when it oc-curred in the presence of her own community, but when strangers were wit-nesses she was not to be comforted; and would speak of her weak heart, or ask for a little water or some food in the attempt to make everything appear natural. Levitation is no uncommon prodigy, and is ascribed on good evi-dence to over two hundred saints and other persons, so that the Bishop of Avila was probably not much surprised when he saw Teresa lifted into the air during Mass, but to Teresa herself it was one of the greatest shames and inconveniences she had to suffer." (Sackville-West adds a note to this paragraph, after the words "Levitation is no uncommon prodigy," suggesting that the reader consult Ezekiel, chapter 8, verse 3—"And the spirit lifted me up between the earth and the heavens"—and recalling Catherine of Siena, as I have done several times. Sackville-West also calls attention to the "truly extraordinary case of St. Joseph of Cupertino," a seventeenth-century Italian saint whose mental capacities were so limited that he was never able to rise above the rank of lay brother. "The accounts of his flights are numerous and amazing," she tells us, "some of them doubtless have gained in the telling, but the residue, related by eyewitnesses, makes up a story sufficient to satisfy the curious. Among the less credible tales is the account of his picking up 'as though it were a straw' a cross thirty-six feet high and too heavy for ten men to lift, and flying with it in his arms to set it in its place. He frequently flew up to holy statues in order to embrace them, and, carrying them off their stands, floated about with them; he sometimes picked up a fellow friar and carried him round the room; on one occasion the sight of a lamb in the garden sent him into such an ecstasy, thinking of the Lamb of God, that he caught up the little creature and rose with it into the air. The lamb was probably not much alarmed for it was said of this simple though surprising saint that all animals had an instinctive trust in him, the sheep especially coming round to listen to his prayers.")

[22] Auclair, Marcelle. *Teresa of Avila.* Page 96. Walsh, William Thomas. *Saint Teresa of Avila.* Pages 135 and 136. Sackville-West, V. *The Eagle and the Dove.* Page 94.

[23] Walsh, William Thomas. *Saint Teresa of Avila.* Page 136.

[24] Her two names were often run together and in many of the references to her are written as if they were one: that is, Maridíaz.

[25] Mária Díaz, like Mária Vela, was declared a Venerable by popular acclamation soon after her death. This method was then accepted by the Church. Authorities differ as to whether she became a hermit as soon as she arrived in the city of Avila or whether this was after her sojourn with Doña Guiomar and the formation of her friendship with Teresa. E. Allison Peers in his *Handbook to the Life and Times of St. Teresa and St. John of the Cross,* Page 147, subscribes to the former theory and he is, unquestionably, a great authority. On the other hand, Martín Carramolino and Father Efrén de la Madre de Dios, the authorities currently accepted on this subject, through documentation at the Convent of Santo Tomás in Avila, give the account of her progress that I have used.

[26] Auclair, Marcelle. *Teresa of Avila.* Page 112 et seq.

[27] These were founded at the following places, in the following order: Medina del Campo, Malagón, Valladolid, Toledo, Pastrana, Salamanca, Alba de Tormes, Segovia, Beas de Segura, Seville, Caravaca, Villanueva de la Jara, Palencia, Soria, Granada and Burgos. (Peers, E. Allison. *Handbook to the Life and Times of St. Teresa and St. John of the Cross.* Pages 237 and 238.)

[28] This number was later increased to twenty-one as the limit for each convent.

28-a The *seises* are still danced at the cathedral in Seville twice a year—on Corpus Christi and on the Feast of the Immaculate Conception. There is a story to the effect that one of the Renaissance Popes disapproved of this dance, but said he would permit it to be continued until the special costumes the choir boys wore for the occasion had given out. The great ladies of Seville at once took over the task of caring for these costumes and, during the intervening centuries, have continued to mend and patch them with such scrupulous skill that they are still wearable!

28-b Some biographers assert that he actually did get to Mexico, but this is open to doubt, as there is no record of any work he did there.

28-c Alonso Orozco was beatified by Leo XIII in 1882 and it is now believed that his canonization will be celebrated in the very near future.

28-d Auclair, Marcelle. *Teresa of Avila*. Page 114.

28-e Leo van Hove as quoted by Marcelle Auclair. *Teresa of Avila*. Page 185.

28-f Marcelle Auclair does not include any mention of this letter in her well-documented biography, and several other authorities have questioned the authenticity of the communication. However, still other authorities, equally eminent, have testified that they consider it genuine. Among them are the Benedictines of Stanbrook Abbey, the Marqués de San Juan de Piedras Albas, who is one of the foremost experts in Teresiana, Father Zimmerman, Antonio Rotondo—author of the *Historia del Real Monasterio de San Lorenzo*—and Julián Zarco Cuevas, another eminent historian of the Escorial. The last named, in writing to reassure Louis Bertrand, is quoted by that author as saying:

"*J'ai entendu le P. Silverio de Santa Teresa, carme dechaussé, et sans nul doute le mieux informé actuellement, de tout ce qui se rapporte a la Sainte, —declarer que cette lettre lui paraissait apocryphe. Mais les raisons qu'il me donna, fondées uniquement sur des considerations internes de style, ne m'ont point paru suffisamment convaincantes. De prime abord, la lettre me parait sans nul doute authentique. Le papier, examiné par D. Ramon Menendez y Pidal, a été reconnu par lui comme etant bien du xvie siecle. Et les paroles pretées a Philippe II sont tout a fait conformes à l'attitude du roi dans ses audiences. Tous les temoignages concordent, en effet, pour affirmer que Philippe II fut, dans ses receptions, le monarque le plus affable et le plus élégant de son temps et aussi le plus courtois; toujours calme et posé, ecoutant avec patience tout ce qu'on lui exposait . . .*"

("I have heard Father Silverio de Santa Teresa, a Discalced Carmelite and, without doubt, actually the best informed about everything which concerns the saint, declare that this letter seems to him apocryphal. But the reasons which he gave me, based entirely on considerations of style, did not seem to me sufficiently convincing. In the first place, the letter appears to me without doubt authentic. The paper [on which it is written] examined by D. Ramon Menendez y Pidal, has been recognized by him as being of the sixteenth century. And the words attributed to Philip II are in conformity with the attitude of the King in his audiences. Indeed, all witnesses are in agreement when affirming that Philip II was, in his receptions, the most affable and the most elegant monarch of his time and also the most courteous; always calm and poised, listening with patience to everything anyone tried to explain to him.")

In this connection, it is also interesting to note that Sackville-West says: "The saint's range of acquaintance was extensive, partly thanks to her faculty for acquiring friends and retaining them; partly to her own noble birth which enabled her to consort on easy terms with the proudest names in Spain; partly to her profession and the activities connected with her Reform, which brought her into touch with Cardinals, Archbishops, and other high dignitaries of the Church, as well as with the most ragged of friars. She wrote frequently to the King, to whom she used to refer as 'my friend the King,' and met him personally when after their interview he made her 'the most courteous bow I ever saw.' " (Quite evidently her research led her to believe that the interview, described on Pages 115 and 116 actually did take place.)

A further interesting analysis of Philip is found in The Spanish People by Martin A. S. Hume, Page 339: "For Philip was a Spaniard of Spaniards. Brought up mostly in the absence of his father by devout women and priests; surrounded from his birth with the overpowering conviction that he and his had been specially chosen by God to fight His battles; inheriting the religious exaltation of his house, firmly believing that Spain was the only true centre of religion, and that no wrong could be done in the service of the Lord, this reticent, distrustful lad of twenty-one, already a widower with an only son, was an embodiment of all the salient qualities which we have noted as characteristic of the Spanish race. Intense individuality in him, as in so many of his countrymen, was merged in the idea of personal distinction in the eyes of God by self-sacrifice. Through his long life, patient, plodding labour, self-denial, humble submission to suffering, and ecstatic asceticism were his portion. Pain, defeat, bereavement, disappointment that would have crushed the hearts of most men, passed over him without ruffling his marble serenity. These afflictions, he thought, were sent by God specially to him as an ordeal and to distinguish him from other men by the bitterness of his sacrifice, only later to bring a brighter glory to him and to the Master for whom he worked. At heart he was kindly, a good father and husband, an indulgent and considerate master, having no love for cruelty itself. And yet lying, dishonesty, cruelty, the infliction of suffering and death upon hosts of helpless ones, and the secret murder of those who stood in his path, were not wrong for him, because, in his moral obliquity, he thought that the ends justified the means, and that all was lawful in the linked causes of God and Spain."

28-g Walsh, William Thomas. Saint Teresa of Avila. Page 519.

29 A verbena, so-called from the plant of that name, was, originally, a sort of garden party, held when this plant was in bloom, and has come to mean almost any sort of festive occasion, especially one held on the vigil of a saint's day, whether this is the season for verbena or not. Of course, October very definitely is not. But, in Avila, not content with holding a verbena on October 14—the vigil of St. Teresa's Feast Day—the inhabitants also have them on the seventh, eleventh, thirteenth and fifteenth.

NOTES FOR PART III

[1] Some writers refer to this porridge as *polenta*, but I have preferred the word *gachas*—both are derived from *coacta*, a Latin expression for porridge—since the former does not appear in *Tesoro de la Lengua Castellana* by Don Sebastián de Covarrubias (1611) while the latter does. Though the modern *Diccionario de la Lengua* issued by the *Real Academia Española* does give the word *polenta*, the Spanish authorities I have consulted are agreed that the popular word was and is *gachas* or *puches* (from the Latin *puls*).

[2] Most authorities I have consulted are of the opinion that Catalina took all three of her little sons with her from Fontiveros to Arévalo. However, the source most highly regarded by those I have consulted in Avila—namely, *San Juan de la Cruz. Su Obra Científica y su Obra Literária* by Fray Crisógono de Jesús Sacramentado—thinks Luis died of starvation before the others started out and that this was Catalina's main reason for doing so, which seems logical. Moreover, the fact that there are no further references to Luis—at least that I have found, whereas there are many to Francisco—would seem to indicate that the former did not survive to adolescence.

[3] Juan de Yepes was born in 1542; this exodus took place in 1548.

[4] The circumstances surrounding the departure of Catalina Alvarez and her children from Fontiveros for Arévalo and the manner of it are based on reliable record. The story of Juan's song is, admittedly, merely a matter of tradition, but I have permitted myself to follow the wise counsel of Merry del Val to the effect that "tradition, wisely controlled, even in the absence of written documents, gives us manifest proofs of the truths of our beliefs."

[5] Alvarez was not and still is not an uncommon Spanish name. The Don Antonio, in some records referred to as Don Alfonso, who befriended Juan, was not a relative of his mother.

[6] 1564.

[7] Sencourt, Robert. *Carmelite and Poet; A Framed Portrait of St. John of the Cross.* Pages 27 and 28.

[8] Sencourt, Robert. *Carmelite and Poet; A Framed Portrait of St. John of the Cross.* Page 28.

[9] Peers, E. Allison. *The Complete Works of St. John of the Cross.* Volume I, Page xxxv.

[10] Rodrigo went to the New World with Pedro de Mendoza, took part in the foundation of Buenos Aires and accompanied Juan de Ayolas in the campaign up the rivers of Paraná and Paraguay. He, as well as four of his brothers, was in the Battle of Iñaquito and eventually lost his life fighting in Chile.

Marcelle Auclair gives this vivid description of his preparations for departure and the spirit in which it was undertaken: "His [Rodrigo's] outfit and equipment cost Don Alonso [his father] many ducats and Teresa a great deal of work. But Pedro de Mendoza's expedition to which he was to be attached was the most splendid that ever set sail. Juan Osorio, the master of the camp, was from Avila and thirty-two noble families of Spain gave him their eldest sons for the war on the Río de la Plate, which name of Silver River was given to it because men made their fortunes there. The hopes of the future conquistador were so confident that he renounced his inheritance in favour of Teresa, so that a large dowry should help her to make a good match."

The other brothers, to list them alphabetically, were Agustín, Antonio, Hernando, Jerónimo, Lorenzo and Pedro.

Agustín went to America either with the first Viceroy of Peru, Don Blasco Núñez y Vela—the brother of Teresa's godfather, Don Francisco Núñez y Vela—or with the second Viceroy, Pedro de la Gasca. He saw military service first in Peru and later in Chile and became successively Governor of Los Quijos and of Tucumán. Marcelle Auclair says of him: "Agustín was a perfect example of the adventurer whose deeds were gilded over with the fair name of conquistador in order to embellish to the full a fascinating legend. Whereas Lorenzo in his prudence had turned his attention as soon as possible to making a good marriage and amassing a solid fortune, Agustín with his wild ideas had preferred to go on fighting. Having conquered the Araucanians in Chile seventeen times, he had . . . been made governor of an important place in Peru, but [it] did not seem as if he could settle down quietly. . . . In a letter which he wrote to the Viceroy, he spoke of embarking on 'An expedition to the richest land in men and gold that has ever been seen; according to what people say, it's El Dorado . . . I've decided upon this not so much through my eager desire for the place as on account of the certainty that God and His Majesty will thus be well served.' Men with such daring and extravagant temperaments never became rich; when at the beginning of 1582 Agustín contemplated returning to Spain, his sister for all her joy was anxious: '. . . If he doesn't bring back enough to keep himself he will have a lot of trouble, for nobody will be able to pay for his keep, and it will be a great trouble for me not to be in a position to help him.' Agustín was relying on the King's gratitude; Teresa was less naïve: 'It is distressing,' said Teresa, 'to see him undertake such a perilous voyage for money at his age, when we shouldn't be thinking of anything else but preparing ourselves for heaven. . . .'"

For all his talk about seeking El Dorado and returning to Spain, he remained in South America until after Teresa's death. Very little is known of his family life, though it is recorded that he had one illegitimate daughter whose name was Leonor.

Marcelle Auclair describes Antonio as "the gentlest of them all" and says that he was "caught up in his sister's fervor and just as la niña had persuaded Rodrigo to set out with her in search of martyrdom, so now she persuaded this younger brother of hers to leave their father's house at the same time she did and to enter with the Dominicans while she went to join her friend, Juana Suárez, at the Convent of the Encarnación. . . .

One morning towards the very end of October 1536, when as yet the tops of the trees in the garden were scarcely visible in the grey light of dawn, she came out of her room without allowing herself to give so much as one backward glance, walking on tiptoe and holding her breath as she passed the rooms where her father, her brothers and her young sister Juana were still sleeping. Antonio helped her to move the locks of the heavy entrance door silently, to pull it open and then hold it so that it should shut to noiselessly on all those they were leaving. Teresa recalled her flight with Rodrigo thirteen years before: then she had felt no grief, the fact that she had parents had only been a 'major obstacle' for her and the thought of their grief did not make her suffer. Was she more affectionate now? Or weaker? Had her struggles with herself, the first effects of the awakening of the love of Christ in her soul, softened her hard heart? On the threshold she hesitated, but Antonio was there, unfaltering because of his very un- consciousness of what was involved. Teresa's code of honour did not allow her to show weakness before one so young. And just as on a former occasion, in the uncertain light of dawn, two thin silhouettes could be distinguished against the grey façade and were soon lost in the crowd of merchants, servants, worshippers, who were crossing the Plaza Santo Domingo to go to market or to church. But this time, it was for ever; Teresa knew it by the anguish which she felt."

After becoming a Dominican novice at the Convent of Santo Tomás in Avila, Antonio transferred to the Hieronymite Order. Though ill health eventually forced him out of the cloister, it did not prevent him from be- coming an explorer and a soldier and he was one of the four brothers who took part in the Battle of Iñaquito. He was wounded in it and died two days later.

Hernando went to America as early as 1530, joined Francisco de Pizarro, with whom he fought in Peru, and lived there many years. He was a stand- ard bearer at the Battle of Iñaquito and was badly wounded, but recovered to become an Alderman—Regidor—of Pastro.

Jerónimo went to South America at the same time as Lorenzo (1540), lived there for many years, and left there—again with Lorenzo—for Spain, but died "like a saint" at Nombre de Dios before embarking. It appears, however, that this saintliness must have been a characteristic of his later, rather than his earlier life. In any case, he apparently left at least one ille- gitimate child.

Lorenzo is thought to have been Teresa's favorite brother. When, as a young nun, she was given up for dead, after the serious illness which ended in three days and nights of complete unconsciousness, Lorenzo was the one chosen to keep the vigil by her bedside. "He fell asleep; a candlestick over- turned, the bed curtains caught fire and the seemingly lifeless body was very nearly burned." (Marcelle Auclair.) Such inattention under responsibility was, however, apparently far from characteristic, for though "all the brothers were valiant"—with the possible exception of Pedro—Lorenzo was undoubt- edly the most prosperous. He settled in Quito, married the daughter of a conquistador in Lima and finally returned to Spain a very rich man. Even while still abroad, he helped his sister materially with her projects and, after his return, took an active part in the foundation of the Carmelite Convent at Seville. "Heaven sent to her [Teresa] all she lacked by the hands of those who were most dear to her: her brothers, Lorenzo and Pedro arrived from Ecuador. Lorenzo was as rich in gold from the Indies as he was in good disposition," Marcelle Auclair tells us. "In the parlour, behind the grille, one August day Teresa of Jesus lifted her veil as Carmelites are allowed to do in the case of close relatives: her brothers could look upon the face of the sister who, when they left her, was young and beautiful but torn between the world and God; they found her so radiant with inner light that the ravages of thirty years had left scarcely a trace upon her bodily appearance. As to herself, her deep feeling did not prevent her from being amused at the gorgeousness of these Indians (Spaniards who went to the Indies and returned were known as Indians): the serious-minded Lorenzo had acquired ostentatious habits in this country where his important position obliged him to live on a grand scale; how gorgeously he was dressed! Even the children, Lorencito and Francisco, their necks confined in starched ruffs, spread out fingers stiff with rings over their velvet clothes; Teresita, their little eight-year-old sister, was smothered in brocade and carried a fortune in emeralds on ears, chest and fingers. . . . When the time came for them to go, Teresita did not want to leave the convent: they had to promise her that she should come and live with Aunt Teresa. And if Lorenzo rattled his doubloons a little noisily during the conversation, it was to declare that in future he would make himself responsible for the entire expenses of the convent and for the purchase of a house. . . . Teresita, in a frieze dress of suitable size, trotted about the convent 'like a friendly sprite' to the great joy of the sisters who at recreation never tired of hearing her tell 'stories of the sea and the Indians.' "

Lorenzo eventually bought an estate near Avila, which was called La Serna, and remained there until his sudden death in 1580. Marcelle Auclair devotes a whole chapter—"Don Lorenzo de Cepeda, Indian"—to this period of his life in her fine biography of St. Teresa.

Pedro seems to have been the least distinguished of the lot. Unlike the others, he did nothing especially outstanding in the New World; on the contrary, he became something of a hypochondriac. After his return to Spain with Lorenzo, Pedro lived with his wealthy brother and proved a source of embarrassment, not only to Lorenzo, but to Teresa, because of his acute melancholia. Marcelle Auclair describes him as a "ruined remnant of a conquistador . . . nursing a grievance, continually up against it . . . ill-suited to his parasite existence." But he survived his wealthy brother and managed to live fairly comfortably on the legacy Lorenzo had left him.

The house in Seville for which the generous Lorenzo supplied the funds is still standing, like most of Teresa's Foundations, and is still used, almost unchanged, as a Carmelite Convent. In common with many other buildings in the Barrio de Santa Cruz, it stands on a street so narrow that it can be reached only on foot; the façade is blankly forbidding and its massive double doors are studded with heavy ornamental nails which add to their appearance of solidity and security. But once inside the patio to which these doors lead, the atmosphere changes completely, for the patio itself is small and friendly and dappled with sunshine; it is shaded by a pergola and the vines which hang from this are fresh and green and fruitful. The lodge of the lay portress is at the left and she and her children and their pet animals are all friendly, too. At the right is the entrance to the parlor—not the same poor room where Lorenzo and Pedro were received on their return from the Indies, but the one which was happily supplied by the former's prodigality, and which still seems to reflect his warm and generous personality. It lacks the stern quality of so many convent parlors; like the patio, it seems to bid you welcome if you are not an intruder, but have a right to come there. To be sure, in its essentials it is the usual bare, whitewashed reception room of the Carmelites, with a plain wooden cross surmounting the grille; but a fine painting of St. John of the Cross hangs on one of its walls and on another is a plaque, inscribed with the following precept:

> Hermanos, una de dos
> O no hablar, o hablar de Dios.
> Que en la casa de Teresa
> Aquesta ley se profesa!
>
> (Brothers, do one of two things
> Do not speak at all or speak of God.
> In the house of Teresa
> This is the law observed.)

Its pleasant approach, its low ceiling and its very lack of space for superfluous furniture give an air of coziness to this room. The relics of St. Teresa which are kept in the convent and which are passed through the drawer beneath the grille for the privileged visitor to see also lack the gruesome quality of many preserved and shown elsewhere and said more to me than many others I have had the opportunity of seeing: numerous letters exchanged between St. Teresa and St. John of the Cross; the original manuscript of The Interior Castle, carefully folded in crimson silk and kept in a silver-bound leather box; one of Teresa's shoes which her loving "daughters" have covered with gold lace and embroidered in pearls; and the white cape— now lined with blue brocade—in which she was wrapped when she died. Such relics as these are all intimate and touching. They bring the saint very close.

It is easy for me to picture how happy Teresita, Lorenzo's little daughter, must have been in this house, for Teresa not only dearly loved all her brothers, but also their children, whether legitimate or illegitimate. She was delighted with the satisfactory marriages made by the natural daughters of Agustín and Jerónimo, while the natural daughter of her nephew, Lorenzo, who repeated his father's material successes, both at home and abroad, became one of her most dearly cherished young relatives during her last years.

As will be seen from the above quotations, Marcelle Auclair has given us delightful glimpses, all founded on authentic records, into the lives of Teresa's seven brothers. Other outstanding biographers, notably E. Allison Peers, have provided us with helpful resumés of their careers. But, as far as I know, no entire work has been devoted to this subject. I wish it might be, for it certainly would make arresting reading.

10-a "A Vicar General is a deputy appointed by a bishop to assist him in the government of his diocese. He succeeds to the position and some of the powers of the mediaeval archdeacon. He is delegated to exercise episcopal jurisdiction in spirituals and temporals on behalf of the bishop up to the extent of the bishop's reservations and those of law, but he must exercise it according to the mind of the bishop. He forms one tribunal with the bishop, so there can be no appeal from the sentence of one to the other. Even if a simple priest the vicar general takes precedence of all clergy of the diocese and is a prelate with the dress and privileges of a titular protonotary apostolic so long as he retains his office, which terminates at the will, death or translation of the bishop." *A Catholic Dictionary*. Edited by Donald Attwater. Page 516.

10-b "Reform is the bringing back of a religious order to its *primitive austerity* and observance of rule when it has become relaxed either through slackness or by lawful and authorized mitigation. This may be done either by a gradual process throughout the whole order or by the creation of a new reformed branch." *A Catholic Dictionary*. Edited by Donald Attwater. Page 422.

10-c "A Provincial is the superior of a province of a religious order. Provincial is often added to some other title, e.g., prior, vicar, minister. He is always elected for a term of years by the votes of a provincial chapter, but a Jesuit provincial is appointed by the general. The provincial is responsible to his superior general for the administration of his province and for the maintenance of religion therein, chiefly by means of visitations. He convenes the provincial chapter and is a member of the general chapter." *A Catholic Dictionary*. Edited by Donald Attwater. Page 410.

11 Literally, "Bend before breaking." Figuratively, die rather than give up.

11-a "Discalced is an epithet, 'barefooted,' applied to certain religious orders and congregations which are distinguished by the wearing of sandals." *A Catholic Dictionary*. Edited by Donald Attwater. Page 149.

"Calced. Certain religious are distinguished by this adjective, as wearing boots or shoes, from a branch of their order that goes barefoot or sandalled, e.g., the Calced Carmelites." *A Catholic Dictionary*. Edited by Donald Attwater. Page 65.

In common usage, the two terms were used, without further definition, to distinguish between the Carmelites of the Reform, who observed the Primitive Rule, and those who did not.

"The Carmelites, or Brothers of the Order of the most blessed Mother of God and ever virgin Mary of Mount Carmel, have claimed an organic descent from hermits living on that mountain under the direction of Elias and Eliseus. For practical purposes their history may be taken to begin in 1155, when a hermitage of western men was founded there by St. Berthold. The hermits spread to Europe and under a Kentishman, St. Simon Stock, modified their life and became mendicant friars. The reforming activity of St. Teresa and St. John-of-the-Cross in the 16th century resulted in two independent branches of the order. (a) The Calced or Shod Carmelites (properly called 'of the Old Observance') are the parent stem. They have modified their original rule, e.g., as regards fasting, abstinence, night office, and the like, but retain their mediaeval liturgy. . . . (b) The Discalced, Barefooted or Teresian Carmelites say the Divine Office daily in choir, rising from bed for the night office, and mental prayer is also made in common, twice a day. Abstinence is perpetual and there are special fasts. . . .

"The nuns of the order, founded in 1452 with papal sanction under the 'mitigated' rule then in force, spread rapidly, producing among other saints Mary-Magdalen de' Pazzi (1607). From 1562 St. Teresa founded convents under the primitive (non-mitigated) rule, which are now far more numerous than the others. Among them, two kinds of constitutions are in force, differing but slightly, both approved by the Church, and both recognized as Teresian. The nuns live in poverty and have strict enclosure, limited numbers, perpetual abstinence and silence (except two hours' recreation), choir office, mental prayer, and manual work." A *Catholic Dictionary*. Edited by Donald Attwater. Page 76.

12 Marcelle Auclair, from whom this moving account of the time, place and way in which Juan de San Matías took the habit is taken, goes on to say: "It was Fray John of the Cross who was 'the first.' Fray Antonio was not too well pleased at this and John in his charity allowed him the pleasure of boasting that he was Discalced before anyone else. He was also quite willing for him to be prior of the Duruelo house, but quietly stood out against the twists and turns given to the Primitive Rule by a man who had lived more than thirty years in the Mitigation. That was why Mother Teresa put all her energies into obtaining Constitutions for the friars, 'for some were of one opinion and others of another,' and the Foundress was often 'considerably troubled by their differences.'

"All this did not prevent Antonio de Jesus from chaffing Fray John because he had received the habit at the hands of a woman, the very same who, at Valladolid, when she was superintending the completion of the construction of the enclosure, instructed the young friar on the manner of life in monasteries of this sort, and on everything else, 'our mortifications, as well as our fraternal friendship and the recreations which we took together.' In these directives as in those Teresa of Jesus gave her nuns, the keyword was 'moderation.' "

Peers tells the story differently: "The Duruelo foundation was inaugurated on November 28 by Fray Antonio de Jesus (Heredia), St. John of the Cross and a deacon, José de Cristo. The Provincial, P. Alonso Gonzalez, who said their first Mass, and received their vows, revisited them shortly before Lent 1569, and appointed Antonio de Jesus Prior and St. John of the Cross Sub-Prior and novice-master, though some months passed before the small community became any larger. No more is heard of José de Cristo, who probably died, while a fourth Calced friar, Lucas de Celis, who joined the community at the beginning of its history, found its life too strict and returned to the Observance."

As both Auclair and Peers are equally meticulous in their research and both use sources that are, apparently, equally authentic, it seems to the author that the reader may feel free to choose between them. However, Robert Sencourt, another reliable authority, agrees with Marcelle Auclair, for he says: "He [San Juan de la Cruz] and Madre Teresa also welcomed the remoteness and poverty of Duruelo because it enabled him to make a centre of religion among the lonely peasants of the plain. And there was something about this little household that attracted the attention of others. Fray Juan was not alone there. A few weeks after his arrival he had been joined by another member of the Carmelite Convent at Medina. (The italics are mine.) This was a man of sixty years of age, no less a personage than the Prior, Fray Antonio de Heredia. An old friend of Madre Teresa, he, like Fray Juan, had been moved by her to make the sacrifice; he had given up the authority of his position and the amenities of his house to face the hardships and meanness of Duruelo."

[13] Auclair, Marcelle. *Teresa of Avila*. Page 195.

[14] Sencourt, Robert. *Carmelite and Poet; A Framed Portrait of St. John of the Cross*. Pages 58 and 59.

[15] Sencourt, Robert. *Carmelite and Poet; A Framed Portrait of St. John of the Cross*. Page 56.

[16] She is not to be confused with another nun by the same name (in religion) who was also professed at Medina del Campo and who later became not only one of Juan's greatest friends, but one of the greatest sources of inspiration for his writing. She was never at Pastrana.

[17] The number is variously given between 120 and 180. I have selected the one that seems most authentic, in the light of my own recent conferences at Encarnación.

[18] Walsh, William Thomas. *Saint Teresa of Avila*. Page 129.

[19] Auclair, Marcelle. *Teresa of Avila*. Page 238.

[20] Auclair, Marcelle. *Teresa of Avila*. Page 239.

[21] Jerónimo Tostado should not be confused with Alonzo de Madrigal, commonly called El Tostado, who was Bishop of Avila for more than fifty years and the author of more than sixty books. "He has written even more than El Tostado" is a common saying in Avila to this day, when referring to an especially prolific author. His tomb in the Avila Cathedral is one of its most impressive monuments.

[22] Matthew 5:44.

[22-a] Fulop-Miller, Rene. *The Saints That Moved The World*. Page 408.

[23]

1

Upon a darksome night,
Kindling with love in flame of yearning keen
—O moment of delight!—
I went, by all unseen,
New-hush'd to rest the house where I had been.

2

Safe sped I through that night,
By the secret stair, disguised and unseen,

—O moment of delight!—
Wrapt in that night serene,
New-hush'd to rest the house where I had been.

3

O happy night and blest!
Secretly speeding, screen'd from mortal gaze,
Unseeing, on I prest,
Lit by no earthly rays,
Nay, only by heart's inmost fire ablaze.

4

'Twas that light guided me,
More surely than the noonday's brightest glare,
To the place where none would be
Save one that waited there—
Well knew I whom or ere I forth did fare.

5

O night that led'st me thus!
O night more winsome than the rising sun!
O night that madest us,
Lover and lov'd, as one,
Lover transform'd in lov'd, love's journey done!

****

How well I know the fount that freely flows
    Although 'tis night!

1

The eternal fount its source has never show'd,
But well I know wherein is its abode,
    Although 'tis night.

2

Its origin I know not—it has none:
All other origins are here begun,
    Although 'tis night.

3

I know that naught beside can be so fair,
That heav'ns and earth drink deep refreshment there,
    Although 'tis night.

4

Well know I that its depths can no man plumb
Nor, fording it, across it hope to come,
    Although 'tis night.

5

Never was fount so clear, undimm'd and bright:
From it alone, I know, proceeds all light,
            Although 'tis night.

6

Rich are its streams and full—this know I well;
They water nations, heav'ns and depths of hell,
            Although 'tis night.

7

Yea, more I know: the stream that hence proceeds,
Omnipotent, suffices for all needs,
            Although 'tis night.

8

From fount and stream another stream forth flows,
And this, I know, in nothing yields to those,
            Although 'tis night.

9

The eternal fount is hidden in living bread,
That we with life eternal may be fed,
            Although 'tis night.

10

Call'd to this living fount, we creatures still
Darkly may feed hereon and take our fill,
            Although 'tis night.

11

This living fount which is so dear to me
Is in the bread of life, which now I see,
            Although 'tis night.

These translations are taken from *The Complete Works of St. John of the Cross*. Volume II, Pages 417, 431 and 432, by E. Allison Peers.

[24] Some authorities say seventeen and believe this number corresponds with the number of times he was flogged; others think as many as thirty stanzas may have been composed there, and do not connect these specifically with the number of floggings.

24–a

1

Oh, living flame of love That tenderly woundest
    my soul in its deepest centre,
Since thou art no longer oppressive, perfect me now
    if it be thy will, Break the web of this sweet encounter.

2

Oh, sweet burn! Oh, delectable wound! Oh, soft hand!
Oh, delicate touch
That savours of eternal life and pays every debt! In
slaying, thou has changed death into life.

3

Oh, lamps of fire, In whose splendours the deep
caverns of sense which were dark and blind
With strange brightness Give heat and light together
to their Beloved!

4

How gently and lovingly thou awakenest in my bosom,
Where thou dwellest secretly and alone!
And in thy sweet breathing, full of blessing and
glory, How delicately thou inspirest my love!

This translation is taken from *The Complete Works of St. John of the Cross.* Volume III, Page 16, by E. Allison Peers.

[25] Sencourt, Robert. *Carmelite and Poet; A Framed Portrait of St. John of the Cross.* Page 188.

[26] The story of this inscription is charmingly told in *Leyendas de Avila* by José Belmonte Diaz.

[26-a] It may be helpful to the average lay reader to have concrete definitions of the ecclesiastical offices and conferences mentioned in the following pages and not already described, since the duties they involved and the power with which they were invested played such a large part in the destiny of San Juan de la Cruz.

Definitor. A *definitorio* was a governing chapter or assembly of a religious order. Therefore, the First Definitor was the head of this and the Second, his assistant.

Consilario. He is a councilor or a member of the Advisory Board to the Superior and would be consulted by the latter over many matters of importance.

Apostolic Visitor. "He is a legate of the Holy See specially deputed to carry out a visitation and report on the religious state of a given ecclesiastical district or of a house or province of a religious order." *A Catholic Dictionary.* Edited by Donald Attwater. Page 520.

Master General. "He is the head of the order of Friars Preachers. He is elected by the priors provincial and the definitors of each province for a period of twelve years. The friars' professions are all received in his name. He has the curious distinction for a mendicant friar of ranking as a grandee in Spain with the right to remain covered before his Catholic Majesty (when there is one). The head of the Mercedarians is also called master general." *A Catholic Dictionary.* Edited by Donald Attwater. Page 313.

At the present time, the Master General of the Carmelites is called the Father General. He is the Head of the Order and resides in Rome.

Papal Nuncio. "He is a legate of the Holy See sent as ambassador to a foreign court as the permanent diplomatic agent of the pope and accredited accordingly to the civil government. He also has the duty of watching over the welfare of the Church within the country of his mission. There are nunciatures in most of the principal countries of Europe and the Americas, excepting Great Britain, U.S.S.R., and U.S.A." A *Catholic Dictionary*. Edited by Donald Attwater. Page 347.

General Chapter. "This is a canonical conference of the provincial and other superiors and representatives of a whole religious order or institute, for the purposes of legislation, discipline, election of officers, etc."

Provincial Chapter. "This is a canonical conference of the superiors and other representatives of the local province of a religious order or institute." A *Catholic Dictionary*. Edited by Donald Attwater. Page 89.

Commissary General or Provincial. "He is the provincial superior of the Friars Minor and Conventuals where there are not enough friars to form a real province; he is dependent on some other province. If dependent on the minister general he is called Commissary General." A *Catholic Dictionary*. Edited by Donald Attwater. Page 107.

[27] Auclair, Marcelle. *Teresa of Avila*. Page 262.

[28] Auclair, Marcelle. *Teresa of Avila*. Page 259.

[29] Auclair, Marcelle. *Teresa of Avila*. Page 345.

[30] Auclair, Marcelle. *Teresa of Avila*. Page 293.

[31] Auclair, Marcelle. *Teresa of Avila*. Page 352.

[32] Sencourt, Robert. *Carmelite and Poet; A Framed Portrait of St. John of the Cross*. Pages 205 and 206.

[33] Sencourt, Robert. *Carmelite and Poet; A Framed Portrait of St. John of the Cross*. Page 206.

[34] Sencourt, Robert. *Carmelite and Poet; A Framed Portrait of St. John of the Cross*. Page 208. In Note 19 on this page, Sencourt gives as his reference for this quotation E. Allison Peers, *Works*. Volume III, Page 298. The edition which I have of Peers' *Works* quotes this letter in slightly different form in Volume III, Page 275.

[35] Ana de Peñalosa's niece.

[36] Peers, E. Allison. *The Complete Works of St. John of the Cross*. Volume III, Pages 275 and 276.

[37] I thoroughly agree with H. V. Morton's estimate of St. John of the Cross as expressed in *A Stranger in Spain*. In this, he says: "Of all Spaniards who ever lived, St. John of the Cross is the most appealing and the most ethereal. He drifts across the religious history of sixteenth century Spain like a spirit, indeed he scarcely seems anchored to the earth at all. In his search for infused wisdom this great spiritual explorer was always wandering out at night to adore God in the darkness. He wrote love poems to God which are the most beautiful ever written by a saint."

To this analysis may be added the one by Sackville-West:

"Among the crowd of friars, confessors, prioresses, nuns, princes, and ladies who pullulate with such actuality through the records of Teresa's life, St. John for all his elusiveness shines with a light of his own. We never seize him; he possessed more than any man the *pudeur* of suppressing his own personality. He is an essence, volatile, imponderable, floating in a rarefied atmosphere difficult for us to breathe, his one desire to pass unnoticed, the better to lose himself in the only preoccupation which held any significance for him. Like the ideal soul of which he writes, he is 'free, perfect, solitary, and pure.' Free indeed; for he had divorced himself from all attachments, 'such as to individuals, to a book or a call, to a particular food, to certain society, to the satisfaction of one's taste for science, news, and such things.' Does it make any difference, he asks, whether a bird be held by a slender thread or a rope since it is bound and cannot fly until the cord that holds it be broken? the solitary bird which can endure no companionship, even of its own kind. He himself had broken all bonds:

> Forth unobserved I went
> In darkness and security,
> By the secret ladder, in disguise,
> In secret, seen of none.
>
> Oh night more lovely than the dawn!
> Lost to all things and myself,
> And, amid the lilies forgotten,
> Threw all my cares away."

The Eagle and the Dove. Pages 79 and 80.

NOTES FOR PART IV

1 The other column, according to legend, was erected across the Straits of Gibraltar, when Hercules joined the Atlantic and the Mediterranean.

2 Freely translated, this reads:
Hercules built me,
Julius Caesar girded me
with high walls and towers,
the Saint King won me
With Garcia Perez de Vargas.

3 It will be remembered that Francisco Núñez Vela, Teresa de Ahumada's godfather, was the brother of this viceroy.

4 Like the forbears of Doña Luisa de la Cerda, these grandparents of María Vela could claim that they had royal blood in their veins.

4-a No less than a dozen tombs of the Blásquez family are located in a chapel of the Avila cathedral. This chapel was founded by one of its Deans, a noble of the great family of the Medinas, whose history is closely associated with that of the Ahumadas. The slabs on the floor, which mark the earlier tombs, and date from the twelfth to the fourteenth century, were almost certainly transferred from another location when this chapel was built in the sixteenth; the inscriptions on these are difficult to decipher as the lettering is obscured by age. But fortunately, the inscription of the sepulchre on the wall, dating from 1559, is entirely legible and authenticates all the others, every one of which is ornamented by a full coat-of-arms with a clear-cut carving of five hats in the upper left-hand quarter! These hats, however, appear in two different shapes on different shields: some are in a simple mushroom shape; others are adorned with topknots and simulated ribbons, the latter obviously copied from those designed to be tied under the wearer's chin and hang from under the wide brims. The beribboned hats are those which belong to the period of the chapel's founder.

5 This privilege, at first applying to all matrons of Avila, was later confined to the female descendants of Doña Jimena, who eventually renounced the right of their own volition.

6 E. Allison Peers, in his Handbook to the Life and Times of St. Teresa and St. John of the Cross, says of Isabel de Santo Domingo: "Born of a good family at Cardeñosa, near Avila, she realized her vocation while still young, proposing to become a Discalced Franciscan. St. Peter of Alcántara, however, whom she consulted, recommended her to St. Teresa, and she was one of the first to embrace the Reform (c. 1563) after the foundation of St. Joseph's, Avila, making her profession on October 21, 1564. In 1569, she went with St.

Teresa to make the foundation at Toledo and was left there as Prioress—the first nun to hold that office in the Reform who had not come from the Incarnation. After a few months, she was sent as Prioress to Pastrana, where she handled particularly difficult situations with unusual tact and skill. Transferred to Segovia with the Pastrana community, she became Prioress there (May 20, 1574). She was considered for the same office at Malagón but not appointed there. In 1588 she went from Segovia, also as Prioress, to make a foundation at Zaragoza and in 1598 she became the first Prioress of the convent at Ocaña. Before her triennium was completed, she returned to Segovia, at the unanimous request of the community there, which found itself in material straits. In 1604, she returned to St. Joseph's, Avila, where she was Prioress from 1606 to 1610. She died on June 13, 1623. Both in spirituality and as an administrator, she was one of St. Teresa's outstanding daughters, in request everywhere and exercising a notable influence on the Order."

It is interesting to note that, whereas Teresa was born in the capital city of the province, many of its other most prominent figures were born in its villages—Isabel in Madrigal, San Juan de la Cruz in Fontiveros, María Díaz in Vita, María Vela and Isabel de Santo Domingo in Cardeñosa, San Pedro Bautista in San Esteban del Valle, Diego de Espinosa (see p. 115 and p. 145) in Martín Muñoz, and Juan Sedeño in Arévalo. The last named was both a warrior and a writer. (See Prologue Notes—Page 292.)

7 This grille and retable was ordered made by the magnificent lady Señora Doña Isabel Rivera, daughter of the magnificent knight, Francisco de Valderrabano, in honor of Santa Barbada in the year 1547.

8 This is the same shrine that is described on page 119.

9 A *fanega* is a little more than a bushel and one-half; a *celemin* is about a peck.

10 The convent also contained, and still contains, so-called cells, similar to the more desirable ones at Encarnación, comprising a bed alcove and a small sitting room, which could be used as an oratory. These were and are available under special circumstances, formerly both by religious and lay visitors. In addition to these, there were and still are the very large rooms like those occupied by Isabel, which are no longer used as sleeping quarters.

11 According to *A Catholic Dictionary*, General Confession is:

"A repetition of all previous confessions either of one's life or over a considerable period of time. It may be made necessary by previous confessions having been wilfully incomplete or lacking in true penitence, or by the confessor having been without jurisdiction. Such a general confession is customary before first communion, ordination, monastic profession, etc., and may be allowed in order to remove doubts and scruples in respect of past sins. Except for such or other good reasons, the making of a general confession is strongly discouraged by ascetical writers and confessors as being an occasion of scrupulosity and generally harmful."

12 Dr. Miguel González Vaquero, María Vela's first biographer (1618) and last confessor, who was largely responsible for her *Autobiography*, writes thus of this episode and its sequel, "He had never thought of entering religious life, but all he read on the sly seemed to him God's call. Before following

it, he confessed his guilt to Doña María de Avila and then took the habit in a certain Order, where he has become a very spiritual man and a great preacher. When he comes to this city, he drops in to see me and talk about the sanctity of María Vela. Upon her death, I wrote to him to confirm this story and he readily owned to his peccadillo and the signal favor he had received through it."

[13] Vaquero, Miguel González. *La Mujer Fuerte.* Part I. Chapter 31.

[14] Vaquero, Miguel González. *La Mujer Fuerte.* Part I. Chapter 33.

[15] Vaquero, Miguel González. *La Mujer Fuerte.* Part I. Chapter 33.

[16] "As early as 1602, requests for the beatification of Teresa of Jesus began to pour in at Rome. In 1614, seventy galleons left Genoa under the command of the High Admiral of the Fleet, Don Carlos Doria: they were bringing the news of the Foundress's beatification, to Spain. In 1622, Blessed Teresa became Saint Teresa of Jesus. During the canonization ceremony, doves and a multitude of other small birds were let loose in St. Peter's. In 1926, the Cortes nominated St. Teresa patron of all the Spains. But Spain already had a patron in St. James, and his clients caused the decree to be revoked. But if St. Teresa has not this official glory, at least she retains the prestige non-officially." (Auclair, Marcelle. *Teresa of Avila.* Page 435.)

[17] Dietary rules vary greatly in different Orders and at different periods. For instance, the Carmelites, before the Reform, had great latitude in this respect; now, they never eat meat. At the time about which we are writing; the Cistercians were permitted, by Papal dispensation, to eat meat on Tuesdays, Thursdays and Sundays.

[18] Vaquero, Miguel González. *La Mujer Fuerte.* Part II. Chapter 1.

[19] Vaquero, Miguel González. *La Mujer Fuerte.* Part II. Chapter 11.

[20] Vaquero, Miguel González. *La Mujer Fuerte.* Part II. Chapter 11.

[21] Vaquero, Miguel González. *La Mujer Fuerte.* Part II. Chapters 11, 12 and 13.

[22] It is interesting to note that this charge of singularity is the one that was brought against the heroine of *The Nun's Story*, the book by Kathryn Hulme, which has recently been enjoying such well-deserved success and acclaim.

[23] Vaquero, Miguel González. *La Mujer Fuerte.* Part II. Chapter 20.

[24] Vaquero, Miguel González. *La Mujer Fuerte.* Part II. Chapter 22.

[25] Vaquero, Miguel González. *La Mujer Fuerte.* Part II. Chapter 36.

[25-a] Vaquero, Miguel González. *La Mujer Fuerte.* Part II. Chapter 36.

[26] Vaquero, Miguel González. *La Mujer Fuerte.* Part II. Chapter 37.

[27] Vaquero, Miguel González. *La Mujer Fuerte.* Part III. Chapter 3.

[27-a] It is interesting to note that one of the greatest philosophers of modern times, George Santayana, whose father was an *Abulense* and who himself spent much of his early life in Avila and has written most beautifully and feelingly about it, says that "a certain joy and beauty did radiate visibly from the saints"—and this, despite the fact that, alas! in his later years he became an agnostic. As the Santayana family house, which has now passed into other hands, is directly across the street from the Convent of Santa Ana

and George Santayana frequently refers to this institution in the course of
his writings, it is quite possible that this statement of his was based, at
least in part, on what he had heard about María Vela.

This statement about the radiation of beauty and joy was vividly recalled
to me during my latest perusal of Agnes Repplier's *Mère Marie of the
Ursulines*, in which she quotes it. The final quotation in Miss Repplier's
book, which comes from a source unfamiliar to me, also seems appropriate
to María Vela, though, of course, it is not used in that connection:
"Courage was cast about her like a dress
Of solemn comeliness."

[28] Vaquero, Miguel González. *La Mujer Fuerte*. Part I. Chapter 3.

[29] Vaquero, Miguel González. *La Mujer Fuerte*. Part II. Chapter 48.

[30] Vaquero, Miguel González. *La Mujer Fuerte*. Part II. Chapter 48.

[30-a] Auclair, Marcelle. *Teresa of Avila*. Page 23.

[30-b] Valencia, Bartolomé Fz. Op. Cit., Fol. 30.

[31] Vaquero, Miguel González. *La Mujer Fuerte*. Part III. Chapter 18.

[32] Vaquero, Miguel González. *La Mujer Fuerte*. Part III. Chapter 1.

[33] Vaquero, Miguel González. *La Mujer Fuerte*. Part III. Chapter 18.

[34] Vaquero, Miguel González. *La Mujer Fuerte*. Part III. Chapter 18.

[34-a] Vaquero, Miguel González. *La Mujer Fuerte*. Part III. Chapter 4.

[35] Vaquero, Miguel González. *La Mujer Fuerte*. Part III. Chapters 7 and 8.

[36] Vaquero, Miguel González. *La Mujer Fuerte*. Part III. Chapter 18.

[37] Vaquero, Miguel González. *La Mujer Fuerte*. Part III. Chapter 6.

[38] Vaquero, Miguel González. *La Mujer Fuerte*. Part III. Chapter 17.

[39] Vaquero, Miguel González. *La Mujer Fuerte*. Part II. Chapter 46.

[40] It is still carefully preserved at the Convent of Santa Ana. The parish priest
of Cardeñosa, in writing about it in 1917, remarked that "To this day it
retains its [the blood] natural color, though somewhat pallid." (I saw these
garments during the summer of 1956 and can make the same observation.)

[41] "Here lies the body of the Venerable Doña María Vela, the strong woman, a
nun in this House and native of Avila. She died on September 24, 1617.
From her first sepulchre she was transferred to this one by Don Francisco
Gamarra, Bishop of Avila, formerly of Cartagena, with the consent of the
Faculty of Theology of Salamanca, on August 5, 1623, under the Pontificate
of Urban VIII, the reign of Philip IV and the rule of Governor Juan de
Beaumont y Navarra, Doña María Dávila being the Abbess of this Convent."

[42] "It is established beyond all doubt that the remains of certain persons, even
after the lapse of centuries, have not suffered the ordinary decomposition
of mortal flesh. On this point there can be no argument at all. Nor do the
conditions following upon death and burial appear to affect the matter;
it is influenced neither by damp, nor quicklime, nor by delay in interment
(and in many cases the reluctance of the devout to be separated from the
object of their devotion has led to an abnormal procrastination, St. Bernardine of Siena for instance remaining unburied for twenty-six days, St. Angela

Merici, Foundress of the Ursulines, for thirty days, St. Laurence Giustiniani for sixty-seven days), nor by such exceptional circumstances as those which occurred in the case of St. Josaphat, who was murdered and thrown into the river Dwina, retrieved after spending six days in the water, found then to be fresh and beautiful, and preserved his incorruption for many years afterwards. From the moment we begin to glance, however cursorily, at this subject, the more baffling does it become. For one thing, the marvel of incorruptibility is extremely erratic in its incidence, and would seem not necessarily to be associated with the degree of sanctity. Thus, neither St. Francis, St. Bernard, St. Dominic . . . nor . . . St. Thérèse of Lisieux was spared the common lot of decay. On the other hand, this remarkable favour attends some of the most famous names in the Calendar, St. Charles Borromeo for example, dying in 1584, was found almost entire in 1880 despite a damp and leaky coffin; St. John of the Cross, dying in 1591, was still incorrupt in 1859 . . . and, coming down to more recent times, [we] may note the case of the renowned Curé d'Ars, Jean-Baptiste Vianney, and that of St. Bernadette Soubirous of Lourdes, who, dying in 1879, was exhumed thirty years later and found to be without any trace of putrefaction. Erratic indeed; inconsistent, even whimsical, would appear the bestowal of this most strange dispensation." Sackville-West, V. *The Eagle and the Dove.* Pages 5 and 6.

43 The coffin was opened again in 1664, 1808, 1812 and 1943. I have in my possession the sworn statement, in Spanish, of the Abbess who officiated on the latest occasion and of which a translation reads, as follows:

"When the most excellent and Reverend Bishop Dr. D. Santos Moro Briz made his canonical visit on November 6, 1943, the Reverend Abbess, who was then Manuela Santos, asked him as a special favor permission to lower and view the body of the Venerable María Vela which, at present, is [entombed] between the upper and lower choirs in view of both the church and the cloistered choir—a favor which, without making any difficulty, he graciously granted at once; and on the fourteenth day of the same month, after previous notice, at four in the afternoon, the afore-mentioned Bishop came in person to the monastery accompanied by his Mayordomo, D. Jesús Jiménez, and the Chaplain of the Community, D. Flavio Aguilera. When they had entered the cloister, the Bishop ordered the nuns to lower the casket, which contains the body, while the afore-mentioned dignitaries went, with the Superiors, to the room of Isabella the Catholic there to see and examine the books and *The Life of the Venerable,* written by this nun herself, which they did with admiration, both for the excellent state of preservation in which they found these documents and for the beautiful handwriting.

"With indescribable emotion and enthusiasm, the nuns who remained in the choir proceeded to lower the sarcophagus, which is covered with red damask and curtained with green velvet. Once lowered, it was placed on the table which had been prepared beforehand, and the waiting Bishop, Superiors and other dignitaries were notified. When the community, the Bishop and the Abbess were all together again, they opened the sarcophagus and saw that the body was intact, except for part of the eyes, nose and lips.

"By order of the Bishop and Superiors, the body was removed from the casket with great care and respect and placed on a white cloth. This removal occasioned no disturbance whatsoever in its condition, except for the loss of a tooth which the Abbess offered the Bishop, but which, through delicacy, he did not accept; instead, he insisted upon leaving it with the community as a relic. The Venerable's woollen habit, which had disintegrated, was removed, but her undergarments were like new, fresh and whole. Another favor, which he granted with his usual graciousness, was then asked of the Bishop: namely, that the body might be left where it was for three days, in order that a new habit might be made for it, like those at present worn by the community; then she was clothed in a cowl, hood and veil, all very clean and well arranged.

"On the 17th, at seven in the afternoon, the Bishop, accompanied by his Mayordomo Jesús Jiménez, Flavio Aguilera, Leandro Martín and Venancio Moro, met the community and again viewed the body of the Venerable, now dressed in her new habit. The sarcophagus was closed with two keys, one of which remained in the keeping of the Abbess and the other in the keeping of the Bishop. Once the sarcophagus was closed, these dignitaries went to the apartment of Isabella the Catholic and ordered that the sarcophagus be raised again to its niche. When it was again in place, they were advised, so that they could confirm this, which they did. Then they took leave of the community with every indication of affection and admiration.

"The body of the Venerable has now been uncovered on several occasions: first, six years after her death and again, forty years after. Later, because of the French invasion, it was safeguarded from impiety by concealment underground. Today, it rests, enclosed in a sarcophagus, in a niche between the upper and lower choirs.

"Royal Cistercian Convent of Santa Ana of Avila.

October 15, 1956."

NOTES FOR PART V

[1] The exact date of Pedro Bautista's birth has not been authenticated, but most authorities put it in this year.

[2] A *Guardian* is the Superior of a Franciscan Convent; a *Custodian* is the Superior of all the friars in a region where there are fewer than ten convents; a *Provincial* is the Superior of a region with ten convents or less, if it has been elevated to the category of a *Provincia* by the Pope; a *Comisario* is the delegate of a Provincial, or a General, to found convents or to visit them.

[3] "*Beata* is the term used for a woman wearing religious habit, but living in her own house, practising prayer and works of virtue. But the term is applied loosely in Spain to devout ladies given over to prayer and good works of all kinds." (Marcelle Auclair. *Teresa of Avila.* Page 38.)

[4] Ribadeneira, Marcelo de. *Historia de las Islas del Archipiélago Filipino y Reinos de la Gran China, Tartaria, Cochinchina, Malaca, Siam, Cambodge y Japón.*

[5] See Note 2.

[5-a] There are eleven letters of San Pedro Bautista's in the Archives of the Indies. I have had the privilege of examining these and thus doubly authenticating other source material.

[6] A modern American writer—Thomas J. Campbell, S.J.—suggests in his excellent history of the Jesuits that, since 1589 was the year when two Christian women declined to enter Cambacu's harem, and thereby infuriated him, this refusal may well have been responsible for the edict.

[7] 1590–1593.

[8] *American College Dictionary* published by Random House.

[9] My poem, entitled *Permanence*, included in the volume, entitled *The Happy Wanderer*, sets forth this feeling very clearly.

[10] "In 1479–80 the Catholic Kings had specifically recognized by treaty the exclusive rights of Portugal to all lands she should discover in Guinea and off the coast of it, except the Canaries; and on June 21, 1481, Pope Sixtus IV had confirmed this treaty, and also the grants under his predecessors' bulls. Since that time the Portuguese had rounded the Cape of Good Hope and followed up the east coast of Africa to a point beyond Algoa Bay; clearly, in view of the prevailing ignorance of geography and the doubts as to the exact location of the lands Columbus had found, it was essential that Rome be immediately notified of the Spanish pretensions. Ferdinand and Isabella had every reason to believe that their claims would not fare ill at the hands of the recently elected pontiff, Alexander VI, who, in addition to being of Valencian birth, was beholden to them in a variety of different ways. Their foresight was

justified by the event; in all the ensuing negotiations the pontiff was less an arbiter, than an instrument in the hands of the Catholic Kings. In April, 1493, he put forth the first of the two famous bulls *Inter caetera*, granting to the Spanish sovereigns exclusive right and possession in all the lands and islands discovered in the West, towards the Indies, in the Ocean Sea, as well as in all others yet to be discovered in that region. On May 17 the bull was dispatched to the papal nuncio in Spain. It was doubtless Alexander's hope that the very vague phraseology which had been employed would safeguard the rights already granted by his predecessors to Portugal 'from Cape Bojador towards Guinea and beyond,' and at the same time satisfy the demands of Ferdinand and Isabella; but he was destined to be disappointed. By the time that the bull arrived in Spain, the sovereigns had had time to discuss the whole affair with Columbus, and to learn the full extent of his achievements and of his hopes. They had also opened negotiations with John II of Portugal, and had been informed of the counter-claims which that monarch had to urge. The wording of the first bull was clearly inadequate: it did not settle the question of the dominion of the Atlantic, particularly to the southward, which Spain was most desirous to secure. Columbus urged the advisability of a demarcation line; and the sovereigns, acting on his suggestion, again applied to Rome for an amplification and extension of the rights already conferred upon them. The result was the second bull *Inter caetera*, which was issued in June and reached Spain in the middle of July. It granted to their Catholic Majesties all lands found or to be found both to the west and to the south towards India and all other regions, provided they had not been occupied by any other Christian prince previously to Christmas, 1492; and it established a line to be drawn, north and south, a hundred leagues to the westward of the Azores and Cape Verde Islands, beyond which no foreigner was to venture without a license from the Spanish sovereign. Furthermore, a supplementary bull *Eximiae*, issued in July, reiterated and emphasized the rights and privileges to be enjoyed by Ferdinand and Isabella in the territories in question; while a final one, dated September 26, provided—in flat contradiction to the earlier instrument—that previous occupation by other Christian potentates should not constitute a title, and annulled all grants 'to kings, princes, infantes, or religious or military orders' in the regions assigned to the king and queen of Spain.

"Clearly all these stipulations were aimed directly at the Portuguese; Alexander, who, on account of the political situation in Italy, was like wax in the hands of Ferdinand and Isabella, was being steadily led on to more and more open infringement of the rights of their rival. Naturally, under the circumstances, King John regarded the course of the negotiations between Spain and the Vatican with steadily increasing dissatisfaction. In addition to all their other advantages, the fact that the Catholic Kings were holding their court at Barcelona, whence they could reach Rome twice as quickly as could the Portuguese monarch, doubtless convinced the latter that little was to be gained by an attempt to outbid them there; his best hope was to deal directly with Ferdinand and Isabella themselves. He therefore instructed Ruy de Sande, his representative at the Spanish court, to lay his case before them; moreover he assembled a powerful fleet, probably with the idea of threatening a descent on Columbus's discoveries if his protests should not be heard. The negotiations dragged slowly along far beyond the date of Columbus's departure on his second voyage, but both parties were desirous to avoid a quarrel, and Ferdinand and Isabella saw no harm in yielding to the argument of King John that the original line—one hundred leagues west of the Azores and Cape Verde Islands—limited too closely Portugal's opportunities for expansion in the Atlantic. On June 7, 1494, a treaty between the monarchs was accordingly signed at Tordesillas, by which the line of demarcation of their respective claims was drawn north and south at a point three hundred and seventy leagues west of the Cape Verde Islands—that is, about half way between them and the islands that Columbus had discovered; everything beyond that line was to fall to the Catholic Kings, everything to the east of it was to belong to the Portuguese. The line hits the north coast of South America just east of the mouth of the Amazon, and of course ultimately served to secure the Portuguese title to Brazil. On the other side of the globe it passes just west of New Guinea, but it was a long time before the facts were accurately determined, and in the meantime Spain made good her hold on the Philippines, which lie on the Portuguese side of it. (In view of the difficulty of ascertaining exact positions in the Pacific, the sovereigns of Spain and of Portugal made a treaty in 1529, by which a line was drawn from north to south 297 leagues east of the Moluccas, to serve as a boundary between the areas claimed by the two realms pending a scientific and accurate determination of their respective rights. This arrangement put the Philippines in Portuguese territory even more conclusively than the Tordesillas line would have done; but the Spanish monarchs chose to ignore the facts, and tacitly assumed the right to conquer them.)" Merriman, Roger Bigelow. *The Rise of the Spanish Empire in the Old World and in the New.* Volume II, Pages 200–204.

Two items in this summary are especially interesting to the present chronicler: one, that the first firm agreement, regarding the demarcation line, was signed at Tordesillas and that its official title, according to Webster's New International Dictionary and the American College Dictionary, is the Treaty of Tordesillas. Since this city is so closely associated with the story of the Catholic Kings—See Pages 36, 39 and 40, Part I—and their unfortunate daughter, Juana—See Note 20, Part I—it seems strange that this designation is not in more general use. Two, if the agreement actually conceded the Philippines to Portugal, rather than to Spain, it seems strange that the former country did not make an issue of this, considering all the dissension about Japan. Furthermore, this author finds it hard to believe that Isabel was guilty of deliberate duplicity in this situation, as such double-dealing is not typical of her. She may well have been in ignorance of the exact boundary line—as indeed everyone seems to have been—but that she was deceitful is, I think, open to grave doubt, though her husband may well have been. He had a much less candid and forthright character than his wife. There is a well-authenticated story to the effect that, when the King of France complained that Ferdinand had deceived him twice and Ferdinand heard of this complaint, he gleefully exclaimed, "Twice! I have deceived him ten times!" Obviously, he gloried in his powers of deception.

"Well down in the sixteenth century, navigators of the American shores supposed that they were still feeling their way along the shores of Asia. Indeed it is quite probable that the first appearance of the coast of the United States on the map is due not to the observation of any adventurer who had really seen it, but to the certainty which Marco Polo had given two centuries before, that the coast of Asia trended in that direction. . . . With the supposition that the Pacific was so narrow, the Philippines were brought twenty or thirty degrees nearer to America than they are. Really they belonged within the Portuguese half of the undiscovered world. But Magellan put them into the Spanish part, and there they have remained to this day. It was not till Anson's voyage of 1743 that this great error was exposed to Europe.

"Government so extensive—more than imperial,—or any definition of empire which the world had known until now, was administered by Charles, —while he was in the field perhaps, perhaps in fight, perhaps in his Mediterranean adventures, perhaps engaged in those perplexing diplomacies in which theology bore so large a part, and where, as it has proved, Charles bore himself so unwisely. No wonder, then, if in the details of the administration much went wrong. In that eventful half century between the reign of Ferdinand and the end of that of Philip, Spain had won, through most of the world, the reputation of the blackest cruelty. . . . But, after granting this cruelty, yet making allowance for it, in memory of its sources, none the less is it true, that in discovery, in adventure, in colonization, in all that part of her work which fell outside of Europe, Spain showed the noblest courage, patience, and foresight. She illustrated some of the grandest qualities of man. It is not by cruelty and treachery that the people of a poor peninsula, just emerging from a long war of races, obtain possession of half the world. It is rather by such faith as led Columbus, by such manhood as gave Magalhaens his supremacy over discontented rivals. It is by that proud hospitality, in which Spain welcomed such leaders, and gave places of command to these two men, and to Cabot and Vespucius, who were only not their peers. It was by such prompt decision or heroic audacity as once and again saved Cortés,—it was by the wisdom of Ximénes, by the humanity of Las Casas, by the chivalric courage of thousands of unnamed soldiers, and the Christian constancy of thousands of unnamed confessors, that Spanish names were placed on half the headlands of the world. Everywhere the modern world, tracing back its recent history, looks with mysterious curiosity to that land which sent out such men as Columbus, and Balboa, and Cortés, and Magalhaens, in the age of Charles V, of Leo, of Michel Angelo, of Leonardo, of Loyola, and of Luther." *The Story of the Nations—The Story of Spain* by Edward Everett Hale and Susan Hale. Pages 338–340.

[11] 1583.

[12] "Coelho seems to have been a worthy but earthy type, with a strong belief in the prevalence of demons in his garden after dark. Francis obviously liked him and was not above teasing him, though the honest soul did not perceive the banter in his guest's eyes. They became very intimate, as how could they not sharing the same kitchenette and bed-sitting-room? For the only

time in his life the Saint indulged in reminiscences of his youth, and confessed to the Vicar, as mentioned above, how far from edifying had been his early years in Paris. Those years obviously still lay heavy on his conscience and may very well be the explanation of something that Coelho, who slept soundly, believed to be devilry pure and simple in his compound." Brodrick, James, S.J. *Saint Francis Xavier* (1506–1552). Page 225.

13 To the present author, admittedly not an authority in such matters, it would seem that Pedro had valid reasons for using the Brief of Sixtus V as authority, since Sixtus succeeded Gregory, but that he was not on such firm ground as far as Paul III was concerned, since the latter had reigned nearly half a century earlier.

14 The modern Kyoto.

15 Robles Dégano makes no further mention of Cobo's fate. According to Ribadeneira and the Dominican historians, his name was spelt Cobos, not Cobo, and he died in a shipwreck off the coast of Formosa on his return from Japan. These authorities also believe that San Pedro Bautista was sent to find out not the fate of Father Cobos, but the result of his embassy. Since the authorities seem to be equally dependable, the modern reader may take his choice among them.

15-a This Provincial should not be confused with the Governor of the Philippines. Pedro and Gómez are both names in very general use.

16 All direct quotes in this narrative, unless otherwise noted, are from the book entitled *Vida y Martirio de San Pedro Bautista* by D. Felipe Robles Dégano, Pbro.

17 At this point, Robles Dégano comments, with considerable feeling, how little Pedro cared whether the Jesuits were Portuguese or Chinese. On the other hand, they could not bear him because he was a Spaniard.

18 Thomas J. Campbell, S.J. places the figures much higher; he says that, in 1589, the number of Christians in Japan was 300,000. *The Jesuits 1534–1921.* Page 183.

18-a When the tidings of this procession reached Organtino who, as we have already learned, was one of the only three persons in Meaco who interfered with Pedro, the Italian immediately wrote a letter of protest; the action seemed to him "most imprudent." Pedro replied to this and other complaints with a courteous letter; but, as Organtino's excitement did not subside and Pedro feared that some desecration might ensue, he decided to go no further with his plans.

19 "In the middle years of Philip's reign there was one project of great moment in Spanish history which he pushed to a successful conclusion,—the annexation of Portugal. While the ultimate importance of this event was to be lessened by the later separation of the two kingdoms, they were united long enough (sixty years) for notable effects to be felt in Spain and more particularly in the Americas. The desire for peninsula unity had long been an aspiration of the Castilian kings, and its consummation from the standpoint of the acquisition of Portugal had several times been attempted, though without success. The death of King Sebastián in 1578 without issue left the

Portuguese throne to Cardinal Henry, who was already very old, and whom in any event the pope refused to release from his religious vows. This caused various claimants to the succession to announce themselves, among whom were the Duchess of Braganza, Antonio (the prior of Crato), and Philip. The first-named had the best hereditary claim, since she was descended from a son (the youngest), of King Manuel, a predecessor of Sebastián. Antonio of Crato was son of another of King Manuel's sons, but was of illegitimate birth; nevertheless, he was the favorite of the regular clergy, the popular classes, some nobles, and the pope, and was the only serious rival Philip had to consider. Philip's mother was the eldest daughter of the same King Manuel. With this foundation for his claim he pushed his candidacy with great ability, aided by the skilful diplomacy of his special ambassador, Cristóbal de Moura. One of the master strokes was the public announcement of Philip's proposed governmental policy in Portugal, promising among other things to respect the autonomy of the kingdom, recognizing it as a separate political entity from Spain. A Portuguese Cortes of 1580 voted for the succession of Philip, for the noble and ecclesiatical branches supported him, against the opposition of the third estate. A few days later King Henry died, and Philip prepared to take possession. The partisans of Antonio resisted, but Philip, who had long been in readiness for the emergency, sent an army into Portugal under the Duke of Alba, and he easily routed the forces of Antonio. In keeping with his desire to avoid giving offence to the Portuguese, Philip gave Alba the strictest orders to punish any infractions of discipline or improper acts of the soldiery against the inhabitants, and these commands were carefully complied with,—in striking contrast with the policy which had been followed while Alba was governor in the Low Countries. Thus it was that a Portuguese Cortes of 1581 solemnly recognized Philip as king of Portugal. Philip took oath not to appoint any Spaniards to Portuguese offices, and he kept his word to the end of his reign. Portugal had now come into the peninsula union in much the same fashion that Aragon had joined with Castile. With her came the vast area and great wealth of the Portuguese colonies of Asia, Africa, and more particularly Brazil. If only the Spanish kings might hold the country long enough, it appeared inevitable that a real amalgamation of such kindred peoples would one day take place. Furthermore, if only the kings would have, or could have, confined themselves to a Pan-Hispanic policy, embracing Spain and Portugal and their colonies, the opportunity for the continued greatness of the peninsula seemed striking. The case was a different one from that of the union of Castile and Aragon, however, for a strong feeling of Portuguese nationality had already developed, based largely on a *hatred of Spaniards*. This spirit had something to feed upon from the outset in the defeat of the popular Antonio of Crato and in the discontent of many nobles, who did not profit as much by Philip's accession as they had been led to expect. It was necessary to put strong garrisons in Portuguese cities and to fortify strategic points. Nevertheless, Philip experienced no serious trouble and was able to leave Portugal to his immediate successor." (The italics are mine.) A *History of Spain* by Charles E. Chapman, Ph.D. Pages 251–253.

"... Henceforth the Iberian Peninsula was completely unified under the same sceptre. Philip, heir through his mother to the crown of Portugal, annexed this kingdom to his states (1581). Apart from Castile and Aragon, he had inherited the kingdoms of Valencia, Naples, and the Two Sicilies, Tuscany, the Milanese and Liguria. From his father, heir of the House of Burgundy, he held Flanders." The History of Spain by Louis Bertrand and Sir Charles Petrie Bt. Page 225.

20 Countless historians bear out these statements. Mary Watters says, "The work of the missionaries began in Venezuela early in the sixteenth century. With the conquerors there came friars to evangelize the Indians." A History of the Church in Venezuela 1810–1930. Page 6.

"On the second voyage of Columbus several of the clergy were included in the company." Three Centuries of Advance by Kenneth Scott Latourette. Page 86.

Charles F. Lummis states, "Indeed, within a year after the arrival in Mexico of the first transcontinental traveller [Cortés] two more of our present States were found [Arizona and New Mexico] by his countrymen [Fray Marcos de Nizza and Francisco Vásquez de Coronado, Governor of the Mexican Province of New Galicia] as the direct result of his narratives. . . . In 1581 three Spanish missionaries . . . started from Santa Barbara, Chihuahua, with an escort of nine Spanish soldiers." The Spanish Pioneers and the California Missions. Pages 78, 80 and 86.

"There has already been frequent occasion to mention the two representatives of the church who accompanied Cortés in his conquest of Mexico. . . . It was inevitable, however, that the task of conversion should pass out of the hands of the conquerors, and that the church should undertake the evangelization of the people." Religious Aspects of the Conquest of Mexico by Charles S. Braden. Pages 130 and 131.

Bernard De Vaulx in his excellent book uses as a chapter title, "Dans le Sillage des Découvreurs," ("In the Wake of the Explorers") in describing the early Jesuit activities in North America. (The italics are mine.)

21 This is the church at Paracuellos de la Ribera, Province of Saragossa.

22 It seems very important to the present author that the reader should continue to bear in mind what has been pointed out already, namely that rivalry between Spaniards and Portuguese had, at this period, reached a very high point, and that this intensive feeling about nationality had its effect on clerics as well as on laymen. We have already seen how much Juan de la Cruz was called upon to suffer because Doria, an Italian, hated Gracián, who was a Spaniard. Likewise, in the story of the same saint, we have seen how much hard feeling questions of ecclesiastical precedence could cause; he was continually bewildered, grieved and abused because provincials, bishops and papal nuncios could not, or would not, agree—especially when they were not fellow countrymen—as to who had the final voice in what he should do.

We should also remember that the period under consideration was essentially one of persecution, and that this was not confined to any one country or any one form of faith, though we are better informed about some aspects of this persecution than we are about others. For instance, almost every educated person has heard of the Protestants put to death by Mary Tudor, who has come down in history with the horrible designation of Bloody Mary; yet no one refers to her successor as Bloody Elizabeth; and though the afore-mentioned educated persons have usually heard of Sir Thomas More, I venture to say that few of them could name half a dozen others among those victimized by Elizabeth on account of their religion. By way of example, I may mention a play produced in 1950 which was called *Design for a Stained Glass Window*. It was based on the story of Margaret Clitherow, a devoted young wife and the loving mother of several small children, whose only crime was fidelity to her Faith, but who was martyrized for this by being crushed between two millstones in 1571. The play, magnificently staged and beautifully acted, opened in Boston and went from there to New York; however, it ran for only a fortnight altogether. I saw it myself in Boston and the reason ascribed for its failure by everyone who spoke to me about it was that it was too far-fetched to be convincing! Yet it was based on the same amount of sad and sober truth as the various plays about the execution of Joan of Arc and of many other incidents, the details of which we do not know as well as we should.

Our own age, alas! has not been free from hideous persecution, especially of the Jews, and racial, as well as religious, elements have had a part in it. Even so, this persecution has not been sufficiently widespread or sufficiently condoned for us to judge the period of Pedro Bautista by our own. This was known in Spain as its "Golden Century" and, as Louis Bertrand rightly says in his *History of Spain*, the contribution made by Spanish theology during this Golden Century was really incomparable. "Saint Theresa of Avila, Saint John of the Cross, to mention only the greatest among the Spanish mystics and to consider them only on the purely intellectual side of their work, veritably opened unknown worlds to psychological introspection. They corresponded, in the spiritual sphere, with the discoverers of America and the conquistadors." (Page 243.)

This is supremely true. But intolerance and the crimes committed in the name of Christianity by Catholics and Protestants alike, in Spain, England and elsewhere, are among the greatest blots on that otherwise glorious era. We can and should regret and bewail this, but we cannot intelligently estimate it or judge it.

Taking all this into consideration, heroic and moving as is the story of Pedro Bautista, his fate would not seem as tragic to me as that of San Juan de la Cruz, had it not involved twenty-five other persons with him, among them three innocent and trustful children. His persecutors were not of his own Order or of his own country and the chief instigators of his abuse were not even of his race, whereas Juan de la Cruz was tortured by other Carmelites and other Spaniards and though two Italians helped to bring about his ultimate ruin, they were not primarily responsible for it.

[22-a] This crucifix, according to Cosme, was covered with the blood which flowed from Pedro Bautista's ear when it was cut, and is still preserved in the chapel of the saint at San Esteban del Valle.

[23] He had obviously never heard the old saying, attributed to the Jesuits, "Give me a boy until he is ten; after that, anyone may have him. He will be a good Catholic all his life."

24 The list of the crucified, as given by Robles Dégano, is as follows: Fray Pedro Bautista, Fray Martín de la Ascensión, Fray Felipe de Jesús, Fray Gonzalo García, Fray Francisco Blanco and Fray Francisco de San Miguel; Pablo Miki, Pablo Ibarki and Juan de Goto; Francisco Cayo, Cosme Takeya, Pedro Sukeshiro, Miguel Kosaki, Diego Kisay, Luisito, aged twelve, Antoñito, aged thirteen, the boy Tomé Kosaki, Matías the cook, León Karatsuma, Ventura, Joaquín, Francisco Kichi, Tomé Danki, Juan Kizuya, Gabriel Duisko and Pablo Suzuki.

In telling the story of Pedro Bautista, I have followed, as faithfully as possible, the records in all the source material I have been able to obtain and which I believe is authentic. However, in order to let the reader judge for himself what happened—as well as is possible after this lapse of centuries, and allowing for possible prejudice on the part of some narrators, or possible tampering with reliable records on the part of others—I think I should also quote from Father Campbell's brief mention of the Franciscans' ministry in Japan, which reads as follows:

"Unfortunately, the Spanish merchants in the Philippines just at that time [1589] induced the Franciscan missionaries of those islands to go over to Japan, for the rumor had got abroad that the Jesuits in Japan had been wholly exterminated, although there were still, in reality, twenty-six of them in the country. It is true they were not in evidence as formerly, for with the exception of the two army chaplains, they were exercising their ministry secretly. Of that, however, the Spaniards were not aware and probably spoke in good faith. The Franciscans, on arriving, discovered that they had been duped in believing that the persecution was prompted by dislike of the Jesuits' personality, some of whom no doubt they met. Nevertheless, they determined to remain, and Taicosama permitted them to do so, because of the letters they carried from the Governor of the Philippines, who expressed a desire of becoming Taicosama's vassal. Meantime, a Spanish captain whose vessel had been wrecked on the coast had foolishly said that the sending of missionaries to Japan was only a device to prepare for a Portuguese and Spanish invasion. Possibly he spoke in jest, but his words were reported to Taicosama, with the result that on February 5, 1597, six Franciscans and three Jesuits were hanging on crosses at Nagasaki. The Jesuits were Paul Miki, James Kisai, and John de Goto, all three Japanese. On the same day a general decree of banishment was issued." The Jesuits 1534-1921. Pages 183 and 184.

It will be noted that Father Campbell does not mention even Pedro Bautista by name in giving the number of Franciscans crucified and that he does not refer at all to the other seventeen victims listed by Robles Dégano; all twenty-six were beatified September 14, 1627 by Urban VIII and canonized June 8, 1862 by Pius IX.

The Catholic Encyclopedia, published by Applegate in 1911, gives the following account, with the following cross references, of the circumstances which led to the wholesale crucifixion, the crucifixion itself and the subsequent beatification and canonization. (Histoire des 26 martyrs du Japon crucifies à Nangasaqui by Bouix. Published in Paris, Lyons, 1682; Le Catholicisme au Japon; II L'Ere des Martyres 1593-1660, by De Place. Published in

Brussels, 1909; Lives of the Saints and Blessed of the Three Orders of St. Francis, I [Taunton, 1885], pages: 169–223; *Acta Apostolicae Sedis*: Feb., 729–770; and *Cronica de la provincia de San Gregorio Magno de Religiosos Descalzos de N.S.P. San Francisco en las Islas Filipinas, China, Japón*, etc. I [Manila, 1892].)

"PETER Baptist and Twenty-five Companions, Saints, d. at Nagasaki 5 of February 1597.

"In 1593 while negotiations were pending between the Emperor of Japan and the Governor of the Philippine Islands, the latter sent Peter Baptist and several other Franciscans as his ambassadors to Japan. They were well received by the Emperor, and were able to establish convents, schools, and Hospitals, and effect many conversions. When on 20 Oct., 1596, a Spanish vessel of war, the 'San Felipe,' was stranded on the Isle of Tosa, it became, according to Japanese custom, the property of the Emperor. The captain was foolish enough to extol the power of his King, and said that the Missionaries had been sent to prepare for the conquest of the country. The Emperor became furious, and on 9 Dec., 1596, ordered the Missionaries to be imprisoned. On 5 Feb., 1597, six friars belonging to the First Order of St. Francis (Peter Baptist, Martin of the Ascension, Francis Blanco, priests; Philip of Jesus, cleric; Gonsalvo Garzia, Francis of St. Michael, lay brothers), three Japanese Jesuits (Paul Miki, John Goto, James Kisai) and seventeen native Franciscan Tertiaries were crucified.

"They were beatified 14 Sept., 1627 by Urban VIII, and canonized 8 June, 1862, by Pius IX."

I am indebted to Father Rudolph Arlanti, Chancellor of the Diocese of Lafayette, Lafayette, Louisiana, for bringing this final reference material to my attention and also, for furnishing or verifying several other names and facts contained in the text.

My thanks are also due to Miss Marie Mamalakis, Associate Professor and Circulation Librarian of Southwestern Louisiana Institute, who has also been most helpful in supplying me with additional reference material, especially for the Notes on Part V; and to Dr. J. Frank Davis, Professor of Foreign Languages at Southwestern Louisiana Institute, who was of great help to me in authenticating my translation of certain passages in *The Life of San Pedro Bautista* by Robles Dégano, where archaic or colloquial forms of Spanish were used and where I could not trust my powers as a translator. Dr. Davis has also been kind enough to read Part V from beginning to end, along with the reference material on which I based it, and has assured me that, as far as he can see, I have neither omitted nor misrepresented any essential fact contained therein.

BIBLIOGRAPHY

BIOGRAPHIES AND HISTORIES (English)

History of the Reign of Ferdinand and Isabella, The Catholic, by William H. Prescott. Three Volumes. Published by Charles C. Little and James Brown.

Isabella of Spain, by William Thomas Walsh. Published by Sheed & Ward, Inc.

Isabella the Catholic, Queen of Spain, Her Life, Reign and Times, by M. Le Baron de Nervo, translated from the original French by Lieut.-Colonel Temple-West. Published by Smith, Elder & Co.

Isabel of Castile and the Making of the Spanish Nation, by Ierne Plunket. Published by G. P. Putnam's Sons.

A Queen of Queens and the Making of Spain, by Christopher Hare. Published by Harper & Brothers.

Seek the Darkness, the Story of Juana la Loca, by Amarie Dennis. Published by the successors of Rivadeneyra Press, Inc.

The Eagle and the Dove; A Study in Contrasts, St. Teresa of Avila, St. Thérèse of Lisieux, by V. Sackville-West. Published by Doubleday & Company, Inc.

Saint Teresa of Avila; a Biography, by William Thomas Walsh. Published by the Bruce Publishing Company, Milwaukee.

Teresa of Avila, by Marcelle Auclair, translated by Kathleen Pond. Published by Pantheon Books, Inc.

Handbook to the Life and Times of St. Teresa and St. John of the Cross, by E. Allison Peers. Published by the Newman Press, Westminster, Maryland.

Carmelite and Poet; A Framed Portrait of St. John of the Cross, by Robert Sencourt. Published by The Macmillan Company.

The Complete Works of St. John of the Cross, translated and edited by E. Allison Peers. Three Volumes. Published by the Newman Press, Westminster, Maryland.

Poems of St. John of the Cross, translated by Roy Campbell. Published by Pantheon Books, Inc.

St. John of the Cross, Doctor of Divine Love and Contemplation, by Father Gabriel of St. Mary Magdalen, translated by a Benedictine of

Stanbrook Abbey. Published by the Newman Press, Westminster, Maryland.

Saint Francis Xavier (1506–1552), by James Brodrick, S.J. Published by Burns, Oates & Washbourne, Ltd., London.

Mère Marie of the Ursulines, by Agnes Repplier. Published by the Literary Guild of America.

The History of Spain, by Louis Bertrand and Sir Charles Petrie Bt. Published by The Macmillan Company.

A History of Spain, by Charles E. Chapman. Published by The Macmillan Company.

The Jesuits 1534–1921; A History of the Society of Jesus from its Foundation to the Present Time, by Thomas J. Campbell, S.J. Two Volumes. Published by the Encyclopedia Press.

The Rise of the Spanish Empire in the Old World and in the New, by Roger Bigelow Merriman. Four Volumes. Published by The Macmillan Company.

Three Centuries of Advance, A.D. 1500–A.D. 1800 (Volume III of *A History of the Expansion of Christianity*), by Kenneth Scott Latourette. Published by Harper & Brothers.

A History of the Church in Venezuela, 1810–1930, by Mary Watters. Published by The University of North Carolina Press.

The Spanish Pioneers and the California Missions, by Charles F. Lummis. Published by A. C. McClurg & Co.

The Spanish People, Their Origin, Growth, and Influence, by Martin A. S. Hume. Published by D. Appleton and Company.

The Story of the Nations—The Story of Spain, by Edward Everett Hale and Susan Hale. Published by G. P. Putnam's Sons.

Religious Aspects of the Conquest of Mexico, by Charles S. Braden. Published by the Duke University Press.

Ambassador on Special Mission, by the Rt. Hon. Sir Samuel Hoare, Viscount Templewood. Published by William Collins Sons & Company, Ltd.

Cervantes, the Man and His Time, by Sebastian Juan Arbo. Published by the Vanguard Press.

The Dark Virgin, The Book of Our Lady of Guadalupe, edited by Donald Demarest and Coley Taylor. Published by Coley Taylor, Inc.

The Grace of Guadalupe, by Frances Parkinson Keyes. Published by Julian Messner, Inc.

A History of Spain, by Rafael Altamira, translated by Muna Lee. Published by D. Van Nostrand Company, Inc.

The Structure of Spanish History, by Américo Castro, translated by Edmund L. King. Published by Princeton University Press.

A Catholic Dictionary, by William E. Addis and Thomas Arnold, M.A. Published by B. Herder Book Company.

A Catholic Dictionary (The Catholic Encyclopaedic Dictionary). Edited by Donald Attwater. Published by The Macmillan Company.

The Saints That Moved the World, by René Fülöp-Miller. Published by the Thomas Y. Crowell Company.

Saints at Prayer, compiled and edited by Raymond E. F. Larsson. Published by Coward-McCann, Inc.

FICTION, TRAVEL BOOKS, ETC.

Ferdinand and Isabella, by Herman Kesten. Published by A. A. Wyn, Inc.

The Queen's Cross, by Lawrence Schoonover. Published by William Sloane Associates, Inc.

Raquel, by Lion Feuchtwanger. Published by Julian Messner, Inc.

Set All Afire; A Novel of Saint Francis Xavier, by Louis de Wohl. Published by J. B. Lippincott Company, 1953.

The Cities of Spain, by Edward Hutton. Published by Methuen & Company, Ltd.

Fabulous Spain, by James Reynolds. Published by G. P. Putnam's Sons.

Journey in the Sun, by Dane Chandos. Published by Doubleday & Company, Inc.

The Soul of Spain, by Havelock Ellis. Published by Houghton Mifflin Company.

The Spanish Pageant, by Arthur Stanley Riggs. Published by the Bobbs-Merrill Company.

Spring in Spain, by MacKinley Helm. Published by Harcourt, Brace and Company.

A Stranger in Spain, by H. V. Morton. Published by Dodd, Mead & Company.

Understanding Spain, by Clayton Sedgwick Cooper. Published by Frederick A. Stokes Company.

The Tourist Guide-Book of Spain, compiled and edited by Herbert W. Serra Williamson. Published by *The Times of Spain*—The British American Publishing Company.

BIOGRAPHIES (French)

Sainte Thérèse, by Louis Bertrand. Published by Librairie Arthème Fayard, Paris.

La Vie de Sainte Thérèse d'Avila, by Marcelle Auclair. Published by Éditions du Seuil, Paris.

Les Plus Beaux Textes sur les Missions, by Bernard De Vaulx. Published by Éditions du Vieux Colombier, Paris.

BIOGRAPHIES AND HISTORIES (Spanish)

El Principe Juan de las Españas, 1478–1497, by Antonio Veredas Rodriguez. Distributed by Sigirando Diaz, Avila.

Corónicas, by Alonso de Palencia. (N.B. The present author was greatly interested in the tribute paid by Prescott to Palencia [*History of the Reign of Ferdinand and Isabella, The Catholic*, Volume I, Part I, Page 136, Note]. This says, in part: "The historian cannot complain of a want of authentic materials for the reign of Henry IV. Two of the chroniclers of that period, Alonso de Palencia and Enriquez del Castillo, were eyewitnesses and conspicuous actors in the scenes which they recorded. . . . He [Palencia] was raised to the dignity of royal historiographer by Alfonso, younger brother of Henry IV, and competitor with him for the crown. He attached himself to the fortunes of Isabella, after Alfonso's death, and was employed by the archbishop of Toledo in many delicate negotiations, particularly in arranging the marriage of the princess with Ferdinand, for which purpose he made a secret journey into Aragon. On the accession of Isabella, he was confirmed in the office of national chronicler, and passed the remainder of his life in the composition of philological and historical works and translations from the ancient classics.")

Los Reyes Catolicos, by Hernán Pérez del Pulgar.

Other contemporary chroniclers as indicated in the notes.

Obras Completas de Santa Teresa de Jesús, edited by Luis Santullano. Published by Aguilar S. A. Ediciones, 1951.

Cartas de Santa Teresa de Jesús. Four Volumes. Published by Josef Doblado, 1578.

Cartas de Santa Teresa de Jesús. Published by Francisco Foppens, Brussels, 1674.

Obras Completas–Santa Teresa de Jesús. Edition prepared by Father Efrén de la Madre de Dios, O.C.D., and Father Otilio del Niño Jesús, O.C.D. Published by Autores Cristianos, 1951.

Obras de la Gloriosa Madre Santa Teresa de Jesús. Two Volumes. Published by Josef Doblado, 1578.

Senda Emocional de Alba de Tormes, by Antonio Alamo Salazar. Published by Talleres Tipográficos Merino.

Polvo de Sus Sandalias, by A. de Castro Albarran. Printed in Toledo, 1951.

Biografia de Santa Teresa, by Father Efrén de la Madre de Dios, O.C.D., B.A.C. Published in Madrid, 1951.

San Juan de la Cruz. Su Obra cientifíca y su Obra Literária, by Fray Crisógono de Jesús Sacramentado.

Obras del Venerable Padre Fray Juan de la Cruz. Published by Gregorio Rodriguez, 1649.

Vida y Obras de San Juan de la Cruz, by Crisógono de Jesús, O.C.D. Published by Biblioteca de Autores Cristianos (Revised and re-edited 1955).

Historia de Avila, Su Provincia y Obispado, by Juan Martin Carramolino. Published by Libreria Española, Madrid, 1872.

Historia de las Grandezas de la Ciudad de Avila, by Luis Ariz, O.S.B. Published at Alcála de Henares, 1607.

Las Grandezas de Avila, El Insigne Templo de los Santos Vicente, Sabina y Cristeta, by Bartolomé Fernandez Valencia, 1676.

Victoria de la Muerte, by Beato Alonso d'Orozco. Published by Gil-Blas, Madrid.

Vida y Escritos del Beato Alonso de Orozco, by P. Fr. Tomás Cámara. Published by Imp. y Lib. de la V. de Cuesta e Hijos, Valladolid, 1882.

Ensayo Ibero-Americano, by P. Vela.

La Mujer Fuerte, Por Otro Titulo *La Vida de D. María Vela Monja de San Bernardo en el Convento de Santa Ana de Avila,* Escrita por el Doctor Miguel Gonzalez Vaquero su Confesor, natural de la misma ciudad.

La Mujer Fuerte—Venerable Sierva de Dios—Doña María Vela y Cueto, Por El Párroco de Cardeñosa. Published by Tipografía y Encuadernación de Sucesores de A. Jimenez, 1917.

Vida de Doña María
   Vela Religiosa Bernarda en el Convento
   de Santa Ana de la ciudad de
   Avila.

Escrita por Ella Misma
   por mandado de su Confesor.
   1617.

Dirigia a Christo Crucificado. Published in Madrid Por la viuda de Alonso Martin, ano de 1618.

Santo, Sabio, Embajador y Martis ante un Centenario. Conferencia Pronunciada, Por el Lic. D. Fortunato Gutiérrez y Gutiérrez Párroco de San Pedro Apóstol de Olmedo en el Centro Cultural Abulense —April 12, 1945. Published by Imp. Católica Sigirano Diaz, Avila.

Vida y Martirio de San Pedro Bautista, by D. Felipe Robles Dégano, Pbro. Published by Tipografía Moderna, S. A.

Historia de las Islas del Archipiélago Filipino y Reinos de la Gran China, Tartaria, Cochinchina, Malaca, Siam, Combodge y Japón, by P. Marcelo de Ribadeneira, O.F.M. Edicion de 1601 en la Biblioteca Nacional, Madrid.

Avila Monumental, by Santiago Alcolea. Published by Editorial Plus-Ultra, Madrid.

El Diario de Avila—Numero Extraordinario. October, 1951.

Monasterios de España—Su Arte—Su Historia—Sus Leyendas, by Federico Carlos Sainz de Robles. Published by Aguilar S. A. de Ediciones, Madrid.

Leyendas de Avila, by José Belmonte Diaz. Published by Publicaciones Alonso de Madrigal. Avila.

Avila, by Camilo José Cela. Published by Editorial Noguer, S. A., Barcelona.

Avila de los Caballeros, by Antonio Veredas Rodriguez. Published by Libreria "El Magisterio" Adrian Medrano, Avila.

Entre Cumbres y Torres, by J. Mayoral Fernandez. Printed by Vda. de Emilio Martin, Avila, 1950.

Cuadros Abulenses, by A. Veredas Rodriguez. Printed in Avila, 1939.

Morañegas, by Constantino de Lucas y Martin. Published by Editorial—Tip. y Enc. de Señen Martin, 1946.

Tesoro de la Lengua Castellana, by Don Sebastian de Covarrubias.

Diccionario de la Lengua, issued by the Real Academia Española.

Index

Acapulco, 234
Acosta, José de, 197
Acuña, Alonso Carrillo de; see Carrillo
Acuña, Don Pedro de, 27
Adaja, River, xviii, 51, 66, 119, 181, 184, 300
Africa, 60, 109, 135, 294, 332, 336
Agreda, 29, 300
Aguila, Don Rodrigo de, 202
Aguila, Suero del, 97
Aguirre, Doña Ana de, 181–83, 185, 186
Ahumada, Doña Beatriz, 67, 69, 81
Ahumada, Teresa de; see Teresa de Jesús
Akashi, 241
Alarcón, Juan de, 198, 199, 202, 204, 213
Alba, Dukes and Duchess of, 38, 45, 62, 98, 103, 104, 108, 115–18, 121, 140, 142, 292, 294, 337
Alba de Tormes, 99, 104, 108, 116–18, 141–43, 310
Albi, Cardinal of, 22
Albornoz, 115, 116
Alcalá, Brother Francisco de, 218
Alcalá de Henares, 37, 38, 44, 143, 148, 152, 159, 165, 168, 169, 292
Alcántara, 50, 101
Alcántara, Fray Pedro de, 101–4, 108, 229, 232, 326
Alcarar, Fernando de, 37
Alcideus, 180
Alderete, Diego Gracián de, 165
Alfonso, "King of Avila," 4–7, 9–12, 14, 17, 45, 48, 59, 130, 183, 294
Alfonso VIII of Castile, 182, 186
Alfonso XI of Castile, 4, 12, 293

Alfonso V of Portugal, 3, 7, 8, 18–20, 26, 29, 38
Alfonso XII of Spain, xxii
Alfonso of Portugal, Prince, 44
Alhambra, 162
Almagro, 8
Almodóvar, 157, 158
Alvarez, Don Antonio de, 130, 131, 313
Alvarez, Father Baltazar, 193
Alvarez, Catalina, 127–30, 160, 184, 313
Amakusa, College of, 253
Amezua, Don Agustín, xx, 297
Andalucía, 158, 159, 161, 164, 166, 167, 170, 173, 229
Angeles, Ana de los, 161
Antonio (Japanese boy martyr), 256, 271, 281, 282, 286, 340
Aragon, 7, 18–23, 25, 28, 34, 35, 45, 46, 57, 297, 301, 337, 338
Aragon, Catherine of; see Catalina, Infanta
Aranda de Duero, 29, 300
Arenas de San Pedro, 229, 287
Areto, Diego Alvarez de, 181
Arévalo, xvii, xix, 4, 5, 7, 8, 17, 25, 36, 42, 43, 45, 48, 127–30, 183, 292, 313, 327
Arima, Seminary of, 253
Arnalt, Hernán Núñez, 44
Asaka, 241
Ascensión, Fray Martín de la, 256, 263, 265, 267, 268, 274, 340, 341
Ascent of Mount Carmel, 157, 158, 164
Asturias, 16
Asuna, Fray Francisco de, 82
Atlantic Ocean, 135, 333, 334

Auclair, Marcelle, xiv, xix, 305–8, 310, 311, 314–17, 319, 320, 324, 328, 329, 332

Augustinian Monks, 114, 132, 235, 259

Augustinian Nuns, 65, 73, 75, 76, 112

Avila, xi–xxi, xxv, xxvi, 3, 4, 7, 9, 11–13, 15–17, 34, 43, 44, 46, 50, 51, 53, 61, 62, 65, 66, 69, 76, 81, 82, 86, 90, 97, 99, 101, 104, 106, 108, 112, 114, 117–21, 128, 135–38, 145, 150, 152, 153, 158, 160, 161, 166, 170, 171, 177, 179–84, 186, 187, 192, 193, 195, 197, 201–3, 206–9, 212, 214, 218, 224, 226, 229, 230, 233, 235, 238, 261, 284, 287, 288, 290–94, 297, 300, 301, 303, 309, 310, 312–14, 316, 320, 326–29, 339

Avila, Gaspar de, 190–94, 207

Avila, Father Gonzalo de, 202

Avila, Bishop Don Juan Arias de, 39, 40

Avila, Julián de, 204, 206, 213, 215, 216

Avila, Doña María de, 44

Avila, Doña María de, 179, 189, 196, 198, 207, 211, 214, 215, 220, 225, 226, 328, 329

Baeza, 159, 160, 165

Barbada, Santa, xviii, 183–85, 289, 327

Barcelona, 22, 333

Barco, 150

Barco, San Pedro del, 150, 151, 289

Bautista, San Pedro, xviii, 229–39, 241–54, 256–60, 262–90, 327, 332, 336, 339–41

Beas, 158, 161, 165, 166, 310

Becedas, 81, 83, 86, 87, 91, 102

Belén, 258, 265, 268

Beltraneja, La, 6, 11, 20, 28, 29, 31, 33, 38, 299

Benavente, Count of, 40

Bernardino of Avila, 280, 281

Bizerta, 145

Blanche of Aragon, 6

Blanco, Fray Francisco, 256, 271, 340, 341

Blasques Villacastín, Cataline, 231, 233

Blasques Villacastín, Francisca, 231, 233

Blasques Villacastín, Inés, 231, 233

Blasques Villacastín, María, 231, 233

Blasques Villacastín, Pedro; see San Pedro Bautista

Blásquez, Doña Jimena, 182, 183, 326

Bobadilla, Beatriz de, 8, 9, 29, 30, 39, 40, 59

Bobadilla, Mosen de, 39

Borja, San Francisco, 262

Brazil, 241, 334, 337

Briceño y Contreras, Doña María de, 65, 66, 68–72

Brussels, 59

Bujalance, 165

Burgo de Osma, 24

Burgos, 48, 49, 134, 161, 181, 310

Burgos, Bishop of, 21, 22, 58, 59

Cabrera, Andrés de, 29, 30, 32, 39–42

Calatayud, 45

Calvario, El, 158, 164

Cambacu; see Taicosama

Cano, Melchor, 133

Caravaca, 164, 310

Cárdenas, Gutierre de, 19–23, 32, 33

Cardeñosa, 11, 183, 184, 187, 188, 218, 326, 327, 329

Cardillejo, Convent of, 232

Carlos of Viana, 7

Carmelites, Calced, 115, 116, 152, 153, 165, 166, 168, 169, 318

Carmelites, Discalced, 115, 116, 139, 157, 159, 165, 166, 168, 169, 213, 226, 318, 319

Carrillo, Archbishop of Toledo, 7–15, 17–21, 23, 25–27, 30, 32–34, 37–39, 147, 294, 299

Carrión de los Condes, 119

Cartuja de Miraflores, 48, 134

Carvahal, Pedro Gonzales de, 246, 248, 249

Casada, Doña Teresa de, 80

Castellanos de la Cañada, 68, 73–76, 81, 83, 102

Castile, xvii, 3, 4, 6, 8, 10, 12, 14, 16–20, 23, 25, 28, 31–36, 38, 40, 42, 45, 46, 51, 53, 57, 61, 62, 97, 114, 130, 136, 145, 158, 168, 179, 182, 186, 202, 212, 293, 297, 299, 301, 304, 337, 338

Castillo de la Mota, xxiii, 58

Catalina (Catherine of Aragon), Infanta, 44, 45, 48, 54–57, 148, 303

Catalonia, 34, 301

Catholic Kings (Isabel and Fernando),

35, 43, 44, 48, 55, 58, 66, 72, 147, 148, 165, 290, 292, 332–34

Caturla, María Luisa, xiv–xvi, xxiii

Cavite, 238

Cayo, Francisco, 256, 271, 275, 279, 340

Cebreros, 128

Cepeda, Don Alonso, 67–69, 76, 78, 80–84, 86, 87, 150, 306, 314

Cepeda, Don Francisco, 67, 68, 70

Cepeda, Don Pedro, 73, 74, 82, 83

Cepeda y Ahumada, Agustín, 68, 314, 317

Cepeda y Ahumada, Antonio, 68, 77, 135, 314, 315

Cepeda y Ahumada, Hernando, 68, 76, 314, 315

Cepeda y Ahumada, Jerónimo, 68, 314, 315, 317

Cepeda y Ahumada, Juana; see Ovalle

Cepeda y Ahumada, Lorenzo, 68, 86, 108, 146, 314–17

Cepeda y Ahumada, Pedro, 68, 146, 314–17

Cepeda y Ahumada, Rodrigo, 68, 76, 78, 109, 313–15

Cepeda y Ahumada, Teresa; see Teresa de Jesús

Cepeda y Henao, Juan, 68

Cepeda y Henao, María, 68, 73–75, 81, 83, 85, 305, 306

Cerda, Doña Luisa de la, 102–4, 108, 117, 138, 326

Charles V of Spain, 56, 60, 76, 112, 114, 142, 165, 212, 290–92, 300, 303, 335

Chichimecos, 234

China, 200, 273

Chosokabe, 259, 260, 264, 266, 267, 272

Cobo, Juan, 243–45, 336

Cochinchina, 243

Coelho, Gaspar, 241, 335, 336

Coimbra, 262

Colegio de los Niños de la Doctrine, 130

Columbus, Christopher, xix, 42, 45, 49, 61, 240, 302, 332–35, 338

Commentaries, 157, 158, 164

Conceptos del Amor de Dios, 151

Confessions of Saint Augustine, 93

Córdoba, 43, 44, 119, 164, 182

Córdoba, Gonzalo de, "Golden Youth," 32

Cortes, xxi, 6, 16–18, 37, 43, 60, 297, 328

Cortés, Hernan, 262, 290, 335, 338

Coruña, La, 54

Cotelo, Pedro, 267

Crisóstomo, Francisco, 173

Cristeta, Santa, 98, 150, 289

Cuenca, 132

Cuestra de la Parra, 231

Cueto, Diego Alvarez de, 181, 183

Cueto, Doña Isabel de, 186–93

Cueva, Beltrán de la (Duke of Alburquerque), 6, 8, 10, 11, 32, 35

Danki, Tomé, 266, 340

Dark Night of the Soul, 156–58, 164, 166

Dávila, Fernán Gómez, 43, 289, 290

Dávila, Juan, 46, 50, 301, 302

Dávila, Sancho (Bishop), 4, 12, 186, 289, 292, 294, 295

Dégano, Felipe Robles, 237, 286, 289, 336, 340, 341

Dennis, Amarie, 302, 304

Denys, the Carthusian, 135

De Soto, Hernandez, 262

Deza, Fray Diego, 51

Díaz, María, 101, 102, 215, 289, 310, 327

Dilao, 236, 239

Dominic, St., 170

Dominican Monks, xix, 44, 52, 77, 124, 202, 211, 236, 243, 259, 314, 336

Dominican Nuns, xix, 214, 315

Doria (Fray Nicolás de Jesús María), 165, 169, 170–72, 338

Dueñas, 24, 27–29, 44, 50, 299

Duisko, Gabriel, 256, 266, 340

Duruelo, 138–41, 148, 152, 155, 319, 320

Eboli, Princess of, 110, 142

Ecija, 165

Ecuador, 108

Edward IV of England, 7

Encarnación, Convent of the, 75, 78, 80, 81, 83, 87–90, 92, 93, 99, 101, 103, 104, 106, 118, 135, 142–44, 146, 151–53, 156, 158, 184, 314, 320, 327

England, 48, 54–56, 114, 148, 291, 339
Enrique IV of Castile, 4–12, 14–16, 18–20, 22, 23, 25–31, 33, 38, 42, 43, 55, 294, 299
Enriquez, Don Fadrique (Admiral of Castile), 19, 20, 23, 25–27, 33, 297
Enriquez, Don Fadrique III, 48
Enriquez, Juana, 21, 22, 45, 297, 299
Escalona, 16, 17, 127, 158
Escorial, San Lorenzo del, 115
Espinosa, Diego de, 115, 145, 327
Estrada, Ambassador to England, 56
Extremadura, 101

Facada, 274
Fajiba; see Taicosama
Faranda, 243–47
Fazamburo, 274–82, 284
Ferdinand III of Castile (The Saint), 32, 301
Fernández, Padre Gregorio, 106
Fernando, Infante, 58, 59
Fernando of Aragon, 7, 18–28, 32–36, 42–46, 50, 52, 54, 55, 57, 58, 60, 62, 212, 297, 299–302, 304, 332–35
Figen, 274
Figueredo, Ruy Mendez de, 269, 275, 286
Firando, 241, 246
Flanders, 48, 49, 56, 58, 59, 140, 142, 291, 292, 294, 295, 338
Fontiveros, 127, 128, 130, 138, 184, 229, 232, 233, 313, 327
Foricava, 249
Frances of Rome, St., 95
Francis of Assisi, St., xvi, 134, 230, 232, 234, 249, 251, 268
Franciscans, Order of, 230, 231, 233, 235, 236, 238, 239, 241–44, 248–54, 256, 257, 259, 264, 265, 268–70, 273, 275, 277, 287, 288, 332, 340, 341
Frías, Dukes of, 114
Fuente, Don Francisco de la, 52
Fujimi, 250, 259, 260, 264, 265, 267, 270
Fungen, 246, 248, 249

Gamarra, Don Francisco de, 226, 329
García, Gonzalo, 236, 239, 243, 245–47, 249, 251, 257, 265, 269, 271, 281, 340, 341

Garrovillas, Juan de, 254
Gaspar, 243
Generalife, 162
Geraldino, Alessandro, 46
Geraldino, Antonio, 46
Gerona, 22
Gibraltar, 8, 18, 61, 326
Giron, Don Pedro, 8, 10, 20
Goa, 236, 241
Gómez, Pedro, 246, 252, 253, 276
Gonzalo, "Great Captain," 58
Gotarrendura, 81
Goto, Juan de, 265, 270, 281, 340, 341
Gracián (Jerónimo de la Madre de Dios), 165–72, 338
Graham, Mrs. Cunningham, 171
Granada, 25, 42–44, 54, 61, 62, 160–62, 164, 165, 170, 171, 293, 294, 301, 310
Grande Chartreuse, 134
Gredos, 119, 229
Gregory XIII, Pope, 233, 241–43, 245, 252, 336
Grenoble, 134
Guadalcazar, 165
Guadarrama, Valley of, 134
Guenifoin, Viceroy, 248, 249, 251, 252, 260
Guevara, Diego de, 267
Guienne, Duke of, 18, 22, 28, 29
Guzmán, Domingo de, 132
Guzmán y Barriento, Don Martín; see Cepeda y Henao

Hare, Christopher, 299
Haro, Count, 38
Henry VII of England, 55, 56
Henry VIII of England, 54, 56, 114, 148, 303
Hercules, 179, 180, 326
Heredia, Antonio de (Antonio de Jesús), 137, 139, 141, 157, 166, 173, 174, 319, 320
Hidelsugu, 244, 248, 256
Hideyori, 270
Hieronymite Monastery, 15
Hohenlohe-Langenburg, Princess von, xx
Hortigosa, 73, 75, 76, 81
Huescar, Duke and Duchess of, 116–18
Huete, 16, 297
Hungary, 48
Hutton, Edward, xii, xvi, xviii, xix, 292

Ibáñez, Padre Pedro, 107
Ibarki, Pablo, 256, 271, 340
Indies, 45, 110, 146, 172, 233, 237, 243, 291, 316, 317, 333
Indies, Archives of, 237, 332
Infantado, Duke of, 38
Inquisition, 106, 118, 133, 134, 145, 168, 205
Interior Castle, 111, 317
Isabel, Infanta, 27, 34, 35, 39–41, 44, 53, 299
Isabel of Castile, xvi, xix, xx, 4–9, 11–46, 48, 50, 52–62, 69, 111, 127, 130, 136, 147, 179–83, 212, 289, 293, 294, 297, 299, 300, 302, 304, 327, 330–34
Isabel of Portugal, 3–5, 8, 25, 43, 45, 48
Isabella II of Spain, xxi
Isabella, Empress of Spain, 68, 112, 212, 261
Izquierdo, Ana, 130, 160

Jacuin, 264, 270
Jaén, 158
Japan, xviii, 200, 234, 236, 239–46, 248–55, 260–64, 273, 281, 285–88, 334, 336, 340, 341
James, St., 97, 328
Jesuits, 130, 131, 192–94, 197, 202, 212, 230, 235, 236, 239–43, 245, 246, 248, 250–52, 257, 262–66, 270, 277–79, 288, 292, 318, 332, 336, 338–40
Jesús, Ana de, 143
Jesús, Ana de, 158, 160–62, 164, 165, 171, 172, 307, 320
Jesús, Fray Felipe de, 259, 271, 282, 340, 341
Jesús, Fray Jerónimo de, 249, 251–53, 263, 268, 269, 273, 287
Jesús, Fray Pablo de, 238, 244, 249
Jibunoyo, 265, 266, 270
Joachim (Martyr), 258, 265, 340
Joan of Arc, 97, 205, 308, 339
John of Lorraine, 22
John of the Cross, St.; see Juan de la Cruz
Joyo, Cosme, 256, 265, 272, 281, 287, 339
Juan, Infante, 44, 45, 48–53, 60, 61, 301–3
Juan (Japanese boy martyr), 256, 258

Juan of Austria, Don, 145
Juan de la Cruz, xvi, xx, 90, 97, 98, 111, 112, 127–62, 164–68, 170–74, 184, 195, 204, 205, 229, 263, 284, 289, 290, 310, 313, 317–20, 322–27, 330, 338, 339
Juan II of Aragon, 21, 25, 33, 36, 297, 299, 301
Juan II of Castile, 3, 4, 14, 25, 43, 48, 127, 129
Juana la Loca, 44–46, 48, 56–60, 62, 300, 334
Juana of Portugal, 6–8, 11, 14, 16, 28, 29, 33
Julius Caesar, 15, 69, 179, 180, 326

Karatsu, 274, 275
Karatsuma, León, 249, 251, 254, 255, 257, 266, 340
Kichi, Francisco, 255, 256, 271, 340
Kisay, Diego, 265, 270, 340, 341
Kizua, Juan, 271, 340
Korea, 243, 244, 274
Kosaki, Miguel, 271, 340
Kosaki, Tome, 258, 340

La Espina, Convent of, 188
Laguna de Bay, 238
Landecho, Don Matías de, 259, 261, 267–70, 272, 276, 277, 280, 281, 285, 286
Lego, Monsignor Felipo, 233
León, 16, 28, 32, 301
León, Luis de, 132–34, 136, 141, 145
Letters of Saint Jerome, 74, 82
Lisbon, 20, 164, 240, 251, 295
Living Flame of Love, 164, 322, 323
Llano, Lope de, 243, 244
London, 54
Louis XI of France, 18, 19, 28
Louis XII of France, 58
Loyola, St. Ignatius, 131, 132, 240, 290, 335
Luisito (Japanese boy martyr), 256, 271, 275, 282, 340
Luther, Martin, 147, 335
Luzon, 237, 247, 266

Macao, 262, 285–87
Madrid, xi, xx, xxv, 30, 33, 57, 114, 115, 145, 165, 168, 169, 171, 233, 294
Madrigal de las Altas Torres, xvii, xix,

3, 21–23, 30, 38, 43, 60, 128, 183, 300, 327
Malacca, 243
Málaga, 164
Malagón, 138, 310, 327
Maldonado, 39, 41
Mancera, 140, 141, 143, 148, 152
Manchuela de Jaén, La, 164
Manila, 235–39, 241–45, 247–49, 251, 254, 256, 257, 259, 262, 263, 269, 273, 283, 286, 287
Manoel of Portugal, 44, 50, 53, 54
Margaret of Austria, 46, 48–50, 53, 55
Margarita of Austria, 212
María, Infanta, 44, 45, 48, 54, 301
Marinas, Don Luis Pérez las, 249
Martín Muñoz, 327
Martínez, Don Pedro, 262–64, 282–86
Martínez, Father Pedro, 198, 202
Martire, Pietro (Peter Martyr), 46, 49, 301
Mártires, Los, 160, 162, 165, 170, 171
Mártires, Santa María de los, 285
Masuda, 259–61, 264, 267
Matías (Martyr), 271, 340
Matías, Fray, 287
Matías, Juan de San; see Juan de la Cruz
Maximilian I of Austria, 46
Meaco, 244, 248, 250–60, 262–68, 270–74, 336
Mechuacán, 234
Medinaceli, Duke of, 29, 103, 138
Medina del Campo, xxiii, 5, 16, 17, 43, 58, 59, 62, 116, 118, 127, 130, 132–37, 139, 143, 148, 152, 153, 156, 158, 160, 257, 304, 310, 320
Mejia, Rafael, 139
Mendoza, Don Álvaro de, 230
Mendoza, Don Bernardino de la, 138
Mendoza, Pedro de, 76, 313, 314
Mendoza, Don Pedro González de, 30, 31, 34, 37, 40, 41, 43, 60, 147, 157, 300
Mercado, Cristóbal de, 260
Mercado, Don Luis de, 164, 173
Mercado, Doña María de, 192
"Mercies" of María Vela, 191, 193, 194, 195
Mérida, 233
Mexico, 114, 171, 233–36, 258, 262, 286, 290, 311, 338
Michiu, 271

Miguel of Portugal, Prince, 53, 56
Miki, Pablo, 265, 270, 275, 340, 341
Molina, 16
Mombeltrán, 230
Montalvo, Alonso Díaz de, 43
Montefrío, Count and Countess of, xx–xxiii, xxv, 121
Moors, 19, 25, 43, 46, 109, 135, 182, 291
Moraleja, La, 153
Morejón, Pedro, 257, 270, 308
Morton, H. V., xviii, 303, 324
Muñoz, Illana, 186

Nagasaki, 239, 245, 246, 251, 253, 254, 258, 262–64, 268–70, 272–74, 276–80, 283, 285–87, 340, 341
Nagoya, 244, 246, 248
Navarrete, Don Luis, 287
New World, 45, 61, 92, 98, 100, 109, 181, 240, 291, 313, 316
Nieto, Doña Inés, 115, 116
Nobunanga, 239
North American Martyrs, 240
Núñez y Vela, Don Blasco, 98, 181, 314
Núñez y Vela, Don Francisco, 98, 314, 326

Ocampo, María de, 106, 107
Ocaña, 17, 20, 21, 291, 327
Olandia, Francisco de, 267
Olmedo, 10, 11, 16, 17
Omura, 276
Organtino, 250, 336
Ormaneto (Papal Nuncio), 153, 167, 168
Oropesa, 114, 230
Orozco, Blessed Alonso, xxii, 112, 114, 289, 311
Osaka, 257, 259, 263–65, 267, 268, 270–74, 281
Ovalle, Juan and Juana de, 68, 78, 103, 104, 108, 109, 142, 315
Our Lady of Grace, Convent of (Las Gracias), 65–67, 69, 71–73, 76, 90, 112

Pacific Ocean, 234
Padua, San Antonio de, 251
Palencia, Alonso de, 20, 21, 23, 32, 297
Palencia, Bishop of, 62

Pardiñas, Juan de, 93
Parilla, Fray Francisco de la, 245, 246, 265
Pasio, Fray Francisco, 264, 276–79, 282
Pastrana, 141–44, 148, 152, 164, 168, 310, 320, 327
Paul III, Pope, 243, 336
Paul V, Pope, 224
Paular, El, 134, 138, 141, 152
Peers, E. Allison, xix, 310, 313, 317, 319, 322–24, 326
Peñalosa, Ana de, 164, 171, 173, 324
Peñaranda, Convent of, 232, 236
Peñuela, La, 172, 173
Pérez, Francisco, 257
Pérez das Marinas, Don Luis, 238
Pérez das Marinas, Don Pedro Gómez, 238, 239, 242–45, 247, 248
Perpignan, 33, 299
Peru, 76, 98, 181, 241, 291, 314, 315
Peter, St., 97, 284, 328
Philip the Fair, 46, 55, 57–60
Philip II of Spain, 68, 69, 76, 112, 114–16, 145, 165, 166, 169, 181, 212, 236, 238, 239, 241, 252, 261, 262, 291, 293, 294, 303–5, 311, 312, 335–38
Philip III of Spain, 212, 291, 292, 305
Philip IV of Spain, 291, 292, 329
Philippine Islands, xviii, 233–36, 238, 239, 242, 243, 246, 249, 250, 258, 261, 273, 334–36, 340, 341
Pius II, Pope, 25
Pius XI, Pope, 245, 340, 341
Pizarro, Francisco de, 76, 291, 315
Plasencia, 11
Plasencia, Fray Juan de, 235, 236, 241
Plunket, Ierne, 299
Portsmouth, 54
Portugal, 16, 18, 29, 36, 38, 44, 48, 50, 54, 55, 168, 236, 240, 241, 261, 262, 291, 295, 332–34, 336–38
Prescott, William H., 304
Primitive Rule, 107, 109, 137, 318, 319
Puebla, Ambassador to England, 55
Puente, Luis de la, 198, 218
Pulgar, Hernán Pérez del, 34, 35, 297, 300

Quixote, Don, 127

Ramon, Pedro, 250

Rangél, Bartolomé Rodríguez, 267, 277–80, 284, 285
Reform Movement, 137–39, 154–58, 165, 166, 168–70, 312, 318, 326–28
Remedios, Los, 169
Repplier, Agnes, 308, 329
Reyes, Ana de los, 215
Ribadeneira, Fray Marcelo de, 234, 249, 251, 252, 255, 257, 263, 274, 287, 332, 336
Río de la Plata, 76, 314
Rodríguez, Fray Agustín, 249, 258, 263, 274
Rodríguez, Fray Juan, 250, 265, 276–80, 282
Rojas, Cristóbal de, 169
Rubco, Juan Bautista, 112, 137, 167, 168
Ruiz, Fray Padre Bartolomé, 245, 246, 249, 253, 263, 274

Saavedra, Antonio Arias Pardo de, 103
Sabina, Santa, 98, 150, 289
Sacay, 257, 264, 272, 274
Sackville-West, V., xi, 100, 305, 307, 309, 310, 312, 324, 330
St. Augustine, Convent of, 245
Salamanca, xii, xvi, 4, 46, 50, 51, 66, 81, 99, 114, 118, 131–33, 137–39, 141, 145, 152, 158, 159, 181, 196, 197, 214, 221, 230, 232, 235, 243, 292, 303, 310, 329
Salcedo, Father Francisco de, 193–99, 202–4, 207, 218
San Andrés, Convent of, 231, 232, 236
San Antonio, Convent of, 202
San Bartolomé, Ana de, 117
San Benito, Mariano de, 167, 168
San Bernardino, Convent of, 233
San Eliseo, Fray Gerónimo, 213, 214
San Esteban del Valle, 229, 230, 283, 284, 327, 339
San Francisco del Monte, Convent of, 238, 243, 286
San Gabriel, Angel de, 143
San Gregorio, Custodia de, 235, 236, 238, 241, 243
San José, Convent of, 107–9, 112, 117, 118, 135, 137, 142, 143, 152, 154, 158, 160, 162, 204, 326, 327
San José, Hospital of, 254
San Lázaro, Hospital of, 252, 285
San Matías, Fray Germán de, 153

San Miguel, Fray Francisco de, 271, 340, 341
San Salvador, 61
Santa Ana, Carmelite Monastery of, 131, 156
Santa Ana, Cistercian Convent of, xvi, xix, xxiii, xxiv, 3, 4, 7, 9, 12, 13, 15, 17, 38, 53, 112, 177, 179, 186, 187, 189, 195, 197, 203, 208, 211–13, 226, 291, 293, 294, 297, 328, 329, 331
Santa Ana, Hospital of, 254
Santa Hermandad, 60
Santa María, Juan de, 156
Santa María de los Angeles, Convent of, 236, 237
Santa María de Guadalupe, 31
Santander, 48
Santo Domingo, Isabel de, 183, 326, 327
Santo Tomás, Convent of, xix, 44, 50, 52, 61, 107, 118, 179, 198, 301, 303, 310, 315
Saragossa, 23, 30, 300, 327, 338
Sedeño, Antonio, 245, 248
Sega, 168, 169
Segovia, 5, 8, 11, 28–34, 36, 37, 39, 40, 42, 43, 53, 58, 134, 152, 165, 170, 294, 299, 310, 327
Segundo, San, xviii, 97, 183, 184, 212, 284, 289, 308
Sencourt, Robert, 313, 319, 320, 323, 324
Sepúlveda, 29, 300
Serra, Fray Junípero, 262
Severo, Don, 150
Seville, 43, 44, 121, 147, 167, 233, 237, 291, 310, 311, 316
Shikoku, 259
Siam, 243
Siculo, Lucio Marineo, 46
Siena, St. Catherine of, 97, 205, 216, 308, 310
Silva, Ruy Gomes da, 142
Sixtus V, Pope, 172, 238, 242, 243, 336
Song of Songs, 133, 146, 174
Sonogi, 276–78
Sonsoles, Shrine of, 119, 120, 185
Soto, Domingo de, 133
Sotomeyer, Fray Gregorio de, 226
Spanish Civil War (1936–39), 119, 120

Spiritual Alphabet, 82, 91
Spiritual Canticle, 155, 157, 158, 164
Suárez, Juana, 75, 78, 81–83, 85, 103, 314
Sukeshiro, Pedro, 275, 279, 340
Susuki, Pablo, 254–56, 258, 266, 340

Tagalog, 236
Takeya, Cosme, 265, 340
Taicosama, 239, 240, 242–52, 256, 259–61, 264–67, 269, 270, 272, 274, 276, 279, 287, 332, 340
Talavera, 114
Talavera, Fray Hernando de, 43, 58, 301
Tavera, Pardo de, 103
Tello, Don Francisco, 286
Teresa de Jesús, xiii–xx, xxii, xxiii, 65–73, 75, 76, 78–81, 83–87, 89, 90, 92–112, 115–19, 121, 123, 124, 135–44, 146–54, 157–62, 164, 166–68, 170, 171, 183, 193, 195, 204–6, 210, 215, 220, 224, 232, 234, 284, 289, 290, 294, 305–10, 312, 314–20, 325–28, 339
Terezava, 251–53, 274
Thérèse of Lisieux, 79, 98, 224, 330
Tokitsu, 277, 278
Toledo, 7, 13, 23, 27, 32, 38, 43, 44, 57, 58, 62, 66, 102–4, 108, 114, 127, 130, 138, 139, 141, 147, 152, 153, 157, 165, 168, 233, 246, 292, 310, 327
Tomé (Japanese boy martyr), 256, 265, 271
Tordesillas, 36, 39, 40, 300, 333
Tormes, River, 104, 150
Toro, 36, 39, 42, 60
Toros de Guisando, 15–18, 20, 26, 27, 43, 69, 127
Torquemada, 42
Torres, Father Juan de, 198, 202
Tostado, Jerónimo, 153, 154, 168, 320
Tostado, El (Alonzo de Madrigal), 289, 320
Trevino, Count of, 24
Tudor, Mary, 114, 338

Ubeda, 16, 17, 172, 173
Ulloa, Doña Guiomar de, 101–3, 106–8, 215, 310
Ungasavara, Pablo, 248
Urakami, 278, 279
Urando, 259, 260, 266, 267

Urban VIII, 291, 329, 340,341
Usaca, 273

Valdes, Diego de, 267
Valdivieso, Petronilla, 187, 210
Valladolid, 9, 23, 24, 26, 27, 30, 43, 66, 137–39, 141, 164, 165, 198, 207, 218, 291, 310, 319
Vaquero, Dr. Miguel González, 214–16, 218–26, 327–29
Vega, 162
Vela, Don Antonio, 181
Vela, Don Cristóbal, 181
Vela, Diego, 182, 188–90, 196, 206, 208, 213, 214, 218, 219
Vela, Isabel, 182, 188–90
Vela, Jerónima, 182, 186–90
Vela, Don Juan de Acuña, 181
Vela, Lorenzo, 182, 188, 190, 206, 213–15, 218
Vela, María, xviii, 177, 179–99, 201–16, 218–27, 230, 234, 289, 310, 326–31
Velázquez, Juan, 46, 50–52, 302, 303
Velázquez, Doña Juana de, 46, 302
Ventura (Martyr), 256, 266, 340
Vera, Don Santiago de, 241
Vicente, San, 98, 150, 179, 289
Villareal, 8
Villena, Marqués de (Juan Pacheco), 6–12, 15, 16, 18, 21, 22, 28, 29, 31, 35, 37
Vita, 101, 102, 215, 327
Vitoria, Francisco de, 133
Vivero, Juan de, 24, 26
Vulgate, 134

Wales, Arthur, Prince of, 48, 54–56
Walsh, William Thomas, 294, 297, 299, 300, 304–6, 310, 312, 320
Way of Perfection, The, 111, 224

Xavier, St. Francis, 240, 241, 248, 335, 336
Ximénez, 62, 300, 335

Yepes, Francisco de, 127–30, 160, 313
Yepes, Francisco Gonzalo de, 127, 128, 184
Yepes, Juan de; see Juan de la Cruz
Yepes, Luis de, 128, 129, 313
Yuste, Monastery of, 112

Zamora, Fray Juan Pobre de, 254–57, 259, 260, 266, 267, 287
Zoilu, San, 119
Zuazola, Andrés, 261, 267
Zumárraga, Fray Juan de, xix, 233, 262
Zuñiga, Doña Ana María de, 189, 218, 219, 222, 226

ANTES QUEBRAR QUE DOBLAR

AVILA
TIERRA DE CANTOS Y SANTOS

PROVINCIA VALLADOL

MA
AL
7

FONTIVERO

A SALAMANCA 55 K.

DE SALAMANCA

A ALBA DE TORMES 27 K.

PROVINCIA

ORTIGOS

Provincia

SANTA TERESA DE JESVS

BECEDAS

ISABEL LA CATOLICA

PROVINCIA DE CACERES

SAN JVAN DE LA ✝

PROVINCIA

S. Merino